Imperialism in the Twentieth Century

IMPERIALISM
in the
TWENTIETH CENTURY

by

A. P. THORNTON

UNIVERSITY OF MINNESOTA PRESS □ MINNEAPOLIS

. . . and, whosoever considers that the
nature of men, especially of men in
authority, is inclined rather to commit
two errors than to retract one, will
not marvel that from this root of
unadvisedness, so many and tall branches
of mischief have proceeded.

CLARENDON

ACKNOWLEDGMENTS

Writers are unable to acknowledge whatever knowledge they have no recollection of having acquired: accordingly, this note does not adequately thank all those in my life and friendship who have so markedly helped my thinking and myself. The generous leave policy of the University of Toronto made it possible for me to begin this book, and its research funds to complete it. The University of Edinburgh gave me the use of its splendid library, and I owe much to the kindliness, which many others also know, of George Shepperson. My friend James Conacher, chairman of the department of history at the University of Toronto, generously and doubtless quite improperly gave me some respite from departmental duties while I was in labor. William C. Berman cast a sternly helpful eye upon my fifth chapter. Cecile Sydney typed the manuscript, but did more: her diligence and intelligence signally added to its clarity. I have also greatly appreciated the editorial skill of Victoria Haire of the University of Minnesota Press and the continuous support of John Ervin, Jr., its director, and William Wood. But I hardly need to make the point, standard but seldom sincere, that all faults in this book are my own.

On page 7, I say that no book is ever written without conditions of quiet. Only a writer's wife knows what those conditions cost — and to mine, I dedicate this book.

1 July 1977

University College,
University of Toronto

FOREWORD

In the nineteenth century Sir Archibald Alison filled fifteen volumes with a narrative account of events in Europe between 1789 and 1815, and followed these with another ten, bringing the story to 1852 — and even after this prodigious achievement would often tell his friends how much he regretted having left out. This single volume could not try and does not try to provide an in-depth account of the past seventy-seven years. Instead, it develops a single theme from these years: the theme of imperialism, hereafter defined.

It examines how the policies of imperialism were organized, and by whom. It sets out how imperialists saw the way of the world and how they gathered its public affairs into a framework of their own devising. It tells what assertions were made against them, and how they dealt with these. It shows how they developed no new strategy in the face of this challenge and how as a direct consequence they watched the moral initiative pass to the dissidents, usually called nationalists, who based their case on liberal principles like self-determination, which were often preached but not as often practiced among them. It discusses the ideas and the tactics of the spokesmen for these dissidents, who spent the years between the two world wars attaining credibility, durability, and, ultimately, a national following.

It asserts also that although the imperial framework at first held firm under this pressure, it was pressure from within that finally broke the image the imperialists had made of both empire and themselves; for in World War II the ambitions of Germany, Japan, and Italy put the matter of power to the test so thoroughly that, although they were defeated, they took with them down to defeat their rivals' hope that the vast areas of the extra-European world, over whose ground much of the war had been fought, could continue to be controlled from metropolitan centers. And it tells how, after the war, this exhaustion of imperial assurance cleared the way for the success of the colonial assertion against it that had long been publicized.

This assertion claimed first the name and then the rights of nationalism. But its chief claim was one of imperialism's own: a claim to control the future. For nationalism also set out to colonize the minds of men and to build a world at the far side of empire wherein its principles would animate free societies and promote free interchange among free nations, loosed from the imperial bondage and thus inspired to develop the best that was in them. Yet it turned out that in the twentieth century the filing of such claims was not covered by sufficient insurance. For any such policy the premiums were too high. In this book an attempt is made to explain why this was so and how it came about that the record of our own times tells how long-term plans and policies of whatever kind, wherever and by whomever made, came apart or came to grief under the pressure of events.

It can of course be said that this has been and will continue to be the fate of all the best-laid schemes of men, who in no generation have ever commanded the lightning. But this century has been singular, in that it has witnessed a series of struggles fought less for limited and therefore possible ends than for ideas which often evaded clear formulation and made their strongest appeal to the emotions. The potent phrase "the revolution of rising expectations" has been elected to preside over a series of aspirations. But it does not summarize them. They are too diverse. Since the concept makes its appeal to the spirit, its essence will survive: but it will always lack substance, because the revolution it evokes is not actual, is not to be found in the record. It has never yet been able to find itself a general staff. If expectation is to have a strategy, it must, like any other strategy, first get itself its own tacticians. Tactics if they are to be effective must refer to experience: and in the field of imperialism there is no one common experience, only a set of experiences, also as diverse as they can be. To know that the doctrine of the rights of man exists will perhaps put heart into a man in a dungeon, but it will not loosen his staple from the wall. What one dissident learned about the nature of imperial power in Kazakhstan in Soviet Central Asia does not usefully or sensibly compare with the view of the same taken by another dissident in, say, the British colony of the Gold Coast in West Africa—since the former would never have been heard of by the latter or indeed by anyone else at all.

Moreover, casualties in the wars of this century have been heavy: so many dead men, so many vanished hopes. Among these casualties – and whether it should be listed as terminal or as among the walking-wounded was something still not clear as the century's final quarter began—has been the belief that there was such a thing as progress, that the best guarantee for its vitality and continuance is to be found within a system of order and a framework of control, and that the people best fitted to be in charge of both are those whose own progress is too obvious to be questioned by anyone laying claim to common sense. Whether a majority of people (supposing them to have believed this) stopped believing it for the reasons Jacques Berque has suggested—that they either had suffered a loss of will or had come to realize how "a subtle, uneasy shift in the tone and accent of life, a sense of inauthenticity, betrayed injustice under the cloak of order, and disease under that of health"[1]—or from some other less sensitive but more easily identifiable cause is another of the topics examined here.

But it is also emphasized that although territorial empire relinquished its political grip, the economic control of the world's business remained with an affluent minority, consisting of the comfortably industrialized nations which did not take long to discover that the possession of such an empire was not a *sine qua non* of power. In these circumstances the assertions of nationalism and the proliferation of nation-states often seemed irrelevant, and national leaders found out that full independence, if it was anywhere, was still beyond the horizon. At the far side of empire another country lay.

Many new flags flew over it; many new men held authority in many parts of it; but, for all its unfamiliarities, it was still a country much like that which had already been traveled—a country populated by controllers and controlled.

No examination of or argument about anything can be made until matters that were and are by nature disorderly have been put into order. Because this is so, and because orderliness may become as much an enemy as an ally of the truth, the book runs the risk common to all histories of one's time, namely, of playing the censor's part—that is, of treating the immediate past as a country that, had only a little more intelligence and a lot more imagination been applied to its affairs by its inhabitants, would have prospered better than it did and left to its inheritors a brighter prospect than they have. The writer can only say he has remembered the risk—although a reader may think that its consequences have not been avoided.

Yet why people think what they do at the time they think it is certainly a question to which historians may properly address themselves—provided always they are ready to answer, without resentment, the same question when it is put to them in turn. No harm ever comes of holding fast to the reminder from Carl Becker that all historians approach their subject with at least one preconception: which is, the fixed idea that they have none.[2]

The following pages, therefore, set out a particular and considered statement on a subject which lives in a context of controversy: and it is not supposed that they will lay that controversy to rest.

A. P. T.

CONTENTS

TERMS OF REFERENCE

Imperialism as it appears in the eyes of its various be-
holders. Its pervasive influence beyond the political
sphere. The framework it made for its subsequent
action. The emotions it arouses and the problems
these cause.

1

TERMS OF REFERENCE

Nothing is filed under the heading "imperialism" in the archives of any nation-state that owned an empire. Foreign affairs, or external relations, are catalogued there, and a place is found for imperial administration and colonial trade; but "imperialism" is always a listing in someone else's index, never one's own. It is not the name a government uses to classify the policies it sets in motion. It is the name given them by those who adopt a particular attitude.

An imperial policy is one that enables a metropolis to create and maintain an external system of effective control. The control may be exerted by political, economic, strategic, cultural, religious, or ideological means, or by a combination of some or all of these.

In our time the attitude toward this control is hostile.

Imperialism is a critical term for activity let loose. It deals in dominance. In every age on record the dominant have been at work, imposing on others, themselves, their structures, and above all, their conviction that they alone know how to size up and exploit a situation, now and in the future. It is they who both define and seize an opportunity. Only they know how to distinguish between what is significant and what is irrelevant. They are convinced their power proves their superiority. They make their own moralities and judge others by them. At the turn of the twentieth century they were

3

willing to accept the name of imperialist, as fairly describing those who actively promoted the national interest beyond home bounds. If they do not accept the name now, it is because they object more to the unfair implications they find in it than to the policy itself. They expect to meet opposition and are ready to deal with it, but they do not spend time looking for its philosophical basis. When they are told that self-interest does not square with theories of social behavior, they reply that they do not agree with the theories or respect those who construct them. Their mentors are gone but not forgotten. The English imperialist Alfred Milner wrote in 1893 that the people of Egypt neither understood nor desired popular government. "They would come to singular grief if they had it. And nobody, except a few silly theorists, thinks of giving it to them." Theodore Roosevelt remarked in *The Winning of the West* (1889) —whose title correctly implies the presence in western America of other people who lost—that "this great continent could not have been kept as nothing but a game preserve for squalid savages."[1]

But only in the twentieth century have so many been free to make a case against the dominant while they were still at work, still about their business. German critics of national socialism in the 1930s had to leave Germany to be heard, and if they did not do so in good time, they were destroyed; and only the exile from the Union of Soviet Socialist Republics has been able to give the world at large any image of what life is like for the average Russian—an image which to this day is unclear. But in the "Third World"—the name a continuing imperialist attitude gave in the 1970s to areas that the western imperialists evacuated in the 1950s and 1960s—free speech on the evils of imperialism is a popular activity warmly encouraged by government. All this says something about the century, which a commentator on its events must account for. It says something too about those who bring the charges. It says nothing at all about the future, which may follow another fashion.

For the century is not over. Many of the issues that have troubled its inhabitants are still alive and well. Imperialism is one of these: power, like murder, will out. Accordingly, anyone who sets out to isolate this theme has to behave like a photographer, taking a stance and using the best available equipment to make the picture. The photographer then fixes and frames this theme within its own context, that is, a particular time of a definite day. It therefore becomes at once a piece of historical evidence. This evidence, when collected in an album, can tell how things looked. It does not tell how things were, for life is fluid, not fixed. The "I am a camera" claim is vulnerable on another count—and so are you and so is he or she. Whoever owns the superior apparatus, whoever stands in a clearer light with a keener eye in a different place, may do the subject better justice. Who is the best judge of justice and of what it means begs another question. Where one should stand to make that judgment is also unresolved. Perspective is a term better left with the painters, because it applies more to things than to happenings and more to insight than to distance.

Hindsight and insight are not necessarily first cousins. Every generation or so, analysts of public affairs practice what they call revisionism. For example, a recent (1965) editor of J. A. Hobson's *Imperialism* (1902) says that the study of mistaken or partly valid theories is important to the task of contemporary theory-formation and refers to "time-bound" disciplines such as history without being struck by the notion that theory-formation, like all the thoughts of man, may also be time-bound and may be dismissed as mistaken.[2] And many begin the work of revision with the preconception that their seniors, who lacked their own advantage of later birth and longer views, got it all wrong: but again, this is not necessarily so. A "last word" on anything may only repeat the first word ever said about it, and the research of the living may merely justify the perceptions of the dead. The obvious can be twice-born.

If judgment depends not on justice but on the predilections of the judge, at least the context of time stays the same for everyone. In the eighth decade of this century we can reasonably assert that what European or western imperialism destroyed in the world has not been restored and that what it set going has not been seriously disturbed.[3] Up-country a plantation-economy still follows the routines laid down by departed foreigners. In the towns the statues to their various pioneer heroes were removed from the public squares, but the squares themselves are still there, as are the other monuments to alien achievement. Only a few of these are bronze. Most of them are concrete: the towns themselves, the docks, the roads, the markets; the bills of lading, the manifests, the warehouses, the insurance offices, the banks, and the clerks who keep tally; the collars, the ties, and the jackets; the dinner tables and the limousines; the airport and the most traveled road in the territory, the one that leads from the airport to the luxury hotel where a middle-class elite walks on carpets which their countrywomen in a part of town they do not visit have worked fourteen-hour days to weave—all these things still exist in Dakar, Jakarta, Manila, Calcutta, and all points east and south. Westerners do not now sit behind the desks in government offices, but everyone of importance there knows where and how to reach them. The territorial empires disappeared—but not the impulses that helped to build them and not the system of power and its relationships in which they played their part.

This is clearest to those who, having watched these impulses and this system at work, did their best seriously to disturb them. As Cuba's Fidel Castro exclaimed in 1962, "It is not for revolutionaries to sit in the doorways of their houses waiting for the corpse of imperialism to pass by!"[4] No such corpse has passed by. Imperialism has not been buried, for the good reason that it is not dead.

In the preface to his *Imperialism*, dated August 1902, J. A. Hobson called it "the most powerful movement in the western world." He addressed his book to those who desired to understand political forces so that they might direct them. Imperialism, although under new auspices and in a different dress, has not lost its power in the western world—which, like its eastern counterpart, is unlikely ever to run short of those who desire to understand political forces so that they may direct them. The study of imperialism, Hobson says, "is distinctively one of social pathology."[5] He assures his readers that his account of it will not try to "disguise the nature of the disease" and expresses regret that the pioneers in the science of sociology were inclined to take biological conceptions too literally. He is right: health and disease are not analogies that clarify analysis of public action. Comparison with a similar context serves it better. In 1867 one eminent Victorian, charged with all the careless confidence of the imperial West, told students in Calcutta that "except the blind force of nature, nothing moves in this world that is not Greek in its origin."[6] To adapt the words of Sir Henry Maine, much of what moves this world is western in both its origins and habits.

Imperialism fashioned the framework within which modern states operate, whatever the strength of their private traditions.

For, just as their culture outlives the Greeks, so the framework for action built by the departed empires has not been broken. The map of the world is now different from what it was and what it will become, but what occurs in the world and will continue to occur in it would not have surprised an intelligent diplomat of the nineteenth century or, indeed, a well-informed Roman senator in the age of Augustus. Within the frame, people change places, as they always have. Front ranks become rear ranks. Nations lose power, they get power, they go up, they go down—or indeed vanish entirely, which was the fate not merely of the Roman Empire but of the Romans themselves. The departing captains and kings, described in Kipling's poem "Recessional," are elbowed even as they are leaving by the incoming crowd of still more captains and yet more kings. The movers and the shakers of one era become immobile in another. What shocks them is that such a thing could happen to them, not the novelty of the thing itself. Power is frequently best appreciated when lost—and the opportunity to appreciate presents itself often, since those who lost power can watch in action those who gained it, and can be struck by the resemblance.

Power still has its prestige, "national interests" are still defined and defended, and in an age of "summit meetings" people certainly believe it better to meet at a summit than be left in an abyss. No one admits to imperialism or describes one's own policy as imperial, but everyone can find a use for weapons made in the imperial foundry. There is no reason to suppose that the frame will enclose a different scene tomorrow. Any observer of that scene will also be living in an imperial context: the dominant will still be around. And whatever assessment that observer will make of the past, which is our present, one thing will remain true: the observer will always be someone in a privileged position, with time on his or her hands and food on the table. It will accordingly still be the observer's business, as it is ours, to recognize how both were come by. Books must be written, and books must be read, in conditions of peace and quiet. It is certain that many a manuscript did not come down to us because the monk writing it was broken in on by a Viking with an ax. A good question to ask at any time is, how can conditions of peace and quiet be arrived at? Or, as Castro would certainly put it, at whose expense?

The other limitation within which any assessment must be made has already been indicated. This is time itself, the time of the assessor's particular day. Disruption is as regular a fact of history as continuity; and so, despite all sensible expectation, the scene caught by the camera this morning may not survive sunset tonight. Anyone trying to sum up the public business of the twentieth century needs to keep in mind what Shakespeare's soothsayer told Julius Caesar, who had jeered at him that the Ides of March were come. His reply was, aye, Caesar, but not gone — and, as it turned out, he had a point. Nobody looking in the past for clues to explain the future will consult a history of the eighteenth century published in the year 1775, which is inevitably ignorant of two revolutions and a Napoleon to follow. The risks implicit in writing about one's own time are enormous, and a writer can only accept this and hope to be given as much luck as judgment. The writer should not forget Polybius's warning that only people of practical affairs should write history, and Walter Bagehot's reminder that the reason so few good books are written is that so few people who can write *know* anything. And people who know things know them best through their impact on themselves: when men of practical affairs take to print, they write not history but autobiography, often *With Prejudice*, as many high-ranking memorialists of World War II proved.[7]

Bagehot could have added that the verb "know" does not mean the same things to all people. Knowledge, like cloth, can be cut on the bias, and the result is just as much a matter of fashion and taste. A retired British colonial official remarked of an American analysis of the British colonial service that it manages to be penetrating and balanced, but at the same time it "subtly misunderstands the whole subject, so that one suspects this is really the historical process at work, and this is how all historians get their pictures slightly wrong." Or even entirely false: Sir Roy Harrod complained that contemporary history had been wrongly written under his very eyes. So although every picture tells a story, no one is ever certain what the story says. A recent, sympathetic biography of the English socialist thinker R. H. Tawney, written by an American, remarks that Tawney "tended to espouse reform of the Empire rather than to demand its speedy, total dismantling as an institution" and "failed to confront the issue of colonialism." This is to colonize the past with present assumptions, for in Tawney's lifetime nobody in England outside of the British Communist party advocated dismantling the empire (and even they were not sure whether this was a good idea), and nobody then had ever heard of colonialism. Historians who are irritated by the course that history actually took are not perhaps the best guides to it. The problem is often called ideological. The Indian communist editor of a work called *Communism in India*, originally a set of "secret and confidential" documents brought together in the 1920s by the Intelligence department of the government of India and now excavated from its archives, acidly dismisses its author, Cecil Kaye, as being little acquainted with the fundamentals of communism and complains that the officers of Kaye's department were "mostly persons incapable of writing strictly objective reports on all they and their agents saw and gathered." No wonder, then, that the documents should be "one-sided, distorted, and described from a perverse point of view." Perversity can as easily be born of simple bewilderment. Frances Fitzgerald wrote of American activity in Vietnam in the late 1960s that although the Americans saw themselves as the builders of world order there, "many Vietnamese saw them merely as the producers of garbage from which they could build houses."[8]

And there are always some stories that are not acceptable at all, some pictures nobody will look at. There are some actions, things done and things caused, that words, however well chosen, will not encompass. There are things that do not translate. One great charge against imperialism is that by invading the past and wrenching it from its context, it has distorted and stultified the present. This is not logical, but it makes emotional sense. The continent of Africa, and generations of Africans, would have had, should have had, another history entirely. That they did not has not been forgiven. Had Frantz Fanon lived longer he would have gone on writing versions of *The Wretched of the Earth* (1965) without ever managing to rid either the matter of imperialism or his own heart of everything he felt about it. Putting on paper the experience of humiliation does not resolve it. It is not one of the emotions that the poet recollects in tranquillity. It is never so recollected, by anyone.

In fact, the colonial world was never a unit. What Senegalese and Annamese, Ibo and Kikuyu, and all the unnumbered under the sun had in common was their state of subordination. To the nationalist historian, this often seems enough: the target of imperialism is plainly viewed, and his or her assumption is that the subjected everywhere, since they shared an identical emotion, can be identified as a rank of comrades, shooting their weapons in unison at the target until it shattered and fell. Yet, just as the sum of your toothache and his or her headache is not a generalized pain but is nothing— since nobody is experiencing it—this proclaimed clarity of vision can mask a serious distortion. Frantz Fanon came from Martinique in the French Antilles, and he was reacting less to French fashions of imperialism imported from Paris than to the Creole culture which ruled the conventions above and around him when he was young. Cultural rage, not political oppression, bred his thesis on *les condamnés*, since colonialism in the Caribbean, as Trinidad's present (1977) prime minister Eric Williams agrees, was "something you touched, saw, heard, and felt every day everywhere."[9]

Another Trinidadian, Selwyn Ryan, urges however that a colonially reared historian must be especially cautious and must try "to prevent the poison in his system from interfering with his objectivity." In his opinion, nationalism in the West Indies was driven more by hostility to the racial exclusiveness of the settler community than it was by political frustration. The Indians in Trinidad, he notes, were never ardent "nationalists" (his quotation marks), since they distrusted the blacks much more than the Creole whites and the British Colonial Office, "which the majority of them viewed as a form of political insurance."[10]

Nevertheless, the inevitable embroilment of imperialism with matters that were once collected under the heading of "the native question" or "the race question," and that are now usually listed as "racism," worsened a bad reputation. Attached to the arrogance of imperialism is the display of certainty that its culture is superior. A movement that met with opposition, but not with much, and that provoked argument, but not from those who could carry their point, encouraged its leaders to develop prejudices which were enlarged by their own success. The invasions imperialism launched were actual and physical; they were also psychical. They startled and bewildered other peoples. They disoriented ideas and displaced customs. They enforced an experience on others which was not wanted but which could neither be avoided nor coped with. That the extra-European world was open to such invasions caused its inhabitants to lose any chance of winning and holding the respect of those who came among them and ordered them about.

From the time of Vasco da Gama, the whites believed that places they had not "discovered" could not be said, in any true sense of the verb, to exist. What does not exist necessarily lacks essence, presence, and future. Many variations were to be played on this theme, but at no time did they change the nature and course of the statement. Europeans who encountered other peoples at a different stage of development assumed that they had not developed at all. Columbus, as we are still taught, "discovered" America, but it is as true to say that he broke into a different era and that his ships were the equivalent of the time machine H. G. Wells imagined in 1895. The areas uncovered by European action presented an appearance of immobility, but their resistance, which had never before been so tested, proved to be low. Hubert Lyautey, arriving as resident-general in Morocco on May 13, 1912 to establish the French Protectorate there, found that there were no roads in and no maps of the territory. It has been said accordingly, that he came into the midst of a medieval society;[11] but, since nothing in the history of, say, Touraine or the Franche-Comté can truly be compared with the condition of early twentieth-century Morocco, the comment shows only that the adjective "medieval" reveals one more western assumption about the continuing nature of development and can be accurately applied to western societies exclusively. The social and religious structure of India, the political structure of China, the unascertainable customs of Africa—all were to splinter alike under the impact of European energy and its brand of dynamite. Consequently, European sappers and miners early developed a confidence not only in their ability to destroy but also in their right to build. Segregation of thought and insulation of understanding accompanied the pride they took in their distinctiveness of purpose and their speciality of technique. They did not allow their misgivings, if they had them, to surface. "By thinking the worst of their subjects," remarks V. G. Kiernan of these *Lords of Human Kind*, "they avoided having to think badly of themselves."[12] The strong have no time for the weak; indeed, they actively dislike them: for their very weakness stands as a warning of the fate that the strong, too, if ever they stop proving their strength, will finally know.

Alien masters preferred native subjects who were "friendly" rather than those who were "hostile," but it did not greatly matter which they were. In Europe when the Powers fell out, they sent one another stiff notes or made diplomatic *démarches*; but when problems arose outside Europe, they sent gunboats. Naval gunnery provided the "grand passport to the East." Hinterlands which were impenetrable by the navy could be shown the sight of the Maxim machine gun. If it is true that a person or a people "can only know themselves through the test of action,"[13] imperialism everywhere provided the opportunity of getting this knowledge; but of course the results of these tests under fire were always sweepingly in favor of the self-constituted board of examiners, the men with the guns. When the guns stopped firing, the posture of "present arms" was still universal: the police patrol replaced the military expedition, and "law and order" became the rule of the day.

The Europeans' determination to make and fix a social discipline wherever they went laid down the bedrock for their arrogant attitude. It was their set test of action, and of courage in action, that Joseph Conrad's *Lord Jim* (1900) so notably failed to pass; because, as Captain Brierly remarks in that novel, if a merchant marine present on all the seas of the world lacks a code of behavior, what else is it but a collection of tinkers? Overweighted by the sense of his own superiority and by the isolation it has brought him, Captain Brierly soon afterward commits suicide—thereby underlining the point made by Conrad, and many since, that thought and doubt together made up the true white man's burden. But still the hero who failed to carry this without stumbling, like Jim, has to redeem himself by some new act of assertion before the western reader is again ready to identify with him.

Yet collections of tinkers, renegades and outsiders, were always to be found in the interstices of white colonial society. In times of exuberant national expansion, odd characters emerge from wherever they have bred their oddities and expand them in the full light of a bright day. That a code of behavior was so firmly insisted on is the best evidence that it was often broken. The code provided a hand-book of regulations to govern all public contingencies. In the heyday of tropical empires the life of the colonial expatriate was lived in public, before the eyes of those who, although not in the least comprehending his daily routines, still shared his humanity and would gladly have taken advantage of any occasion that arose to emphasize this. No such occasion was therefore allowed to arise. Not letting the side down, playing the game, keeping a straight bat and a stiff upper lip, not going native, dressing for dinner, showing the flag—all these clichés were useful, because they provided timbers for a palisade built to reinforce a personality that had to live not according to its own inclinations but in obedience to tenets it thought proper for the colonial situation in which it found itself. Within this stockade, even speech itself became a guarded form of communication, a form of oral shorthand, laced with irony and understatement in order to dissociate itself and those who spoke it from everything lush and overblown (and what was not?) around them. A white man, that is to say a "real" white man, does not show fear. He does not show embarrassment. He does not show anger. He does not lose his dignity. He cannot relax. He cannot be taken by surprise. So devoted is he to fixed routines that he cannot even be late. If he has a sense of humor, he conceals it, because nothing is so perilous to a posture as a joke. His efficiency can never be in question, or be seen to be in question, so one white man must cover up for the mistakes made by another. He must exhibit *sangfroid* and *savoir faire* in all normal situations as well as in those that are abnormal, some of which he himself creates: for what was big-game hunting in origin but a need to draw attention to one's superior courage and skill? Native prudence retires from the presence of the tiger or the rhinoceros, but a white man must pit wits with him. And large, rampant beasts must be felled with a single shot.

No wonder, as has been remarked, Europeans in the tropics became neurasthenic.[14] The tensions induced by living according to this negative creed—for every thing that was "done," there were at least three things that were not—were great. It is not surprising, or especially censurable, that the club became a refuge to retire into, a white man's cave where an honest opinion might be aired and an honest temper lost. Nor is it odd that in a social life lived largely after sundown and from which the natives were totally excluded, the white colonial could feel free from both the pressures of the day and the restricting conventions of his homeland. No lower classes were present to observe how the energies and emotions of the self-repressed found their outlet, for one convention that had been safely translated from home experience was that servants were invisible and saw nothing. White colonial society was always a young man's empire, over which young women presided. Kipling's Mrs. Hauksbee queening it at Simla in the 1880s, the lady at Quetta who lent the benefit of her experience to all the cadets as a matter of course in the 1930s,[15] sum up for two separate generations a range of behavior which, although never officially approved and never hinted at by anyone other than mischief makers, never drew any official rebuke unless it got "out of hand"—which was of course the worst thing that could happen to anything or anybody.

Officialdom in public played the policeman's role: which is, in western society, to uphold the status quo and the powers that be. The police view all those who have to be kept in order, so that the status quo can indeed be maintained, as potential troublemakers. Beyond that they have no individuality. Any other role they aspire to can only be minor. No real relationship was therefore established between the controllers and the controlled. This is the insult that has not been forgotten. The same dissociation was true of every contact made, even the one that was universal in all the empires but is not documented in the imperial histories. On the matter of sexual relations in a colonial society, Kiernan has a comment that deserves to stand as the last word: "If respect and esteem between two races do not grow by daylight, they will not grow by moonlight."[16] More accurately, it was by half-light that the scene of these contacts was staged. It is by half-light that we look at it still. The white expatriate is summarized and dismissed in the caricature of a comedian caught unawares; the races he controlled appear also as caricatures, though of what is not clear. In the resultant obscurity there is room for both prejudice and fantasy, and the accumulation of these has been thick enough to stop anyone from claiming convincingly that one can strip the whole business down to its essentials. One person's essentials are not likely to be anyone else's. Accordingly, no universally persuasive history of race contact, racialism, and racism is likely to be written until all these issues have been removed from the agenda of human problems. That time is unlikely to be soon.

The implications of this question were readily acknowledged in the case of Zionism, whose impartial history, says Walter Laqueur, "will be written, if ever, only when the subject has ceased to be of topical interest."[17] Impartiality has always had a better reputation than the number of its admirers has warranted. Racism is the name given, and not cordially given, to explanations that assess a culture and a society in terms of a belief concerning the biological structure of certain races. It is the attitude that holds: they do it because they can't help it, and what they do is nothing to admire. With this for its basis, racial prejudice is still alive and well and living among black and brown and yellow as well as among white people. Those who incline to it usually hide their motives for doing so from themselves and certainly do not want to be told why they behave as they deny they behave. Comments made from beyond a predicament are resented by those who are trapped in it. What can outsiders know, it is asked, of the strains and pressures of a situation in which they are not involved? Judgment comes easily, for the price of this detachment is paid not by the outsiders but by others. That nobody has the right to force the payment of this bill on anybody has long been the attitude of the white citizens of the Union (since 1961 the Republic) of South Africa.

The observer of the past plays the same role as the outsider in the present and can also be accused of making judgments without having to pay for them. The observer's protest that he or she is only trying to get at the truth is likely to bring on the answer that everyone else is trying to do the same. At any time in history it is not what is true but what is thought to be true that is significant. What men think about the nature of the present inevitably affects their estimate of the shape of the future. This future is seen as a nebulous block of time somewhere out there, beyond the area of anyone's responsibility. Since nobody has in fact experienced it, it is not real, and the imagination can roam over it at will. But our own present was, once upon a time, someone else's future, and it is not easy to argue that people in the past were not responsible for it. (If there is such an argument, the young do not accept it.) Yet it is unlikely that the fantasies conjured up by even the most imaginative people

a century ago envisaged the shape the present has actually taken—
although Jules Verne among others divined much of its gadgetry.
The past also came as a surprise. Every account of it deals not only
with what is real, since indeed it happened, but also with the unexpected, with events that nobody foresaw.

To envisage the Chinese occupying, say, Ireland, is a fantasy—
but two hundred years ago the Chinese, few of whom had heard of
England, would have thought any prophecy that Hong Kong would
be occupied by the English to be outright nonsense. Imperial territorial expansion is a closed book now, but it was once the most
surprising serial extant. Anyone can "look it up," for example, to
find out how India came and stayed under British rule; but no one
has yet conclusively answered the really interesting question "how
could this possibly have happened, so strange is this turn of events?"
Guidance through the country of the imagination is best offered by
those who colonized it. Walter Scott, who was fascinated all his life
by questions of this kind, gave his novel *Waverley* (1814) the subtitle
'Tis Sixty Years Since. He made his history come alive by confronting the attitudes of one age with those of another. He did not forget that three generations are alive at any one time; he did not believe that any of them were composed of vipers or of hypocrites or
of fools; and he did not suppose that the opinions of the grandson
would ever confirm the convictions of the grandfather. These are
useful guides for anyone trying to find out what people thought
and why they thought it.

There are other, more dogmatic teachers. One of the earliest and
greatest of English "contemporary" historians, Edward Hyde earl
of Clarendon, saw himself as a survivor of a generation in the main
composed of vipers and hypocrites. He therefore drew a moral from
the tale he told and forced it on his readers. He begins his *History
of the Great Rebellion* with this declaration of intent: "That posterity may not be deceived by the prosperous wickedness of these
times." This clearly assumes that posterity, having read him, would
come to what Clarendon believed ought to be its senses and base
its view of the past on the estimate he made of his own present. It
has not done this, although no account of the mid-seventeenth century in England can ignore him. To say he had a bias is not to dismiss
his testimony as valueless. The bias of all history is in the direction

of clarity, which is not what life deals in. To make sense of its mass of material, the historian must classify and thus impose on the past an individual judgment of what makes sense. These classifications are then collected into groups and given names. "Society" is one such collective. Nobody can see society or discover it in action, but everyone assumes it exists. It is an invention, mothered perhaps by necessity but certainly fathered by the imagination.

"Class" is another. Class, says Joseph Schumpeter, "is a creation of the researcher, and owes its existence to his organizing touch."[18] Applying this touch is a necessary exercise. For we cannot, as we say, "deal with" people at all until we have decided what kind of people we are dealing with. The image we have in mind may turn out to be wrong, but we have to start somewhere. At this point the student of empire and imperialism meets with a particular difficulty. The starting point is deserted. The images that are examined are unpopular The assumptions that explain them are now rejected. The student knows, for example, that the mid-Victorians called certain of their own contemporaries, on whom they had happened in amazement, savages; and knows that his or her own contemporaries in the late twentieth century call the same human beings preliterate, pretechnical (but not prelogical) people. At best both images are shorthand classifications. It is still necessary to find out why one age used one style and its successor another.

The question is easier framed than answered. To whom will any answer carry conviction? Anyone can ask at once, what makes you think you are objective? In times when black and brown and yellow men attack the history written by white men, when articulate women diminish as self-serving the history produced by chauvinist males, we need not expect white, masculine imperial history to be granted much charity. It was once said admiringly of the English historian C. H. Firth that he knew the seventeenth century as though he had lived in it. Today's questions would be—lived where in it? Doing what? The assumptions anyone has, it is insisted, are the product of the place one occupies.

Moreover, it is only when assumptions have weakened or collapsed that they come under critical study. Until then they are, as we say, "taken for granted"—an expression that means, if it means anything, that they are not to be questioned, that it would indeed be wrong to question them. Who or what "granted" anything is not explored. It was, for example, in South Africa at the turn of the century that J. A. Hobson, still the most famous analyst of imperialism, arrived at his conclusions. He protested what the imperialists around him, his own countrymen, were doing, yet—

like so many other liberal intellectuals brought up in the pacific climate of an Anglo-Saxon country he also assumed the existence of such institutions as a police force, law and order, and an incorruptible administration.[19]

One's own assumptions are always perceived to be so natural and commonsensible that they are not even classified as assumptions.

But imperialism is certainly like racism and like Zionism: it is a subject which has not ceased to hold topical interest. People come out into the streets with banners denouncing it. Because there is no excuse for it, it is also supposed that there is no reason for it, which is the point at which reason and emotion part company. To deal with the history of imperialism is to deal in terms and classifications that have, amid the sensitivities of the 1970s, become out-moded. This makes them presently unthinkable. But the record knows nothing of these later judgments. It presents itself in the terms that were the commonplaces of their particular day. It deals in natives and tribes and fetishes; in settlers and traders and mineral "rights"; in missionaries, returns upon investment, profit and loss, and all other calculated risks. It lives in the atmosphere and among the assumptions of what Kipling called "cities and thrones and powers." Since it shows the view taken from above, a charge of intellectual arrogance is easily leveled at anyone who aligns oneself with it, and what one says about it is often discounted on the ground that there is nothing else one *could* say. Scholars who after the second world war began to construct the history of Africans in Africa soon came to suspect, sometimes with justice, that historians of the Europeans in Africa shared the opinions of their own protagonists by assuming that Africa had no history of any importance—"a quarrel of kites and crows"—until the Europeans arrived.

What is said usually depends on what one is trying to do. Two historians of both Africa and the British Empire in the nineteenth century, to illustrate the point, cite Madame de Staël's roseate account of the Germany of her day. She saw it as a land of philosophers, poets, and pious peasants. This reading was sardonically annotated by her contemporary, the poet Heinrich Heine, who stressed some details she had omitted to observe: "our jails, our brothels, our barracks—and all to needle the Emperor [Napoleon I] whose enemies we were at the time."[20] But these writers run the risk of a similar attack when they add that "to western scholarship belongs the credit of pioneering the social sciences in Africa, and of recreating the African past."[21] In other words, western scholarship plays the part of an imperialist cultural agency, which supposes its task is to develop the right approaches to the right themes. At once, an African historian of Africa, Godfrey Uzoigwe, comes forward to play Heine's part and speaks of "the battle of African history, the mopping-up operations of which are still going on."[22] This military metaphor has its point. Anyone who has tried to reassemble the sequence of events that took place on a battlefield long since "mopped up," some meadow now become a housing development, knows that if this reconstruction is to have any value it must both reconstitute the facts and restore the context to which they belonged. Something now hidden has to be revealed, and clearing away the accretions involves as much art as craft. Art, Paul Klee stated in 1920, "does not reproduce what can be seen: it makes things visible."[23] History has the same task.

But to paint a picture, or to tell a story, one has to choose one's own ground. Uzoigwe objects to the western view of African history —but that is the only view of African history that westerners can have, and it is pointless both for them to claim any other and for anyone else to attack them for it. Recognizing a bias will not necessarily, or even often, get rid of it. At best, it can be compensated for. Nobody can be everywhere at once. Nobody can hold "universal"—that is to say, nobody's—views. There is a view from above and a view from below. Nobody can experience both at once: nobody can photograph both at once. Nobody should try, and nobody need apologize for not trying. James Bryce's study of *The American Commonwealth* (1888) remains a classic account, enhanced by the fact that he was not an American. The Irish interpretation of Anglo-Irish relations certainly differs from the English but is not less valuable. History relies on honesty, not on nationality, and on judgment, not on color. If, for example, the claim were really true that a study of the life and personality of Gandhi is for the historian the best way into the complexities of Indian public affairs, the history of those affairs could not be written at all in terms that could be generally understood, since few men living or dead are anything like Gandhi. Moreover, where too much is expected from the sympathetic approach, revisionism can rebound on itself. The following passage shows how the historian of *Gandhi's Rise to Power, 1915-1922* may find that by examining the evidence she is forced to face in an unexpected direction. Judith M. Brown writes that

The older tendency to write Indian history in terms of the initiatives of the imperial government has rightly yielded to an emphasis on initiatives from within Indian society, on the indigenous forces pushing men into public action. However, the balance of emphasis can swing so far in that direction that it is possible to underestimate the *raj* as a vital component of Indian public life and a constituent element of Indian society. It held the arena of public life and its actions, directly or indirectly, were the cause of much public activity by Indians. In one area of public life particularly, the new style of politics, it created the objects and to a very large extent decided the rules of the political game.[24]

That "older tendency" referred to certainly had the virtue of common sense, for those who leaned toward it had never thought of underestimating the *raj* as a vital component of Indian public life. The dilemma of members of the Indian Congress in the period 1915-1922, and for very much later, was indeed exactly what the officials of the *raj* kept saying it was—the congressmen did not know whom they represented and were often afraid that in fact they represented nobody.

This reluctant latter-day acceptance of what was once obvious to everyone can be construed as further evidence of the loss of the imperial confidence which once informed all writing produced in the West about its own past. Because imperialism has become so disliked, any effectiveness, and certainly any appeal, it once had must somehow be explained away. If an honest historian like Brown cannot bring herself to do that, the tone of regret—that the realities were what they were—still shows through.

Two historians of Southeast Asia commented on this attitude. In recent years, say John S. Bastin and Harry J. Benda,

the tendency has been to pay greater respect to the majesty of the South-East Asian infrastructure, and to view the Dutch, let alone their Portuguese predecessors and competitors, as mere tangential influences on the course of South-East Asian history. Arresting and welcome as this corrective is, it is easily possible to overstate and exaggerate it. . . . The Dutch Company . . . profoundly affected the economy and the social structure of those parts of Indonesia where it exercised quasi-sovereign political control.[25]

Evidence of internal development is eagerly looked for. External contributions, external impacts, and external causes in general are relegated to the background. These peoples were bemused and confused by imperialism: it did not help, it positively obstructed, their development. Gandhi saw imperialism in India as a mask on the face of India, as something that distorted and constricted all its natural expression.

Behind the modern tendency emphasized by Bastin and Benda lies the wish to see — and perhaps the hope that one would have been honest and humane enough to see, even if in the employ of the Dutch Company or the British *raj* — the other person's point of view. To take two antique and therefore less controversial examples: who, reading *Ben Hur*, aligns oneself with the Romans, or reading *Uncle Tom's Cabin*, with Simon Legree? But an insistence on sympathy for the downtrodden, or even for the unknown, does not contribute to a genuine understanding of either condition. In the upshot, nothing comes of it. T. S. Eliot once issued a message about this. In his *Notes towards a Definition of Culture* (1948), he warned against having too great a degree of identification —

The man who, in order to understand the inner world of a cannibal tribe, has partaken of the practice of cannibalism, has probably gone too far: he can never be quite one of his own folk again.[26]

"Probably" is certainly one of Eliot's grimmer jokes; but "his own folk" is the key. There is only one inner world, one's own. I do not have yours, you do not have mine, and his or hers is something different again. Unwarranted invaders are as unwelcome in these areas as they are everywhere else. The blacks resent white liberals who misapply their sympathies for what they suppose to be the blacks' view of their own condition. The whites, when their overtures are rebuffed, are dismayed by what they call black chauvinism. When understanding is not reached, it is usually because it is not wanted. Who are you, to understand me? Insistence on understanding may seem to be one more example of paternalist condescension. To be understood is to be known, is to be weighed. This knowledge and weight will very likely be recorded somewhere for future reference.

The age-old superstition that to tell the stranger your name is to put yourself in his or her power still has some life. To be safe, it is essential to keep oneself close, to guard an identity, to claim a justified exclusion. The assumed name of one of this century's anticolonialist heroes, Ho Chi Minh, means "he who enlightens"—but, however sincerely he believed in the eventual victory of international communism, the people he spent his days trying to enlighten were his own.

With luck, a sympathetic approach will bring historians to a state of empathy. But they are out of luck if they reach, or think they have reached, a stage of identification, for at that point they will have lost the capacity to judge. Certainly, they will say nothing of value, least of all to themselves, if they take on a burden of guilt. To apologize for the past is to lose any true sense of it: things do not happen so that they may later be explained away. They can, however, be accounted for. Why did people who were not fools, not vipers, not hypocrites think about nationalism and imperialism—or, for that matter, about baptism and feudalism—in the manner they did? Why were they the way they were? Why, in particular, were certain things taboo, not to be told, not acknowledged to exist? The thought that is unthinkable, the thing that cannot be said—or, if said, will never find print—makes sense of what can be thought and said. Anyone who in the 1970s draws up a list of what is not politically, socially, or morally practicable (and everyone will have one's own list) will begin to appreciate that the people of the 1870s or the 1930s had some reason for thinking and feeling as they did. And during this mental exercise, charges of bias and folly may die before they are made.

Consider this passage from the journal of a French explorer-imperialist of the 1860s. It may strike a modern ear as so much romantic gush, but it is the tone of that day and cannot be dismissed either as hypocritical or as unimportant:

On the afternoon of 18 October 1867, five months after our departure from Luang Prabang, and sixteen months away from Saigon, after crossing a high ridge, we came across a great plain spread out before our eyes. Far away against a hill stood a town with red walls and brick roofs. We were about to set foot on one of the most ancient and least-known lands in the world. Tears filled our eyes: all hearts beat with emotion. If I had been fated to die on this expedition, I should have liked to die there, like Moses at Mount Nebo, gazing for the last time upon the land of Canaan.[27]

That afternoon Louis de Carné obviously thought he was not only on the border of Yunnan but also on a frontier of knowledge: he would not have understood any accusation that he had no right to be there. A regular omission in the accounts of imperialism is the high hope that took many of its enterprises to the farther places of the earth. No human artifact is so hard to trace as an echo: and of an enchantment, no factual record ever remains.

Posterity may indeed be impressed by "the wickedness of these times " But there will be plenty of wickedness about in its own. Every observer has to remember that he or she is a part of the scene and may share the general assumptions of the day or deny them. But whichever course is taken, whether the observer conforms to them or rebels against them, the assumptions are still there, conditioning the nature and depth of his or her loyalty to them or reaction against them. As for posterity, it is just another collective, as fictitious as most. There is no such thing as "history," which is going to issue any such thing as a "verdict." It is men who pass judgment on other men, whether their contemporaries or their forebears, and they always have their reasons for doing so.

Their judgment on imperialism has already been delivered. It differs in kind from that on, say, feudalism, which has no "topical interest" for the educated — although uneducated Iranian peasants, if asked, would bring in another verdict on feudalism experienced first-hand. It differs in degree from that on matters which educated opinion thinks not to be of topical interest but which nevertheless contrived to insist themselves on everyone's notice. In the last quarter of this century it became obvious that in Northern Ireland it still mattered very much who was a Protestant and who was a Catholic; but the reason for this was not at all clear to outsiders who thought all religious disputation to be outmoded, something akin to the quarrel between pope and presbyter which had surely long ago been buried under the masonry of the European Enlightenment. Similarly, the emergence in 1965 of the racially unreconstructed state of Rhodesia, which by all the liberal canons should never have emerged at all, startled those who had reckoned the verdict of history in advance. These two homes of obscurantism were freakish survivals, obviously. The general consensus was that they belonged in dinosaur country: they would die soon of their own stupidity.

One trouble with this diagnosis is that nobody really knows how long the dinosaurs lived or what finally killed them off. (It cannot have been an impatient public opinion, however.) Imperialism is also a survival. It still roams the earth, crashing into structures and susceptibilities alike. What it did can still shock, what it may yet do can still frighten. Claiming to see it plain can still cause anger, as A. J. P. Taylor found out when he reappraised *The Origins of the Second World War* ten years before anyone in western Europe was ready for a new assessment.

But the reputation of empire is something else again. Reappraisal has not changed it much. Empires are ascertainable places. They were formed as a result of action: in them things were done which can be traced as good of their kind and true to their purpose. Greece and Rome are famous yet, Alexander and Augustus have not been removed from the halls of the great, and there are indeed corners of foreign fields that are forever England, where men have truly died *pour la France*, where the sons of the Fatherland and of Mother Russia paid their accounts at the last. Empire owns a logical story. It has a unity of time and place. It can make a roll call, of both heroes and unknown soldiers. Its name is celebrated at rallies, on trophies, and in exhibitions; it is found on the stamps and on the matchboxes, on the regimental colors, and on the monuments in the museums, churches, cemeteries, and public squares.

Imperialism is not a story. Its name is celebrated nowhere, and it has no one place to call home. It has an image, but no face; notoriety, but no fame; a reputation, but one which few defend. Nameless men immured in unidentifiable boardrooms, and uniformed men in undiscoverable headquarters are assumed to be working ceaselessly to extend its range of operations. They are known as "They" or "Them," who keep in the background of whatever wickedness is happening in the foreground. All their actions are machinations, all their plans are plots. They do not work with people, they only put people to work. Their language is thin and depersonalized, forever proclaiming the interests of England or of Germany, insisting the honor of France will not permit this or the unalterable will of the people will not allow that. Their attempts at romanticism have the same texture as concrete blocks: blood and iron, the new order, the revolution. Their maps are filled with place-names describing not the places themselves but their relationship to other areas judged more important: the Middle East, the Far East, Southeast Asia. (The Chinese in rebuttal classify the Middle East as West Asia.) There are spheres of influence, scientific frontiers, and power vacuums. The sea itself is not excluded from this exercise: in the 1970s the North Sea, once the German Ocean, has been partitioned into areas where the bordering countries can enter unhindered to look for oil on its bed.

Imperial policy at any time can bring all these abstractions to life. Swaths of jungle, desert wadis, unheard-of villages can be suddenly heard of, indeed promoted to worldwide prominence so that in the name of one or another national interest men may be ordered to take and hold them at all costs. As long as this process stays close to common sense, men will do as they are told. When it does not, they will not. A man who will fight for "king and country," or its equivalent, does not willingly die for an abstraction he cannot attach to anything he knows. In the late 1960s citizens of the United States of America, whose foot was caught in the gin trap of an undeclared war in an unknown country, experienced this revulsion. Since their purpose was not clear, their self-image came under an attack fiercer than any the mysterious enemy could mount. The nature of the war and the name of imperialism contaminated the ideal of patriotism, and an army of men came to believe they were doing something they could not honestly account for, which would never be remembered with pride. It was a reaction very similar to that which had in England at the turn of the century overtaken those who found themselves pursuing a war in South Africa against "backward" farmers, in the name of empire and in the cause of civilization. The description of imperialism then—as something self-serving and spurious, immoral and self-destructive—did not change at all in the seventy years following.

But the emotions which the name of imperialism lives on and lets loose do not spring simply from the rage men feel against the existence of power and its inevitable misuse. The uproar is not solely caused by the ideological clash between Left and Right. The name itself is imprecise, for it describes, but cannot identify, a relationship—the interaction, itself not definable, between the weak and the strong. Relationships are not finite. They are only with difficulty even observed. Imperialism is not, for example, as distinctive a

relationship as marriage, which in part is based on a doctrine of contract—nevertheless, who has ever thought he or she can discourse
with assurance on the history of marriage? If, as C. Wright Mills said,
it is the historian's business to represent the organized memory of
mankind,[28] in the case of imperialism the historian is plainly in
trouble. For such a thing as a common memory of a relationship, a
memory equally true for both parties to the relationship, nowhere
exists.

IMPERIAL ASSUMPTION

The attitudes of the Imperial Powers and why they adopted and maintained them. How these attitudes governed their international action.

2

IMPERIAL ASSUMPTION

Ll the argument about the context of imperialism—sometimes
going around in circles, sometimes shooting off at tangents,
and sometimes hitting its target—says as much about those
who argue it and the context they argue in as it does about the subject itself. Imperialism is a phenomenon, it exists. About it can be
said what H. G. Wells said about liberalism: "It is something greater
than unfavourable comment on the deeds of active men."[1] And
it was said of the study of economic history that it concerns itself
with proving or disproving current economic theories, to the consequent neglect of the social aspects of the subject.[2] This is also
true of many "studies" in imperialism. One version revises another
version, one doxy confronts another doxy, with the expectedly
shrill results. But there is a case, and it is one which this book will
adopt throughout, for taking imperialism—the medium through
which control is extended—as a datum, as something given. There
is a case for treating it as scholars consider feudalism, as the context
for the social action of an era—as something of clear utility, serving
its day, and at the same time serving the self-interest and purposes
of an elite. Feudalism was as much a milieu as a structure.

And so is imperialism. Within it operate the processes by which
the power of a metropolis expands. Expansion is born of confidence. it carries its own dynamism. It explodes among the passive,

apparently without harm to itself. It changes the polity; it changes
the social structure; above all, it changes the mind and life-style of
those among whom it comes. Expanson lives without rules and
happens where it can: that there is a gambler's element in it has
not helped its reputation. That there is a cruelty in it has worsened
it further—but this was also true of feudalism and can become true
even of political systems that are not overtly or directly authoritarian: "constitutional questions, if fully thought out," as a rough-
tongued English jurist once upsettingly remarked, "are all questions,
not of law, but of power."[3] All systems are best judged in action,
not in textbooks: one will not discover the way of an eagle in the
air by looking at a stuffed specimen in a glass case. In the imperial
age this was usually admitted without an accompanying feeling that
anyone need be much upset. "We do not primarily think of Turkey,"
observed Arnold Toynbee in 1923, speaking for Europeans in general, "as the home of fellow human beings." This was also the attitude toward a great many other places on the surface of the earth,
and fifty years later it was still doubtful how far ideas of fellowship
and fraternity had penetrated the thinking of mankind. Toynbee
picked his example carefully. Turkey at the close of World War I
was seen as a lay figure, one in poor condition whose flaccid limbs
were falling apart, indeed falling off. Outsiders managed its affairs,
reckoning it would be in everyone's best interests if Armenia and
Kurdistan were lopped off, if all Arabia "went." In Toynbee's opinion, the treaty of Sèvres of 1920, with the simultaneous tripartite
agreement among France, Great Britain, and Italy regarding French
and Italian spheres of influence in Asia Minor, was one of the most
striking examples of modern western imperialism. The high hand
was evident throughout. When they entered Constantinople on
March 15, 1920, the British and French deported nationalist Turkish
leaders to Malta, a British colony often used as a receptacle for undesirables. The same cavalier style was used soon afterward in Egypt,
whose government and independence was "recognized"—in fact,
created—by the British government on February 28, 1922, when
the country was still Turkey's own legal property.[4]

These were the ingrained habits of imperial behavior. It was then
still common to speak and write of "the Great Powers" without

either embarrassment or envy. It was taken for granted that they would be present in the world and would run its affairs; that a "Power" should call itself such, act at will, and take advantage of anything that could be made to further its own interest. Why else have power at all? A traditional example of this attitude, one that reached the textbooks, is the comment of George Canning, when he was British foreign secretary in 1823, that "Spanish America is free, and if we do not mismanage our affairs sadly, she is English." Canning spoke a little loud; his contemporaries saw this remark as in poor taste, his posterity have called it arrogance. But he was telling a truth nonetheless: it was a perfectly viable calculation to make. Nobody now talks like Canning in the 1820s or writes like Toynbee in the 1920s, but the policy of pursuing the national interest has not changed. Power still lives. Because of its varied and variable attributes, imperialism has been hedged around with metaphor. But if metaphor is really needed, let us use one to clarify, one that does not criticize but simply describes: magnetism, that is, a central source of power within a field of force wherein that power is exercised.

It is never difficult to discover agencies of imperialism everywhere one looks, if one is so minded: in Uganda in the early 1970s Idi Amin identified imperialism with white faces and with white minds concealed by African or Asian faces. But is it possible to isolate the essential elements in a political, an economic, or an ideological imperialism? The effort should be made if imperialism is to be disentangled from influence. Two elements stand out. First, the imperial agency must be recognized as a presence that imposes an *unwelcome* system, a disliked regime. A great deal of power that is used in the world is not thought of as imperialistic and never will be. Religious communicants do not believe themselves to be the subjects of religious imperialism. Communists do not revile Marx and Lenin as cultural imperialists or see themselves as empire builders. Zionists from the outset saw their cause as self-evidently just and all who opposed it as persecutors, actual or potential. Citizens of the United States of America do not think of themselves as ideologically dominated by a set of documents written largely in the interests of a group of eighteenth-century landlords. As I have said, the first essential element is that the power used must be categorized as oppressive.

When this judgment has been made, an immediate tension results, and the second necessary element in imperialism discovers itself. The imperialist agency, once identified as something to be opposed and condemned, is recognized as controlling a context within which everything has to find, or fall into, a place: a context that dominates all thought and feeling. It has the power ultimately to impose itself. In the 1970s in Latin America, Canada, and the countries of the Caribbean, many complained of the shape and substance of the branch-plant economy which controlled the commerce and therefore the life-style in all these areas, although they were unable to convince the majority of their countrymen that this sensitivity, even if true, was of any value. A similar acquiescence to the status quo was found in areas of Eastern Europe that the Union of Soviet Socialist Republics judged as essential to the health of its own national economy. Both the economic systems predominating in the later twentieth century, however different their ideologies, have had power over millions of people, and it has been a power which could be, if someone decided it should be, enforced.

Four special privileges confer and accompany power: will, room, time and money. Imperialists are the impresarios who successfully put these to work. Money is the component that has attracted the most vigilance—money reckoned as a power in its own right and modern imperialism seen as both the product and the buttress of capitalism. But when all four conditions interlock, their combined strength makes imperialism an instrument of cohesion. It works between margins. It calls the options. It does the day's work.

And those indeed were the days. Insisting on their privileges, setting their margins, and calculating their options, the Great Powers built a framework within which the world of the nineteenth century grew and prospered. It did this so spectacularly that intelligent people everywhere believed they were the masters of an age of progress and the servants of a civilizing mission. In any age civilization has never been easy to define; but its absence has always been painfully obvious. The agents of the Imperial Powers, wherever under the sun their enterprise took them, never spent any time thinking that what they were exploring, invading, manipulating, and ultimately demolishing had any value whatever. Even the natives who caused trouble, were frankly hostile, were assessed according to western values. The man who held his ground at the far end of your rifle, like the Pathan, and the man who was eager to come over and fire yours against everyone else, like the Gurkha, won admiration. If to this day these hill-races together with the Sikh, the Zulu in Africa, and a host of Amerindian tribes hold their place in white man's history, it is because Europeans graded them according to the warrior virtues by which they themselves set such store. But they saw them also as the exceptions to the rules they lived by, rules which laid it down that the first test of character is courage and that the best proof of courage is stamina, and where that test is not passed and that proof is not made, no further attention need be paid.

When the circumstances dictated that at least some attention be paid, imperialists became irritated and resentful. In particular, the various *pashalics* of the Ottoman Empire outside of Asia Minor were seen as areas wherein Europeans had a right to entrench themselves. The premier of Italy, Giovanni Giolitti, whose government launched a sudden war against Turkish Tripolitania and Cyrenaica in 1911, made a latecomer's comment on this: "when we thought it convenient to move the field of war from Libya to the Aegean, everywhere we turned we found British, German, Russian, French and even American, but never Turkish, interests."[5] Indeed the Italians' attitude toward imperialism reflected everyone else's assumptions. Watching the Great Powers and urgently wanting to become one of their number, Italy calculated that a principal reason for their greatness and certainly the most spectacular symbol of it was their possession of overseas territory which they claimed as part of the national patrimony. Nowhere in his memoirs does Giolitti indicate that he ever had a second thought on this matter or that there was a second thought to pursue. One characteristic of modern colonization, he remarks, was an insistence on the decisive importance of the commercial element in determining the validity of political as well as traditional interests. If a country had a secure economic base, it could do anything. Since Italy did not have such a base in its home territory, and was losing to the emigrant stream a great deal of its manpower as a direct consequence, the country must look to the world outside to provide it with the base and the political security that would come with it. Others had done so, were still doing so. Taking a view southward from the Italian peninsula and from Sicily, Africa appeared as a dish to be carved. But it was unfortunately one whose best portions were already distributed among other European Powers. Giolitti quoted another popular metaphor, dating from 1882, that the keys of the Mediterranean were in the Red Sea—"but we have never found them there." Others had come and pocketed them. So Italy must shoulder its way forward; and if this created problems, well, a good imperialist assumption was that creating problems was a proper imperial task, as well as defining and solving them. The biggest problem was timing: but, plainly, to take advantage of time, one must get started, must seize the day and make it one's own.

Intent on putting the globe into a single Eurocentric framework, the Imperial Powers intended to develop the resources upon which the ignorant and the uncaring sat. They would sow the desert if they could. This was the task of the time; to prove itself, a nation had to take its share, had to compete. There was virtue in action, there was nothing but decadence in passivity, and the surest sign of the latter was absence from the busy scene. From imperial action wealth would result—not mere money but the prestige which only power had a right to claim. "Civilization" was not then, and never had been, an abstraction: its concrete base was privilege and property, two types of wealth which in the minds of those who owned it had only the remotest kinship to exploitation and loot.

This was Giolitti's stance. The Italians were nineteenth-century latecomers, students of all that had happened before. They were a nation, yes, without ethnic problems: but how to convince the Great Powers that they were there at all? Clearly, by talking the imperial language and copying the imperial actions. One sorts life into "questions" and "problems"; one assumes that thought and intelligence, and a touch of romance, will solve them. From the time he entered parliament, Giolitti says, "I had shown that I was taking the importance of the Mediterranean-African problem into consideration and the necessity of Italy's inclusion in its solution." After Italy's soldiers had been routed at Adua in Ethiopia on March 1, 1896, the Rudiní government wanted to abandon Africa *in toto*. Giolitti thought this was going "too far, and not . . . in keeping with the national dignity." Luckily, matters improved. In the first decade of the century the time seemed ripe to "solve the Libyan problem," despite a crafty Turkish attempt to involve Italy in a "Mesopotamian problem" instead. Therefore, as soon as the "Moroccan question" between France and Germany was settled peacefully, he judged it was time to take action, the more so since "our prestige and national dignity were in danger." Italy thus found itself obliged for inevitable reasons to disturb the peace of Europe. The British foreign secretary, Sir Edward Grey, promised Giolitti his moral support, in other words, that England would not interfere; but Grey insisted that Italy should avoid any appearance that England's inaction

was determined by any desire on our part to obtain an economic position based on particular interests granted to us by Turkey. This would render it difficult for him to uphold in Parliament the sympathy and the moral support he intended to give us.

Thereafter, on September 26, 1911, Italy served an ultimatum on Turkey. This rehearsed how often Italy had urged Turkey to put an end to "the state of disorder and abandonment into which Tripoli and Cyrenaïca had sunk, instead of their being brought up to the level of the other countries on the Northern littoral of Africa. This desirable transformation . . . was required in the general interests of civilisation." War began three days later. On November 4, 1911 Italian sovereignty over Libya was proclaimed. Giolitti says this was done at such speed "for fear of an intervention of the allied and friendly powers."[6]

These allied and friendly Powers saw the Italian action as crude and possibly dangerous, but they accepted it as legitimate nonetheless. They had done the same kind of thing themselves, if not often with such startling suddenness. Imperialism saw itself, and its promoters saw themselves, as the moving force of the civilization of the metropolis. They recognized no counterclaim against this assertion as valid. What had the Senussi or the Somali to say to the Italians, heirs of all the ages, that was worth hearing? Giolitti's attitude was faithfully reflected a generation later by Benito Mussolini: "I think for Italy," he said on July 31, 1935, "as the great Englishmen who have made the British Empire have thought for England, as the great French colonizers have thought for France." He would therefore imitate to the letter those who were then lecturing him concerning his ambitions in Africa. On the day Addis Ababa was occupied (May 5, 1936), he shouted from the balcony of the Palazzo

Venezia that Abyssinia was "Italian by right, because with the sword of Rome it is Civilization which triumphs over barbarism!"[7] A conviction like that has always carried the convinced a long way.

Civilization had to be fought for. It had also to be worked for. Because all civilizations have depended ultimately upon the efficient organization of a labor force, it is no surprise that the agents of empire should have spent so much time on that particular business: the "Native question" began in the imperial mind as a problem not of race but of method, a matter of time and motion. Where work is to be done, a premium is put on efficiency. Standards of competence are set up. The concepts of loyalty, responsibility, and diligence are broadcast and appealed to. Competence was to Europeans a hallmark of their own value in the world, and they everywhere equated its presence with character. "Can we trust you to do this?" was their question—and not its corollary, "can you trust us?" Their disappointment when they assessed the answer was everywhere evident: the same thread of complaint runs through the skein of every empire. These people will never learn, they will never understand: people who cannot even be punctual will never be anything. This sigh of weariness has kept company with the imperial ethos since its earliest days.

The Romans in their heyday looked down upon the Greeks. Greeks were knowing, cynical, and untrustworthy, the exiles from a collapsed civilization, mocking the virtues they no longer had the strength to emulate. Cicero thought that Greeks had no character at all, Juvenal exclaimed that Greeks brought with them "any character you please."[8] In 1909 the English statesman Arthur Balfour took up much the same attitude, although he could find little that was Greek in the contemporary scene. It was after centuries of arduous effort that the races of Europe had won for themselves great rights and privileges. They were now in the process of giving the same rights and privileges to other races who had not won anything for themselves, races who were

quite incapable, by themselves, of fighting for them at all, or obtaining them at all. That is the plain historic truth of the situation, which it is perfect folly for us to attempt to forget.[9]

He implied here that he and those who thought as he did would waste no time on any such attempt. The judgment was from on

high, and it was one of many. Although imperialist assumptions
varied, all of them were patrician. Arriving anywhere in any European territory overseas, a white official at once found himself in a
privileged position because of the color of his skin. He became a
member of a *noblesse de peau*. The atmosphere of sycophancy and
falsity that surrounded him on his coming to India, as Gandhi later
pointed out, demoralized him—"as it would many of us."[10] One
young cadet descending on Bengal cried, "At home I was nobody"—
but now he was a somebody with two servants, for whom he had
to think up daily tasks in order to justify their existence to himself
and to them. White men gave the orders, and if experience taught
very many of them that these would seldom be thoroughly carried
out, it also taught them that their self-proclaimed right to give them
would not be challenged. High concepts of policy and strategy were
not discussed in offices or bungalows and remained a mystery to
the man in the street and to the woman at the well.

In this context the claim to paternalism so often put forward on
imperialism's behalf, not infrequently by its own practitioners, looks
dubious. Parents, however good or bad they may be in the role, at
least make daily contact with their children. They know their youngsters' names and can make an educated estimate of what they are
likely to do next. Imperial officials indeed dealt daily with people,
but they did it as though through a grille—and not a confessional
grille, either, through which a lot might be learned, but one which
their own administrative style used more as a mask than as a channel
of communication. Knowing what they expected to see and hear,
they often assumed they had seen and heard exactly that. This self-
deception was widespread. To the informed viewpoint of imperial
officialdom, natives were natives, much the same everywhere. They
disliked alien governance and always created trouble where and
when they could. That was a datum, the point from which governance had to begin. But the time spent on a minute examination
of local peculiarities and customs might well be time wasted, since
the upshot was going to be the same. When you had seen one native
village, you had indeed seen them all. Prefacing a sociological study
of a Tunisian township, Cecil Hourani remarks that

paternalism in government . . . rests on the assumption that the authorities
know better than the governed the interests of the community: but the concepts

of the authorities are formed and shaped not by the real collective life and needs of the different communities which constitute the society, but by ideas which in part reflect the problems and experience of other societies.[11]

The view from above is wide-ranging, but in fact it does not take in much. It sees the forest but not what is going on in the shadow of the trees.

But however myopic, white imperial administration continued to conduct itself in the fashion of a medieval guild. It intended to attract to its craft apprentices drawn only from its own young, people with the right stuff in them. Empire was seen as an administrative construct, not as a political problem. What was needed to serve it was ability and integrity, not radical theory or classroom nonsense. In taking this attitude, imperialists abroad were no different from their cousinhood in government and civil service at home; in their circles also men from the streets were unwelcome and therefore did not appear. The high tone taken by Joseph Chamberlain, Britain's most autocratic colonial secretary (1895-1903), was now muted, but the assumption it spoke for did not change much as the century progressed. Chamberlain had remarked that he had never thought wishes and rights were necessarily identical, or that, for example, it was sufficient to find out what the majority of the Irish people desired in order to grant their demands at once.[12] Indian politicians found out that this assumption included their fates too. In October 1916 Mohammed Ali Jinnah, who forty years later would become the father of Pakistan, remarked that even if the Indian Civil Service were to be manned by angels from heaven, the incurable defects of a bureaucratic government must pervert the best of intentions and make it the foe of political progress. Officials, he considered, were beset by the prejudices and limitations that marked them as a class apart. They were naturally conservative. They had a rooted horror of bold administrative changes and constitutional experiments. They were reluctant to part with power and to let Indians participate freely in the government of India. Apparently, their main concern was to work the machine smoothly. They were content to go through their common round from day to day, and they felt bored and worried and upset by the loud, confident, and unsettling accents of New India.

Digesting this, the then viceroy, Lord Chelmsford, was able to comfort himself with the thought that Jinnah represented the growing self-respect and self-consciousness of the Indian people and that these were "plants that we ourselves have watered."[13] Viceroys were, however, brief visitants to India, often Whig and patrician in a style that did not indulge in the pleasure of ordering other people about. They were imbued, too, with the kind of modern metropolitan liberalism of which their own subordinates, long cut off from new styles in politics were naturally suspicious. But the sense of righteousness was shared. Whatever its manners (and perhaps because of them), imperialism stayed secure in its rectitude. It did not need to go looking for a doctrine based on a specific ideology. This attitude of superiority strayed beyond the official frontiers of empire into some surprising places. President Franklin D. Roosevelt, like the country he led, would have shied at the accusation that he had imperial ideas. But he was certainly a patrician to whom the high hand and the high tone came naturally, as it did when he reminded General George Marshall in March 1943 that Chiang Kai-shek was the chief executive in China as well as the commander-in-chief, and "one cannot speak sternly to a man like that or exact commitments from him the way we might do from the Sultan of Morocco."[14] Within its own circles of governance, imperialism did not find any sophisticated credo necessary. Busy agents of empire had neither the time nor the inclination to go parsing the principles of political science among those they met and instructed during their daily round.

The French system, in this as in so many other things clearer-sighted than most, testifies to this. The French never strayed from the Jacobins' principle of universalism: to examine their doctrine of *la mission civilisatrice* is to come to the conclusion that it meant the French believed in France. There was of course nothing narrow in such a belief. The absence of color prejudice among the French came from their certitude that they could make a black man a Frenchman in a relatively short time. That they were often right to think so is testified to by many French West Indians, who, with a history behind them of three hundred years of assimilation, were to guide French West Africans toward the wilder shores of French revolutionary thought. Maurice Violette, who was one of France's most forward-looking colonial administrators, wrote in 1925, when he was governor-general of Algeria, that

Muslim students, while remaining Muslim, should become so French in their character that no Frenchman, however deeply racist or religiously prejudiced he might be . . . will any longer dare to deny them French fraternity.

The whole aim of assimilation was to achieve this fraternity. Violette admitted that not all his compatriots were as sanguine as he was about the outcome of the process. He realized also that not all of them believed in fraternity in the first place. He upbraided his colleagues on their attitude to colonial peoples: "When they protest against abuses, you are indignant: when they applaud, you are suspicious; and when they are silent, you are afraid."[15] Yet the senators would not have been afraid of silent French, so even in Violette's thinking a distinction was being made. And it continued to be made. The French took with them wherever they went their vivid sense of political life and thus thought it understandable that a body like the *Parti du Peuple Algérien* (P. P. A.) should emerge in 1936; but what *bêtises* might they not expect to be committed by a *Mouvement pour le Triomphe de Libertés Démocratiques*, which by 1947 that same P.P.A. had become?

The fear that things might reach that pass (and go on to worse) was precisely why French conservatism had always protested any relaxation of the authoritative principle which, despite all liberal theory, underlay and upheld all colonial governance. They had never seen any need to rethink their position or consider seriously the possibility that colonies and protectorates could take any road into the future other than that laid out in advance, on the best principles known to man, by French engineers. Why then spend time on what did not deserve it? Their colonial policies and practices were therefore basically negative. The methodologies of *association* and *assimilation* caused more doctrinal wrangles among *savants* and their students than they were worth; for they were both processes that suppressed or ignored the local structure and the local culture — whether these were Berber, West African, Malagasy, Annamese, or Polynesian. They replaced them with a colonial structure, backed up by a colonial system of education. These, since they were invented by Frenchmen, were certainly French, but they were also

very different from anything existing at the same level in metropolitan France.[16] Natives who had been through the system passed
muster, they were acceptable, and no further thought was spent on
them. Premier Georges Clemenceau told Winston Churchill in 1920
how he had observed that officers in the British army were rough
with Indians and did not mingle with them at all. That surely, he
said, was the wrong way round: "Frenchmen would be much more
intimate—but we should not allow them to dispute our principles
of government."[17]

Indeed they would not. Although subjects of the British Empire
were devising a politics of complaint and learning to develop an
expertise in it, the French controllers of empire took the view that
since there was nothing to complain about, there was no need for
any politics—and, since there was no need for it, no right to it either.
Not many French subjects were in any position to dispute French
principles of government. Even while Clemenceau was chiding
Churchill, a total of only eighty-four men in French West and French
Equatorial Africa were full French citizens. In such circumstances
the vital question "who is in charge here?" was always easily answered. Premier Painlevé, in the lee of the Rif revolt of 1921-1924,
exclaimed that to abandon Morocco would be to abandon North Africa, under disastrous conditions. It would mark the end of France's
colonial empire. It would mark the end of France's economic independence, which was of course impossible without the colonies. It
would mark the end of French prestige and influence in the world.[18]
No French leader thought otherwise or thought it possible to think
otherwise. Even the *Front Populaire* of 1936, whose very existence
caused a trauma among officers of the French army from which few
of them ever fully recovered, took the line that freedom for the
colonial populations could come about only by extending to them
French political and social institutions. Independence was out of
the question. Was not *la liberté* itself a French invention? And since,
by definition, liberty required a vigilant, must he not of necessity
be French?

Ideologists make fewer friends than pragmatists, as a study of
the internal relations within the British and the French empires can
show. Rhetoric was something the British did their best to avoid.
They did not insist they were upholding a culture, they asserted

instead that they were doing a job. The temperature was therefore always lower, and their feelings were not seriously wounded when they met with rejection. By contrast, the French, founders and keepers of the civilization of Europe, expected a great deal—and in the end, *à l'heure du gendarme*, they made Annamese and Algerians pay very heavily for cruelly disappointing this expectation.

But the ways of the alien remain alien ways, and thus the imperialist ideas about civilization made few intellectual converts, whoever exported the civilization. Sun Yat-sen saw it as an equation of George Washington plus Thomas Edison—scientific, utilitarian and materialistic.[19] Gandhi did the same. So also did Bertrand Russell, who wrote in 1920 of "the mechanistic outlook" as something that existed equally in imperialism, in Bolshevism, and in the Y.M.C.A.: a habit of regarding mankind as so much raw material.[20]

Russell was joking, but the best jokes tell the truth. This has indeed been a long-standing habit among the strong-minded and high-spirited. It has animated the brightest and most energetic of their day. Anybody who sets out to shape and mold another individual, or a family, or a society, in the way he or she thinks best stands necessarily on a ground of self-assurance. This assurance has been acquired elsewhere, and it needs only to be applied afresh. The conditions may be different, but they are never all that different. It was when he was an assistant master at a preparatory school in England, Sir Meyrick Hewlett told readers of his *Forty Years in China*, that he learned lessons which were to prove of real value in his subsequent relations with the Chinese. He discovered, for example, when to exact obedience by firmness, when to promote loyal devotion by sympathetic understanding, and when to share joyfully in innocent fun.[21] The responses of the Chinese could be assumed to be those of other people in the same position. As already noted, colonies and other areas of governance were reckoned, by those professional civilians and soldiers who had the most to do with them, to differ more in degree than in kind. The problems that arose in one place were very much like the problems that had already been met with in some other place and should be coped with in much the same way. The competent official carried his rule book in his head, together with his common sense. The missionary did the same. Christianity in colonies became associated with a distinctively western

style of living, in housing and dress as well as in language and conduct; and it displayed, as it had to, an unrelenting hostility to the
traditional religious authorities there. Thus the outcome of imposing
a religious system among people who, to become Christian at all,
had to wrench themselves away from their own context, and of importing a political system among people to whom politics was as
great a mystery as calculus, was the creation of a comprehension
gap which no amount of paternalism ever managed to bridge. The
absence of any voluntary response, of any active inquiry, from the
mass of the people widened this gap, and in self-defense imperial
officialdom invented the notion of the "the silent majority"—this
term indeed seems to have been coined in 1929 by a reminiscent
servant of the British *raj* in India, Sir Reginald Craddock.[22] By its
very silence the majority was assumed to be giving not only tacit
but loyal consent to whatever officialdom was doing, however in-
explicable it might be. A sense of moral responsibility thus grew
up among officials which was private and incommunicable but not
the less potent for that: a responsibility toward the people of the
"real" India, or of the "real" Indochina, the same people whom
their own homegrown elites, should they ever get power, would
certainly oppress and exploit.

Accordingly, many English civilians in India and most French
military in Indochina and Algeria reached the decision that to cut
the imperial tie would be a scandalous desertion of both persons and
principles. They got little public sympathy for this attitude, since
in the event India quit the British Empire while the British people
were immersed in a fuel crisis, and Indochina was able to generate
excitement only on the extremes of French politics, Left and Right.

But the sentiment itself deserves attention. The ground of assurance on which the patrician/paternalist had always stood, together
with the assumptions he had always lived by on the same ground
were not diminished in the least by the pressure of events—or, as
officers of the French army saw it, by the pressure that politicians
put upon events. In the interwar years the military journals and colonial newspapers that were most widely read by the French overseas
general staffs and garrisons evoked the frightful cry of communist
subversion whenever they dealt with Indochina, North Africa, and
the Levant. Syria and Saigon must therefore be kept clean of the

microbes that assuredly swarmed in the barracks of Trèves and Mayence. A code of behavior formed itself around the idea of purity, purity from political corruption of all kinds. St. Cyr had given the officers enough of a modern education to make them equate colonialism with economic oppression and social injustice, and in the 1950s this was to enable them

to skirt around the basic problem, that of Algeria's political independence. How could they be colonialists, since they set the example in their military existence of austere living and of a certain concern for quality?[23]

Thus the French army, which had prided itself on its private virtues and dignified silences — *la Grande Muette* — finally became vocal. What it voiced was its conviction that France and its great ideals were being betrayed by a set of weakling politicians — among whom Charles de Gaulle stood out, in the army's bitter eye, as one more self-deceived than most and more guilty because he was himself *St-Cyrien*, a son of the army. The last stand of all the imperialist assumptions is epitomized by the rhetoric of Air Force General Maurice Challe, on trial for treason against the Fifth Republic after the failure of the military coup d'état in Algeria in April 1961. Treason like everything else was in the eye of the beholder. Certainly obedience, discipline, and duty — of which his accusers made so much — had always been his own standards: but then no law in the world could require a man to make perjury his daily bread.[24]

The most successful paternalist of this century, Marshal Lyautey of Morocco — whose body was being transferred from Rabat to Les Invalides in Paris even while Challe and the others were laying their plots — had once declared his soldier's view that the adversaries of today were the collaborators of tomorrow.[25] The generation of French officers who succeeded him found out that in fact the reverse was true. But systems everywhere, and imperial systems no less, deal hardly with individuals who profess antique principles at inconvenient times.

Rhetoric goes out of style faster than slang. Power does not. It only changes hands. Not in the least out of style is the assumption that to the powerful belongs the right to arrange both the strategic map and the local outlook to suit imperial requirements, and to decide what people should do and what role places should play without

being contradicted. The history books are full of examples, of which
the following is an assortment:

The Ottoman Empire in the nineteenth century was cast as "the
sick man of Europe." The assumption here is that those who so dismissed it were themselves well men, on which the best comment is
that the phrase was coined by a tsar of Russia. In 1885 Prime Minister Lord Salisbury in the midst of the Irish Home Rule controversy
made it clear that England could not look with favor on any proposal
to resolve it that menaced the first condition of England's position
among the nations of the world, namely its security. Three years
later his colleague Lord Derby, in the teeth of much evidence to the
contrary, announced his refusal to believe that, when every tangible
grievance had been removed from Ireland, the dream of a separate
nationality which had no historical existence would continue to
influence Irish minds.

The imperialist assumption that even dreams could be brought
to order was not, however, widespread. In 1910 and 1911 Sir Edward Grey as foreign secretary held suitably global and practical
views concerning two different areas where other powers might be
allowed their share of imperial responsibility without detriment to
England's own. Of the Central American republics he wrote that
they

will never establish decent government themselves—they must succumb to
some greater and better influence, and it can only be that of the U.S.A. . . . .
The more we can support the U.S. contention for the Open Door in other parts
of the world the stronger our position will be morally in contending at Washington for the Open Door in Central America.[26]

He also thought that Japan "might reasonably claim to expand in
China," and his colleagues Arthur Balfour and George Curzon
thought this was reasonable too. Six years later Balfour reminded
the Imperial War Council why Grey thought this, and how right he
was:

Lord Grey held the view that if you are going to keep Japan out of North America, out of Canada, out of the United States, out of Australia, out of New Zealand, out of the islands south of the equator in the Pacific, you could not forbid
her to expand in China. A nation of that sort must have a safety-valve somewhere.[27]

Looking for safety valves was certainly more sensible than letting the machine overheat. In 1920 a United States's commission of inquiry into the affairs of the Middle East, an area lately forcibly vacated by the Ottoman Empire, came to the entirely accurate conclusion that the allocation of both a National Home for the Jews in Palestine and a French mandate over Syria would cause nothing but trouble, a trouble with no foreseeable end.[28] The British and the French paid no attention whatever to this, on the assumption that the assumptions of outsiders were bound to be irrelevant. In 1920 also the settler pioneer in Kenya, Lord Delamere, declared that if England truly believed in its civilization, it would make every effort to keep its African subjects free from the influence of oriental civilization until they were fit to judge for themselves. At the time he spoke, 9,600 Europeans in Kenya presided over the destinies of 22,800 "East Indians" and about 3 million Africans. The outcome of adopting Delamere's notions, as a historian of the East Indians in Uganda pointed out, was that the Africans came to look upon the East Indians as a group of mischievous aliens, a point of view which was not counteracted throughout the colonial period by any educational or social example set by the colonial officials.[29] In 1935 Foreign Secretary Sir Samuel Hoare told the House of Commons that "we admit the need for Italian expansion."[30] In 1936 his successor Anthony Eden believed that as a last resort the only fundamental solution to the Egyptian problem was to make Egypt a formal part of the British Empire;[31] and twenty years later, when he had become prime minister, he set out to prove he had not changed his mind. In 1949 a governor of Cyprus told his fellow peers he thought it was a little early for people who could not even run a fire brigade to be asking for self-government.[32]

The very extent of empire allowed its component parts to be thought of and used as political receptacles for failures and irritants alike. Unsatisfactory higher civil servants were removed to the West Indies or the Straits Settlements in Malaya: the epitome of this policy was the appointment of the duke of Windsor to the governorship of the Bahamas. Malta in the Mediterranean and the Seychelles Islands in the Indian Ocean were used as receptacles for deported Egyptian and Cypriot leaders. In 1942 the secretary of state for India advised the viceroy that if Gandhi really became too troublesome he could be flown out to join Burma's nationalist leader U Saw in Uganda. Out of reach, he remarked, had something of the same effect as death: "People forget all about them."[33] But on this as on other things there was also a view from below to consider. Other people might come to look upon the imperial expanses as convenient for their own purposes. Ranging a view over Asia's population, Australia's R. G. Casey warned in 1951 that unless his own country's population doubled, "in a generation our children will be pulling rickshaws."[34]

World War II came and went, but the empire of assumption survived. The British Labour government's foreign secretary, Ernest Bevin, bred not to middle-class socialism but to the pragmatism of trade union and shop-floor politics, told the House of Commons on May 16, 1947 that he could not accept the view that England had ceased to be a Great Power and the contention that it could no longer play this role.[35] After 1949 American politicians cast about, and with success, for scapegoats who had brought about "the loss of China"—the assumption here being that people not Chinese had owned China in the first place. It was a notion that was transferable, and it died hard. David Halberstam recounts an exchange between U.S. Air Force General Curtis LeMay and presidential adviser McGeorge Bundy in 1964. LeMay said he could not understand it:

"Here we are at the height of our power. The most powerful nation in the world. And yet we're afraid to use that power, we lack the will. In the last thirty years we've lost Estonia, Latvia, Lithuania, Poland, Czechoslovakia, Hungary, Bulgaria. China . . ."

"Some people," said Bundy, "don't think we ever had them."

LeMay, with a wave of the cigar, a quick flick of the ash: "Some people think we did."[36]

In the interim, in 1954, President Eisenhower had followed this line by declaring that the loss of Indochina would cause the rest of Southeast Asia to fall to the communists like a set of dominoes.[37] This domino theory was to haunt international relations for the next fifteen years.

From playing dominoes, it is a short if sophisticated step to playing chess. In 1962 Adolf A. Berle, Jr. began his book *Latin America: Diplomacy and Reality* by stating that the region, the whole continent, had to be placed on a vast checkerboard. It is at once clear who is playing the game and who is a piece on the board, for he goes on to say that the implacable criterion of his judgment has to be the safety of the United States.[38] Apparently, George Canning is still at large, talking in an American accent. Latin America in particular, whose scholars have not forgotten its place as a Mecca in the minds of nineteenth-century capitalists who were looking for 12 percent interest on their investments, provides excellent evidence for those who insist that modern imperialism needs no foreign flag, like some piece of Victorian prudery, to drape it. The same scholars point to a telling statistic. Between 1945 and 1960 the total capital inflow into Latin America amounted to $8.7 million, but the transfer of profits elsewhere totaled $15.5 million. The process is known as decapitalization, but the imagery of President Kubitschek of Brazil is more vivid. He said that Latin America resembled a man getting a transfusion in one arm while donating blood from the other.[39]

With these assumptions the empires of Europe did their day's work. To list them is to begin understanding the assurance of right with which they did it. It was an assurance based on the belief that only within a system of authority could anything worth doing ever be done at all. "We have learned," wrote the senior American "China expert," John K. Fairbank, in 1967, "that international stability must be undergirded by some structure of power relations—something we did not like to contemplate during most of our early history in Asia."[40] Throughout runs this feeling of justification, and no empire ever existed whose agents did not rely and call upon it. They saw an attack on their position as a denial of common sense itself. The nations of the twentieth century have worked within an altered framework, but they have adhered to terms of reference which the Powers of the nineteenth century would easily have recognized. If the latter were able to get their way more easily, this was because they owned more physical property. But privilege is an intangible property, and although this has to date (1977) come under heavy attack, it has not in fact been extensively redistributed. There are nations who "have"—even granting that they do not have as much as they did—and nations who "have not," though they have more than they once had.

In the former empires of property, problems of authority did not arise; or if they did, they were quashed rather than answered. The imperialists of that day were landlords. They were also policemen, working within a pale of government of their own construction, as the Plantagenets had once done in Ireland. Within a pale, a stockade mentality develops. And as a result of this development the imperial systems began to reveal their first signs of weakness.

Empire was the assumption of superiority and optimism made concrete. But more was taken over than could usefully be put to work. Maintaining and managing empire brought problems which had never bothered the men who "built" it, to whom action was the only creed that counted. Imperialism was their declaration of energy. It was dynamic, a "happening"—as the spread of railways in India and the discovery of oil in the Persian Gulf, in the North Sea, and on the Arctic slope were and are happenings. Imperialism infiltrates and invades. Most vividly, it inquires: it finds out things about an area which its own inhabitants never knew. Larger than any one territory, it relates this territory to an outside and unheard-of world whose purposes can only be conjectured. But the wish to know, rather than to guess, how all these things are done, is almost at once implanted. Imperialism thus creates new kinds of thinking and new states of mind. By scrapping old routines and substituting new ones, it creates new needs. At the same time it creates new kinds of people, people who have found a new awareness and are resolved not to lose it. It sets up new social and economic structures and, quite literally, dislocates and disorients those who had their place in the old social and economic structures. While doing this, it presents for the first time both a set of alternatives and a frame of mind that can recognize them—and so the possibilities of freedom, or at least of movement, insert themselves into areas of life which had never known them.

Imperialism is therefore like the old-time religion: it is a mover and a shaker. Intent on progress through order, it brings as much disorder with it. It has a bad name it will never lose, but all those who gave it that name had to borrow metaphors that signifiy *motion*: encounter and impact, shock and exploitation, aggression and confrontation. And winds of change build up to become Draza Mihajlovic's "gale of the world," to carry everything away.

The source of all this motion is the metropolis. From there philosophical equipment was issued which was not put to much use in the daily life of the colonial world. The principles of the rights of man, the liberty of the subject, the worth of the individual; the doctrines of equality and fraternity—all these were part of the Europeans' psychic baggage before they ever went empire building in nineteenth-century Asia and Africa. The empire builders were merchants and soldiers and adventurers, not philosophers or intellectuals. But they were still the products of their time. They were guided by common rules. They followed accepted habits of conduct, conduct which had been laid down in books they had not necessarily read. Although they might choose to take a risk and ignore the consequences, they knew when they were breaking the rules and that they might not be able to "get away with it." They had a shrewd idea of what would cause trouble "at home." So on the whole they preferred to follow rules that had order and method in them, that made sense. No one was so firm in his devotion to the social proprieties as the Old China Hand in Shanghai and the treaty ports, whose niche in history will forever be that of the exploiting foreign devil. The total nature of the cultural imperialism that made a conformist out of the imperialist will always be hard to trace, for its roots lie in custom and folklore, and its evidence has to be looked for between the lines of what is written down. The things that the whites in the tropics looked on as "not done" were never things, after all, that were impossible to do.

The Romans had despised *rustici* and *barbari*, people without vision, people without a horizon: the European imperialists when they threw the ring of governance around jungle and outback and bush did not suppose that any ideas worth considering would ever grow in its soil or thrive in its undeserted villages. On the contrary, they thought that in so hostile an environment they had to take special care of their own ideas, to see to it that these were not dissipated and lost. Because the French believed so thoroughly in their own great principles, they believed them to be safe only in their own hands. The British, by contrast, took their stand not on universalism but on individualism and believed in that as thoroughly. Their liberal doctrine on colonies was set down in the Report on British North America which Lord Durham handed to his own surprised government in 1839. This has turned out to be a "civil rights" charter which has needed no revision or reissue, since it put the entire British imperial system at risk from its own colonials, of whatever color, by pronouncing that the business of a people is best managed by that people themselves. Such were the thoughts, however seldom expressed in the course of a harassing day, that lay "at the back of the white man's mind." They are thoughts that look forward and upward. They are a long way from, they have little to do with, routines of police work and patrol, or tax gathering and nominal rolls, of naval bases and the balance of power.

This paradox penetrated the conscience of the best colonial officials both nations produced. Their trouble was that their left hands did in fact know what their right hands were doing. The paradox arose because the new empires were made and maintained at the same time that this philosophical revolution impacted upon the European habit and the European mind. The essence of empire is not motion, it is control. Continuance of empire depended upon the acceptance of this control. Empire has fixed structures, none of which adapt to motion or to hurricane or to seepage, and none of which are insured against any of these. The colonial way of life, the expatriate pattern of behavior, very quickly becomes a cement of the imperial structure itself, to pick and chip at which is to put the whole system in danger. Empire is an organized institution, run by a bureaucracy, with set routines within stated territorial bounds. What its agents do within these bounds ought, ideally, to be equally rigid in purpose. But purposes can multiply, and when they do they play havoc with consistency. British officials in Malaya, for example, saw it as their duty to create conditions of political stability and ordered government along western (that is to say, the "right") lines. Economic progress could not be made, the country's natural resources could not be harvested, until this had been done. But simultaneously they wished to justify their presence by promoting the welfare and advancement of the Malay people within the framework of the traditional Malay society.[41] Yet both things could not be done at once. They contradicted one another. It was as if a stage director, while busy supervising the building of an elaborate set, should strew the boards with gunpowder.

Directing a play involves one in its success. So does running a governmental machine. Noises offstage are not wanted. Criticism is thought to be not only unnecessary but impertinent, if not downright subversive. This was particularly so when it came from below, from people who, although they were constantly in the forefront of the official mind, were seldom met with off-duty. Here was (as will be argued later) more a class than a race prejudice. The Portuguese who lived in British Guiana were not classified as Europeans, because they had entered the colony via the indentured immigration program. A coolie was a coolie, and since coolies were by definition not white, a white man who in fact had coolie status lost his definition and his color with it. The opposite also applied: in the British and French West Indies, as in both the colonial Guianas, a man was treated as white, whatever his color, when his income rose above a certain level. This confused logic remained operative in Guiana until 1946, when the Portuguese were classified as "other Europeans"— other, that is, because unequal. That system in turn lasted until 1960, when these nice distinctions in a country now ruled by blacks, East Indians, and various admixtures seemed no longer sensible to anyone.[42]

Barriers designed to prevent social intercourse were equally effective in preventing any leap into the political arena from some unexpected quarter. Politics in any language has a dialect of its own, as much social as technical: only the initiated can use it. Since men who were officially invisible could not be initiated into anything, it was not likely that they would be officially heard from. In Kenya under British rule the Civil Service reflected the social structure of the colony with an entire accuracy. It had three racial tiers, with different rates of pay for each race, even if members of each were doing the same job. Social contact at the Europeans' level of living was thus impossible. Any official setting out to change this state of affairs would have involved himself in what was called "politics"— and this was a zone barred to him by every rule in the book. A man who persisted would soon find himself docketed (to borrow from British Colonial Office jargon) as "temperamentally unsuited to the Service."[43]

Imagination is rare in anyone's behavior. Only a glimpse of it is ever caught in public life. In the public life of colonies it was seldom present. The ablest and most intelligent expatriate could not effectively counteract his isolation from the context of life and thought in the metropolis, the context which had nourished his ability and intelligence in the first place. At home among his own kind, an official may not welcome change, but he is not likely to think of it as intrinsically dangerous. But in colonies the imponderables are so many that change can hardly be anything but dangerous. The colonial official, the European settler, set down in clusters amid people who did not have, did not want, and did not develop any sense of community with him, kept the future at a distance by doing his best to perpetuate the conditions of the present. His resolution was that tomorrow the sun would rise, and set, on exactly the same scene. This was not the ground to nourish imagination.

One result of this attitude was that little innovation took place in the area where it was most needed, in agriculture. The subjects of empire were, almost exclusively, peasants. Not much "westernization" came their way. The ring of governance was thrown around the countryside, but aliens left few marks on its ground. The village was not modernized, and no new horizon was revealed to the peasant. One viceroy, Lord Mayo, had in 1870 declared that the progress of India in wealth and civilization was directly dependent on its progress in agriculture. He was right: but no equivalent of the eighteenth century's "Turnip" Townshend ever descended on the Indian plains. His absence was not noticed by either the ruler or the vast majority of the ruled. Valentine Chirol, who wrote good books on India and knew it first hand, was probably right in saying that no race had been so successful as the English in ruling primitive and backward peoples who did not aspire to equality, but were content, as children were, to be treated in the spirit of kindliness and fair play which most Englishmen possessed.[44] Yet although many people may act as guardian with honor, few kindle to the prospect of assuming a perpetual role as ward. For no amount of kindliness and fair play could do much to give people a life in place of an existence. Whether or not they aspired to equality, they aspired to *something* —and because the majority of the English did not know what this was and did not intend to find out, because their officialdom could not even prevent poverty from falling into misery, Gandhi in the 1930s brought his most wounding charge against the English, the more cutting because he couched it in language he had first learned among lawyers in the Middle Temple in London. The English in India, he said, were both incompetent and irrelevant. They were busy with tasks that had nothing to do with anything that mattered to the life of India. Their work was perpetually beside the point.

So it came about that the revolutionary equipment, which was indeed stored in the armory of imperialism as it was in that of all other western movements, was put into the hands of men whose time was fully taken up in patrolling the bounds of empire and keeping the peace within them. These conservatives, holding the ring of government, were not commissioned to lay plans for some very different kind of future. They had not heard of any revolution of rising expectations, and if they had they would not have understood what it meant. Their business was not to promote expectation in anyone. It was a going concern, which it was their task to keep going, along the same lines. In fact, they worked within the narrowest of bounds, while thinking them to be the widest of horizons. They were modern men. The imperial way made sense because it was modern, and it was profitable for the same reason. Who should complain of this? What right of complaint was there? The world was a place of action, not of complaint. If man on this earth had before him a "manifest destiny" at all, it was to make progress: and no assertion from below had yet brought any evidence forward to contradict the white man's view of what progress meant. Indeed, the ablest imperial subjects were thoroughly indoctrinated with it and had never denied it.

Accordingly, to the imperial mind, exploitation was simply a description of progress, not a criticism of it. Gandhi's criticisms came from a world it did not know, a world it doubted existed—or, if it allowed its existence, consigned it to the shadow of fantasy and sentimentality. Gandhi was in undergraduate company in the University of Oxford on October 24, 1931, telling these future empire managers that he did not want them to determine the pace of other people's progress, pointing out to them that "consciously or unconsciously, you adopt the role of divinity." He answered the question "how would you distinguish exploitation from trading with a nation?" There were two tests:

The other nation must want our goods which should in no case be dumped on it against our will. The trade should not be backed by the Navy.

A month later he made a similar point to a like audience at Cambridge. No scheme of Indianization in the army could serve any useful purpose, inasmuch as, "until the last moment, the command will be British." In an army orders were orders, as the story of the massacre at Amritsar had shown. "Who was it that shot people at Jallianwala Bagh, if it was not their own countrymen?"[45]

But whatever impact he may have made on these English young, he was not talking a language their seniors could translate, and they were as unlikely to listen to any précis of it made by their juniors as they were to one made by Hindus. Empire, they continued to insist, was an administrative task. It had absolutely no place in politics, and only the foolish and the subversive wanted to transfer it into that arena. Certainly, since human beings were fallible, there were some things done that might be better done; sensible changes were therefore to be welcomed by sensible people. But such changes, when made, must be those that squared with their own ideas of good management. The future was always a potential menace to the status quo, but, surely, insisting on good management now would serve as an investment in security, would force the future into an acceptable shape? To be worth reaching at all, it had to be the kind of future capable of being intelligently handled by people like themselves. From this standpoint the future was itself a colonial territory, part of the patrimony of the just and the powerful, a heritage to be passed on to their own posterity for them to colonize and exploit. If the idea of progress meant anything at all, it meant that someday one would arrive at what Winston Churchill liked to call "the broad uplands," and what would be the point of arriving at broad uplands that were occupied by someone else? Charles de Gaulle, touring French Africa in January 1944 under the banner of Free France, declared that the civilizing labors of France in the colonies excluded all possibility of colonial development outside of the French system and insisted that no form of self-government was envisaged, "even in the distant future."[46] And after World War II so staunch an English socialist as Stafford Cripps was still convinced that the British Empire still had a long history ahead of it—provided, of course, that it was rejuvenated with a zeal for the economic and social welfare of all its subjects.

Good management was, of course, another concept which was reinforced by unexamined assumptions. It was bred in and belonged to the western industrial world, and since this world was still ex-

panding—a process which the two world wars did a great deal to
assist—it would continue to be a necessity everywhere. Westerners
saw no alternative to it: anything else was fantasy, the last thing
anyone needed. In their view, the evidence plainly showed how
much inefficiency and incompetence, which were perhaps not the
worst vices of weak and conquered peoples but which certainly
hobbled them enormously, were still abroad and how much, therefore, the western work ethic still had to do to eradicate them. Colonies were colonies precisely because the people who lived in them
had not known how to manage themselves, their environment, their
present, and their future. They had in fact known nothing worth
knowing. They had to be shown, they had had to be told; and the
showing and the telling could not be done in a day. Obviously, good
management had to expect to meet head on with hindrance and
misunderstanding and open hostility, but these things honed and
sharpened it and made its virtues shine the brighter in "Darkest Africa," behind God's back, in all the other parts of the forest, all the
parts of barbary. It became the habit of the European imperial official to believe that if plans and programs went astray, it was not
because there was anything wrong with the plans and programs. He
brought with him a mental apparatus that assumed it was natural
that appointments would be kept, a word would be honored, truth
would be told, females would not be exposed at birth or circumcised
at puberty, gin and rifles would not be bartered, prisoners would not
be sold or mutilated, travelers would not be robbed and murdered,
sand would not be mixed in with the concrete, and men would stay
unbribed. The more he found out that others did not think these
things were natural, the more he was convinced that their only salvation, or anyway some glimpse of it, lay in his own continued
presence.

Around this central problem of management other difficulties
ranged themselves. One minority was perpetually dealing with
another, in an alien language whose structure was understood but
whose idiom was not. "What is it that the white men write all day
at their desks?" is a famous question out of the colonial world. What,
indeed. Their memoranda and instructions were all related to the
same terms of reference. The controllers controlled the assessment
of what was in the local interest and connected it to their assessment

of what was in the imperial interest. They were not there to lose other people's money or to waste their own government's money. They were not there to be displaced by enemies, whether internal or external. They were there because they were there, with a job in hand, and the more people they could get to help them do the job, the better for everyone, on both the local and the imperial scene. They had the power to enforce the application of these imperial ideas, and this fact often caused them to lose sight of the other fact that they held imperial ideas at all. They took a particular view of law: its aim was to preserve order—and the expression they so often and so fervently used, "Law and Order," in fact meant peace and order. It meant an absence of public foolishness, an absence of violence, a guarantee of unhindered travel from one place to another. It had little if anything to do with any abstract concept of justice, an imperial idea which always lacked for jurists. And this was precisely what Jawaharlal Nehru had in mind when he said that any imperial system must be the enemy of any true international order.[47]

In any society how things are done depends on the assumptions of those who are in charge of it. A historian of anarchism made this point best, seeing it sideways. Law is the body of legal norms; and a legal norm is

one which is based on the fact that men have the will to see a certain procedure generally observed within a circle which includes themselves. . . . It instructs us not as to what is good but only as to what is prescribed.[48]

What a man can do has always kept company with what he cannot. The other side of the coin of prescription is proscription, as all records of empire show. In the West Indies and in Ireland law was long identified with oppression by an elite. To the Hindu any notion of equality before the law was meaningless because he did not suppose men to be equal in the first place, and the European image of justice as a blindfolded woman seemed to him not only ridiculous but sinister. Justice was anyway not something to be got from aliens. Sir Henry Maine remarked that the corpus of English law was a law-library of some thousand volumes. Could there be conceived, he asked, a more intolerable hardship than having the civil rights of 150 million people dependent on a system contained in records which were inaccessible to them, which they could not translate, and which, even if they could translate, they could not understand?

It was no argument, he added, to say that a like state of affairs prevailed in England itself: "That was true, but it was a peculiarity of England, and not an honourable one, and not one which Englishmen should carry all over the world with them." The government of India, he concluded, might be defined as a despotism limited by the capacity of its officers to do more than a certain amount of work.[49]

The controllers of empire were not apt to be diffident about their capacities, but the best of them felt, probably not without a degree of wishful thinking concerning the length of their own careers, that however competent and able everyone was, the work itself would never be done. There was just too much of it: it was a task for Titans, as Joseph Chamberlain said. They had to prepare their charges for self-government, in the British system. They had to make not only adequate but exceptional French people out of them, in the French system. The Dutch, intent on money, saw no end to processes that would multiply the ways in which more money might be made. The Portuguese held onto their property overseas because it *was* their property overseas: it reminded them of the great days when they had also had a purpose overseas. Theirs was the empire of fantasy, appearing to outsiders as "inveterably quixotic"—and perhaps as a result of this attribution their *missão civilisadora* and their *mapa côr de rosa* were to survive, as though enclosed in a twenty-year time lock, into the 1970s. Portugal's empire remained an anachronism, not to be classified among the categories that analysts made, since in its case Thorstein Veblen could be taken as a surer guide than Hobson—"the Veblenian notion of conspicuous consumption seems nearer the mark than the urgings of Hobsonian capitalists bent on enlarging export markets in improbable places."[50]

Russia under Communism, less willing to realize the implications of Lenin's theorems on imperialism than some analysts expected, held onto its own Central Asian properties with a similar traditional tenacity and in an autocratic fashion which Tsar Alexander II and his victorious General Skobeleff would have approved. And although China's own Celestial Empire disappeared with the Ch'ing dynasty in 1911, and its new republican state-structure began to disintegrate amid the quarrels of warlords whose political notions did not extend beyond loot, these banditti were still able to hold fast to the idea of the nation still alive and in being, though beset by troubles—China, its own—despite the expectancy of foreign devils that the country would ultimately collapse, if only because of exhaustion, into a passivity of a kind wherein the Far East might at last be made over into a replica of the Midwest.

But however and by whom the imperial task was seen, it was commonly agreed that it would take time, a great deal of time. What was done in this time must be, and be perceived to be, in the best interests of the subject people. In the 1920s this became a much publicized axiom, concrete enough to bury whatever programs emerged for using the time for some specific purpose. A paternalist doctrine did not necessarily contain a blueprint for change, or even a definition of aim. The language of the Victorians was still used, but it could not be made to mean very much beyond the Victorian context, in the twilight of the Victorian trust in progress. Going through the motions was easier than movement. A striking example of this occurs in the report of an official British commission which investigated the affairs of Palestine, published in 1937 and largely written by the imperial historian Reginald Coupland while simultaneously drafting a new constitution for British India. Having rehearsed, with exceptional skill and cogency, the history and extant state of enmity between the Arabs and the Jews—with such persuasiveness that a reader is convinced (as many contemporary readers were also) there is nothing any outsider can do about it—this report spells out the unthinking imperialist assumption in a straight line: "Obviously, Your Majesty's Government cannot stand aside and let the Jews and the Arabs fight their quarrel out."[51]

Another thing that took time, a great deal of it, was development. No accepted definition of this exists. "Development, like any other major idea," says Robert Nisbet, "is a perspective," and he adds that the whole theory of social evolution provided a marvelous justification for the ascendancy of the West. The assumption here was that the recent history of the West could be taken as evidence of the direction in which mankind as a whole would move, and, flowing from this, *should* move. Its criteria were technology, individualism, secularism, democracy, and egalitarianism. Bearing these on their banners, westerners find themselves confronted with what they see as darkness, backwardness, superstition, primitivism, ruralism, and immaturity, the whole encased in a context of irrelevance. They therefore set out on a victory campaign, to plant their banners triumphantly somewhere within this country of the blind. Imperialism is, above all, functional: it sends out a task force. "At no point in the history of European thought," adds Nisbet, "has this combination of comparison and developmentalism been really absent."[52] Whether the comparison reveals a Noble Savage, or merely an unregenerate being in a state of nature, is only a matter of mood.

The questions surrounding development are, however, likely to remain so long as rich and resourceful nations set out to promote it in places that have resources but are not rich. It is enveloped by the kind of mystery that was once attached to economics and by an idealism similar to that found in imperialist history itself. A distinction can be made between "modernization," which is another name for westernization and is seen as something done by someone to a subordinate, and "development," which semantically infers a growth, which is something achieved by someone. Semantics are a notorious trap in politics, but it makes sense to suppose that the concept of development argues, indeed makes essential, the presence of a developer, armed with a plan. Like the imperialist, such a one may be short of character witnesses, since the edge between development and exploitation is razor-thin. (The name of developer, attached to someone whose business deals with city blocks, high-rise apartments, etc., is not necessarily given in admiration.) The development of the United States of America, as one of its angrier late twentieth-century critics pointed out, includes the slaughter of the indigenous population and the importation of another alien population as slaves.[53] The target is familiar. It is neither impossible nor overstrained to classify the modern western devotion to development as one more imperialist activity. It goes through the same motions as the standard actions of imperialism and proclaims the same ends. It can even produce a similar pedigree. It is, in fact, the most up-to-date version of the French imperialist concept *la mission civilisatrice*: a blueprint for someone else's future.

Colonies were long categorized as undeveloped, and have latterly been classified as underdeveloped, estates. An estate is a property, an area, and its value is judged by what it can produce. That the area has its tenants, that people live there, is known but is not at the forefront of the developer's mind. That the people themselves have an economic value is also known: indeed, it is notorious. Having digested the report of a royal commission on Indian expenditure, published in 1900, Romesh Dutt figured that the Indian taxpayer, earning little more than his food, was taxed 40 percent more than his contemporary, the taxpayer in the United Kingdom. The annual remittance to England of £17 million for "home charges," added to the remittances made by European officers employed in India, represented nearly one half of the net revenues of the country.[54] Albert Sarraut, a generation later, in his book *Grandeur et servitude coloniales* (1931)—itself a title filched from the Romantic tradition in France—may have had this kind of thing in mind when he said that colonialism had the right to distribute resources that incapable owners held without profit to themselves or to anyone else.[55]

But whatever form development takes, all of it begins with research. Research in turn is based on motive. It must start, as Gunnar Myrdal pointed out, from a set of analytical preconceptions. People armed with analytical preconceptions can, however, become as arrogant as the forgotten figure in a *topi*. For holding this particular preconception, Myrdal himself was charged with arrogance by others in his line of work who prefer to call development-studies "normative."[56] Yet the only alternative to making an analytical approach to anything is to fall silent altogether. Emile Durkheim, who rejected individualism and believed that the antecedent state did not produce the subsequent but that the relation between them was purely chronological, once attacked Auguste Comte and Herbert Spencer for identifying human development "with the idea they had of it"; but it is hard to see what else they could have done. The only preconceptions one can have, after all, are one's own. (Durkheim's solution to the problem was to eradicate all preconceptions, which is easier said than done.)[57] In the field of imperial studies, "development" has kept its good name because it is seen to own both a scientific basis and a progressive tradition. For another example, a student might examine the enclosure movement in late eighteenth-century England, which was a piece of local imperialism put in hand by a developing, modernizing squirearchy, in everyone's best interests. The common land vanished. In the highlands of Scotland a generation later, a similar development took place: the land was not enclosed, it was thrown open for sheep to roam in, and as a result the crofts vanished and the crofters with them. In modern South Africa the construction of the enclave of Bantustan, to house the black unassimilables whom the white rulers of the republic do not need, illustrates yet another enclosing policy, arranged in the general interest. And the greatest enclosure movement of them all is still at work—the movement that westernizes, industrializes, and modernizes. The imperialism of modern technology, of development identified with progress and given into the hands of technocrats who speak only their own language, has never yet had any bounds set to it by anyone, since nobody wants to see this done. Great indeed is the empire of the controllers of our own time—the empire of what Sir Peter Medawar has called, in a high romantic enthusiasm, "that huge, logically-articulated structure of ideas which is already, though not yet half-built, the most glorious accomplishment of mankind."[58]

A structure of ideas argues the presence of a builder with a blueprint. The doctrine of development therefore has to include educational progress. How fast it goes depends on the definition of progress laid down by the developing agency. How far it goes nobody ever knows. Education, let loose imperially into the world with its means accounted for but not its ends, turned out to be less a theory than a thing, whose effects are much like those of a land mine. Mission schools were everywhere established and staffed by the Christian pioneers of European imperialism, working with heart and will: it was not their fault that the classroom door opened only into an area of uncertainty. The best of those who went through it were supposed to be of use thereafter to the imperial regime—but beyond that requirement, no theory covered the continuing existence of the remainder. In 1835 two Englishmen in India had looked at this prospect from two different points of view. The orientalist Henry Hayman Wilson forecast exactly what Gandhi and Nehru would say a century later about western education and its results:

to make a whole people dependent upon a remote and unknown country for all their ideas, and for the very words in which to clothe them . . . [must] degrade their character, depress their energies, and render them incapable of aspiring to any intellectual distinction.[59]

The Whig politician T. B. Macaulay, in India to write an "education minute" which was to have a profound effect on the Indian future, urged that the task of English-language education should be to create a class of interpreters, middlemen who would pass on to their illiterate kin the wishes of their superiors. This would both ease the burden of government and involve in the political process as many of the subject race as possible. But Macaulay also realized that a time would come when the post of go-between would not be the only employment an awakened mind would want and that some other outlet for intellectual energy would have to be found. He did not say what or where this might be, and in this omission he was followed by an entire posterity of officialdom. Europeans believed in the virtues of education. They saw themselves as the standing example of its value, and they could not have brought themselves to run an administration that had no educational policy. But they related it to youth and to the classroom: they did not make the connection to life. In the imperial arena they laid down a running track that did not end at a winning post. It ended in the mist.

Students who graduated into a world that did not especially want them, like them, or respect them, crowded into the field of government work or into journalism and the law. Or they took to the streets. Schoolteachers became Irish martyrs. Egyptian nationalism owed them much. The success of the May Fourth movement in China (1919) owed them more. But to the officials, students were just another collective, one much less durable than most. They had a voice, but it was a voice that faded, and it never said a word worth listening to. People who thought that subversion and conspiracy were other names for idealism, who threw rocks and burned books, were plainly people whose other views, on anything at all, were not worth discovering.

So if education remained low among the items on imperial budgets, this was partly because awakened minds had proved to keep company with awakened emotions, among people who did not think and would not learn that common sense, compromise, and acceptance were obvious virtues. Imperialists delayed dealing with this dilemma for as long as they could. When they did look into it, they recommended not more education but better education: to use the English name for it, higher education. Writing of the program for the development of higher education in British colonies after World War II, the educationist Sir Eric Ashby tells that advice was given, decisions were made, and a great deal of money was spent within a framework of assumptions which he and his colleagues never had time to examine, still less to question. These assumptions, when examined, turn out indeed to be what one would have supposed them to be. The underlying assumption, which made a massive foundation for everything built afterward, was that the structure and curriculum appropriate to a university in London or Exeter or Manchester was ipso facto suitable in a new institution in Nigeria, the West Indies, or Malaya. This was, says Ashby, "almost an axiom."[60] Yet it makes no sense to raise an eyebrow at this axiom, since it was not likely that British people would want to introduce French, American, or other foreign educational systems into British colonies. The French, Americans, and others would equally have preferred what they themselves knew best and thought best.

The British government appointed in August 1943 a royal commission on higher education in the colonies. At that time there were only four institutions in the colonies classifiable as "higher"—in Malta, in Ceylon, the Hebrew University at Jerusalem (whose foundation stone had been laid in 1925 by Arthur Balfour himself), and in Hong Kong, then in Japanese hands. In its report, issued in 1945, the commission decided it could consider only the next few decades, but the commissioners saw the establishment of universities as an inescapable corollary of any policy aimed at achieving colonial self-government. In colonies, where education as a whole was backward, effort was most rewarding when it was directed to the higher levels. How high these levels were, only the initiated could know; accordingly, no premature grant of degree-giving powers was envisaged. Each new alma mater would have its own grandmother. But the new institutions must be true universities, not mere technical schools. There should be in each of them a senior lecturer or professor of philosophy. The commissioners did not want to see utilitarian results demanded from the research activities of faculty members, or their work judged by its immediate bearing upon practical problems. English would be the language of instruction, although it was recognized that far too little had yet been done in Britain itself to explore the nature and range of the problems that arose in the teaching of English as a foreign language. But what good would it serve, one of the commissioners asked, to perpetuate the native African languages?

"The world would not have gained if the pre-Roman languages of Spain and Gaul had survived instead of giving place to a great common tongue."[61] That one educates others along one's own lines can also, like imperialism itself, be taken as a datum.

That others respond to such cultural assurance is also an axiom: if they did not, the assurance would not exist. Its acceptance in the world beyond the classroom, and admiration for it, governed the local reaction to the syllabus prescribed. Should the classics and English literature be taught at the colleges at Fourah Bay and Achimota? Yes, insisted the majority of West African intellectuals in the 1920s and 1930s, certainly they should. They were not to be fobbed off with something else, something different which, just because it was different, was clearly inferior, unlike what Europeans taught to their own young. Wordsworth's *Daffodil* thus stayed a subject of study for those who had not seen a daffodil and might never do so. But this did not matter. As one Hindu prince asked, shall I shut in my son's face the door through which I myself have passed?[62] Western education, in this view, was the key that unlocked a golden treasury. By others it was looked upon as fraudulent: it was a key, perhaps, but where was the lock it fitted? Both Gandhi and Nehru described the British system of education as a thing that emasculated. "It has torn us from our moorings," Nehru said; "it has made us hug the very chains that bind us." And the poet and seer, Rabindranath Tagore—known to the Indian Intelligence department before 1914 as "suspect number 12, class B"—called western education an almsbowl and a dustbin.[63]

Yet these were the best receptacles available. Western education alone could issue political concepts to the assertive, could give them a vocabulary of expression to coin the slogans emblazoned on the banners they would march beneath. It alone could equip them with a *lingua franca* which would bring them worldwide attention. Nehru knew this was so. He asked, after listing all the Anglo-Saxon race prejudices he could think of, a list at whose end stood the entire populations of Asia and Africa,

Is it any wonder that their vision grows dim when they look toward us, and that we should irritate them when we talk of democracy and liberty? These words were not coined for our use.[64]

Indeed they were not. But a currency once issued will circulate, whatever the prejudices of the mint master. For example, the *dusturi* (constitutional) party of Tunisia asked for: an assembly consisting of French and Tunisians, with equal rights and universal suffrage; a government responsible to that assembly; a separation of the legislative, executive, and judicial powers; the "Tunisianization" of the public services; equal pay for French and Tunisian workers; elective municipal councils; freedom of the press and of association; and a compulsory system of education. They asked for all these things in March 1920, and they were speaking in a language that owed all its concepts to the imperial context from which it sprang.[65]

However it was seen and characterized, western education remained an essential part of imperial policy. If education was hard to define, so was policy. Since statesmen have always spoken of policy in grave tones, much of the same solemnity invaded the histories that discuss it. But in hindsight the dictum of the third Lord Salisbury that his main business as foreign secretary was to put out boathooks, to ward off collision from the ship of state, seems less a confession of incompetence than a testimony to his acute sense of the possible. The Imperial Powers were not naturally inclined to political adventure. The very concept of the "balance of power," to which they all paid homage and in which most of them, despite the evidence, believed, conjures up an image of an assessor, cautiously reading the runes. The chief political business of an empire was to remain an empire, and since the record shows that not one empire succeeded in doing so, the accolade of genuine imperial statesmanship in truth belongs finally to nobody: if Bismarck is still admired, this is because the German Empire, while he was in charge of it, did make an accurate assessment of the relationship between diplomatic means and imperial ends.

Certain aspirations were held in common. There was, always and everywhere, a general policy of self-preservation. Foreigners must not be allowed to take over one's own satellite area: trespassers must be prosecuted. There was a policy of internal security, since no business could be done in conditions of danger. There was a policy of attracting to colonies Europeans who would settle there and produce exports which could be taxed, at the same time encouraging or coercing the local inhabitants to produce cash crops which would also provide resources for taxation. But imperial policy, in any larger sense, was rare. One attempt to provide it occurred when the British cabinet approved what became known as the Balfour Declaration on November 2, 1917, which "viewed with favour" the founding in British colonial Palestine of a National Home for the Jews. Similarly, the French effort to spread their civilization abroad became an exercise in the exportation of French dominance, a policy which in the good revolutionary tradition produced *cahiers de doléances* to suit. This did not happen because these policies or their authors were spurious and hypocritical, but because they had bypassed, to their own peril, a major fact of imperial life—that what controllers can accomplish is limited by what the controlled will accept.

In practice, imperial policy reduced itself to coping with the problems that the facts of empire, evidenced by the incoming mail, brought up. The tidy desk, the quiet street, the busy harbor, the lower statistics on hookworm, the absence of plague and famine – why should a harassed official look for larger aims than these? On this ground, which was surely wide enough, some limited victories might be gained. Beyond it, a policy would have to find massive financial backing from headquarters, and before it could get this, it would have to be explained and then more money would have to be allocated, entailing an interminable wrangle with the Treasury at home. There was no end in sight to such a campaign and no assurance at all of victory at the close of it.

Moreover, imperial officials knew that the majority of the people they controlled were, like themselves, interested only in the present, in surviving the day and living out the week. Aspiration beyond that they saw as the exception, not the rule—and about this fundamental matter they were not mistaken. Everywhere, the majority of people conformed, and would always conform, to the powers that were. Conformity makes no headlines, attracts little attention from historians: they are the nonconformists who bear witness to the struggles they endured to come up from below and who, when they have been successful, write the books that make success appear inevitable. In their autobiographies they tell how they perceived the struggle. They do not diminish their difficulties, but they explain how their especial acumen allowed them to exploit the local situation to their own advantage. But, because they are indeed exceptional men, they cannot and do not throw much light on the people and the background from whom and from which they emerged. Conformists in the imperial world lived in an area whose bounds have not been accurately measured either by those who governed it or by those of their own kin who lived in it, then burst out, and broke free. Conformists were the apolitical, the unaware. For them no alternative existed, since they did not know that any alternative had ever been presented.

This state of blankness among the majority accounts for the actual physical flimsiness of alien control. At the turn of this century, there were only 750 officers in the covenanted civil service in India, one for every quarter million of the population. In the higher judicial and executive services there were about 2,600 officers. Within the substructure worked a subordinate civil service staffed by Indians — and "subordinate" was part of their official title — which had about 110,000 employees. Jawaharlal Nehru had this organization and situation in mind when he wrote that while he was an inmate watching the working of an Indian prison, it struck him how it resembled the way the British governed India itself, with "convict warders and convict overseers." The French used the same system. On January 1, 1938, among the 30 million inhabitants of Cambodia, Laos and Vietnam were stationed 11,000 soldiers and 292 police officers.[66]

Empires always depended for their existence on the collaboration of a substratum of native clerks, native soldiers, and native policemen. Colonial governments were, all of them, multiracial, plural societies in miniature. This did not come about because political theorists were applying a liberal policy. It arose out of plain necessity. There were never enough aliens present to do the administrative work which the aliens had created for themselves. They organized a government for the people and then recruited to it the ambition of the people themselves. The ambition was often enough simply getting enough to eat. Within that social context a process of intellectual lend-lease was constantly at work. The taught adapted to the teachers, the teachers adapted to the taught, and the pace of the government office adapted to the capacities of its inmates. The same things happened also at home, for no institution anywhere is ever any better, or does any better, than the people who staff it; but the transplantation of western institutions overseas brought about a transformation of not only the kind of activities the institutions performed but also the kind of people inside them. But, as was true everywhere else too, the officers were always instantly distinguishable from the other ranks. The former drew up the agenda, declared their intentions, issued the information, and defined the method by which the objective should be reached.

Yet every authoritative system has room in it for the element of bewilderment. The serving soldier does not take long finding out about the fatuous side of the army. He learns that total unreason (*Catch-22*) lurks inside its cage of regulations, which can at any time play havoc. In a situation where his officers are actual aliens, no amount of insight will help him know what stage of affairs has been reached or what is and what is not absurd. Where there is no common frame of reference, everything may seem absurd: and because it seems so, it is so. Because of the breadth of this comprehension gap, rather than from any obsession with race, colonial noncollaboration and nonconformism ultimately spread. The very busyness and activity of the administration appeared irrelevant to the lives people were living and to the thoughts (whatever they were) they were thinking. "We are the enemies of life," was W. R. Crocker's judgment on his own generation of officials in West Africa.[67]

Accordingly, although the imperial files now fill libraries, there are gaps on all the shelves. What can be seen and cross-referenced may get more attention than it strictly deserves. The Indian Congress party is a case in point. India's political life was lived not among the jealousies and posturings of Congress but in the provincial legislatures, the law courts, the newspaper editorials, the universities, the town councils, the temple committees, and the office of the *tahsildar*.[68] In these arenas the British *raj* was more a looming than an actual presence. An imperial government, although officially monarch of all it surveyed, did not in fact survey very much, so it did not often know a lot about what was actually going on. Its historians, who in Gilberto Freyre's words are men "islamically trapped in the mystique of the written word,"[69] can too easily assume that the things that are well documented are the only things that either happened or mattered. In imperial history this notion takes nobody far. Corruption, rife in all empires, was by its own nature an undocumented activity. So was crime, since it is only on discovery that crime, unlike sin, exists at all. Moneylending kept its documentation to itself—

but Nehru's own word on it is that the root cause of the tension between Hindu and Muslim in Bengal was the exploitation of the Muslim tenant by the Hindu landlord and *bania*.[70] No government, however totalitarian, has yet managed to penetrate into every area of life: George Orwell's *Nineteen Eighty-Four* (1949) scared everyone because it envisages a future where this will be possible. The imperial world was, despite all the efforts expended by cadres of devoted administrators, undergoverned. Since no European Power either wanted or was able to post a soldier behind every native over whom its flag flew, the quick-witted among these subjects always had the opportunity to become invisible when they chose to do so, to "get away with it," to exploit the preoccupations of controllers who had their hands full with external problems and whose judgment of the true state of internal affairs was always hesitant at best.

Europeans in time came to know the appeal and the motivation of this style of behavior well enough. During World War II every "resistance movement" in German-occupied Europe, many of which had other things in mind than simple patriotism, made it a moral imperative to get away with everything possible. In imperially occupied Asia and Africa resistance was more sporadic, because the need for such a close-knit organization was not recognized: but the resisters, the nonconformists, took the same hard line, and by the sixth decade of the century had got away with empire itself. And they did this not by storm and siege but by pushing open doors. The movements of resistance pressed against what was itself moving — but not moving forward and no longer resisting.

To assess how this came about; how the assumptions that had carried Europeans far failed to carry them farther; how their assurance ran out; how the gap grew between what was seen and what was true; how, even on the narrow ground it had taken for its own, imperial policy could no longer find and keep an acceptance; how the margins of power shrank and the number of options diminished; and how the politics of complaint invaded the areas where for so long imperialism had sheltered behind a sound barrier, it is necessary to look first at the world as it was when the century began and then at the structure of authority which its imperial framework enclosed for the next fifty years.

IMPERIAL FRAMEWORK

The world the imperialists made, and how they governed it.

3

IMPERIAL FRAMEWORK

Imperialism makes use of other people: coercion is its natual habit. The ultimatum waits at the far side of all imperial diplomacy. The record of the first half of the twentieth century owns no testimony more telling than this, dictated by Sir Miles Lampson, the British ambassador in Cairo on February 4, 1942: "Unless I hear by 6 p.m. that Nahas Pasha has been asked to form a Cabinet, His Majesty King Farouk must expect the consequences." On this occasion Lampson's retinue at His Majesty's Abdin Palace was a posse of armored cars. He presented his ultimatum, which was accepted. He wrote in his diary that night: "So much for the events of the evening, which I confess I could not have more enjoyed."[1]

It did not signify, at a climactic time in the life of the British Empire, that junior officers in the Egyptian army, like Gamal Abdel Nasser—who, trained in Britain's Royal Military Academy at Sandhurst, looked on their own king as their commander-in-chief—resented both the thought that such a statement could be made by a foreigner and the knowledge that it was not only possible to issue but easy to fulfill. Diplomacy is a branch of manners, and imperialism has few. In wartime it has none. The unstated assumptions of a Great Power then become public, and its politicians act upon them, the more harshly perhaps because peacetime gives them few chances to speak their true minds. In October 1940 Anthony Eden had told Lampson he was coming to the conclusion that the only thing to do was "to kick the boy [Farouk] out";[2] now, sixteen months later, the "boy," though not "kicked out," was effectively shackled in the keeping of a chief minister who, it was known, would conform to British ideas of what ought to happen in Egypt. Such an event makes it plain that no uproar about imperialism can affect the facts of power. Where its base is secure, no argument can shift it, any more than the existence of the science of meteorology can change the course of the weather. "Power" was defined by a historian of the oil business as a resource necessary for ordered action. The resourceful are those who know how to assess and assemble their resources. They know how to succeed. It is also possible to define "empire" (at least, it has been done) as "an a-symmetrical power relationship"; but this is a notion bred in the schoolroom, one which could have been reached only by those with the leisure to formulate second thoughts about other people's activities.[3] It belongs to bystanders, more accurately described as privileged than as innocent.

But the unprivileged, too, have their own thoughts. One pioneer bystander, the black intellectual Edward Wilmot Blyden, took a ranging view over the future. In his 1881 inaugural address as president of the college of Liberia, he remarked that the black people had had their history written for them and then tried to act upon it, "whereas the true order is, that history should be first acted, then written." Sixty years later the Indian dissident Subhas Chandra Bose made the same point, answering someone who had urged him that the history of the Indian National Army, a force recruited to the service of imperial Japan, must be written: "Let us make it, someone else will write it." In the first half of the century, making history and writing history were privileges thought by white people to belong exclusively to white people. It was their world, their property; so they alone kept the books of the estate. No outside auditors were needed or wanted. A speaker at the Royal Colonial Institute in London was able, with no sense of omission, to give a paper on "Our Future Colonial Policy" that mentioned no part of Africa other than South Africa—which was of course seen as another white man's country. Our hindsight demonstrates that his foresight reflected the distorted view natural to imperialist arrogance; but this was not the way it looked in the year 1902.[4] Or in 1942 either, as the "ruler" of Egypt found out.

Everything, including the horizon, was white man's country. Because this was so it had a magnetism that drew the enterprising to it. They wanted to leave bystanding behind, to make sure that, when they stood up, they would be counted. They wanted no part of impotence. Imperial service offered at least a life, a choice, and a role. Irishmen therefore joined it throughout the long history of the British Empire, however many songs and wrongs of Ireland they had learned at their mothers' knee. The English patrician Lord Durham, having watched the ways of French-Canadians subject to an alien overlordship in British North America in the 1830s, referred to "the vices of a weak and conquered people."[5] One of these was mendacity: and a person need not be *Canadien* or Irish or Afrikaner to know what this vice was and to want a life free of it. Having an option about what to do with oneself; knowing how best to express oneself; being on the side of progress and partner to those who were making it; sharing in some great enterprise; being in at the death; and leaving some sign of having passed that way—these were all among the normal ambitions of the imperialists' young, who by the fact of their youth were compelled to take the bystander's role. It was to these youngsters that such English writers as Rider Haggard and G. A. Henty (*With Clive to India* and *With Kitchener to the Soudan*) made so vivid an appeal in the 1880s, and their books were still in print fifty years later. But beyond this fortunate circle of youth, in due course to come into its own, were all the other outsiders, whose severance from the world of action did not end at age twenty-one.

Nobody romanticized these people, or wrote books for them, for nobody noticed them. But among them, since they were human, grew the same ambitions and the realization that only by their own efforts could they draw attention to themselves. A sense of national self-respect begins when one people tries to measure itself against another people's standards. Success is an obvious standard; so, watching the successful at work may teach, if not how to live, at least how to make a mark.

To behave, therefore, as the whites behaved—that is, to cope, to learn styles of fortitude and loyalty and aplomb—in time these things were to become, as has been noted, humorous clichés concerning European behavior and the ideals it set for itself in far places. But many men who were not white and had no wish to mimic social mannerisms or dress for dinner in the jungle responded to the direct appeal of the code that belonged to the master of circumstances. If courage was a passport to success and recognition in this exclusive field, courage they would show. They did this not as sycophants, hoping for the casual nod of approval. They did it to win their own respect and to be assured of their own manhood. It was for one such community of men, famously brave, that the maharaja of Nepal spoke when on August 3, 1914, he told the British resident at his court to inform the viceroy of India, "and through him the King-Emperor, that the whole military resources of Nepal are at His Majesty's disposal."[6] It was a stance the Gurkhas had not changed in 1939; and they were to win ten Victoria Crosses for valor during World War II.

For this reason "the Regiment" in imperial history was always more than a military formation consisting of white officers and native other ranks, more than a monument to imperialist guile and colonialist conformity. It provided a social and a personal status which could be acquired nowhere else. It provided a purpose which could be found nowhere else. To be ranked at all, to stay in close order with comrades for the attainment of some common and specified objective, was one certain way of expressing both a personality and a presence. The *sepoy* in India, the *spahi* in North Africa were not forerunners of the future, and accordingly the later nationalist historians have paid them only slighting attention: yet they are the best witnesses imperial history has on call to testify to the prestige of empire itself. That success, power, and the *mana* that both confer are all tangible marks of heavenly approval are not Christian ideas: nevertheless, the Christian Imperial Powers behaved as if these ideas were real also for them, and they were ready to make use of races who thoroughly believed in such ideas, proclaimed them wholeheartedly, and were swift to bow to heaven's will by following the imperial drum — cheerfully, and sometimes with bagpipes and bells.

An army, whatever else it is, is an organized system, in which everyone knows his place and acts according to it. Empire was a larger system, equally devoted to order. Everyone it controlled, whether he complied or complained, had to live somewhere within its framework. There was no other available: but perhaps some day there would be. With this hope in mind Blyden had made his point, a point which was true and would stay true only as long as there was no other history of events for anyone to refer to. The imperial view was that those who had not acted, who had done nothing, had no history. Without history, they were not people. To be sure, they had a past, since they now existed: but their record consisted of having occupied time and space. They occupied these now, since they were visible. But that was all. Such were the conclusions reached in colonial institutes and other imperial bureaus.

It was certainly the habit in all the chancelleries of Europe not to include these people in their diplomatic and strategic calculations. Paul Cambon at the Quai d'Orsay told Lord Lansdowne at the Foreign Office on August 6, 1902, that France saw Morocco as an extension of Algeria, which in its turn was an extension of France. Morocco was the open door to the French Empire in Africa, and it could have only one guardian. Not for any price could France allow the establishment of a force there that would be beyond French control. As France and England began to negotiate their *entente*, concluded in 1904, similar notions multiplied. Reckonings made — whether the French fishing rights on the Newfoundland coast should or should not be exchanged for an English cession to France of the Gambia colony in West Africa—were reminiscent of the recurrent negotiations of the eighteenth century, when all of French Canada was weighed in the same balance as the sugar-rich West Indian island of Guadeloupe and when Goree in Senegambia was likely to change hands at every international peace settlement. Meanwhile, Russia's price for consenting to the new English freedom of action in Egypt, now agreed to by France, was the exaction of an English promise not to establish a protectorate over Tibet.[7] During all this nothing was heard of the preferences of Tibetans, Egyptians, or Moroccans.

Nor did any European set out to discover what these preferences were. Routines cannot be pursued in times of crisis, and therefore no administrator has ever lived who wants to create problems. To ask people what they think about anything, is to do so, for this is much more apt to create ideas than to elicit them. This is true whether there is a crisis or not. Officialdom therefore continued to follow its routines and developed a set of attitudes to dignify them, attitudes which sometimes parted company with reality. The radical George Orwell, on whose thinking his service in the Burma police left an indelible mark, often noted that these routines, however honestly adhered to, had a dishonest effect, because they disguised the real reasons officialdom was there in the first place, why the territory was a colony at all.[8] The officials were in the territory to manage the exploitation of its commerce and commodities. Colonies were producers of primary materials. Local conditions had to be organized so that these products could, at the cheapest possible cost, be brought to the markets of the industrial western world. Wages, health, education, in fact everything, had to be linked to this necessity. H. W. Nevinson, a senior radical journalist whom Orwell knew and admired, had set it all down in 1903. It was all a question— Nevinson said, looking around him in the newly acquired British property of Nigeria—of soap and candles:

It is for this that district commissioners hold their courts of British justice and officials above suspicion improve the perspiring hour by adding up sums. For this the natives trim the forest into golf-links. For this, devoted teachers instruct the boys and girls in the length of Irish rivers and the order of Napoleon's campaigns. For this the director of public works dies at his drain and the officer at a palisade gets an iron slug in his stomach. For this the bugles of England blow at Sokoto, and the little plots of white crosses stand conspicuous at every clearing.[9]

"Oh, who would not sleep with the brave?" the English poet A. E. Housman had asked. Not radical journalists, seemingly. Nevinson came to make a judgment on a scene in which he was not involved. Those beneath the white crosses, at Sokoto or anywhere else within the European imperial parish, could not afford such detachment about what they had accomplished and what they had left for their successors to do. They would not have made much sense of all the theories of capitalist imperialism that have since been devised to account for the existence of this parish and for their own presence in it. They would not have thought the theories relevant to their position, one that constantly asked them to act, to do a day's work. And indeed some of the theorists on occasion sympathized with this attitude. As E. M. Winslow pointed out in his *The Pattern of Im-*

perialism: a Study in the Theories of Power (1948), the general term "economic imperialism" had by his time of writing come to be applied to every suspected attempt, no matter how ancient or how modern, of any group to further its economic interests by expansionist policies.

Thus used, it appears to fit the ambitions of Caesar as well as those of the modern capitalist seeking foreign markets or concessions, and to apply equally to the self-seeking people of Plato's day who were bent upon obtaining "a slice of our neighbor's land " and to a present-day schoolmaster buying a foreign government bond.[10]

Winslow objected to this oversimplification, and thirty years later specialists are still agreeing with the objection. "Popular textbooks like P. T. Moon's *Imperialism and World Politics* (1927) embodied rather than tested the economic hypothesis," says Charles Wilson in his foreword to D. K. Fieldhouse's *Economics and Empire, 1830-1914* (1973); and Fieldhouse himself takes it to pieces.

Whether the imperialism of the last quarter of the nineteenth century was a political phenomenon—the result of rivalries within Europe, the outcome of frontier quarrels that overseas empires developed wherever their lands adjoined—or whether it was caused by economic forces inherent in the character of European capitalist society thus remains a subject for great debate. The need, says Fieldhouse, is clearly for a synthesis "which, on the principle that correct answers flow only from proper questions, can be used as the starting-point of the precise relationship between economics and the construction of Empire." Germans, Belgians, and Italians clearly thought they were being left behind in some kind of race, and Lenin later took it for granted that the competitive element among the rival imperialisms was one of the root causes of World War I. Colonies promised to expand the trade of a metropolis. They opened up markets and made new sources of raw materials accessible. They provided areas for profitable investment of capital. Industrial Europe and North America hoped to find these things in Africa and China, but they did not expect to find them all present and available at the same time in any given area: "Italian imperialism clearly did not spring from the existence of an 'overripe' capitalist economy, or from the need to export surplus capital." But, Fieldhouse adds, the most commonly held and dangerous myth connected with the modern Empires is that they were great machines deliberately constructed by Europe to exploit dependent peoples by extracting economic and fiscal profit from them. . . . It is really as meaningless to ask whether a colony such as Nigeria was "profitable" to Britain as to ask whether Wales or England was.

The vital link between economics and formal empire, he concludes, was neither the economic need of the metropolis for colonies nor the requirements of private economic interests but the secondary consequences of problems created on the periphery by economic and other European enterprises for which there was no simple economic solution.[11]

That correct answers flow from proper questions is a sound, but subjective, principle. People of principle are slow to recognize one another because they are quick to impute motives to those who disagree with them. They read between the lines of the credentials that entitle anyone to voice his or her particular question, and accordingly there is no definition of what is "proper" and what is not. Nevinson's view of empire as a facade masking the self-interest of merchants and bankers was shared by another distinguished journalist of his day, his friend H. N. Brailsford, who contradicted Fieldhouse long in advance when he pointed out in his *The War of Steel and Gold* (1914) that regarded as a national undertaking, imperialism did not pay; but regarded as a means of assuring unearned income to the governing classes, it emphatically did. Sixty years later V. G. Kiernan, in his *Marxism and Imperialism* (1974), stayed at Brailsford's side, putting Edward Elgar's secular Edwardian hymn in its place with the comment that English children were "taught to lisp in honour of their Empire, turning economics into song, 'wider still and wider, shall thy bounds be set.' "[12]

Song and dogma are two different ways to convert the heart. The critical reports filed by Nevinson and Brailsford predated Lenin's theories on the relations of capitalism and imperialism, but it was the fate of these theories to be converted into theorems, all easily demonstrable by proof—at least by those who had any ideological sense. Lenin diagnosed that capitalism was hurrying to its fall and, itself aware of this, was busy looking for protection, physical and fiscal. To maintain its profit margins it was intent on exploiting limited and protected markets. The men who controlled this operation, the finance-capitalists grouped in banks and trusts, thought it was more profitable to employ surplus capital abroad, where a high interest return could be obtained, than in domestic industry. (Imperialist exploitation, as David Landes remarked, is the employment of labor at wages lower than those obtaining in a free market.) The extent of overseas investments necessitated that some form of political control be established over the areas concerned—as in a "semi-colony" like Argentina, which in theory was controlled by colonels but in practice by corporations. Formal and direct colonial rule was, however, more certain, even if more costly: and accordingly since 1870 all the Powers had rushed to pick up colonies wherever they could and so bring all the world into their imperialist-capitalist framework. Interimperial wars would naturally follow, which in turn would produce proletarian revolutions in the imperial metropolis, thus bringing down imperialism and capitalism with it.

Fieldhouse and all later analysts have had to take Leninism into account; but when they do this in ways judged "improper," they must expect severe handling. The belittlers of Lenin's argument, Kiernan states flatly, have found no better interpretations. And, along the same line, one reviewer of Fieldhouse's *Economics and Empire, 1830-1914* irritably insists that Fieldhouse is attacking a caricature of what Lenin said; that he does not understand what Lenin meant; and that even if he did understand it, he would still be out of touch with the truth because Lenin's analysis of imperialism underwent "many significant clarifications and corrections within the Marxist tradition of social science over the last sixty years."[13] As indeed it did, like many other topics within this created tradition.

Over this trampled ground no one has been, or will ever be, allowed a parting shot. Since whatever is taking place on it—open war, ideological conflict, or great debate—has for seven decades been less intent on discovering the truth than on satisfying the soul, the topic is unlikely to be argued out of existence. Commitment is the real issue here: stands are taken and held. "Economic imperialism," D. C. M. Platt accurately remarked in 1969, "is a political rather than a historical label: and political polemicists know what they want to say long before they find the evidence to support it." Because the professional focus differs, one man's evidence is another's irrelevance.

The diplomatic historian, Platt adds, bypasses trade and finance; the economist has no patience with diplomacy. He notes that regarding the British invasion and occupation of Egypt in 1882, the thesis that its motive was to rescue foreign bondholders from their financial predicament there has now so firmly become a part of the folklore of economic imperialism that scholarship is unlikely to shake it. Examining this notorious case, which has riveted the attention of J. A. Hobson and Rosa Luxemburg, H. N. Brailsford and John Strachey, Parker Moon and Harold Laski, he agrees with two contemporary judgments on it made by men who had been personally and politically involved. Sir Stafford Northcote, an elder Conservative statesman, said in 1884 that England's policy in Egypt was "of an imperial character, and with the minimum of interference to maintain the position of that important country, so important in the chain of our communications." Cromer told Salisbury a decade later that Egypt was impossible to evacuate, not because of trouble on the periphery, like the dervish problem in the south—although, he was ready to concede, "this was an excellent working argument"—but because of the utter incapacity of the Egyptian ruling classes. Platt concludes decisively that Egypt was conscripted into the British Empire not because it offered a field for the investment of surplus capital, not because existing British bondholdings were insecure, but because the trade and even the existence of the empire were threatened by anarchy within.[14]

Theory may swing between abstraction and folklore, but property is a tangible. Its owners expect property to have a yield, an economic value. To develop the property is, one hopes, to increase its value, and to expand the property is to exploit its potential for further increase. On this, what is "commonly held" is not likely to be soon consigned to any realm of myth. Analysts of imperialism do indeed, as Hobson himself noted, resemble pathologists: they may disagree about what emphasis should be placed on economic factors, about how these worked and what was the upshot, but all admit that the body lies there on the table, awaiting a correct autopsy. That empire and profit were intended to be natural partners is not denied even by those who most enjoy pointing out the many places under the imperial sun where no profit accrued, and where Hobson and Lenin, to name no others, misread the evidence they had themselves selected.

(Still, if Lenin fell short as an oracle, his gift of diagnosis is hard to confute: he did foresee, for example, the "complete division of the world among the great international trusts.") John Strachey, writing *The End of Empire* nearly a generation ago (1959), had intellectual affinities with both Hobson's socialism and Lenin's Marxism, but he set forth the case with particular clarity. We were told, he wrote — although he does not say by whom — that any analysis made in terms of economics was now out of date; that men sought power rather than wealth; and that the whole modern imperialist process had to be seen as a competitive struggle for power among the great nations. Yet what was power but wealth, if anyone thought seriously about either? And

how can we possibly deny a connection between [the] outpouring of British and European capital in foreign investment between 1870 and 1914, and the vast annexations that took place? . . . Is it not perverse to deny that it was primarily in order to open the way for, and then to safeguard, these outpourings of foreign investment that the western European capitalism annexed or dominated so much of the world between 1870 and 1914?[15]

Certainly, one should not downgrade the outpourings: £692.3 million in 1870, £1,189.4 million in 1880, £1,935.1 million in 1890, £2,396.9 million in 1900, £3,371.3 million in 1910, £3,989.6 million in 1913.[16]

Those crosses at Sokoto therefore illustrate a particular case, at the same time symbolizing a general rule. The British had gone to "Nigeria" (which did not exist before they went there) to trade. They stayed to protect the area where the trading was done, and in doing this many men died. Nevinson in his day, and the less theoretical analysts of empire since, were right to emphasize facts of life. Soap and candles were a form of property: all forms of property had to be protected. This sort of simplicity made sense; it was the other sort, like the wide claim put forward regarding "civilization" and its values, that bordered on the simple-minded. If one had to talk about civilized values, it was well to remember that managerial skills were certainly not the least of these, for only by exercising such skills would anything useful, and therefore beneficial, get done at all. Those who insisted on this point of view were nonromantics, easily irritated by the tinsel trappings and the individual posturing that seemed inextricably entangled with the presence of empire.

Did it really matter twopence who had been at school with whom, who was and was not invited to His Excellency's dinner table at Government House, and whom his lady invited to call? It did not even matter who His Excellency and his lady were in the first place. Excellencies came and went; the property stayed fixed. The purpose of empire was not to provide an exercise ground for upper-class mannerism, it was a commercial enterprise geared to profit. Soap and candles, rubber and sisal, oil and nickel, tin and copper, copra and bananas, cocoa and coffee, bauxite and manganese, wool and wheat, tea and sugar, jute and cotton—these were the things that mattered, that always had and always would. The true business of imperial officialdom was to hold the ring, while, and within which, the continuing exploitation of all these products, and more, took place.

Romance and analysis do not keep close company. Telling planters and merchants and their wives that they were at the center of colonial affairs, when their social experience of colonial life told them very clearly they were not, did not please them, cause them to smile on cynical journalists like Nevinson and Orwell, or even bring them to read what they said. A backhanded compliment is no compliment at all. For nobody anywhere has ever wanted to be told one lives by bread alone and might as well take pride in one's healthy appetite for it. The pomp and circumstance of empire gave its citizens not only pleasure but also a sense of belonging to something larger than a countinghouse and bigger than themselves. It was not the governor sweating under the sun who wanted to wear gold braid and goose-feathers on his hat, not the natives who were impressed by this: it was the white community that insisted on an uncomfortable formalism, an imperviousness to climate itself, as a mark of their superiority and distinction. In Hong Kong and Singapore and Shanghai the European community did not exceed 75,000 at any time, and it therefore made no place for eccentricity, for people who saw the funny side of things and liked to categorize the normal as something odd. Artists were absent, as were socialists; and although adultery was acceptable if not permissible, homosexuality was neither. Addiction to sport not only killed time but also attested to character. Social segregation kept natural company with this attitude. The lower orders numbered in the millions, but they were not counted and, accordingly, did not count. The "other ranks" were likewise ignored: the European soldiers and sailors who reached the ports of the East were left to make their way off-duty "on the shabby frontier of debauchery," fit company for all those rice Christians, lascars, Chinese, and Portuguese half-breeds who made good enough seamen in fair weather but were "of little use in a storm or a fight."[17]

The desired amount of social segregation was not hard to achieve amid native races that had always organized their lives in *kampongs* or quarters and were prepared to accept the business enterprise of these pink and energetic barbarians as a useful corollary of their own. The social exclusiveness of the Chinese and the Malays helped reinforce, and even justify, the stockade mentality of the British, since neither were bothered by the unfortunate "neurotic itch,"[18] so observable in the educated Hindu, to become, if not English, at least an acceptable equivalent. Unlike their counterparts in the Middle East, adrift among Muslims whose own sense of superiority was profound, Europeans in the Far East did not have to contend with a visible culture that insisted on measuring its own standard with theirs. China and Malaya and Siam and Burma and Annam kept their cultures to themselves and had no wish to communicate them, neither to aliens nor to one another. The imperial rulers were therefore able to treat them all as equally invisible, and the Old China Hand could congratulate himself on not being able to speak a word of Chinese. As the golden afternoons of the first forty years of the century passed, he and his fraternity, staring unseeingly at the multitude from the verandas of their villas and clubs, could safely continue to know nothing at all about China or wherever. On the Shanghai bund and in downtown Singapore the routine of a City of London working day was steadily observed; and then, this rite having been attended to, its practitioners could retreat to green suburbias made even lusher by the presence of servants, five of whom could be kept at a total cost of £20 a month. At the office the ledgers dealt only in black ink. The Shanghai Opium Combine survived all attacks made upon it by Victorian morality and did not dissolve until 1917; and Malaya, which in 1901 had produced 130 tons of rubber, had by 1928 become the source of 95 percent of the world's supply.

These were the only kinds of spoils such victors had ever wanted —but that they had got what they wanted, and so spectacularly, had

convinced them of their own worth and, with that, of their right
to be masters of the East. If they did not talk about a mandate of
heaven, they nevertheless believed in it. "Most people who ride a
wave of history," George Woodcock pointed out, "as the British
did from 1815 to 1914, believe, without necessary hypocrisy, that
God is on their side."[19] But when waves of history smash against
one another, God too becomes invisible, as the *tuans* of Penang and
Singapore and Kuala Lumpur, local lords of humankind, found out
when the Japanese came in on their own tide of destiny and made
it brutally plain that the British Empire in the Far East was, after
all, made of cardboard—a useful commercial commodity but not
one that can stand strain.

Yet under the limelight it looks solid enough. The commercial
context made sense to people whose skills in barter and bargain were
great. The judgment of historians is much the same as George Orwell's: the various imperial administrations left a far weaker imprint
upon the local populations than did the commercial companies and
the technical departments of government, whose daily demands and
schemes for development altered the tempo and disrupted the pattern of native life.[20] If, meanwhile, white settlers and other officials
insisted on listening to a different drum, this was their own affair:
it could not affect what was actually happening.

Since what transpired was, by definition, routine, nobody wanted
to see it elevated to the status of an event. Imperial officials could
be annoyed—and, being human, usually were—by the knowledge
that nobody back home cared a centime for the daily affairs of
Dakar or wagered on the weather in Batavia or counted how many
memorandums accumulated in Simla during the summer. But half-
knowledge in stay-at-homes irritated them more than total ignorance
ever did. Half-knowledge brought up a "question in the House,"
which, whatever the answer to it, had the demerit of alerting a cabinet minister who was best left undisturbed and who doubtless preferred it that way. Or some radical editorial would appear to throw
an excessively lurid light on a transaction that had a perfectly logical explanation to which nobody would now listen. Such things did
happen, but not very often. The affairs of empire were conducted
by a minority which had convinced itself it was acting in the interests
of the majority of its kin, and in return for the service the majority

was expected to express only a minor interest in these affairs. The principle of trusteeship was popular among trustees for this very reason; that is, it allowed them to go their own way unimpeded. What was true for the British was true also for the French and the Germans, to whose populations their empires were as remote in thought as in geography.

In these circumstances, those who conducted imperial business had a good chance of doing so in a state of seclusion. Steadily denying, without much hypocrisy, that whatever they did had anything to do with "politics," officials claimed that the peace and quiet granted without question to the affairs of every well-regulated public corporation should, in justice and in commonsense, be granted to themselves. Politics, in the civil-service and military mind, was something inescapably attached to uproar. Did raucous voices echo in, were unauthorized persons allowed to enter, the chambers of commerce or the bureaus of government in Europe? No, they did, and were, not. Why, then, should other standards be applied to the imperial institutes, which in doing the world's work were also ensuring its civilized future? Anyone who could read a balance sheet could surely grasp this: for example, between 1901 and 1914 the value of the cocoa export from Britain's Gold Coast colony rose from a mere £43,000 to £2.3 million.

Long before 1914 a series of rebuttals to these assertions had been made. But none were reckoned irrefutable in their turn. There were, there always would be, those who railed, those who complained, the kind of people who would find fault with the organization of heaven itself. This was a mark of their own insecurity: it gave proof not of capacity but of envy. In 1901 H. G. Wells diagnosed that the tradition of self-respecting inferiority was being wholly destroyed in the world and that this would have incalculable results.[21] Wells reckoned, however, that he could calculate one result. From such a situation would spring new expectations and new demands. Notice would be served on employers and on everyone else now in a place of privilege. Voices would be heard that had never been heard, from people who had never been heard of. Things would be said that had never before been said openly. A politics of complaint would draw up an agenda to which all politicians, however much their minds were set on other plans and policies, would in future have to attend. But these were thoughts bred out of Wells's own harsh experience of life below stairs and behind counters: they said something he dearly wanted to be true but had no means of proving. To the young Jawaharlal Nehru, who in 1907 was an undergraduate at Cambridge, the evidence seemed to point the other way. "We saw around us," he remarked, "an assured and advancing order of things — and this was pleasant for those who could afford it."[22] The English ruling class, with whose sons Nehru was then mixing, could certainly afford it and were determined to go on doing so. The sons agreed with their fathers. The Colonial Office agreed wholeheartedly when its governor in the Malay States urged that what the Malayan Civil Service needed was "a number of young men of good physique and an energetic and fearless disposition, of moderate attainments, and if possible well brought up. High scholarship was unnecessary."[23] There was not then, nor was there ever going to be, a lack of available young men with these qualifications.

So the process Wells noted was only a process, something still operating, and therefore as capable of being defeated as of being victorious. His book outlining it he called *Anticipations*. Well, of course, everyone had a right to anticipate, but by definition it was only an exercise in conjecture. The men in charge of affairs — the pragmatic imperialists, whom Wells was to designate in 1912 the "New Macchiavellians"— did not want to see the future as an item on their daily agenda. The future could wait. (The traditional culture, says C. P. Snow, responds by wishing the future did not exist.) The only future worth thinking about was one that mirrored the present. Present thinking should thus be devoted to arranging matters so that they could perpetuate themselves: effective work now would propagate effectiveness for tomorrow. The English Conservative leader Bonar Law said that so long as the English were strong, India was a strength to them; but the moment they were no longer believed to be strong, it was a source of weakness.[24] The essential belief, the one that had to be guarded as carefully as any imperial base or fortress, was a belief in oneself.

Curzon as viceroy of India used a more high-flown style than others did. In August 1904 he assured the members of a white club in Calcutta that he could not conceive of a time as remotely possible when it would be either practicable or desirable for the English to "take their hands from the Indian plough." The same year African doctors were excluded from the West African Medical Service on the ground that English colonial officers, with their wives and families, would have no confidence in them. A few years later (1911) Sir Frederick Lugard announced that the establishment of the University of Hong Kong would be welcomed by all those who were "interested in the maintenance of British prestige in the East."[25] Clearly, the plough had a long way to go, across a field whose boundary lay somewhere over the horizon. Or, possibly, the rainbow.

The French in their empire did not use metaphors; they spoke and wrote a language designed to be understood. It could not be supposed, said Governor Angoulvant in the Ivory Coast in 1908, that the only mission of the administration was to please. A moment must come when it must make demands. Therefore, any signs of impatience or disrespect toward French authority, or any deliberate lack of goodwill, were to be repressed without delay. This process was customarily known among French officers as pacification: in this case the more honest description, "a punitive expedition," was left for English officers to use. In French Equatorial Africa over a limited territory and at the price of "systematic action" during an eight-year period, this officer managed to break the people's capacity to resist When, for example, a railway track was damaged, the traders along the route, the mahogany growers whose timber yards lined it, suffered loss and hardship so severe that, in the official view, the most severe repressions were justified. The villages captured were razed. No quarter was given to prisoners, and severed heads were set up on poles beside the railway stations. In March 1910 another French governor declared himself to an approving *Union Coloniale* banquet in Paris: the French who had gone to new territories had done so by virtue of the right of a civilized, fully developed race to occupy lands that had been left fallow by backward peoples plunged in barbarism and unable to develop the wealth that lay around them. "If anyone denies this, you should firmly maintain that it is a right." Since such was the view of authority, who could be surprised that the right to French citizenship in France's colonies was very closely guarded indeed? The decree of May 1912 laid down the regulations for this citizenship in French West Africa. A man must have been born and domiciled there. He must be twenty-one years old. He must give proof of his means of existence and of good conduct. He must also have shown devotion to French interests or have put in ten years of service in some public or private enterprise. Few qualified. Few were expected to, because the educational budget for the whole of French Africa in 1914 was 2 million francs. As colonial minister Albert Sarraut explained, it was certainly France's duty to instruct the natives—but this duty was a low priority, to be performed only after France's obvious economic, administrative, military, and political duties had been fulfilled.

As a republic which was also a Great Power, France was the exception among the monarchies that ruled Europe between 1900 and 1914, but it shared with them a profound faith in the powers of the state. The sovereign rights that by many treaties had been secured to the chiefs of the ancient African states were unilaterally annulled in French Equatorial Africa by the "fundamental decrees" of 1899 and in French West Africa by the decree of October 23, 1904. Only rarely did the Chamber of Deputies in Paris exercise its right to legislate for the colonies. These therefore were largely administered by a decree that had descended from Napoleon III's Second Empire. In practice the minister for the colonies, acting in the name of the president of the Third Republic, held full powers over the overseas territories.[26] Harmony between himself and his agents there was essential, for no law or decree issued in Paris came into force until it was promulgated by the order of the governor-general, who could choose when to issue it. He was in fact a proconsul in the old Roman style, far more so than any British colonial administrator to whom the name was sometimes loosely given. Cromer himself, beleaguered by cosmopolitan bickering in Cairo which his personality but not his powers controlled, recorded his honest envy of the untrammeled position of the French official who ruled at his ease in Tunisia.

Overseas the state expected from its subjects what it expected from them at home. It did not debate this. It required, and was ready to punish the absence of, "loyalty"; Curzon was to write irritably in 1919 about the existence of "a disloyal movement" in Egypt to expel the British.[27] In fact the number of imperialists who, when they bothered to think the matter out, really believed that their foreign flags were followed with enthusiasm was small. If some civilians thought so, soldiers did not; but so long as they were convinced they could command the obedience of their levies, they did not concern themselves with analyzing the motives of those who carried out the orders given. As the new century began, the Europeans had taken their expansion far, but they were not finished with it. They held 80 percent of the world's surface, and more of it was falling into their hands. What was reckoned as no-man's-land was being taken from the unrecognized inhabitants, those "who hung back," in Lord Salisbury's words, "from the movement of the world." One day the imperial framework would include the whole globe, the resources of which could then be organized and systematized. This was still more a hope than a blueprint, but it did not seem fantastic either to hold to the one or to make sketches for the other. More and more it was becoming clear that the exhortation carved into the plinth of the statue of Sir John Lawrence set up at Lahore in the Punjab—"Will you be governed by the pen or by the sword? Choose!"—had not in reality given people a choice at all. They were to be governed by both.

The early years of the century presented many occasions for these exercises. The manipulation of other people in the pursuit of one's national interest had become a commonplace. In 1903 President Theodore Roosevelt engineered the "independence" of the province of Panama from its parent state of Colombia, thus ensuring a secure grip by the United States on the isthmian canal, then under construction. Simultaneously, France's professional troubadour of empire, Paul Leroy-Beaulieu, pronounced that the basin of Lake Chad would become one of the jewels of Africa: here was a new Egypt, indeed a greater Egypt, in the making.[28] To France, Egypt itself, despite the irritating presence of a British army and of "the Lord" (Cromer) himself, was already profitable enough, since French stockholders held 62 percent of its foreign debt—a profit far in excess of anything yet extracted from Algeria, which seventy years after the first French arrival there had still not been thoroughly "pacified." In May 1903 William d'Arcy, a gold millionaire from Australia, agreed with the Persian government to establish an oil-prospecting venture, which, aptly titled the Exploitation Company, did its work so well that it became reconstituted on May 20, 1914, as the Anglo-Persian Oil Company: its charter decreed that it must always remain an independent British concern, registered in England and with its head office there, and that every director must be a British subject. In July 1903, in what was to become known as Northern Nigeria, the British captured Kano, causing Lady Lugard to exclaim that her compatriots were justified in thinking of themselves as a people which might face, with reasonable hope of success, still vaster questions of tropical administration.[29] An even vaster question, which fortunately received a negative answer, was put the same year when the British government offered some six thousand square miles of a Uganda plateau to the Zionist movement.

In 1904 the British sent a punitive expedition from India to Lhasa in Tibet. In 1906 they dealt harshly with a Xosa uprising in Natal. Meanwhile, the Germans were coping with the Maji Maji rebellion in their East African Protectorate between 1905 and 1907, and in 1906 with the Herreros in South-West Africa. In 1905 Europe's ablest imperial pupil, Japan, made off with the southern part of the island of Sakhalin and five years later with the peninsula of Korea. In 1908 the Dutch were at last able to put an end to the Atjeh war in Sumatra. All these events were duly noted in the world press, but none of them were promoted to celebrity; it was accepted that this sort of thing would be part of the day's work. Nor was much attention paid to England's colonial secretary, Lord Elgin, who one day in 1908 told the governor of British East Africa (Kenya) that it was not consonant with the views of His Majesty's government to impose *legal* restrictions on any particular section of the community there, but as a matter of administrative convenience grants of land for settlement in the upland areas of the territory were not to be made to Indians. But this act of administrative convenience was to govern events in that quarter for the next four decades; and as a result East Africa did not become, as some pioneers like Sir Harry Johnston had hoped, "the America of the Hindu."[30]

In 1909 the northern states of Malaya were removed from their vassalage to Siam and placed under British control. The Spaniards began to occupy a zone of Morocco. In 1911 the Italians set out to occupy Turkish Cyrenaica in Libya: since this task was not completed until they had taken Syrte in November 1924, Giolitti's cry at a triumphal Turin banquet on October 7, 1911—"There are facts which impose themselves as a veritable historical fatality!"—might have been read two ways.[31] In 1911 also the Portuguese government reissued and clarified a regulation of 1899, a document that concisely summarized an accepted imperial attitude. It stated that

all natives of Portuguese overseas provinces are subject to the obligation, moral and legal, of attempting to obtain through work the means that they lack to subsist and to better their social condition. They have full liberty to choose the method of fulfilling this obligation, but if they do not fulfill it, public authority may force a fulfillment.

Public authority was not slow to do precisely this; and as a result, an observer likened the situation in Angola and in São Tomé to the position in the southern states in America during the early part of the nineteenth century. (The Portuguese riposted, "how did he know?")[32] Also in 1911 the first commercial shipment of oil left the British West Indian island of Trinidad, whose governor was simultaneously informed by "a committee of representative gentlemen" that they were opposed to imposing a graduated income tax, owing to the inquisitorial character of proper tax assessment and other technical difficulties incidental to it.[33] The French took Fez in Morocco. They took Marrakesh in September 1912: by then one could say that they had made off with Morocco itself, since by the Franco-Moroccan treaty of March 30 they were pledged to support His Sharifian Majesty against any danger that might threaten his person or his throne or might compromise the tranquillity of his dominions.[34] Immediately afterward, General Hubert Lyautey began what was to be a long and famous proconsular career, in order to ensure that this tranquillity was not compromised.

Everything should fall into line and order be imposed on places that had never known it. Method was to be introduced into ramshackle structures which only the force of inertia kept up. What sensible person could complain of this? None—and so it followed that those who did complain were not sensible. Their views, accordingly, did not merit attention. Germany's Gustav Schmoller, "at whose feet a whole generation of future economists, administrators, and diplomats had sat," defined the task that presented itself to all civilized, progressive, sensible people in these terms:

He who is perceptive enough to realize that the course of world history in the twentieth century will be determined by the competition between the Russian, English, American, and perhaps the Chinese world empires, and by their aspirations to reduce all the other, smaller, states to dependence on them, will also see in a central European customs federation the nucleus of something which may save from destruction not only the political independence of those states, but Europe's higher, ancient culture itself.[35]

But the most articulate and visible spokesman of this dismissive opinion was not bred in Europe: he was America's Theodore Roosevelt, to whom common sense and manliness were keys that unlocked the problems of life and of the day. American imperialism borrowed freely from, and acknowledged its debt to, European practice, while setting a distinctively national stamp on all its expansionist action. Roosevelt himself was an eccentric, but in an acceptably American style. Civilized peoples had barbarian neighbors. Very likely, they would always have them. Only by subduing them could they keep the peace. The more they reduced their number, the better it would be for mankind at large. This task was certainly extensive and expensive — but it was also exhilarating, not to be shirked. The white man's burden that Rudyard Kipling had in 1899 exhorted Americans to pick up in the Philippines was one that Roosevelt was eager to shoulder. Once the United States had established a stable government there, another fair spot of the world would have been snatched from the area of darkness. He told his Democratic opponent, William Jennings Bryan — who had exclaimed that these notions denied the sacred doctine of the consent of the governed — that such criticism did not hold much water. In the United States, "aren't blacks governed by whites without the consent of the governed?" Those who speechified against the unrighteousness of the American occupation of the Philippines, he added, might with as much justification incite the Sioux and the Apache to rebel against the United States' government, on the ground that it had no right to retain South Dakota or Arizona. (A day was indeed to come when exactly this would be said.) And in his presidential State of the Union message of 1906 Roosevelt insisted that the commitment in the Philippines had added dignity to the nation, for it had proved that Americans were capable of bearing honorably and efficiently "the international burdens which a mighty people should bear."[36]

Imperialism was not patented. It was therefore, as Italy's Giolitti would have agreed, in the public domain. The English had held the same assumptions for so long that they no longer thought it necessary to talk about them, but in private they continued to repeat them. The British *raj* in India must be a sorry affair, Liberal Lord Morley told his viceroy, Conservative Lord Minto, in April 1906, if it trembled before a pack of unruly collegians. Minto agreed. It was the line of thinking used by his predecessor, Curzon, who had also scoffed at the actions of "immature striplings."[37] The attitude of all three explains why in Bengal between 1907 and 1917 students formed by far the largest element of the population in the jails. By 1917 Curzon, now in the Cabinet, had not changed his views. In a memorandum that dealt with the future of the enemy colonies, he noted it was "generally conceded" that the higher standards of civilization which white people had developed had conferred on them "a general right of entry into the darker places of the earth where superstition and barbarism prevailed." Those who did not concede this were of no importance. The truth was that the epithet "imperialism," like its brother "capitalism," had become "one of the cant formulas of the doctrinaires of revolution." The rescue of a subject people from cruelty and oppression, which was hailed as a virtue if achieved by a small nation, became a crime if accomplished by a great empire. This was all great nonsense. Did anyone seriously propose a Hottentot republic?[38] Indeed, nobody did. In all the debates about what to do with German colonies in Africa and in the Pacific once Germany was defeated, no one ever suggested that they ought to be undisturbed, handed back to those who lived in them, left without any master at all. Nothing better underlines the imperial assumptions of the day. Places and peoples had to be organized and positioned within the frame: they could not be left, to borrow from the language of the West Indian planter, "in ruinate." Even Gokhale, the leader of the moderates in the Indian Congress, declared in his last will and testament, published in 1916, that German East Africa should be reserved for Indian colonization. There were many plans, and most of them were imperialist. Sir Reginald Wingate wrote from Cairo he did not think it was impossible that in the dim future a federation of semi-independent Arab states might exist under European guidance and supervision, linked by racial and linguistic bonds, owning spiritual allegiance to a single Arab primate, and looking to Great Britain as its patron and protector.[39]

So imperialists had their own dreams. These were extensions of the present, not contradictions of it, like the dreams of the subjected.

The world they dealt with was a visible world; and whenever "unrest" became visible, they had no doubt they could deal with this too. Life was always hard and usually unfair. Too much sensitivity was weakness, and weakness of any kind would always be exploited by those on the watch for it. Lord Lansdowne was not the only viceroy of India to believe that "half our troubles could be avoided if a little more gentleness and consideration were manifest by some of our officials."[40] Viceroys could afford these sentiments: they came and, in four years, went. To the other half of their troubles the officials themselves, who were fixtures, paid the most attention. They had long understood that they could not see far and did not know much. They knew that beyond the lighted circle of their immediate parish of governance lay an area of darkness. Many of them were therefore happy to see at least some of their unknown subjects quitting the area to declare themselves and their purposes, however subversive, in the light.

There was an analogy here with that image of "darkest Africa" which had so haunted the mind and imagination of the mid-Victorians. Many prophets of the Victorian era had foreseen that bringing people against their wishes out of the darkness—which to them was life itself—into the western orbit, into "civilization," would create difficulties enough. Refusing thereafter to admit the consequences of this action, denying to these people any genuine fellowship, any place other than that at the foot of a ladder whose lower rungs only would be available to them, would merely compound the problem. This dilemma was now troubling the conscience, if not as yet the practice, of the masters of the world. When in 1919 French politicians referred to France's "incontestable rights" in Syria, they did not mean that those rights were not contestable or that they were not in fact being contested; and when in 1930 a celebrant of France's centenary in Algeria wrote that the hypothesis of an independent Algeria was inconceivable, he did not mean that the hypothesis had not been conceived.[41] They meant only that it did not signify: they would pay no attention to those who were doing the contesting and the conceiving.

The language used on both sides showed that the Victorians had indeed correctly diagnosed the depth of the trap that lay in wait for their posterity. But they had not spelled out how best to avoid it.

This was due as much to a lack of accurate information as to any idleness or failure of intellect. In the European literature of imperialism Rudyard Kipling holds a place that has not been accorded to any other writer. It is a place quite independent of whatever degree of dislike or admiration people grant to him and to his ideas, for he is seen as a man who reported what his generation truly felt, not what its members believed they ought to have felt. Liberals always disliked Kipling's guidebooks to humanity at work because they were unable, despite themselves, to call him a liar. People ought not to be as Kipling saw them—but, unluckily, a lot of them are.

Kipling's picture of "Anglo-India," catching the *raj en déshabillé*, was composed during the 1880s. It made mischief, then and later, but it never needed revision and kept its acceptance because no other portrait half as accurate was ever produced by anyone else. Certainly no memoir by a retired soldier or civil servant ever ventured much beyond anecdote. It recorded no misgivings or dilemmas, since to admit that these things existed would have risked an accusation, from the only people likely to read the record, that the memorialist was letting down the side. The readers would not want to know what was embossed on the reverse of the medal or even to be told it had one. But the "Anglo-Indian" official tolerated Kipling's portrait not because he liked it but because it at least made sense of what he was doing. It gave him, as a human being, a place to stand. The ordinary expatriate Englishman, caught up in an extraordinary situation of a kind literally incommunicable to anyone who had not experienced it, had never been able to "see" or place himself at all. He had never managed totally to convince himself of the value of what he was doing, since everything he did had to be done over again, and explained over again, from one end of his career to the other. Whatever kind of Grub Street jokes he went in for, Kipling always made his context clear and gave his readers assurance that they were not forever stranded, Crusoes beset with Fridays, in a world of the incomprehensible. They were, instead, men with a task, men with a burden, making a mark on their time and a name for their country, who must stay to guard what they had built and then hand over their duties to their juniors when the time came.

These guardians of empire, patrolling exotic battlements far out of sight of their homekeeping compatriots, were pioneers in the business of constructing an "image" for themselves. They did this so well that all the caricatures later made of it could not destroy it. Rather the reverse: *pukka sahibs* and Colonel Blimps were no doubt comical, but they could strike nobody as sinister. However much they blundered about, everyone expected them to die at their posts if they had to, and courage has never been something people are ready to ridicule. Guardians were asked only to patrol with success, to ensure that what was called at ceremonial dinner tables "the heritage" was not lost or spoiled. Cast in this single and singular role, a guardian, not surprisingly, tried to perfect a characteristic behavior to suit it. But unlike a professional actor, he lacked a regular and a sympathetic audience. At best, there were onlookers, who drifted in and out. He got no encouragement on the local scene. The servant in the bungalow, the clerk in the office were too busy playing their own parts. No genuine relationship could ever develop with people who did as they were told and smiled as they did it. In Africa the same repertory was performed. The ready laughter of Africans was noted by explorers, settlers, and visitors alike — and usually with surprise, for what on earth had Africans to laugh about? The consensus of white opinion was that it did not express any real mirth. Instead, it was a cover behind which bewilderment or fear took refuge in order to play for time, time in which to devise the right reaction for coping with an unexpected situation, time to work out the best way of avoiding compliance with some demand or other, which by the very fact of its issue was unwelcome. It was no bad guess, since this was often true; but the thought that Africans might also be laughing *at* them did not occur to them. The idea that Africans might reckon white people were as dishonest as everyone else they had ever known did not occur to the whites either. When they spoke of standards of conduct, they assumed that these were self-evidently just and reasonable. But the justice and the reason were not clear to those on whom the standards were imposed, who thought them to be a series of cunningly contrived traps, into which all those who were not white must inevitably fall.

Here African simplicity joined hands with Indian sophistication. In 1902 the bishop of Calcutta complained that Indians did not understand the true intent and dignity of education; for had they done so, surely they would not seriously have suggested that one suitable memorial to the lately deceased queen-empress would be to lower, at least for a time, the standards of examination for an academic degree. Yet that the student body had asked for this should not have startled the cleric. It was the natural outcome of a system wherein, by 1900, only 32 percent of the candidates for government service were passing the intermediate Bachelor of Arts degree, and only 19 percent the final one.[42]

A student body—like the peasantry, the taxpayers, and the labor force—is a collective. Imperial governments habitually dealt in collectives. They had nothing else they could deal in. They could not conduct their collective business with individuals, because they had to place all individuals within their own collective group before they could begin to understand them. The upshot was that everybody was always making a series of rough approximations. Nobody could be sure of having understood the other person. Nobody could be sure that the other had listened to what had been said. It was rare in the imperial context for a direct question to elicit a truthful answer, since on neither side were the definitions of directness and truth the same. As a result truth was neither told nor heard, and if at any time it insisted on emerging, it had the impact of shock. The resulting confusion was often acute. This was never exclusively a problem affecting "natives." Everyone in contact made approximations, accommodations, and adjustments, sometimes to a point where individual personalities disappeared. Many loyal wives of European district officers exclaimed in their diaries and letters home their enchantment at the picturesqueness of some mud village in the bush—when what they really meant to say, if only there had been some acceptable language in which to say it, was that here was just another nasty, stinking hole which had not changed in centuries and was not going to do so now no matter what anyone did about it, and wouldn't it be nice when John or Jean was transferred to what could be thought of, at least relatively, as an outpost of civilization?

For there was such a thing as the imperial posture, which everyone was expected, on pain of ostracism, to take up: the hero of George Orwell's sad and bitter *Burmese Days* (1934) is ruined and brought to suicide because he will not do so. When attitudes harden they express themselves in platitudes. Thought and idea, experiment and innovation, could not take root amid the stones of the imperial soil. Situations were not resolved, they were only stereotyped: the topics of conversation in an Indian army officers' mess in 1870 did not differ greatly from those aired in 1910 and even 1940, and the fact that this was so could be hailed as yet another example of the fortifying processes of "tradition." The genuine reluctance expressed by English politicians to stay in Egypt and "run" it after their hasty invasion of July 1882 was bred from their conviction that the Egyptian peasantry, the *fellahin*, would always be, like the Indian *ryot*, just another peasantry, just another problem for "law and order," just another collective obstacle in the path of progress, just another headache for those who had to oversee the peasants' collective activities.

A mystique of empire was, therefore, always more easily found among its observers than among those who worked within it. South of the Mediterranean and east of Suez were worlds belonging to another order of time, worlds wherein any likelihood of self-government in any ascertainable future seemed to those who inspected and patrolled them impossible to entertain and remain within the bounds of common sense. Time never made inroads on this imperial attitude. Even when, in the 1950s and the 1960s, the imperial governments abdicated their control, their agents never truly believed that the day of genuine partnership, of civilized brotherhood and real equality, had in fact come. Imperialism kept to the last its fundamental contempt for its subjects.

The amount of genuine communication that was established between ruler and ruled was generally, therefore, more a matter of luck than of judgment. Nehru wrote from jail in 1936, "As soon as one begins to think of the other side as a mass or a crowd, the human link seems to go."[43] It is arguable that it was ever there. Human links did not make up the bonds of empire. In the British case, where these links existed at all, they joined only the branches of the race that in the nineteenth century had taken themselves to Canada, Australia, New Zealand, South Africa, or to the managerial cadres of the tropical colonies — or even to South America, where "they built up for themselves a home in the lands of the stranger," says a memorialist of the Scots who settled on the Río de la Plata.[44] The links ran direct to the metropolis, to the mother country, to "home." Empire had no link of circumference, even among its white cousinhood: no Canadian was ever taught about or cared to learn about the life-style in New Zealand. It was curious, Nehru added, how each person judged the other race—not by the individual with whom one was in contact but by others about whom one knew little or nothing. Now and then, thankfully, one was able to create a recognizable stereotype: for who did not admire the grizzled, bemedaled *subahdar-*major, steady as a rock, a fine fellow indeed, the salt of the earth? But it was equally clear that he was a very marked exception to all that teeming humanity to be found every day on the Chowringhee Road.

Administrators kept their emotions a long way down their sleeves. But the petitioners who came to them wore their hearts upon theirs, and the office was often the scene of noise and weeping. The official was likely to be prejudiced more against emotionalism than against color, but in the course of a lengthy career in a colonial service he was likely to equate the one with the other and so relate his irritations to both. He was also more inclined to believe he was dealing with a lower *class*—but again, since this class was composed entirely of a different race, the attribute of inferiority could without difficulty, or even without thinking, be transferred to the race itself. The senior official was never even in the position of a gentleman who might by some freak of chance find himself in the main thoroughfare of a manufacturing town, rubbing shoulders with the inhabitants. In the East shoulders did not get rubbed. High officialdom lived in a world of landaus and gharrys, of outriders and limousines and land-rovers; and it is still a common view among those who are conveyed about their business by servant-driven vehicles that pedestrians are just a lot of unnecessary people who take up room. In such a situation it was easy to forget G. K. Chesterton's reminder that "a man ought to know something of the emotions of an insulted man, not by being insulted but simply by being a man."[45]

This absence of human links, this state of mutual incomprehension, supplies the truest tally of the price of empire. In India, particularly, this bill had long been presented. The correspondent of the London *Times*, W. H. Russell, was there right after the mutiny of 1857, observing the conditions of its aftermath—conditions shot through with shock and fear. He saw a duty ahead for his compatriots. It was not enough to say, as one authoritative person had already said, that the heart of the English must beat high when they looked at the scarred and shattered walls of Delhi or at the Union Jack flying from the fort at Lahore. Russell wrote that Mayfair was not so far removed from the Mile End Road in London—in feeling, in modes of life, and in thought—as the western "station" was from the eastern bazaar. No link existed: there was no bond of union in language, faith, or nationality. What really went on? The West ruled, collected taxes, gave balls, drove carriages, raced its horses, went to church, improved the roads, built theaters, formed masonic lodges, and drank its imported drinks. The East paid taxes in the shape of what it ate that was grown on taxed land; it grumbled, propagated, defecated publicly, sat in its decaying temples, haunted its rotting shrines, and drank its semi-putrid water. Russell added (inevitably) that between the two worlds was a great gulf. Bridging this gulf, then, was the work in hand for whoever in the future should come to stablize the western empire in the East—"if ever he comes at all."[46]

No one came. Fifty years later the surface owned by the controllers of the world was pitted with the same gaps and gulfs. Was such worth owning at all? Could it really be said that anything was, in truth, owned? In 1910 a ruminative philosopher-politician, Lord Haldane, thought not. He noted that the power of manipulating people was no doubt of a very high value, but it was not obvious to him "that we do not in this country pay too great a price for it."[47]

Everything costs something. Imperialists who were convinced that they put their power to good use could not agree with Haldane that the price was too high. They did not, in the first forty years of the twentieth century, wonder how, when, or on whom to devolve power. The governors in the European empires devoted little time to the thought that one day their colonies would no longer be theirs. They thought only of making their power both more effective and more acceptable. There were certain lands, an imperialist wrote in 1905, "where autonomy was eternally impossible": and this was still the declared British official position concerning the island of Cyprus as late as 1958.[48] The power of the western empires was a benevolent despotism. It constituted and would continue to constitute a civilizing force, however many "pacifications" had to be carried out in its name. At the core of this belief—it was not even an argument—lay the conviction that it would continue because it deserved to do so. Liberals had the habit, then as now, of forgetting that liberalism, like any other successful political theory, is a product of power. Nobody who was not first able to afford the fare for the journey has ever followed a course of liberalism.

In mid-Victorian times, liberalism was still a program fighting to make its way. It had not become an assumption to which all right-thinking people were ready to subscribe without thinking. Nobody raised the issue of price or value. Ten years after W. H. Russell had recorded his feelings of depression in India, a British expedition, assembled in Bombay, went by sea and land to Addis Ababa, the capital of Emperor Theodore's Ethiopia, to avenge a series of insults and injuries he had inflicted on Europeans resident there. It did this and retired from the country. In the House of Commons Lord Stanley, as secretary of state for India, dealt with the affair briskly and accurately. It was an odd but necessary business. The English, he said, rested their position on what was vaguely called prestige. They held it not exclusively by the use of force but also by the knowledge that, however justly and mildly the English power was used, in the last resort the force could not be resisted. The consequence of this was that "whatever it may cost, we cannot allow that idea to be dispelled." This axiom, the base of every imperialist assumption, was to be passed on intact to his posterity. Those to whom Stanley spoke were men who disliked all foreign adventuring, who resented any squandering of money, and who had no love for generals, admirals, or the showing of flags. But they were also men of property and as such were the last to lose sight of the idea of a fair price. So they did not argue the point with Stanley, patrician though he was. When he added that England had not become what England was, and that its empire had not been built up by men who shrank from facing difficulties while performing a clear and obvious duty, *Hansard* recorded, most unusually in that day, the answering cry of "hear, hear!"[49] In other words, the duty laid upon the English brand of liberalism was to propagate itself, wider still and wider. One did not have to be officially liberal to do this, merely English. There were to be many more like Emperor Theodore, in many more places, on whose heads this good-humored, steel-lined doctrine was to be forcibly brought down.

If this kind of experience altered the lives of the controlled, so too did it tell on the habit and thought of the controllers. By the turn of the century both the intelligent imperialist and the intelligent observer of imperialist activities took much the same view. Hobson's *Imperialism*, published in 1902, recognized that although the process of physical expansion must soon end for want of places anyone would think worth annexing, the process of what he called imperialization was only beginning. The control of the tropics was an ongoing task, with no end to it in sight. He saw that it was "the great practical business of the century, to explore and develop, by every method which science can devise, the hidden natural and human resources of the globe."[50] Since these resources lay within the bounds of Europe's imperial properties, government in all of them would direct itself to the rapid, secure, and effective development of these and to their profitable exploitation by native labor under white management.

Since laboring was the role allotted to the races who lived in these territories, it was not likely they would be allowed to aspire to any other. Hard facts were making their impact on older liberal notions, never thought through. In Britain's case the previous generation's work of expansion had almost wholly concerned itself with acquiring tropical and subtropical countries to whose peoples "we had no serious intention of giving self-government." The confusions in India had also left their mark. The idea, Hobson insisted, that there existed one sound, just, rational system of government, suitable for all sorts and conditions of people, embodied in the elective representative institutions of Great Britain; and that our duty was to impose this system as soon as possible, with the least possible modifications, upon lower [*sic*] races, without regard to their past history and their present capabilities and sentiments, "was tending to disappear in this country." Very few English administrators any longer retained the idea that they could instruct or that they were successfully instructing the great populations of India in the western arts of government—"nor is there the least intention that these native officials shall in the future become the servants of the free Indian nation rather than of the bureaucratic imperial government." He agreed with his friend Henry Nevinson, who had declared that the old humanitarianism was dead. It could not be too clearly recognized that another old liberal notion, of educating the lower races [*sic*] in the arts of popular government, was also discredited. If it survived, it was only for platform purposes. This fact would command the shape of the future for the British Empire. "We have taken upon ourselves . . . the responsibility of governing huge aggregations of lower races in all parts of the world by methods which are antithetic to the methods of government which we most value for ourselves." Here Hobson was expressing the current socialist fear that imperialist agents, armed with all their authoritarian prestige, would finally come home to make short work of England's free representative institutions.

In fact the significance of what he said was not in this (which did not happen) but in the antithesis be outlined. Even then English liberalism was being accused of hypocrisy by the subjects within the British Empire who had taken hold of the contradictions between its professions and its practices, and were making this the basis of what was to become an entire politics of complaint. The politics were designed to display the injustices of their treatment. The complaint was directed to the immorality of their controllers' position. The notions Hobson listed might have been discarded by the imperialists, but they were being blown with the wind and alighting where they would.

But although he arraigned the modern methods of imperialism, Hobson did not ignore the privileges that power had brought with it. He did not advocate getting rid of them. Looking back to mid-Victorian times, he recalled how there had then been a purely defensive attitude to empire and a total abstinence from acquiring new territory. (This was a blurred view of what had actually happened, but it was shared by most of Hobson's educated contemporaries.) Such a policy England had been able to afford—and could still afford, for it possessed in its carrying trade by sea the most effective guarantee of obtaining an adequate share of the net gains from the new markets opened up by foreign nations. (Hobson did not define that "imperialism of Free Trade" which was to be disinterred out of Cobdenism by a later generation of historians, but probably he would not have seen anything in their argument to object to.) China was a case in point. In China the curtain was, as he wrote, going up on "the most stupendous revolutionary enterprise history has known." In China the Powers of Europe, together with the United States of

America, were preparing to launch "the great speculative coup of international capitalism, not fully ripened for international co-operation." When this cooperation had been effected, and perfected, the real drama would begin.

The United States had recently "flung itself into a rapid imperial career for which it possessed neither the material nor the moral equipment."[51] If it was not at all clear to the majority of Americans why their government had done this, it was as clear to Hobson as it was to Senator Albert Beveridge of Indiana, who approved it, and to William Jennings Bryan, who did not. To Bryan, "imperialism had its inspiration in the desire of the syndicates to extend their commerce by conquest."[52] Hobson also found the "taproot" of American expansionism in the fact that its manufacturing power exceeded the demands of its home market. In self-defense the magnates had arranged combines and cartels, to eliminate wasteful competition and to restrict the quantity of operative capital. From there to empire, or whatever Americans preferred to call it, was a natural step. Magnates were faced with the dilemma of either spending more than they knew how to spend or forcing themselves into markets outside the home area. They needed imperialism because they wanted to use the public resources of their country to find profitable employment for their capital, "which otherwise would be superfluous." This surplus capital had no legitimate *raison d'être*, since it consisted of rents, monopoly profits, and other unearned increments. Imperialism, therefore, American or other, was only the fruit of a false economy of distribution. It was, Hobson said, "a suicidal economy."

Here was the argument which so entranced Lenin, which he was to seize and make doctrine of. Hobson's cure for the ills he defined was a redistribution of resources at home, brought about by social reform, entailing a social reconstruction on the basis of democracy, on a Danish or a Swiss model. The only safety of nations, he urged, lay in removing the unearned increments of income from the propertied classes and adding them to the wages of the working classes or to the public income so that they might be spent in raising the standard of consumption.[53] Lenin thought this was nonsense: as he insisted in his *Imperialism, the Highest Stage of Capitalism* (1917), the only cure was obvious, a destruction of the capitalist system itself, and imperialism with it. Socialists who talked, like Hobson, of the magic of a "sound system of taxation" were living in a dream world.

Lenin's dreams in 1903 were focused on the future. Other observers, though not so critical as Hobson, had as keen an eye: the fascination of imperialism, then as now, was that it had so many of its goods in the shopwindow, where they could be inspected. Egypt was one of these windows, and inspection was the principal professional duty of Lord Cromer, England's satrap there. On the race question he shared Hobson's opinion: he was convinced that the difference of mental attributes between ruler and ruled constituted the greatest of barriers, and put all thought of westernization out of the question.[54] Paying a visit there in 1903 was Theodor Herzl, the creator of modern Zionism. He was much struck by the magnitude of actions around him. The role of the English, he wrote in his diary in March 1903, was superb. They were cleaning up the East, letting air and light into its dens of filth, breaking up old tyrannies and destroying ancient abuses. But while propagating freedom and progress, they were teaching the *fellahin* the art of revolt. He believed that the English colonial methods must either destroy England's colonial empire — or lay the foundations for England's world dominion. Here was, surely, "one of the most fascinating alternatives of our age! We would like to see, fifty years hence, how it all turned out."[55]

But Cromer, the man in charge, was setting down what he saw as a fact of life. Barriers and obstacles had always littered the path of man. He had probably not heard of Mikhail Bakunin's definition that revolution is never against man but against relations and things; but if he had, it would not have bothered him. He therefore went on dictating his annual reports on the state of Egypt in what his principal English critic liked to call his "first-chapter-of-Genesis-style."[56] The lack of human links in empire did not bother those who had never thought of it in the first place as some kind of debating society or rotary club, wherein *conversazióne* in armchairs should be continually in session, far from the scenes of action. It might be true, as one analyst said, that there was a fundamental disequilibrium between Europe and most parts of the undeveloped world[57] — but was that Europe's fault? Was European enterprise to stay stagnant because 80 percent of the world preferred, or at any rate lived, life that way? The true links of empire were what they had always been: strategic and economic. Outright political dominance was expensive and unpopular with metropolitan taxpayers: accordingly,

in 1914 European and North American interests in the Ottoman Empire, the Persian Gulf, Afghanistan, Siam, Japan, China, and Latin America were still for the most part based on a complex of treaties and informal influence.[58]

While Cromer was ruling Egypt without the title of king, Europe's most exhilarated imperialist, King Leopold II of the Belgians, was still pursuing the program to which he had dedicated himself forty years earlier. His view was clear. The possession of overseas territory was a means of giving a nation a more important place in the world, of opening up new careers for its citizens, and of supplying it with a new financial structure which might, as it had done for the Netherlands in the case of Java, yield a surplus. Belgium, of low ranking in the European concert, would promote itself high once it had developed a national spirit, and this would best be fostered by the pride its nationals could take in gainfully exploiting the great African domains of its king. The Congo in the hands of Leopold's agents had certainly yielded a surplus.[59] Public outcry was shortly to make the gathering of this surplus—"Red Rubber"—a less bloody and ruinous business to those who yielded it, but the structure itself, although passing from Leopold's direct rule to that of a Belgian colonial bureaucracy, remained intact. All the bureaucracies that operated within the imperial structures kept to their accustomed ways: if their members behaved, as their critics accused them, as an Old Guard, there was still no New Guard in sight.

The European bureaucrats therefore put their trust in the continued supremacy of the machine. They were convinced that all the imperial machines belonged, like so many jinn, only to their masters and could never work for anyone else. The Germans in particular saw no need for any change of guard. They would do mankind a favor by organizing the future, according to the best plans available, which were their own. They had inspected everyone else's machinery and had found it faulty in many respects. The British Empire, for example, was only an emporium, operating along countinghouse, marketplace lines. The English were notorious for making virtues of their necessities: they needed peace in order to prosper and would subordinate everything to getting it, at the same time proclaiming *pax Britannica* as if it was a free gift. The German chancellor Theobald von Bethmann-Hollweg remarked in his *Reflections on the World War* (1920) that the assimilation of the interests of humanity with those of the British Empire, "which is particular to English thinkers, is, of course, unacceptable to Germans."[60]

German thinking on these matters was also, of course, based on clear principles. The interest of the community was superior to, and must therefore override, the interest of the individual. The supreme community, whose authority was unimpeachable, was the state. German gifts of discipline, German powers of organization made Germany the inevitable pioneer in the task of fashioning an imperial framework within which the collective human community would live and prosper. This community, once established, could enjoy no better destiny than to remain under the authority of German culture. *Deutschland über Alles* was thus not a shallow slogan, a piece of jingoistic drum beating: it was a consecrated formula, at once the product and the symbol of the philosophy that governed the teaching of history, and indeed of everything else, within the German state. History was a useful tool in the hands of a scientific investigator who knew what he or she was looking for. So too must the new biology and the evolutionary theories of Darwin be set to the same work. To the strong and the fit went the prizes of life, and who were stronger and fitter than the German people?

Its belief in its superiority did not incline the German Empire to practice reciprocity in its dealings with other nations. No true reciprocity, in such a situation, was possible; and it would be hypocritical, an English but not a German trait, to pretend that it was. The Germans conquered, or planned to conquer, territories and areas, not nations. What Germans needed, above all, if their ideas were fully to develop, was space. If the space was not there, it had to be made, it had to be cleared. They spoke of the *Lebensraum* they needed before they could square to the task that Providence had set for them. They spoke of images that shined. A German Empire, then, a true world state with a true world policy, would be nothing like the British Empire, that humdrum grouping of shopkeepers. It would be something far otherwise, animated by a patriotism of a nobler stamp, incapable of suffering a fall of honor. It would unlock the future. It would usher in that Golden Age for which all peoples, even those who were only dimly aware of science and its wonders, were waiting and hoping. And it went without saying that people who opposed these ideas, or perpetuated conditions that obstructed their fulfillment, were enemies not only of Germany but of all mankind.

Intoxicants of this kind were not essential to carry imperialists successfully through their careers, but they are perhaps worth recalling if only to show how great the empire of enthusiasm could become. But simple pragmatism in the British style, or military efficiency in the French style, continued to serve very well. Anyone who thought differently could still, and very quickly, be brought to a stop: between February 1916 and May 1917 a series of mass trials held before a *Conseil de Guerre* in Cochin China crippled the anti-French movement there for at least ten years.[61] Everywhere, however, a bureaucracy had to select, or sometimes create, a group of agents with whom it could do business and through whom it could get its imperial business done. Such agents were usually anxious, by collaborating with the rulers of their country, to go into business for themselves, of a type whose dividends, whether financial or otherwise, would accrue mainly to themselves. These practical considerations were sometimes too practical for the conscience of theorists. Lugard of Nigeria—who by the end of World War I had graduated to the position of *éminence grise* in the British Colonial Office, one he was to keep until his death at the end of World War II—declared as doctrine and impressed on a troop of official disciples that the interests of a large native population should not be made subject to the will of a small minority of educated and Europeanized natives who had nothing in common with them and whose interests were opposed to theirs.[62] Yet this injunction often had to be sidestepped in the name of expediency. A mission headed by the Colonial Office's other doyen, Lord Milner, arrived in a most unrestful Egypt in December 1919. His eventual report recognized that, owing to the backwardness of the mass of the people, of whom 90 percent were illiterate, it would be many years before any elected assembly really represented more than a comparatively limited class. But he went on to recommend creating such an assembly. In effect, as more rigid theorists angrily pointed out to him, he was making a set of self-appointed politicians, who had no formal authority to negotiate on behalf of Egypt, "a gift of Egypt and its people to milk and misgovern."[63] This problem was to recur, and so was the indignation that it should even exist. As a British police officer in Palestine later complained, when beset by even more unrest than Egypt had produced, if the great imperial and Commonwealth experiment was to deteriorate into a giving of office to the ambitious for the sake of peace and quiet, it was not worth an obituary notice.[64]

That it was a good point, imperial officials had to admit; but they insisted that the argument had a point also at its other end. Still eyeing their machine, they spoke of safety valves. Expediency remained a better policy than no policy at all. The time was gone when one could sit and preside over a totally peaceful scene, if indeed such a time had ever existed. To be sure it was better, that is, more pleasant — as one hardheaded Indian civil servant confided to another — to rule a district than to humbug a raja.[65] But sometimes humbug itself was a useful enough policy. Empire had long been accustomed to the presence in its midst of princes and pashas who bent to the prevailing wind and who turned an expectant face or cheek to the "country power." That these princes and pashas were assuredly humbugs in their turn never disconcerted anyone who knew his business, on either side of whatever transaction was being arranged. When in Rome, sensible strangers did as the Romans did; but sensible Romans kept an eye on strangers nonetheless.

Anyway, public attitudes are at no time entirely free from, or far from, humbug. Even those unaccustomed to empire were never slow or unwilling to get hold of the dividends that the possession of power automatically piled up. In 1922 the English philosopher Bertrand Russell turned a radical and sardonic eye on the style and shape of American hopes for China; and thus early and graphically he laid out precisely what a subsequent generation of Americans reckoned they had "lost" when in 1949 the celebrated "loss of China" (to the Communists) had occurred. It was, he stated, to America's interest to secure in China certain things consistent with Chinese interests and certain things inconsistent with them. The Americans, for the sake of commerce and good investments, wished to see a stable government in China, an increase in the purchasing power of the people, and an absence of territorial aggrandizement by other Powers who were animated by nothing but their own self-interest.

But they did not then nor would they ever wish to see the Chinese strong enough to own and work the railways and mines of China. They resented all Chinese attempts at economic independence — particularly when, as was to be expected, these took the form of state socialism, or what Lenin at the same moment was calling state capitalism. They would keep a dossier on every student educated in colleges under American control and would very likely see to it that those who professed socialism or indulged in radical opinions of any kind obtained no agreeable posts. In short, they would insist that China be made over into a replica of "God's own country" — except that it would not be allowed to keep the wealth generated by its industries.[66]

It was a remarkable forecast, and Russell made it at a time when no definition of "informal empire" had yet been reached or formal attention paid to its habits. Areas of passivity like China were seen as the natural victims of circumstance. Inevitably the type and style of activities within such areas would be decreed by others. Americans in China saw themselves as westerners with a difference, as progressives with clean hands. They were rescuers, not just one more species of foreign devil. The State Department view was also the general view, and it was honestly held: the works of empire and the very name of imperialism were things to be shunned, since they were un-American in origin and application. In his account of World War II, which he called *Crusade in Europe* (1948), General Dwight D. Eisenhower remarked that both Russia and the United States were "free of the stigma of empire-building by force."[67] His innocence of Russian history reflected a like confusion regarding his own country's, as many a Mexican could have told him.

For force had always been a means of everyone's national expansion, including the United States's. That Americans had discovered their manifest destiny in moving westward within continental bounds from one sea to another — defeating en route a series of native peoples and one rival power, the Southern Confederacy — made their history different in degree, but not in kind, from that of other successful nations. Americans, if not prepared to applaud the aims of the European empires, certainly understood what they were: international status, its accompanying self-respect, and the profit that accrued from energies well directed in places well chosen. If the business of America was indeed business, as President Calvin Coolidge said in 1925, America could not afford to stand clear and stay ignorant of the areas of the world where a great deal of this business might be done. But since Coolidge's generation did not make these assumptions clear, preferring to take refuge in such sentimentalities as General Eisenhower was taught to take for granted in his grade-school texts, a series of homebred critics arose in the 1970s who came to look with a cold eye on the foreign policies of their forebears. They refused to award grades for innocence, finding in the record more hypocrisy than shortsightedness. Harry Magdoff repeated the earlier verdict of Bertrand Russell when he insisted in his *The Age of Imperialism* (1969) that the underlying purpose of imperialism "is nothing less than keeping as much of the world as possible open for trade and investment by the giant multi-national corporations."[68] Or as Conor Cruise O'Brien, a less committed but equally critical observer, remarked, the chief characteristic of the open international society has always been that it gives the most benefit to the economically powerful.[69] Power had built the framework, and power was what it enclosed.

What counted was the power to keep an option open. In China the need to have an Open Door had long been asserted. Whose door it was in the first place did not greatly signify. If an Eldorado lay somewhere beyond it, it was axiomatic that an Imperial Power would find the place, an Imperial Power would construct the road that led to it, and an Imperial Power would guard the gate through which the road could be reached. In China the imperial guardians were many, and a jostling confusion of interests bred a like confusion of policies, confusions which China, as much itself as ever, was in the long run able to confound and become free of them all. In Latin America, the door had one warden only, the United States, who took its position so much for granted that it denied it was wearing any imperial uniform whatever. In the Middle East, those who kept watch on its threshold had a lot of trouble doing so, but they always thought it was worth their while.

All these areas of dominance testify to the solidarity of imperial assurance. When miscalculations were made, as in the nature of things they always were, they were merely inconvenient, not fatal. Their principal immediate effect was to cause a passing pessimism, accompanied by a resolve not to commit at least that particular mistake again. The emotional "China policy" of the United States, however it was disguised and whatever course it took at any given time, was always an American luxury, as the event proved: for when the Open Door was shut, bolted, and sealed in 1949, American interests were not greatly damaged. The effect felt in Washington, in business circles, and in missionary headquarters across the United States was psychological, not actual. But this never happened in, and was never the attitude toward, Latin America, an area which had long been locked into the imperial framework. This area was not a country but a hemisphere of countries. All of them were politically independent, but the fact that independence, like everything else, has a context had been made plain to their citizens from the outset. The physical security of North America was predicated on the inviolability of South America, and any South American nation that proposed to argue against this was by definition no friend to the United States. All nations consult their own interest, and if they are powerful they are never too particular how they go about doing this—but the United States, because of its own history of anticolonialism, had laid a special burden of conscience upon itself which the sharp-edged facts of strategy and common sense were constantly lacerating. Geography and good fortune had allowed the United States to expand without having to traffic much in direct colonial rule. Americans had been able to pioneer the development of forms of exploitation that, by the 1970s, had come to be known as neocolonialism. Known to others, that is: such an attribution applied to any American policy whatever, has never been acceptable north of the Mexican border—a border whose very existence kept alive in Mexican memory the old imperialist aggression that absorbed half of Mexico into an alien culture. *Antiyanquismo*, that "crop of the hills and dust,"[70] was one Latin American attitude that was passed intact from one century to the other.

In the western hemisphere it often seemed that the sun rose in the north. The country of the morning threw its shadow on every area of life in the evening south, including the language used there. By what right had the Anglo-Saxons appropriated to themselves the term "American," whose usage denied the fact that there were two Americas? The United States of America accordingly appeared in Spanish translation as *Estados Unidos* N*orteamericanos*; but its attitudes and assumptions were less easily deflected. From the time of its promulgation in 1823 the Monroe Doctrine appeared not so much as a Washington policy to keep Europeans out of the hemisphere's affairs than as a ploy to make North Americans free of them. Within a diplomatic wall of their own construction a "sphere of influence"—Africa later in the century was to be plagued with several of these—was set up; and by the turn of the twentieth century this particular policy of containment was fast changing to one of direct action. By the Peace of Paris of 1898 the United States became the imperial legatee of Spain. It began work at once to make the Caribbean and Central America an enclave of American power, in Panama and in Puerto Rico and in Cuba. Cuba indeed began a new life under its own government and constitution, but it found itself living an old life-style, a life in the colonial mode; for the constitution allowed the United States to intervene on the island if and when Washington thought that good government was in danger and things in general were awry. That things were more likely to go wrong than stay right in areas not governed directly by civilized whites was always the conviction of President Theodore Roosevelt, which he never hesitated to publicize. In his message to Congress on December 6, 1904, he established what became known as a "corollary" to the Monroe Doctrine, expressed in language that could lift no heart in the southern hemisphere:

Chronic wongdoing, or an impotence which results in a general loosening of the ties of civilized society, may in America, as elsewhere, ultimately require intervention by some civilized nations, and in the Western Hemisphere, the adherence of the United States to the Monroe Doctrine may force the United States, however reluctantly . . . to the exercise of the international police power.[71]

Roosevelt knew quite well that there was no such thing as an international police power, but in referring to it he was drawing a weapon from the same imperialist armory that was used by British admirals and politicians, when they spoke at large, particularly on gala occasions, of "the freedom of the seas." For the next thirty years of the century, direct American intervention in Central America became a commonplace, although Washington always refused to see it as anything other than an aberration from the norm. But, if the people there would not act normally, what else could be done?

President Taft sent the United States' marines to Nicaragua in 1911. They stayed there until 1925. President Wilson sent more of them to the Dominican Republic in April 1916, where they stayed until September 1924; and to Haiti in July 1915, where they stayed until July 1934. The policy was always to restore order: alien military occupation was decided on as the best way to stop local militarism. Like the British in India, most Americans at heart thought all Latin American politics were unnecessary. Most of it was noisy, none of it was sound. But however tiresome and expensive the task, the security of the United States was, and would be, in 1902 or 1962 or 1992, the first essential. Official views concerning how this might best be secured varied according to the temperament of the officials. Secretary of State Bryan declared on September 9, 1913, that it was particularly necessary to exert American influence in Haiti, since President Wilson "had no sympathy with those who sought to seize the power of government to advance their own personal interests." That such was the ingrained habit among Latin American military men, to whom politics was their only form of public exercise besides polo, did not deter Wilson, who in a famous burst of idealism that has often been quoted told Sir William Tyrrell, "I am going to teach the Latin American republics to elect good men," right before plunging into the even more complex affairs of Mexico. This sortie, in the opinion of Secretary Lansing, was a duty forced upon the United States "by the impotence of the Mexican authorities"—language which showed how firmly Roosevelt's "corollary" had taken root. Wilson himself kept assuring the factions in Mexico that although the United States did not desire or claim the right to settle the affairs of Mexico, "she could not stand indifferently by and do nothing to serve her neighbor." No imperialist was ever a bystander, as has been noted: but a neighbor who did not wish to be served was not within Wilson's mental compass, and even after his departure the puzzle of how to strike a balance between what was needed and what was wanted did not become any simpler.

On August 20, 1923, Secretary Hughes affirmed that American interest did not lie in controlling foreign peoples. That would be imperialism, in the condemned European style. That would be a policy of mischief and disaster. "Our interest is in having prosperous, peaceful and law-abiding neighbors with whom we can co-operate to mutual advantage."[72] But if they would not, were they to be made to cooperate? This dilemma would not dissolve, either then or later. Certainly the action of President Lyndon Johnson in 1965 underlined it, and again the language invites attention. The people of the Dominican Republic, he remarked on May 17, "must be permitted to freely choose the path of political democracy, social justice, and economic progress." What could better blaze the trail for them than the dispatch of yet another detachment of United States' marines?

That the defense of the western hemisphere was the natural business of the United States was also the European view. "Nothing in this Covenant," stated the League of Nations' Covenant regarding one of its clauses, "shall be deemed to affect the validity of international engagements, such as . . . regional understandings like the Monroe Doctrine, for securing the maintenance of peace." Europeans were not as indifferent to another corollary to American policy, less straightforward than Theodore Roosevelt's but equally true: not only was the physical security of Latin America a United States' responsibility, but its way of life and living seemed also likely to come under a North American wing. In Latin America the public utilities, mineral and petroleum products, the meat-packing and fruit industries had for long been organized and controlled by foreign interests. In 1913 £1,000 million of British capital was invested there. Lenin no doubt had all this in mind when he wrote in his *Imperialism, the Highest Stage of Capitalism* that the countries of South American were "semi-colonies," enmeshed in a net of financial and diplomatic dependence. By 1919 United States' investment in the area amounted to $1.125 billion. By 1934 it had reached $5 billion, by 1962, $10 billion. Secretary Stimson's prophecy that the future was bright was therefore justified: Latin American countries were, and were to remain, producers of raw products suitable for United States' consumption, while providing potential markets for a great variety of manufactures. No imperial structure of the seventeenth and eighteenth centuries had ever had a sounder foundation.

President Franklin Roosevelt's external version of his New Deal —a "Good Neighbor" policy which testified to the removal of his namesake's "Big Stick" from the crumpled papers in the Latin American portfolio—was tied to these shrewdly mercantilist estimates.[73] The notion of a "Coprosperity Sphere" was something too profitable to be left exclusively to Japanese, who had invented it and were busy prospecting in Manchuria. If the southern neighbors were truly neighborly, no stick was needed. At the sixth Pan-American Conference, held in Havana in 1928, a resolution put forward by the Latin Americans, that no state had a right to interfere in the internal affairs of another, was thwarted by the United States' delegation: but the same resolution was accepted by Secretary Hull at the seventh conference, in Montevideo in December 1933. Wilson's adventures in Mexico were not repeated, although the Mexicans nationalized their oil. More than a year before World War II broke out in Europe the planners in Washington were busy mapping out the best role for Latin America to play in the forthcoming drama. When Europe locked itself in battle, the ideas of a Coprosperity Sphere that would exclude all rivals was more strongly emphasized. A memorandum from the office of the coordinator of Inter-American Affairs in 1940 concerned British properties in Latin America, which were still very considerable: three-fifths of the total foreign investment in Argentina remained in British hands. It conjured up a vision of the treasures that might be found beyond yet another open door, could its other janitors be forced by circumstances to retire. As one hardheaded official commented,

there are some good properties in the British portfolio, and we might as well pick them up now. There is also a lot of trash which Britain should be allowed to keep.[74]

Options, margins, a lien on the future—in the first half of the century the United States held and enjoyed all these imperial privileges without ever thinking of them either as imperial or as privileges. They were part, merely, of the Americans' manifest destiny to order their affairs to their own benefit, which clearly could never run contrary to someone else's good.

They were able to think this because at the time it was not in the special interest of any other Power to point out a differing interpretation. The politics of Latin America were more closely discussed in the boardrooms of banks and corporations in New York and London and Berlin (which did not publicize either their opinions or the intentions they decided on) than they were by European politicians.[75] In the world outside, the latter were ready to dignify both China and the Middle East as "questions"; but there never was a

Latin American question anywhere beyond intellectual circles in Latin America, the names of whose leaders were ignored in Washington and totally unknown elsewhere.

European governments after 1919 absorbed themselves in the problems on their home ground or on its immediate periphery. The impact of war had shaken and complicated all these problems. A particular complication was caused by the existence of President Wilson himself, whose imperialism of idealism, had American public opinion allowed it to survive, would have promoted every difficulty to the status of a question, or indeed to that of a cause. What happened to the map of Europe might well have happened in the Middle East: certainly it threatened to do so. Finding that his European associates were very much preoccupied with the future of this other area of previous passivity, Wilson produced ideas about the best investment of the Turkish legacy which no one else he met in the corridors of Versailles would have thought of. They resented having to think of them now. He told the Council of Four on March 20, 1920, that "if we were to send a Commission with no previous contact with Syria, it would at any rate convince the world that the Peace Conference has tried to do all it could to find the most scientific basis possible for a settlement." England's Premier Lloyd George did not believe that politics had much to do with science or that anyone else believed so either. He did not suppose that "the world," whatever convictions it had reached about Syria or anywhere else, had the power to do anything to further them; and from the outset he watched the League of Nations and all its apparatus at Geneva with a skepticism equal to that of the United States' Senate itself. He remarked only that the Turks were entitled to know "who would be the mandatory"; to which Wilson countered, "rather they ought to know how much was to remain Turkish."

Minds that refused to meet continued to signal to one another across steadily increasing distances. But Wilson persevered, finally producing two men, not professional diplomats but a college president and a valve manufacturer respectively, whom he thought particularly qualified to go to Syria "because they knew nothing about it." It happened that Henry C. King and Charles R. Crane were able and intelligent men who issued an excellent report, which accurately defined the flash points of policy, now and for the future, in the

Middle East. But true to the context of Wilsonian detachment, it took no account of the predilections of the Great Powers or of the imperial framework within which all action still had to fit. Since the doctrine of self-determination, if realized, would have splintered the framework, the Powers saw no point in discussing it, or even in taking it seriously. Crane's remark that "even the Bedouin of the desert said, 'We want America to come here and do for us what she has been doing for the Filipinos' "[76] might have alarmed them if they had really believed that any such Bedouin existed, or amused them if they could have checked with Aguinaldo in his Japanese retreat.

To the victor Powers the Middle East was yet another area into which doors could, and should, be opened. In some areas they already came and went at will, with access to oil fields, where the geologist was fast replacing the railroad surveyor as the harbinger of empire. The British had been secure in the Persian Gulf since 1899, in southern Persia since 1907, at Abadan and the Shatt al Arab since 1909, and in a consortium with other Powers in Mesopotamia (Iraq) since 1914. Their agreement at San Remo with France gave them 75 percent of what was thereafter to be found in the Mosul and other Iraqi fields, despite loud American protest that this was not how the United States understood the principle of the open door. These practical advantages were now to supply a basis for a new spiritual adventure in the area. The Middle East was Europe's last area of expansion, its last margin for option and (as it turned out) for error. To it the French, combining Crusaders' dreams with Moroccan and Annamese experience, took a military methodology of administration which had already become stereotyped, but the same British government that had "won the war" and was investing at least some emotional capital in the League of Nations at Geneva decided it was now also time to insert some imagination and a spirit of adventure into an imperial framework that too often had enclosed neither the one nor the other. In what had been Turkish Palestine it believed it could operate a policy that would merge the best elements of imperial paternalism with the current idealism that people had the right to be free. The British sought, therefore, to balance the demands of Arab leaders for a free hand for themselves and their followers with the Zionists' call for universal justice for the Jews. They thought they could best do this by allowing the Jews to make a home in an area inhabited by over half a million Arabs.

Great Powers had always admitted that some things would always be with them, that on some issues the files were never closed. They saw this as a fact of life, to be coped with as sensibly as possible. There had always been, and there was now, a Slav question, a Polish question, an Eastern question, and an Irish question. But the Palestine question was unique because it was deliberately invented by an Imperial Power. It did not arrive on the agenda, it was placed there. Arab assertion and Zionist aspiration had a long sporadic history behind them, but now they simultaneously surfaced to the level of international attention under the auspices of British imperial patronage. From this context both movements were to issue their respective claims in the future. Both well understood the utility of having a fixed address; it was to take a second major war to bring them to reappraise this. Until then they stayed willing clients of empire, for they saw a security in the condition of cliency which they could have got nowhere else.

In the Palestine question, as it developed, all the dilemmas of twentieth-century imperialism appeared in capsule form. Emancipation here took on the form of an act of common justice. The Zionists proclaimed the idea of the subject race as victim: in the case of the Jews as a people subject not to any one imperial controller but to the habits, prejudices, and indifferences of Christian European civilization itself. The Jews had been held down by an age-long and widespread cultural colonialism: Zionists sought at once to have this recognized, expiated, and resolved. They shared the outlook of the Great Powers that the defeated Turkish Empire was a derelict area, fit to be organized anew. The Arabs, like the Chinese, could be manipulated to play their part in a scheme larger than they could ever conceive. They could be handled—and of this handling, European ideas, which included Zionist ideas, would be in charge.

But the ambiguities in Balfour's letter to Lord Rothschild of November 2, 1917, were to worsen and finally ruin the concept of a British mandate for a Palestine wherein everyone would develop and prosper. In a declaration of sympathy to the Zionist Federation, he assured it that the British government "viewed with favour" the establishment in Palestine of a "National Home" for the Jewish people and that it would do its best to facilitate the achievement of this object, it being clearly understood that nothing shall be done which may prejudice the civil and religious rights of existing non-Jewish communities in Palestine, or the rights and political status enjoyed by Jews in any other country.[77]

Cabinet minutes indicate that he meant by the words "National Home" some form of British, American, or other protectorate, under which full facilities would be given to the Jews to work out their own salvation and to build up, by education, agriculture, and industry, a real center of national culture and focus of national life. It did *not necessarily* (my italics) involve the early establishment of an independent Jewish state — "which was a matter for gradual development in accordance with the ordinary laws of political evolution."[78] Here was another illustration of the imperial assumption that there were laws of political evolution, that some of them were ordinary and some not, that these waited on time, and that they could all be controlled by paternalists ordering affairs to everyone's best advantage.

Not everyone in a high place used this line of reasoning. General Allenby, who had brought in both Jerusalem and Damascus as trophies of war, answered the question "What was the value of Palestine?" by saying it had no economic value whatever but that its retention by the British would keep their minds active for the next generation or two — and he was of course right. Curzon, whose imperialism was often overblown but who did not confuse it with omnipotence, was sunk in pessimism before Balfour's letter was approved and sent. How, pray, was it proposed to get rid of the existing majority of Muslim inhabitants and to introduce the Jews in their place? (And as for the Jews' "historical connections," well, on that principle the English had a stronger claim to parts of France.)[79] By 1921 Winston Churchill as colonial secretary, a self-declared Zionist but not one who ever calloused his hands for the cause, insisted that establishing a National Home did not mean setting up a Jewish government to dominate the Arabs. Step by step, no doubt, the British as the mandatory Power would develop representative institutions in Palestine leading to full self-government, but "as in India, our children's children will have passed away before that is accomplished." The elder statesman Lord Grey brought in the judgment that a Zionist home undoubtedly meant a Zionist government over the district in which the home was placed, and since 93 percent of the population of Palestine were Arab, he did not see how anything other than an Arab government could be established without prejudicing their civil rights. "That one sentence of the Balfour Declaration seems to me to involve, without overstating the case, very great difficulty of fulfilment."[80]

Grey was not overstating the case. Fulfillment was never in the cards The declaration, an imperial decree disposing in total fashion of the lives and futures of others, was issued too late for acceptance, by anyone at all. Magnanimity on this scale was reckoned a pose. Balfour himself had of course seen, but had discounted in advance, the point Grey made. He confided as much to Lloyd George in February 1919. The weak point of their mutually agreed position was that in Palestine "we deliberately and rightly decline to accept the principle of self-determination."[81] He knew the aims of the Zionists. He knew their extent, although neither he nor they would spell them out loud. He knew that if and when they could, the Jews would absorb Palestine. His underlings at the Foreign Office, in the dawn of a bad day peering toward a worse twilight, knew this too. One telegram went to Reginald Wingate, overseer of British interests in Egypt, stressing that it was most important that everything possible be done to allay Arab suspicions regarding the true aims of Zionism. Another came back from Gilbert Clayton, supervisor of British interests in Jerusalem, urging that great care was essential in developing a policy which was, "to say the least, somewhat startling to those other elements whom we have been at such pains to cultivate during the past three years and to whom we are morally pledged."[82] Balfour, following his particular dream, might choose to ignore all this, but an imperialist infrastructure outlasts any one imperialist, and it was not long before the British themselves—the controlling group, that is, since the British people were not consulted on high imperial matters—came to look on his declaration as both impolitic and immoral.

This attitude—the "Chatham House Version"—can certainly be attributed to Arnold Toynbee, director of the Royal Institute of International Affairs who was to graduate to seer-at-large. He never changed the view he adopted while clerking at the Middle East desk in Balfour's Foreign Office at the close of World War I. The foundation of British policy should be the setting up of a *Palestinian* state (his italics), with Palestinian citizenship for all inhabitants, whether Arab or Jew. "This alone seemed consistent with Mr. Balfour's letter."[83] In 1967 he repeated this and a swath of other arguments in a letter to J. L. Talmon in Jerusalem; by then the story had developed new dimensions without changing its essence. The Palestine Arabs, Toynbee thought (and in 1974 still did), had suffered injustice. To put it bluntly, they had been made to pay for the genocide of the Jews in Hitler's Europe. The Arabs had been humiliated: first, in the establishment of the Jewish national home; ultimately, in that of the state of Israel (1948). They had never been consulted about either. Balfour's declaration did not even refer to the Arabs by name. It spoke of the non-Jewish communities — rather like describing a group of Swedes as non-Greeks. The Arabs had in fact been treated throughout in the worst old imperialist way — treated as "natives," with no more than subhuman rights.[84]

The Chatham House tone is pitched high, but an overture of it can be heard in the 1937 report of the Peel Commission on Palestine —a report which, coupled with the 1939 white paper that grew out of it, ended any Jewish hope that the British mandate would ever take Zionism back to its inheritance. By then British cabinet ministers were debating not how to pursue Balfour's idealisms but how to cut the knot of the administrative and military tangle of the Palestine question. The Peel Report concluded that it had long been clear that the notion of any cultural assimilation between Arab and Jew was a fantasy. Jewish nationality seemed to reject, whether consciously or otherwise, the very idea of a real Palestinian community.[85] Palestine was a Colonial Office charge—but the name of the place might, however, have been Mauritius or Ceylon, since the imperial role was everywhere the same. The British continued to see it as their duty to guide other races—in the latter's best interests, since the assumption still held that these races would never find either the sense or the energy to distinguish their best interests for themselves. But how could imperialists preside, guide, and judge if at the same time they threw themselves wholeheartedly behind the cause of one of the parties to a dispute—whatever Balfour, dead by 1930, had thought possible and proper?

The official tone therefore did not vary from June 1920, when the Jew and Zionist Sir Herbert Samuel became the first British high commissioner in Palestine, until the issue of the Peel Report itself. Samuel in 1921 declared it the manifest duty of the mandatory Power to promote the well-being of the Arab population: measures to foster Arab progress, the progress of the vast majority, must thus be precisely those which would be adopted in Palestine were there no Zionist question, and no Balfour Declaration either.[86]

The Arabs thought precisely this too. They had a claim upon the British, who during and after World War I had descended among them like a horde of latter-day Franks, who had recast their horoscopes, and who, to justify these actions, ought now to be buckling down to organizing their future. That the British had another protégé in train was no concern of the Arabs—and mounting uproar accompanied their discovery that it was going to be made their concern. So the view of the Arabs—Clayton's other elements, Balfour's non-Jews—was as Toynbee defined it. They never saw any reason to change it. If at any time they did not express it clearly, there were plenty of Englishmen ready to do it for them, partly out of a genuine sympathy for a people who during World War I had been promised no one was quite sure what, and partly because of the quixotic determination so often found among the best British colonial officials not only to see other people's points of view but to point these out in case they had missed them. A British officer early stated the obvious: what the Arabs feared was not the Jews in Palestine but the Jews who were coming to Palestine.[87] Talk about the Semitic cousinhood was all very well, but nobody welcomed cousins who came to take over the house and make it their home.

Samuel by the end of 1922 was reduced to quoting Anatole France: "No one can foresee the future, not even those who make it." The Arabs continued to think, nevertheless, that those who took it on themselves to make the future ought to have some clear idea of what they were doing. They punctuated this argument with risings of varying velocity in April 1920, May 1921, August 1929, and October 1933. The same reasons powered all of them: the Arabs objected to the imposition of the mandate, and they objected to the immigration of the Jews, whose proportion of the Palestine population rose from 13 percent in 1922 to 28 percent by 1935. In April 1936 rising accelerated to revolt: the Arabs had finally decided to face what they called "the mobilised forces of Imperial Britain and the insatiable ambitions of world Jewry."[88] The politics of complaint, transformed into an open rejection of the imperial program, paid a dividend. Peel's commissioners, after a three-month survey of the situation, stated that they were not prepared to recommend the forcible conversion of Palestine into a Jewish state against the will of the Arabs. British imperialists no longer saw it as their task, or their adventure, to solve "the problem of the Jews," and in the white paper of 1939 they reversed a pledge of 1922 to keep Palestine open to Jewish immigration up to the limit of the country's "economic absorptive capacity"—one of Churchill's phrases which neither he nor anyone else, and nobody since, managed to define. Immigration was to continue for another five years, whereafter Arab consent to its continuance would be required. This made it clear that Jews would live in Palestine on sufferance rather than by right, as it was clear enough already that the Arabs were not prepared to suffer anything else at all.

World War II thus descended on a Palestine locked in angry stalemate. The Arabs were listening to the Axis radio, and the mufti of Jerusalem, Rashid Ali in Iraq, their friends in Cairo, and others of like mind were ready to seize any chance the Germans could give them. After the war, although the Germans were gone, their case was the same. They told the Anglo-American Committee of Enquiry in March 1946 that were it not for Zionism and its powerful international friendships, Palestine would long since have been self-governing, would have become a member of the United Nations and a stalwart of the Arab League. And this was true. They denied the claim that the Zionists were the agents of western civilization in the Middle East. What was this, anyway, but the moth-eaten imperialist boast that the West was self-evidently superior to the East in the first place and could go about scattering, by curious hands, a cultural largesse? This argument the Jews, too, could put to their own use. In May 1942 David Ben-Gurion had declared that the policy of Palestine Jewry henceforth was to fight with Britain against Hitler's Germany as if there had been no 1939 white paper and to fight against the white paper as if there had been no war.[89] He said this to an audience of American Jews in the Biltmore Hotel in New York, and, clearly, it served notice that when the war was over the Jews, like the Arabs, would do their best to get rid of their imperial patron.

The major problem confronting Zionism, from the time Theodor Herzl published his *Der Judenstaat* in 1894, had been to get air and elbowroom, to become heard of, talked about, visible at congresses, and ultimately to have itself recognized as an international entity, a fact of public life. Movements need to be labeled and identified at large before anyone will join them. Zionism was, however, the first movement of its kind to infiltrate the interstices of an empire with which it had no direct connection. As noted earlier, views of empire are normally taken from above, the view of the controllers, or from below, the view of the controlled. But Zionism took its view from the wings. Its leaders had to get on stage, appear in a major production before a crowded audience, attract an imperial impresario who would give them more to do than carry spears while cheering Coriolanus. Zionism is philosophically subtle and profound; but one politicial thing about it not in the least subtle or profound, immediately obvious, is its place in the twentieth-century movement of colonial national assertion, contemporary with the Irish and Egyptian movements and forebear of a dozen others. Its nationalism began its international career, necessarily, in other peoples' anterooms. Herzl himself, whose book never mentioned the Arabs and whose diaries express a contempt of them,[90] proposed the notion that if the Ottoman sultan was willing to give Palestine to the Jews, in return the Jews could undertake the organization of the entire finances of Turkey. Within the movement there was continual bickering—about ways and means, about the Uganda project of 1903, and about the central clash with the assimilated Jews in the western world, who, it was charged, had turned their backs on the true and only cause in the vain hope that their assimilation would be accepted by whatever host they had attached themselves to. But everyone was agreed that Zionism must find for itself a forum and a stage on which these and additional arguments could be debated in the limelight, beyond the shadows of an intellectual ghetto wherein angry pamphlets were read, if at all, only by other angry pamphleteers.

This was the famous achievement of Chaim Weizmann, who by force of personality hurled Zionism into the orbit of Balfour and the British. Once this was accomplished, the British might not know what to do with it, but at least they could not pretend it was not there. Nor did they. In 1918 leaflets reprinting the Balfour Declaration were dropped over German and Austrian territory, with the message in Yiddish: "Remember! An Allied victory means the Jewish people's return to Zion." But when the Zionists took and maintained the initiative in seeking Britain as the ruling power in Palestine, they found "that the diplomacy to which they were invited consisted in a management of the balance of power much more than in an appeal to the common conscience of mankind."[91] Others made the same miscalculation. At the end of that grinding war the common conscience of mankind was an exhausted asset: everyone's emotional capital had run out. Yet when Balfour issued his declaration there was certainly no future of blood in his eye, and that generation of Zionists was as innocent, as pacifist, and as clear in conscience as he. It is a long way downriver from "viewing with favour" to the terrorism of the Stern group (1944) on the one side and that of the Black September movement (1970) on the other. Still, it is a voyage people made and one which can be traced.

In attaching themselves to the British imperial institute both the Arabs and the Jews did better for their causes than the troubled history of the mandate might seem to prove. What chiefly troubled this history was the conscience of the mandatory Power. An Imperial Power might otherwise, if not so burdened, have cheerfully used its strength to bring the Arabs into submission and to ignore all calls for justice from the Jews. But Britain's empire was liberal. Nationalism itself, since Gladstone's day, was seen as something benign. Arabs like Jews were thereafter able to capitalize on their opinion that the generosity of the imperial patronage had not gone far enough and on the fact that their overlords were perpetually uneasy about the exercise of their overlordship, calling it by a name — mandate — never before heard of in imperialist history. To be constantly and loudly told by their wards that their trusteeship was doing all kinds of harm was a charge that for thirty years British imperialists parried with increasing ineptitude. Each time Palestine erupted the British brought into action a military-cum-police authority, which on Whitehall's orders did its work with a halfheartedness that at once speeded the arrival of the next effort at revolt and bettered its chances of success. Arabs and Jews who attacked the mandate — the one because it existed at all, the other because it limited Jewish immigration to an average of 18,000 per year — knew that they were not pushing at an open door, but they thought that one more heave with a battering ram would break it. In 1939 Malcolm MacDonald, as colonial secretary, could not bring himself to admit that the mandate was unworkable, but eight years later Ernest Bevin, as foreign secretary, did exactly this, and with some venom.[92]

The mandate for Palestine had reached this point because the Power holding it, believing sincerely in the doctrine of the consent of the governed, had become convinced that the governed were never going to consent to live together within the bounds of a single state. That there were other ways in which imperialism could still conduct itself, other ways to deal with a mandate, a glance at the story of Syria under the French army can show. Palestine's case was exceptional, proving that the old and tried rules still applied. By indulging in an unwonted idealism, England's imperialists ended up without either the ideals or Palestine itself. But the original choice, how they should act, had been theirs to make. Elsewhere within the imperial framework the choices made were of a different kind, but the circle of privileges within which these could be made was still inviolate. If idealism was a stranger there, national interests were not. Palestine would never have become a "question" had it not been a trophy of victory. Other trophies were being sought, and there were plenty of them to seek: "The Spoils" was the frank title of a memorandum put before Prime Minister Asquith in March 1915.[93] There was a newcomer to the circle, who had very recently arrived. On January 18 Japan had presented its "Twenty-One Demands" to China, set down on some sheets of paper watermarked with dreadnoughts and machine guns.[94] The Chinese government accepted these on May 9. Some private diplomatic unease was expressed in both London and Washington, but none in public. The public aim was to secure the future. Why not increase, then, the ranks of the privileged, who were obviously interested in making the world safe for exercising and maintaining their privileges? If this was done, the forces of unrest and subversion, wherever they might appear, would be abashed by a simple tally of the number of opponents. If the United States would not, or not openly, join the ranks of the powerful and associate itself with their purpose, this was due more to America's own internal preoccupations than to any attempt by the other Powers to keep it out, however much they might have experienced the strain of educating these particular newcomers to the proper degree of sophistication.

Especially anxious to bring the Americans into the arena of international politics were the Canadians, who had had to pay a heavy price in manpower for their involvement with the European policies of the British Empire, which in fact meant Great Britain. In August 1918 the Canadian premier, Sir Robert Borden, warned his colleagues in the British imperial war cabinet that the people of Canada were not willing to fight for the mere sake of extending the territories of the empire. The more it was possible to get the United States to undertake large responsibilities in world affairs, the better it would be for the world as a whole and for the British Empire in particular.[95] This thinking was not at all unpopular in London. In line with it many agenda laden with the most intractable problems of the day— including Palestine, Armenia, and the ex-German colonies, but not of course Ireland—were drafted quickly and presented hopefully, but unsuccessfully, to the disdainful American glance.

For the imperial controllers found that they now had the chance to occupy more territory than ever before. Littered around was the debris of three defeated empires, the German, the Austro-Hungarian, and the Turkish. Although war had weakened the European state system, it had not destroyed the assumption that the structure of world power was still naturally Eurocentric, that the center of gravity for all international affairs was still where it had always been. The United States for one reason, the new Union of Soviet Socialist Republics for another, had withdrawn to the sidelines. In the Germanic heartland of the continent a political vacuum existed. Only the victor powers, the twin empires of Britain and France, were present to continue manipulating events, with Italy as an eager client and Greece with Byzantine plans of its own. They were also very willing to set about the task and indeed were convinced that because of the great extent of their recent sacrifices the task was rightfully theirs and nobody else's.

One of the trophies most prized by victors is the right to retain their past. This can only be accomplished by keeping a grip on the present. Although a great many of their plans went astray, imperialists did not suppose that anyone else would have the impertinence to usurp their monopoly of planning. If one plan failed, another could be substituted. Maurice Hankey, secretary to the British Cabinet, reported on December 4, 1918 an exchange between the two premiers, Lloyd George and Clemenceau:

When they were alone Clemenceau said, "Well, what are we to discuss?" "Mesopotamia and Palestine," replied Ll. G. [*sic*]. "Tell me what you want," asked Clemenceau. "I want Mosul," said Ll. G. "You shall have it," said C., "Anything else?" "Yes, I want Jerusalem too," continued Ll. G. "You shall have it," said Clemenceau, "but Pichon [the French foreign minister] will make difficulties about Mosul."[96]

This was the regular and confident tone of the imperialist diplomatic exchanges of the day. Everything was still possible: the important question was, what was practicable? What D. G. Hogarth of the British Arab Bureau in Cairo told Gertrude Bell—who, with a tribe of enthusiastic young Anglo-Indian officers, was disappointed when Turkish Mesopotamia was not made a formal part of the British Empire—was certainly true: "there is no more expansion in us."[97] Expansion for its own sake, in fact one of the rarest of phenomena, was of course to be frowned on as a legacy from a heedless past. But clear fields and broad horizons lay all around: what danger could there be in walking across the one to reach the other? There was still a great deal of administration left in everybody: by 1930 there were as many French officials in Indochina as British officials in India, a country with twelve times the population.

The imperial bureaucracies thus expanded to meet a demand from their own bureaucrats. This bred the natural hope, which grew to a · conviction, that the demand would always exist. The administrators of course expected to have problems, but they expected also to have room and time to tackle them. They did not expect outsiders to interfere. Why should they? Surely, self-determination was a policy which an empire might also claim for itself and thus keep its affairs within a domestic, and therefore private, portfolio. They expected outsiders to protest, because outsiders had always done so. They did so still. Those who were not imperially endowed continued to draw loud attention to the fact that the victor Powers had made off with the world's best surfaces some time ago, leaving for others only what the Powers had thought not worth taking, or indeed worth anything. Mussolini's subsequent snarl that he was not a collector of deserts was understandable. To the "have-not" powers, empire was still the emblem of arrival, the mark of success.

At Versailles the ex-enemy colonies were allocated as "mandated territories" to the victors, who kept them free from any responsibility in the field of external relations. The principle of trusteeship established for these colonies, which were officially designated in the instruments of mandate as territories "not yet able to stand by themselves," was not new, but it had the advantage of being both principled and useful, easily applicable to all colonial situations. It was because colonial peoples had been thought to be unable to stand by themselves that they had become colonial peoples in the first place. They had never had their views canvassed, and they did not have them canvassed now. In 1920 in mandated Syria, overriding a series of protests which graduated through unrest to open revolt, the French established martial law, and retained it as the mode of government for the next four years. They brushed aside all objections: "We could not," said Premier Georges Leygues in December, "without losing our rank as a great Mediterranean, African, and Muslim Power, renounce the action in Syria."[98] This matter of rank was of the highest importance to all patriotic French people. The unchanged opinion of the officers of the French army, devotees less of the Third Republic than of themselves and of the French presence in the world, held that colonial nationalism was the least modern of movements, that it ought *not* to have a future, and that the duty of wise men was to ensure that it would not *have* a future. It was outmoded, properly belonging to the stagecoach era. Here they joined hands with their chief *bête noire*, the dreaded Bolsheviks, who in the same years were busy with the policy of destroying the ambitions and the resistance of all the peoples of Russia who were not and never had been Russian. To men with their eyes on the correct shape of the future, empire, direct rule, and modernity were all aspects of the same issue. Devolution of power was mere weakness, not to be thought of, traitorous even to consider.

It was the rare French officer who was able to distinguish the Bolsheviks from his own unwanted compatriots, the French socialists. In 1936 the socialist premier Léon Blum proclaimed "le self-government"—thus borrowing the English expression for something that the French language could not accommodate, an early example of *franglais*—as the goal of French colonial policy. But it was an ultimate goal, a long way distant. His minister of colonies, Marius Moutet, the first socialist to hold the post, uttered further reassurance on this point. Some thought, he said, that the Left was anti-colonial: well,

maybe some of its members, as a result of misdirected idealism, have seen colonial expansion as being nothing but brutality, violence, and rape. But the greatest number have well understood the immense tasks to be accomplished in taking seriously the civilizing mission which a nation can pursue without forgetting either its traditions or its principles.[99]

These were sentiments with which Jules Ferry in the 1880s, the first promoter of the cause of French capital and enterprise anywhere in the world they could profitably go, would have agreed. Indeed, French socialist views of colonies had always been more French than socialist—if only because an invariable French opinion was that French socialism, like all other things French, was better, more civilized, and more intelligent than anyone else's brand of it, certainly better than whatever might emerge from a colony which was by definition still in a state of tutelage in the arts and crafts of civilization. Moutet was only rephrasing for an Algerian context some thoughts on Indochina that he had declared nine years previously. He had then urged that the French should certainly behave better than they did, noting it was notorious that soldiers of the Foreign Legion, let loose in Annamese villages, paid no attention to doctrines of the rights of man. However, if the Annamese were more equitably and humanely treated, this would be the best insurance for the future: "the natives would have their hearts and their minds turned towards us rather than towards a native nationalism, doubly dangerous both for us and for them."[100] He did not take into account one upshot of this more amiable policy which was later noted by a foreign observer, Virginia Thompson:

When the European treats the Annamite as an equal the latter responds by treating the European as an inferior. Under these circumstances the champion of egalitarian principles feels his ardour dampened.[101]

Blum's Popular Front government proceeded to replace eighteen of thirty colonial governors, and at this the nationalist leader Ferhat Abbas in Algeria expressed his "great joy." But since Algeria remained in the official mind a part of metropolitan France and therefore within the province of the Ministry of the Interior—whereas Morocco, Tunisia, Syria, and Lebanon had at least a shelter within the Ministry of Foreign Affairs, leaving only French Africa, Madagascar, and Indochina to the Ministry of Colonies—nothing much happened that maintained this joy. The Blum-Violette bill, which proposed to make citizens of between 20,000 and 25,000 Algerians who could show evidence of French culture or of service to France, aroused massive opposition. In Algeria three hundred French mayors declared against it. In Paris *Le Temps* on December 21, 1936, exclaimed that the bill would deprive "the masses of Arabs who are sheep"[102] of the French tutelage they would always need, thus once again underlining the truth of H. G. Wells's aphorism that so long as you suffer any man to call himself your shepherd, sooner or later you will find a crook round your ankle.[103] Blum was not prepared to risk his government on the bill, and it dropped. Moutet assured everyone that he was not going to be the gravedigger for French colonies, and even Maurice Thorez from the Communist benches rang the same bell of French unity. As Abbas told Sarraut, "the process of creating hope without satisfying it, promising and then giving nothing, leads to divorce."[104]

Yet there were other imperial areas wherein "divorce" was still unthinkable—using the term this time in the sense that the thought had not been formulated even in the subconscious. "Decolonization" had not been heard of, but in the white dominions within the British Empire a process was forming to which this name might have been applied. The dominion governments called it the assertion of status, and the status they wanted was one of juridical autonomy, a recognition that their independent action was not bound to any system or structure of imperial grace and favor. They wanted the statutory right to it. This was something that no one in Whitehall, still grateful for the combined and courageous war effort of the dominions, wanted to deny them. There was no good reason why a devolution of this kind should not be made to kin who had proved so trustworthy—or even to their white companions the Afrikaners, who were not trustworthy at all but who were at least no threat to anyone's security. In fact nothing much beyond a psychological bonus was granted by the passage of the Statute of Westminster in 1931. The dominions in that year remained what they had been in 1914, small Powers. Status might be accorded to them, but not stature. Their parliaments could be made free to make decisions on foreign policy, but they were not free to choose what the nature of that policy might be, since the decision on this point belonged where it had always belonged, in Great Britain, which controlled the strategy of the empire as a whole and which was the sole Great Power in the system. These things were not affected by calling the locally self-governing areas of the empire a commonwealth. The dominions therefore stayed in their accustomed place, freely associated and equal in status but still as much as ever needing protection in any day of danger. They were right to think that such protection would be automatically afforded them.

London expended no such grace, trust, or affection on the Irish and Hindus. Yet expediency demanded that the same settlement of "dominion status," however mysterious it seemed to Irish republicans, should also be given to the entity that began life as the Irish Free State in 1922. For the Irish, unlike the Afrikaners, were a very serious security risk. Trouble in Ireland had traditionally caused trouble for England. Ireland was too close to home to be treated as a recalcitrant colony full of disloyal subversives, suitable recipients for policies of pacification, systematic action, and the dispatch of punitive expeditions. For three years indeed (1919-21) the English tried to apply precisely these policies: but they did so halfheartedly, because most of their own people, kept regularly informed by the press of atrocities from the other island, would not stomach knowing the kind of thing that, when it went on farther off, they had never bothered either to discover or to question.

Indian "unrest" was not even granted this degree of grudging respect by officialdom, since the physical security of the subcontinent never became an issue. India stayed a British domestic problem. In 1916 one high official of the Indian Civil Service had rightly gauged the future of difficulty when peace broke out. The English would still have to govern India and try to convince the people that a handful of white men could continue to control them. This would be "a task that will not have been rendered easier by indiscriminate eulogy of the exploits of the Indian troops in France."[105] In public a more generous attitude was expressed. The Montagu-Chelmsford Report of 1917 enthusiastically set down as an aim that there should be a progressive realization of responsible government in India as an integral part of the British Empire. An Act of 1919 allowed for the construction of this responsible government in the provinces, although not in the chambers of the central government. But since then the activities of Gandhi, the boycott of the provincial elections by the Congress party, and the rioting and strikes promoted by a host of the as yet unidentifiable followers of both made it plain that the granting of responsible government depended upon the quiet and agreeable cooperation of a sufficient number of responsible persons. This number, it seemed, could not easily be found. There was thus no assurance at all that India under its own rule would remain an integral part of the British Empire; accordingly, nobody wanted to gamble on the matter. Indian leaders seemed as set as ever on taking a leaf from the book of the Irish and on copying their maxims: Tagore resigned from the order of the Knight's Cross of the Indian Empire on May 29, 1919, "an unheard-of impertinence."[106] To the English eye there was no security, principle, or common sense in conduct like this. A massacre in the Jallianwala Bagh at Amritsar on April 13, 1919, set the tone for the next two decades in Anglo-Indian relations: a tone of mutual bitterness and suspicion.

Yet Ho Chi Minh, watching all this from beyond, drew a distinction between habits in imperial behavior. The Gandhis and the de Valeras "would long since have entered heaven had they been born in one of the French colonies."[107]

But the two western Powers agreed that agitation was produced by agitators, not agitators by agitation. They admitted there was trouble brewing; but there was no yeast to it, it would all boil away. The continent of Africa in particular was still virgin ground for experiment. There was still "a tranquil assumption of the long-term character of colonial rule."[108] It might be true for sophisticated European observers that the idea of mandates had raised the whole question of the European presence in Africa and had presented a writ of *quo warranto* to all the European nations that held property there, but the vast majority of Africans had not heard this question and would not have known what to do about it if they had done so. European activists saw their options to be still open. Africa was the place where policy could go to work at will. An English radical, complaining about the feebleness of British policy in Palestine, gave a backhanded recognition to this fact when he asked indignantly, "Suppose Palestine were Kenya, can we conceive the Government calling a conference of insurgent Kikuyu or Masai to sit round a table and discuss terms of settlement?"[109] One day such a thing indeed was to happen, but this day was far over the horizon of the 1920s. Kikuyu and Masai and everybody else were still doing what they were told, as Milner indicated when on July 14, 1920 he noted that the difficulty in the whole question of native labor in East Africa was to steer a middle course between allowing the natives to live in idleness and vice, and using improper means to get them to work. His point was taken up in an official white paper issued in 1925, which repeated these conclusions from Lord Lugard's influential book, *The Dual Mandate in British Tropical Africa* (1923): "We have a duty to humanity to develop the vast economic resources of a great continent." To this end it would be inconsistent with the economic progress of the whole country, and with the advance in civilization of the natives of Africa, to allow them to stagnate in a native reserve, "leaving all the work to the women, the men doing nothing."[110]

In contrast, Egypt, although situated in Africa, was far from being virgin ground; and Milner showed no such confidence about Egypt's future as he did about sub-Saharan situations of which he knew nothing. Sent to inspect and report on Egypt in 1921, he presented findings in which his common sense struggled in alternating paragraphs with his long-held imperialist philosophy. In Egypt, he said, in the face of so solid a phalanx of opposition it might seem at first sight that the English had only two alternatives: either to abandon their position there altogether or to maintain it by sheer force, in the teeth of general and ever-increasing hostility from the Egyptian people. But having encapsulated the situation with such accuracy, he sheered away from its implications. It would be, he urged himself and his readers, "a profound mistake" if such a view was taken.[111] Thinking along these lines would demolish British predominance in places other than Egypt. Accordingly, the thought remained submerged. But Winston Churchill, who followed Milner as colonial secretary, was also in a philosophical frame of mind when he returned from a conference at Cairo in March 1921, at which a great number of frontiers had been drawn in straight lines across the map of the Middle East. Reporting to the House of Commons, he recalled a phrase of Lord Salisbury's. The task of England was to persuade one side to concede and the other to forbear, "but keeping a reasonable margin of force available in order to ensure the acceptance of the position of both parties." Churchill was referring to the situation in Palestine, but his words covered other imperial situations. Like Milner, he knew that an appeal to the older imperial ideas would not rouse enthusiasm. Although he referred to Egypt in the long-accepted style—"this great and splendid monument of British administration, skill, and energy"—he reminded his audience that they were almost completely ignorant of the whole Middle East story and twitted them that the only interest they took in it was to complain about the amount of money that would be taken out of their pockets to finance imperial administration in the area.[112]

But although such committed imperialists as Milner and Churchill knew that power could no longer call up any spiritual support, they were as devoted to imperial efficiency as ever. Churchill's reference to a reasonable margin of force naturally assumed that the judges of what was reasonable would always be found in the same camp as those who had the means of marshaling the force and calculating the margin in which it was to go to work. "Firm government" was still the nostrum of the controllers, still "the idol of the club smoking-room,"[113] a place which was still one of the informal headquarters of formal imperialism. On more occasions than ever before "disturbances" graduated to what were called "outrages." After the British commander in chief and governor of the Sudan was assassinated in Cairo in 1924, Allenby in full field-marshal's regalia led a regiment of cavalry to Parliament House—thus setting the precedent for Sir Miles Lampson's investment of the Abdin Palace eighteen years later. There Allenby delivered a measured tirade to Zaghlul Pasha which spoke of Egypt's heedless ingratitude, invoked the contempt of all civilized peoples, and levied a fine of half a million pounds. Yet this was not thought, except by the Egyptians, to be anything remarkably out of the way. It was only one more example of imperialism losing its temper. The normal tone was more sorrowful than angry. In England the Labour party was in office, and Ramsay MacDonald, as its leader, talked of the affair in terms that would not have been unacceptable to Joseph Chamberlain thirty years earlier. MacDonald declared that England had a duty to preserve order in the Sudan. Since going there, British governments had contracted heavy moral obligations by creating a good administrative system, which they could not allow to be destroyed. They looked on their responsibilities as a trust for the people of the Sudan. There could be no question of abandoning the Sudan until this work was done. No date, of course, was set for this, and the Labour government fell shortly after MacDonald had issued his exhortation. Three months later Joseph Chamberlain's son Austen, as foreign secretary, was uttering exactly the same sentiments (which may indeed have been written for him by exactly the same band of higher civil servants).[114] Imperialism in England, as Nehru and others had divined, was not a party matter: it was still the framework within which all English foreign policy had to fit.

In these interwar years, colonies had attained more of a public face than they had shown before. Their politics of complaint had full publicity. It was recognized that overseas territories presented problems that challenged the domestic political philosophies of the day. But they were still seen as they had always been seen, as satellite areas whose pretensions could not be allowed to reach too high a pitch. Joseph Chamberlain's remark that rights and wishes were not the same thing was still thoroughly believed in by his successors. No case had been made for altering this assessment, for no new evidence had been presented. Colonies were now what they had always been: they had been developed to produce raw materials for a metropolis while importing manufactures and capital from this metropolis. They were complementary parts of a single, metrocentric economy, in much the same category as tariffs, administrative regulations, and currency controls. This was the reality that accounted for the harmony, thought odd only by doctrinaires who never studied hard facts, between the Left and the Right. Neither was prepared to tamper with a structure that was so plainly beneficial to all classes in the metropolis. That the Left was embarrassed by this reality while the Right took it for granted did not alter anything important. The radical George Orwell—in the camp of the Left but never commissioned by its leaders, and often behaving like an "Indian scout" patronizing the greenness of the army on some wilderness frontier —constantly irritated the professional anti-imperialists by pointing out how much they owed to the fact of empire. Who defended their right to be radical? Who but the organisms they so despised. Their collective bible, the Left Book Club, was only a product of Scotland Yard. The Peace Pledge Union was a product of the Royal Navy. The working classes, though ready enough to bawl anticapitalist slogans on stated occasions, still wanted to live in that happy state wherein Friedrich Engels had eighty years ago perceived them to dwell—"merrily sharing the feast of England's monopoly of the world market and its colonies."[115]

Orwell's strictures on English socialism, like those of the Indian Marxist M. N. Roy on Indian nationalism, hit hard because he knew exactly where to aim. Roy could easily have borrowed and applied Orwell's argument to his own compatriots. The English intellectual, Orwell accused, would forever go tilting lances at the wrong windmills, with lances that would forever be made of wood. He was in the position of a young man living on an allowance from a father whom he hated. He had a deep feeling of guilt and resentment, but it was not combined with any genuine desire to escape.[116] Socialists around him naturally did not want to think about this diagnosis or about Orwell either and left it to the pillar of trade unionism in their party, Ernest Bevin, to agree with Orwell's fundamental point that empire involved them all, whatever their views on imperialism. As foreign secretary in 1946, Bevin maintained that if the British Empire fell, "the standard of life of our constituents would fall considerably." And gradually others came to believe that a conviction might have to change in the face of facts. Orwell's gibe that everyone lived by robbing Asiatic coolies remained of course one of his deplorable exaggerations; but John Strachey, a left-wing luminary who had become a respected member of the Labour establishment, underlined the point when, on moving the Overseas Resources Development Bill on January 20, 1948, he remarked that "our national position is really too grave to warrant any indulgence in our particular opinion on the methods of overseas development." Two years later the position was as grave as ever: Lord Trefgarne, chairman of the Commonwealth Development Corporation told a Liverpool audience that what really mattered then was that the United Kingdom had an annual dollar deficit of $500 million. Against this background the productivity of colonial territories had to be viewed, for the simple reason that their products, whether food or raw materials, "were more acceptable to the United States than manufactured goods."[117]

Thus the imperial controllers, whatever their domestic philosophies, always turned in time of emergency —hot war, cold war, debt, and slump —to their durable truths. These truths were not necessarily as principled as those professionally devoted to principle in politics would have liked: Lampson whirling up to the Egyptian palace in a cloud of armored cars in wartime had its parallels in peacetime. There were times so challenging that certain things had to be done, however shocking, and however contradictory of the thousands of placatory words issued in the peaceful past. Emergency made imperialism refer back to the values it truly lived by, and these turned out to relate to what they had always related: to the security, strategic and commercial, of the imperialists.

The controlled had always known these things. Their leaders, who saw life as one extended emergency, had long tried to make political capital out of the knowledge. They had long insisted that imperialists went about in disguise, hiding even from themselves exactly why they had established and still maintained the imperial framework and within it 84 percent of the world's surface (by 1914). To keep control of this surface they would always use what power they had, as ruthlessly as they had to.

How these colonial leaders publicized this knowledge, how they formed their political capital, how they invested it, and what returns it brought in can now be examined.

COLONIAL ASSERTION

Nationalism and the necessary sense of community. The view of imperialism from below: the colonialist experience. How the new assertions made headway. The quest for dignity in the straitjacket of the status quo. Difficulties facing the colonial elites between the two world wars. How they tried to implant and cultivate nationalism at the grass roots. How they succeeded in gaining the moral initiative.

4

COLONIAL ASSERTION

ationalism asserts itself when a community has become aware of itself, has reached a particular state of mind. People who think they belong to a nation, who think they constitute a nation, indeed do so and behave as such. Their problem is less to convince themselves than to impress their conviction on others. The record of many peoples tells that, when their conviction is strong enough, they can accomplish this. Nationalism as a word, a theme, and a cause illuminates every nation's history. To take a single case: historians of modern Italy rightly see nationalism as their focal point, but sociologists at large in present-day Italy accept it as a context and need not pursue it as a theme. Modern Italians have come to take their Italian "state of mind," as well as the state of Italy, for granted, whatever the latter's social and political problems may be.

How to induce this kind of confidence in their followers—or, more accurately, among peoples who had been corralled (as in East Africa, Malaysia, and the Middle East) within boundaries drawn by an Imperial Power to suit not ethnic facts but its strategic, economic, and diplomatic purposes—was the aim of the colonial elites during the colonial period and remains in many cases the aim of the national elites now. The people could not develop a national patriotism or even a sense of community until those who had appointed themselves their

spokesmen found a way to impress upon them that they had to combine and cohere if ever they were to be anything other than the
agents of alien enterprise, if ever they were to make their mark in
the world at all. How, if there was no social awareness, could an
idea of "interest," national or other, be implanted? To infuse purpose into people who lacked identity was a task to tax the ablest.

The members of these elites either had been politically awakened
outside the colony or had been westernized by the alien system of
education within. That they worked in an imperial context impacted
on both the way they saw their problem and the way they handled
it. They shared at least one experience. They all lived beside and
below an apparatus of governance that had been imported by an
alien Power. They all knew how great was the range of authority of
this apparatus: "the administration." So they rightly decided that
if they infiltrated the administration, grasped the levers of the apparatus, and finally seized the powerhouse itself, they could make
their people transfer the acceptance hitherto accorded to the aliens,
to themselves and to their newly proven powers of leadership. The
task was simple enough to state but formidably difficult to carry
out. It was, literally, to change people's minds.

The colonial elites that took European history for their example
knew that all the Great Powers had graduated from the school of
nationalism: imperialism was only one of its diplomas attesting to
success. They therefore had to translate this concept of nationalism
into terms that could be understood by people whose only knowledge of Europe was derived from the presence of its expatriates,
whom they constantly met but seldom understood.

Some found it easier to make the attempt than others. Charismatic
leaders like Egypt's Nasser, Cuba's Castro, and Indonesia's Sukarno
had the gift of communicating at least some of their high visions
of independence to their peoples. Other kinds of spokesmen were
able to reflect only the general discontent: but this, too, had value.
The political and social misfit was definitively explained by A. W.
Singham in his *The Hero and the Crowd in a Colonial Polity* (1969).
Such a one does not pass into history with the great, but he may
provide a more accurate barometer to the colonial weather than
does the man of destiny, groomed for the role of founding father.
For in the colonial situation it was easy to respond to an eccentric

who would not conform to the powers that were, to someone who by the very impudence of defiance indicated that there was, somewhere, another style and dimension of life.

For the peoples, like their elites, also had an experience in common. This was the colonial situation itself: much of a piece all over the world, of many forms but of the same essence. Such a situation bred irresponsibility and lack of self-confidence, since everything important was always controlled by unknown men who did what was not understood for reasons that were not stated. It accounted for a type of behavior that imperialists attributed to a "lack of character": the British in India, particularly, were constantly complaining of this in their subjects. Dr. Singham, having examined such behavior, declares that "one of the greatest myths perpetrated in recent times is that a people can be prepared for responsibility under colonialism": for colonialism most commonly produced not an eager pupil of superior wisdom but a personality type "characterized by *anomie*, rage, compulsion, and withdrawal."[1] It encouraged a state of mind that rejected everything and aspired to nothing, a state of mind basically pathological. The unpleasantness this caused was heightened and compounded when it was incubated within and then released into a "small-island" situation—Dr. Singham deals with one such case, the career of "Uncle" Eric Gairy in Grenada, the British West Indies, but all colonies can, in this sense, be likened to small islands[2]—which served further to turn inward an already withdrawn personality. To be a colonial was to be a prisoner. One's warders, and thus one's enemies, were a collective called "Them": the managers and timekeepers at their desks, the men who drove cars, the men who caught planes, the men who kept big houses and idle women. And it was beside the point what color they were.

So anyone who was able to release a people from this bondage of the spirit, who could ease their burden by openly battling authority —sometimes in doing so exposing sources of it that had till then remained hidden—became a hero. In "standing up for himself" he stood up for all the others who did not, even though he could not politicize and mobilize them, since he lacked an ideology, a banner, and a cause. He might, at best, be a demagogue, a role as much the creature of the colonial situation as the habit of acceptance itself. The process of decolonization, seen from this angle, involves more than getting rid of an imperial governance, more than running up one's own flag in place of someone else's. It includes destroying the psychological bonds set upon a society by colonialism.

Hence the appeal of nationalism depended on the amount of self-knowledge at any given time. Consequently, it became a term as emotional and subjective as "imperialism." Rhetoric like Sukarno's

This I know: we of Indonesia and the citizens of many countries of Asia and Africa have seen our dearest and best suffer and die, struggle and fail, and rise to struggle and fail again—and again be resurrected from the very earth, and finally achieve their goal. Something burned in them: something inspired them. They called it nationalism. We who have followed and have seen what they built . . . we, too, call their inspiration and our inspiration, nationalism. For us there is nothing ignoble in that word. On the contrary, it contains for us all that is best in mankind and all that is noblest.[3]

tells more about the depth of his heartfelt determination to communicate his personal vision than it does about the political realities in the Dutch East Indies at the time. Not enough of those who saw him as a hero were either ready or able to follow him as a leader.

Still to begin was everything. The first exciting step made other steps possible, for it conjured up the image of a journey, of a movement, of *something*—anything—beyond the immediate and the known, where all was subordinate and confined. Assertion illustrated a mental state of independence. A political state of independence was its natural companion, if only people could be made to see this. To reach and capture an audience was the immediate task: and thereafter free minds would begin to envisage the building of a free society, one in charge of its own fate.

But this was strong stuff, too strong for some. Sukarno was not the only national leader to discover that others besides the alien controller distrusted the outcome of such exhortations. The continuing quarrel between traditionalism and modernism in Islam illustrates this. The orthodox fundamentalist Abu'l A'la Mawdudi, for example, did not believe that wisdom would be found anywhere along a western road, or from drinking at a poisoned well placed there originally by infidels. "Muslim nationalism," said he, "is as contradictory a term as chaste prostitute." But Mohammad Ali Jinnah, when in the 1940s his own road toward Pakistan had become clear, would see no such contradiction. To him, Muslims were "a nation according to any definition of a nation, and they must have their homelands, their territory, and their state."[4]

The average alien controller was surprised to learn that a sense of adventure and a will to innovate were stirring among peoples whom he had long since dismissed as incapable of both. Naturally, he did not want to believe that they would ever manage to bring these desires to any effective political point. Since he gave the dissidents no credence, he gave their dissidence even less. When he heard the claim to nationalism being put forward, it was not its substance but the claim itself that kept his attention, for he could perceive it only as a claim to equality with himself—and this was not an idea he could entertain and remain an imperialist. Common sense told him that the danger to his position was not only physical, which he was sure he could cope with, but also moral. Men like Jinnah and Sukarno were obviously convinced they had the right as well as the duty to undermine the very assumptions of acceptance on which the success of imperialism had for so long been based. Although these men had not yet found a master strategy, their tactics were sound enough. They were preaching a gospel and spreading a word. Once this word had been broadcast at large, all assurance in imperial government would come to a halt—and assurance was its essential component, the one thing that, when lost, could not be found again. Gandhi, returning to India in January 1916 after a twenty-two-year exile in South Africa, saw this point at once. Indians must only learn to say no.

Imperial officials were not paid to teach people to say no. Most of them did not even want to examine the philosophical basis of the many colonial assertions voiced by men who, having been educated in western philosophical concepts, made the natural mistake of supposing that western men were guided by these in their everyday conduct. Officialdom was unprepared to relate its ideas on nationalism or social justice or on anything else to what it heard coming from below. It would not dismantle its assumptions amid all this noise.

With the passage of time, it would not be any readier to do so. David Murison had this durable habit in mind when, as late as 1969, he assessed the national status of Scotland—a Scotland not colonized indeed but long saddled with the role of satellite to England. As a lexicographer, he defined nationalism to an academic Edinburgh audience as

the common consciousness of a group of people who have shared political experiences over a long period, have suffered common dangers and successes, have
evolved a common way of life which they feel to be distinct from others, created
common traditions, devised institutions and a system of law and government
to safeguard them, and who will rally against anything which seems to threaten
or to alter them in a manner not in accordance with the community's will.[5]

This was a diagnosis natural in and serviceable to a country whose
nationals were among the most easily identifiable peoples on earth.
But these were not the characteristics, and that was not the behavior,
that the controllers of empire in its heyday were ready to find in
those who protested their control.

According to Edmund Burke, the state is the nation in its collective or corporate character. Wherever they went, the Imperial Powers
brought with them replicas of state machinery they had found useful and gainful at home. A colony was an extension of the parent-
state: and, since its prime purpose was to complement the economy
of the metropolis, its affairs had to be ordered in accordance with
the principles that governed the metropolis itself. These principles
were adaptable, because local conditions had to be allowed for; but,
while allowing for them, the Europeans did not suppose that the
peoples who were a feature of these local conditions had any collective or corporate character. They saw no reason to think otherwise,
since nobody had compelled them to do so—for, if such a collective or corporate character indeed existed, why had it not made
itself manifest in action? Why had it not prevented both the making
and the maintaining of the alien machinery?

Moreover, since the nation-state was the base from which all the
European imperialists had set out, they never thought of it as a concept to be exported or transplanted. As in any classroom, however
idealistic the subject taught, there was a place where the pupils were
expected to sit and a rostrum from which the teacher expected to
speak. Colonies were the property of the colonizers: and it followed
that nobody else had a right to claim them in the name of nationalism or in the name of anything at all. The colonizers did not hesi-
tate to say so: one of the most disliked habits of imperialism was
speaking its mind. In prefacing *Indian Unrest* (1910), a collection
of reports on India written by Valentine Chirol originally for the
London *Times*, Sir Alfred Lyall, ex-Indian civil servant and imperial

poet, announced that "education acts upon the frame of an antique society as a powerful dissolvent, heating weak brains, stimulating rash ambitions, and raising inordinate expectations of which the disappointment is bitterly resented."[6] What Lyall would have been willing to recognize as an ordinate expectation he did not say, but those in India who were then promoting the unrest Chirol recorded could not have said it either.

In November 1898 the United States's envoy at Peking had written that if real progress was to be made in the new century, "Orientalism must give way to Occidentalism."[7] The century then came in, as if on cue, with a strong Chinese statement that rebutted this opinion, taking the form of a rebellion against the ubiquitous presence of the Big Hairy Ones. It was answered in turn by another rebuttal, the dispatch of an international brigade to Peking, to strike the statement from the record.

At the same time the Filipinos were registering objections to their enforced transfer from the old Spanish Empire to the new American one. They ignored a declared American intention to establish good government in the Philippine Islands "not for our satisfaction or for the expression of our theoretical views, but for the happiness, peace, and prosperity of the people"[8] there. The Philippines had a National Assembly by 1907, a 50 percent literacy rate by 1935, and a "closed door" commercial policy throughout. The leader of those who early but vainly opposed the practical application of these theoretical views, Emilio Aguinaldo, did not stay to watch them at work: he quit Luzon in 1902 to make his home in Japan. There until he died in 1943 he told anyone who asked him that the only way to confront the whites, the only way to defeat them and gain freedom and independence, was for all the colonial races to make a combined effort for the common purpose. It was advice more easily given than taken. Manuel Quezon might declaim in 1926 that he preferred a government run like hell by Filipinos to one run like heaven by Americans, but by then this kind of language had become a flourish of a recognizable type, the sort of thing a nationalist leader was expected to say.[9] But the Americans, convinced they were not running an empire at all, could see no point to such an assertion. When they looked at other empires, it was only to intensify their sense of distinctiveness. American taxpayers bore the cost of military expenses in the Philippine Islands, but Indian peasants were paying for these in India; Americans did not encourage the formation of large landed estates, as the French did in Indochina; they did not promote Muslim separatism, as the British did in India; they did not import coolie labor, as the British did in Burma and Malaya; and they gave no official support to opium concessions, the "symptom of social decadence and symbol of imperial hypocrisy in Indonesia, Indo-China, and the Malay States." A Filipino reporter in 1941 traveled throughout East and Southeast Asia "in search of the golden egg, only to find it in his garden." But not everything there was so lovely. The members of the Polo Club and of the Army and Navy Club in Manila behaved like all other white clubmen in the East. "Who knows," wondered one Filipino in 1957, "how much longer we would have remained unaroused if the white man had understood that Asians hold personal dignity above economic or political development?"[10]

Aguinaldo had been aroused about this from the outset, before any such development had been launched. Although few took up his program of outright militance, either in the Philippines or elsewhere, his idea of a combination for whatever other purpose—if only to draw up an agenda for establishing articles of agreement about some purpose—was so clearly useful that it could not be allowed to die.

It was not only useful. It was exciting. The very idea that there could and should be such a thing as a public purpose was one of the most intoxicating in the imperialist distillery. It gave life an aim. It made people, once drawn to this aim, consider the quality of life they were leading and look more closely at the circumstances they found themselves in. They set about taking an inventory of these. The first need was to find themselves a place of assembly, for once they had this, combination for a purpose would surely follow. Assertion fastened itself initially upon small, known things. In March 1900 the Creoles of French Guiana successfully opposed a local measure that would have transformed Cayenne's single secondary school into a vocational institute whose graduates, working as carpenters, would supposedly better "meet the needs of the colony" than the other graduates who had followed the classical metropolitan curriculum.[11] In April Jamaica's capital of Kingston elected its first black mayor.

In July the first pan-African conference met in London, where argument about the style of British imperialism, then in action against another European race, the Boers in South Africa, was running high. This conference was organized by a lawyer from Trinidad, Henry Sylvester-Williams. West Africa's Edward Blyden did not attend it, because he was always suspicious (like Marcus Garvey after him) of mulatto enterprise: mulattoes were by definition "joiners"—collaborators by necessity, since contaminated by the dominant race. But the date is still remarkable. It was only a dozen years after African slavery had ended in Brazil, only fourteen years, in Cuba. Here, certainly, was progress: and liberal opinion everywhere roused itself to combat anything that threatened to get in its way. "We have placed the laboring population where it is," said a British official report in 1897 on the West Indian sugar industry, "and created for it the conditions, moral and material, under which it exists; we cannot divest ourselves of responsibility for its future."[12] But the years immediately following told a story of obstruction. The slow-spreading stain of the tale of how rubber was brought to harvest in King Leopold's Congo (whose revenue from this source in 1908 was 60 million francs); how prisoners were treated in French Guiana and in the New Hebrides, places which, barbarous themselves, barbarized the warders; what happened at Denshawai, Egypt, in 1907 when some English subalterns went out for a little rough shooting among the peasantry—evidence of this sort from lands where the work of civilization was supposed to be under way generated in a concerned and influential minority a sense less of scandal than of sadness.

Such things had happened before. No empire had ever excepted brutality from its practices. But this was *now*, the twentieth century, a time inherited by conscientious and moral people whose duty was to improve on it. Such actions were perceived as too harsh, belonging to a past that should have died, one which liberal idealists thought in fact had died. But as the new century began, complicated by the abrasive and confusing Anglo-Boer war wherein nobody was clearly in the right, who could be sure what would come of the processes that had for so long proclaimed the virtues of western civilization and had supported the actions of the just?

What imperialism did had always been public property, but as its own property expanded, the public had grown larger and more criti-

cal. Imperialism dealt with the world as it was, which was the world
it had made. Liberalism dealt only tangentially with the world as it
was, concentrating its attention on the world it would bring into
being. Not surprisingly, the two were enemies. France's Robert Delavignette was to sigh in 1950, at the close of a long colonial career,
that it was not the lion prowling round the camp that beleagured
all colonies and their administration; it was the "primitive ignorance
of Europe."[13] On their side liberals hailed any news inculpating the
habits of imperialism as evidence that a structure, ill-founded to
begin with, was at last showing signs of decline if not of fall. They
agreed with Tolstoy, who had labeled as erroneous the opinion that
the existing order was unchangeable and must be upheld, "while in
reality it is unchangeable only by being upheld."[14] In truth liberalism
was not so opposed to imperialism as its devotees jointly supposed;
for both parties reckoned they had a natural right to decide the shape
of things to come. Some imperialists accepted this comparison as
valid and were not embarrassed by it. Indeed, in England at the turn
of the century a group of men prominent in the official Liberal
party called themselves Liberal Imperialists, with capital letters.
They saw the proper guidance of empire, the control of its behavior,
as one more item in a list of the great tasks that would confront
every subsequent British government, tasks that must effectively
be squared to if the country was to keep both its position in the
world and its prosperity at home. They did not suppose that this
work would ever be tackled, or even be recognized as existing, by
the kind of conservatism that was content to preside over a domestic status quo and stagnancy in the properties overseas. Imperialists
who used this argument were prepared to agree even with Fabian
socialists who spent much of their time calling down anathema on
empire and all its works. For the latter at least also had a program
and were planning for the future. This future would escape control
altogether if people of common sense and goodwill did not combine
in the present to get rid of poverty and ignorance wherever they
met these, whether in Lancashire slum or pest-ridden village in the
bush.

In France much the same choices confronted much the same type
of man. Many found the contemporary politics of the Third Republic, which appeared to totter out of one scandal only to stagger into

another, unappetizing to a degree. *Outre-mer* life would be found cleaner, by men who kept themselves clean, which meant keeping out of the political arena. This, or course, was not easily done by ranking officers and civilians who followed the well-marked imperial routes to prominence and sometimes fame, and who were compelled to traffic in promotions and lobbying along the way. Yet France in the next forty years was often able to produce, amid general indifference, in harsh climates and on difficult terrain, a band of *dévots* who not only invoked the codes of a chivalric *champ d'honneur* but did their best to live according to them. "The cloudy symbols of a high romance,"once celebrated by England's John Keats, did indeed lead such men forward. If this literate and literary view of empire had ever expressed a reality, if empire had ever been truly capable of becoming what these austere romantics thought it already was — a place of example and of peace, a monastic enclave set down near the market and the camp, in which philosophers were the rightful kings—the history of the twentieth century would be a pastoral tale indeed.

The common kind of liberalism as expressed by people of an easygoing good nature hoped, however, for more concrete returns from its virtues than these. They, with those to their Left who took public matters more acutely to heart, were resolved to rule the century's intellectual empire. Once they had established its bounds, they would continue to propagate within them the views they had long sponsored. They looked forward to a time when the subject races who had adopted these views would apply them against the imperialists and win the day because their cause was just. Liberals did not suppose it was possible that their own views might be adapted as well as adopted and turned to their own disadvantage, since their egotism, as powerful as that of any imperialist, would not allow them to consider the thought that when white men have truly come to believe they are no better than, say, green men, the green men who are sure they are no worse will certainly triumph. Imperialists, being closer to local assertiveness and its habits, were not so ready to take its liberal pretensions on trust. They suspected that a genuine devotion to liberal principles among an ambitious elite that confused social progress with its own advancement might always be hard to find: as Harcourt Butler (the *raj*'s foreign secretary) remarked in

1909, the indigenous system of government in India was a loose, despotic affair tempered by corruption; it did not press too hard on the daily lives of the people.[15] But as long as liberals were dealing in words and the imperialists in actions, the liberals had the better of the argument, since it was always and only the active who were required to account for what they did. The audience, in the meantime, could watch the spotlight swing from one far place to another, everywhere showing the seamier side of public purposes. Every inquiry made, into anything at all, will usually reveal something embarrassing to somebody. Empire, it appeared, passed its time in a welter of such embarrassment.

In 1902 an official commission of inquiry into the habits of the police in India reported that the subordinate ranks of this service, Indian to a man, were universally thought of by their compatriots as corrupt and oppressive. The report was disliked by officialdom and as late as 1971 was still not acceptable to Sir Percival Griffiths, the historian (*To Guard My People*) of this force.[16] Reform of abuse must be put in hand, certainly, if it was necessary; but the judgment of the degree of necessity, and the timing of the reform, could not be allowed to pass within the area of anyone else's decision. Ammunition in the form of facts, figures, and inference must not be issued to those who would assuredly use them for their own very different purposes. Sharpshooters were already sited in the distance; there was no need to bring them closer. In 1908 Mohandas K. Gandhi, resident in South Africa, was there experiencing the effects of a much stronger distillation of European attitudes toward his race than was contemporaneously dispensed in India itself. The experience caused him to assume a stance he never quit. His pamphlet *Hind Swaraj* (Home Rule for India) listed all the complaints that were later to become the working capital of nationalist politics, both in India and elsewhere. Gandhi declared, as he was to do throughout his career in India, that anarchy under home rule would be preferable to order under foreign rule. Few English were ever able to cope with so unthinkable a thought. Foreigners were, arguably, fair game for attack: but order, never. Gandhi always pressed hard on this area of sensitivity, to increase the depth of shock. The English, in love with order, naturally had no idea how to get in touch with anything else. If they did, they would set about replacing their "useless" schools and law courts. They would learn Hindi as a language, a means of communication—not simply as a vocabulary of so many words of command. They would stop importing English textiles into a country capable of producing its own. They would stop spending the peasants' money on railways, police, and barracks. "Of course, it is likely you will laugh at all this in the intoxication of your power,"[17] but such intoxication was suicidal, and the laugh was proof of aberration in intellect.

Even in 1908 this rhetoric was overdone. Laughter was the last thing likely. Few officials supposed that power could afford to become intoxicated or do anything other than walk with circumspection. Everywhere was movement. Editorials converted this to ferment, but the point was there was something to convert. The Indian extremist B. G. Tilak had been one of the first to congratulate the Japanese on their defeat of the Russians in 1905, and when on trial for sedition on June 24, 1908, he made the point again during a speech lasting twenty-one hours. Sun Yat-sen, before starting his Chinese revolution in 1911, saw the Russian defeat of 1905 (or so he was to say in 1924) as the defeat of the West by the East. He believed that socialism could be achieved in China on the basis of radical agrarian reforms, without going through a capitalist phase. Lenin naturally thought this was the worst kind of petty-bourgeois reactionary rubbish, but at the sixth conference of the Bolshevik party, held at Prague in January 1912, he went out of his way to praise Sun for bringing liberalism to Asia and for undermining the domination of the European bourgeoisie. And although Sun's ideological status would continue to defy definition, this did not cause him to lose any face: Mao Tse-tung was to repeat Lenin's praise of the one who began the "anti-imperialist, antifeudal, bourgeois democratic revolution" in China.[18]

The point of all this rhetoric, to those who studied it, was not what it said but that it was being said so universally, by so many disparate types of people. Europeans did not have to look very far into their past to assess the amount of upheaval that intellectual concepts bred in Europe were capable of producing. The European Right had by the 1890s perfected its militarism and with its help was facing the future with far more confidence than it had done in the 1840s: but it was still vigilant over egalitarian ideas, and the thought that these were spreading could not be anything but troubling. Everywhere they looked the Imperial Powers could see dissidents forming groups. There was a new intellectual, modernizing ferment in Islam, as there was in China. The successes of the West were so obvious that even the peoples who most detested the westerners were realizing that they must somehow join the league, organize their culture in concrete terms—like "the nation"—and go to the same school in order to get the education that alone could confront, and possibly confound, those who had already graduated from it. It seemed to them that there was an unguarded framework of ideas, never so static as the framework of power, into which anyone might enter and take one's place. But it was easier to think this than to devise a strategy to implement it. The Young Men's Buddhist Association formed itself in Burma during 1906, assuming perhaps that the secret of temporal power known to the Y.M.C.A. would be revealed to it also. In 1912 were formed both the Party of Young Algeria and the Dutch Indies's *Sarekat Islam* (Islamic Association), whose journal proclaimed its coming as God's will, made manifest so that people might become unhampered in His praise. In 1914 Marcus Garvey established the Universal Negro Improvement Association.

All these bodies had a future, all produced their disciples, some of them remarkable men. But there was no discipline to which everybody conformed. Nothing cohered. No rebel communiqués reported on the battle against imperialism from some headquarters of the likeminded, for the like-minded set up no such headquarters. When in 1919 the Communist International (Comintern) did try to do this, its empire was still one more of rhetoric than of action. Ho Chi Minh (in 1911 a messboy on a French liner) was to fret about this all his revolutionary life. Telling in 1960 why he joined the Communist party in Paris during 1922, he recalled that what he had always wanted to know was precisely what nobody at any of the socialist meetings he attended would ever tell him or indeed would ever discuss. "Which International sided with the peoples of the colonial countries?" was the key question, indeed the only question worth putting, for "if you do not condemn colonialism, if you do not side with the colonial peoples, what kind of revolution are you waging?"[19]

The anarchist Mikhail Bakunin once identified the three escapes available to the downtrodden as the the rum shop, the Church, and the social revolution: whether they were all equally serviceable, he did not say.[20] Ho Chi Minh had seen the first two made easily available to his people in Annam and wanted to test the third. His question was therefore not intended to be rhetorical. Lenin in December 1917 had indeed urged that it was the duty of all peoples to build up their national life freely and without hindrance. It was also their right: and this right, like every other right, like the rights of all the peoples of Russia itself, would be protected by the might of "the Revolution."[21] This language was adopted and inflated by the first manifesto of the Comintern, issued on April 6, 1919. It told the colonial slaves of Asia and Africa that the hour of proletarian dictatorship in Europe would also be the hour of their liberation.

This did not happen, however.

The theses put forward at the Comintern's Second Congress, in 1920, stated flatly that the nationalist movement in the colonial and semicolonial countries was, "objectively, fundamentally a revolutionary struggle, and as such it formed a part of the struggle for world revolution." This was not said with detachment. The armies of the Bolsheviks were then under foreign attack, and the new government of Russia had already admitted that it perceived itself to be "threatened with the fatal danger of becoming a colony of Western Europe or maybe of American or Japanese imperialism." Enemies were everywhere, and even after the foreigners retired from Russian soil, their eternal enmity had to be reckoned with. No one, its secretary Zinoviev assured the Comintern's Fourth Congress in Moscow on November 1, 1922, could speak of a world revolution that would be victorious only in Europe.[22] Many speeches set out the strategy, but still no tactics for implementing it had been devised. It gradually became clear that merely to wait for some grand spontaneous combustion, for history to bring about its own dramatic coup, was not a policy at all but an admission of failure. Such spontaneity simply did not exist among the masses, the *dramatis personae*. It would therefore have to be produced. The Comintern's Fifth Congress, of 1924, thus resolved to devote more attention than it had previously to work in the East.[23] This policy it then instigated in China—and saw come to ruin there. Chiang Kai-shek routed both the Chinese Communist party and the left wing of the Kuomintang (National People's party), ultimately capturing Shanghai in April 1927. Chagrined, the

Comintern's Sixth Congress reversed its "line" in 1928, proclaiming that it had now become necessary "to mercilessly expose before the toiling masses the national reformist character of the swarajist [Indian], wafdist [Egyptian], and other nationalist parties, and in particular of their leaders."[24]

This proved nothing save that dialectics, like people, could bend before the prevailing wind. Lenin was a pragmatist to his death in 1924 and left it for others who were not faced with his extraordinary administrative problems to pursue the purer doctrine of single-mindedness. He was always willing, for example, to listen to the Marxist enthusiasms of India's M. N. Roy, whom he was ready to admit knew far more about "the East" than anyone in Moscow. But he remained convinced that a blow delivered against the English imperialist bourgeoisie by a rebellion in Ireland would be a hundred times more significant than a blow of equal weight delivered in Asia or in Africa.[25] He never resolved the dilemma (which, clearly, he did not think was as pressing as his eastern advisers insisted) whether the Communist movement should expose bourgeois nationalists and fight them in the name of the struggle against capitalism or support them in the name of the struggle against western imperialism. Indeed, he had allowed the Second Congress to approve both courses simultaneously despite their clear contradiction. Roy, "who knew next to nothing about Bolshevism" and was expelled from the Comintern in 1929 for deviationism, could never dislodge his mentor from the theoretical ground that every stage of social evolution was historically determined, and, consequently, the colonial countries must have their bourgeois democratic revolution before they could enter the stage of the proletarian revolution.

Long, divisive, and exhaustive were the quarrels on this point, and they echo in the literature to this day. Feodor Preobrazhensky attacked Lenin's thesis, as set out above, on strictly practical grounds and described what was actually happening:

The commerce-oriented *bourgeoisie* and intellectual upper-crust in the economically backward countries inevitably aspire to solve the national problem *in pretty much the same framework* [my italics] that the big *bourgeois* Powers used in setting up their nation-states.[26]

Chicherin, commissar for foreign affairs, took a more pedagogical view. "To those of us who are not capable of a dialectic argument," he remarked chidingly in August 1923, "the *bourgeoisie*-oriented stand taken at that time by the Soviet government might appear to be a betrayal of Communist principles." This of course was absurd. At present the bourgeoisie, in India for example, was the most progressive eastern class. It was at once a gravedigger for the rotten feudal aristocracy and the leader of the national struggle against imperialism.

Let us then clear the way for the advancing *bourgeoisie*, but let us not join its ranks. . . . The conditions which provide for success in the national struggle lead to the conditions that make the class struggle equally successful.[27]

Stalin, however, was never expert, or indeed interested, in dialectic of this or any other kind. Once Lenin was dead, his views on colonial and national questions were relegated by Stalin among the many other *Problems of Leninism*, on which he wrote a tract in 1925. The question of the rights of nations was not and could not be treated as an isolated and self-sufficient question. It was part of the general problem of the proletarian revolution, subordinate to the whole. It therefore must be considered from the point of view of the whole. The right of self-determination must not be perverted and made an obstacle to the working class in exercising its right to dictatorship. Nationalism and all the emotion-filled slogans it let loose might easily become, in the wrong hands, a facade behind which the forces of reactionary deviationism went to work, hostile to the general good and the general will. Stalin's diagnosis ruled thereafter—and so the Bashkirs were not to inherit Bashkiria; the Turkic tribes, the Caucasus; or the Georgians, Stalin's Georgia. The charge brought against Bukharin in 1938 was much the same as the one leveled at Beria in 1953: that these covert enemies of the Russian people had promoted a bourgeois nationalism, a nationalism inevitably stained with an unscientific, uncritical attitude.

In such ways did revolution in the name of the oppressed peoples of the world draw attention to itself. But it never developed a general staff, an organized body of the like-minded, exchanging notes and ideas how best to get rid of the outrage of imperialism. The "great spontaneous righteous inevitable revolutionary uprising against the forces of imperialism" never got off the ground. The gunpower littered by all the enemies of capitalism both at home and in its overseas outhouses was never heaped into an effectively lethal train for anyone to light, despite all Russian Communist efforts. In March 1920 a "National Congress" of African aspirants in British West Africa was held at Accra in the Gold Coast, but it did not replace India's Congress movement in the official scales of importance, despite the opinion of its organizers that it shook the fortress of officialdom to its very foundations.[28] In September, two thousand representatives attended the first Congress of Eastern Peoples of the Third International in Baku: but its prayer—"May the holy war of the Peoples of the East and the toilers of the whole world burn with unquenchable fire against Imperialist England!"[29]—was not answered. In February 1927 the Congress against Imperialism held at Brussels had four hundred organizations supporting it but only two governments: "Mexico comes in because of its fear of the United States," Nehru noted. Delegates also came from Egypt, Persia, Syria, the Dutch East Indies, Annam, Korea, Morocco, French North Africa, the Union of South Africa, and the black population of the United States. The Arabs were particularly outspoken, perhaps because they were, as Nehru saw them, "wholly untainted with the slave mentality of more intellectual races" (one wonders if he conveyed this opinion to them). The Comintern backed the conference but the Soviet Union stayed away. Every reference to it, however, was cheered. But although the British and the French governments officially protested to the Belgian government that the conference should have been held at all and the French arrested Senegal's Lamine Senghor when he returned to Paris, the European newspapers (except the German, which had their own colonial grievances to publish) ignored it. The following year the Sixth Congress of the Comintern heaped yet more coals on the metaphor of the undying fire: "the vast colonial and semi-colonial world has become an unquenchable, blazing hearth of the revolutionary movement."[30] The language had now become standardized. The Communist party of Indochina, founded in 1930, used it in turn when it inveighed against the counterrevolutionary camp of international capitalism and imperialism —the only touch of originality being its identification of the League of Nations as the general staff in charge of the camp.[31]

What did all this mean? How serious was the challenge here presented? Did it mean anything? Was there a challenge at all? Assessments were necessary.

One assessment had been made before and often enough. Since the time of Peter the Great, the European Powers had grown accustomed to dealing with a suspicious Russia, which forever pursued policies impossible to describe, perpetually inventing its own difficulties and exploiting everyone else's whenever the chance arose — in the Eastern question or in the Far East. One of Bismarck's few axioms had been the necessity of keeping open "the line to St. Petersburg," less because he expected anything useful to be sent along it than to give the tsardom the assurance it needed that Russia indeed played a major role in the European drama, that it was a part of the civilized world whose opinions had authority and would be treated with respect. European statesmen certainly took Russia seriously, since they had to: but Nikita Krushchev's description in his memoirs of himself, of the Politburo, and of Russians in general as "country cousins" expressed a long-standing sense of inferiority.

Yet Russia remained, ever a looming presence, shrouded in an aura of mystery and otherwiseness which its greatest writers had done a great deal to propagate. In the nineteenth century the European chancelleries had little accurate information about Russia's internal condition, but they kept a tenacious watch on all the uncountable ranks that could be mobilized as a mass at a signal from their "Little Father." The shadow of Napoleon retreating from Moscow had lengthened over the years, but it had not faded. There was always the element of surprise. Marx and Engels would have been astonished by the days of October 1917 had they lived to see them, for agrarian Russia was their last candidate for the proletarian revolution. When the smoke from the 1917 revolution had cleared — in part, for it never did so entirely — Russia still appeared as it had always done, as an enigma of uncertain temper and dubious common sense. But once again there was a novel element. A group of ideologues, detesting the halfheartedness of European socialist movements, which, they charged, had achieved nothing beyond a bourgeois complacency, had got hold of both the Russian state and the unknowable hopes of the Russian people and were determined to drive everything forward into a future of their own devising, a future which they alone would devise. Like the French Jacobins of 1793, they enthroned reason. They laid down iron definitions for progress. To them, mankind, or at least Russian mankind to start with, was raw material, so much clay from which the future would be molded. But in a world where folly was still tsar, where irrational notions governed nations of dupes, they clearly had much to do before they could say such a future was assured.

This threat of the Communist International, a basement conspiracy aspiring to world status, troubled the Powers not because they were afraid of Russian armies but because they feared it would contaminate every loyalty on which they had always depended. No one could tell what its effects might be. But its potency was obvious. Idealistic dissidents everywhere were for the next thirty years ready to believe that the state would indeed wither away, as Marx had foretold, once the dictatorship of the proletariat had been established. They were assured, having assured themselves, that there was a light in the East toward which all people, less for their own redemption than for that of history itself, should walk. The American diplomat George Kennan had reasons for his special vehemence when he assessed this at the height of the Cold War antagonisms of the 1950s, but the chord he struck was a true one. It still sounds:

> Communist parties . . . came more and more to be a sort of traditional fixture of the western state: a curious receptacle into which there could be poured, decade after decade, all that fringe of the human species that tended by nature to turn against its human environment and to seek fulfillment of its own ego in the defiance of all that others believed and cherished.[32]

The hope that there exists a system, which has only to be applied to clarify all the problems of life, has deeply entrenched itself among the aspirations of people who cannot find any other faith to serve them.

The system of Communism dealt in certainty, something thought very desirable, especially in western circles that had mislaid the assumptions which had bred their prosperity. Communism described in close detail, if often in incomprehensible language, where this certainty was to be found. It rejected the irrational, the accidental, and the customary with equal and savage disdain. Trotsky told a graduating class of Red Army Academy cadets that it was not compulsory to study the history of any eastern country—only its geography, economics, politics, and military organization.[33] The part of history that was not bogus resembled chemistry. It had elements and properties. The proper combination of these could be discovered (although not perhaps all at once) by applying rational principle. Communism laid down one road to take, one line to follow along the road. Deviation from it was not mere waywardness, it amounted to dangerous subversion, for its example would seduce the weaker intelligences, which were and always would be in the majority. Commitment was therefore a necessary part of everyone's equipment. Once accepted, one could stray neither to the Right, which was fascist, nor to the Left, which was fraudulent.

The European governments, which henceforth had to do their work with this blare in their ears, found that they could reckon on sufficient support from their own peoples—who did not confuse *Das Kapital* with the Koran, despite their considerable troubles—to settle accounts with the minority among them who committed themselves in the name of historical inevitability to the promotion of social unrest—in other words, riot and plot. But when the same governments viewed their imperial properties, they recognized a different scale of difficulty. Here, it seemed, was a new situation. European literates had long held opposing views without necessarily endangering the state; although perhaps, as Napoleon's police chief Fouché had once advised him, all writers would benefit from being locked up at least once in their lives. But in the European context even a police chief could assess the degree of danger. Outside Europe this was not so simple. The daily routines of empire had always included dealing with people whose thoughts could only be guessed, but the controllers at least had been able to assume safely that nobody else was interfering with these thoughts, that nobody else was setting up another system of control. This was the assumption now threatened. Had the Comintern been willing, or able, to break free from the bonds of its dialectic, by which it had calculated the steps leading to the revolution of the proletariat in the industrial West but not in the agrarian East, the imperially privileged would have led a far harder life between the wars than in fact they did.

But an alternative had been presented. It stressed ends, not means, unlike the programs of the territorial empires. How long would it take the subject races to find out that this alternative existed?

"A long time" was the judgment reached by the imperial generation, once it had mastered its first unease. Imperial officials recognized that they now had to continue their work in a new climate of opinion. They realized that all they had ever said about the possibility of natives' participating in their own governance must now find some practical expression. They knew that it was essential to obtain the trust of their subjects if they were to continue to hold these subjects in trust. But as the years passed, it did not appear that matters had changed so greatly after all. At customs and immigration, books were more carefully banned, passports more regularly scanned, and the list of undesirables lengthened and kept up-to-date. Trouble was not invited, but the sense of alarm diminished, for it became clear that those who were graduating from the imperial schoolrooms into the professions of law, journalism, and "politics" and who were making their voices heard in these areas did not at once rush to enroll, whether clandestinely or openly, as agents of Moscow. They did not go the way of Ho Chi Minh, the least secret "secret agent" of them all. Yet the possibility that they still might worked in their favor. They were paid an amount of attention that would never have come their way otherwise. "Moderates" were flattered for their moderation and concessions made to them lest their moderation fail or be suborned by the extremists who stayed in the background.

This was a positive victory for the controlled. They did not deal in ideology, although when it served they used its appropriate slogans. They watched nationalism at work in Europe, drawing up new frontiers to quarrel over. They were ready to use the popular western argument about self-determination. But they had not yet learned how to translate any of this into terms that could be understood beyond their own level. Nobody in their own territories taught them any such exercise: all the imperial educational systems related more to the classroom than to the world beyond its door. Instead, they had to experience long periods of trial and error, while enduring the imperial attitude of disdain that they should be doing such things at all. Gandhi's close friend Charles Freer Andrews, a missionary, knew more about English habits of thinking in India than Gandhi, but even Andrews could not tell him why the English felt, thought, and behaved as they did—since, a radical individualist by choice, cut off from his own kind, he did not understand it himself.

So the actions that the colonial leaders took did not add up to anything approaching effective corporate action. This point needs emphasis, for a century from now people may well see as one of the principal puzzles of the twentieth century, not that India attained self-government in 1950, but that it took fifty years to do so, since the intelligentsia's statements of the 1890s were repeated, often word for word, throughout the 1920s, 1930s, and 1940s. This was true of the other empires. The attitude of the Moroccans to the French before World War I was much the same after it. The Moroccans' exasperation was mirrored by the Syrians. The sense of frustration experienced by the Javanese in the presence of the Dutch varied only in degrees of intensity from one decade to another. Anti-imperialism in full nationalist dress came out into the streets of Peking on May 4, 1919, and in Shanghai on May 20, 1925. Between the two world wars more prolonged outbursts of the same kind occurred in French and British satellite areas in the Middle East. But the status quo, the fact of empire, the fact of its control, was not yet vigorously threatened anywhere. Challenges were made and were recognized as challenges: but they were not thought, by those challenged, to have real significance.

Why not? No theory of imperialism, however intricate or ingenious, can ever discover a fully satisfying answer to this question or to others relating to the same puzzle. Because this is so, the "modern tendency" that Bastin and Benda referred to, i.e., treating as tangential what in fact was central, gained the ground it did. On what, exactly, did the imperialism that arrived on a local scene, so confident and uncaring, impose itself? Imperial diarists like Lugard and Lyautey noted their impressions of particular local scenes, but imperial governments—and Lugard and Lyautey too, once they had become agents of imperial governments—did not deal in impressions. The questions themselves, however, did not disappear.

What was durable and what was permeable? What changes were happening in the local societies in which the imperial machinery set itself up? How far did these changes help its managers, and how much did they hinder them? They had no barometer to consult. They could only guess: at best, they called themselves lucky when the natives were friendly and not hostile. Why the natives behaved a particular way in one place and a different way in another the alien controllers had no means of knowing. Why did the Afghans oppose one front to imperialism, the Annamese another? The West Indian islands after three hundred years' experience of European control had become perhaps the most assimilated culture in the imperial record; does this explain why in two different generations leaders like Marcus Garvey and Stokely Carmichael should have emerged from there to attack the assimilation of the blacks on the North American mainland?

Did the social importance attached to government employ, or to service in the imperial army or the police, outweigh the "alienation" it was supposed, by those who knew what alienation was, to bring with it? How much conscious role playing took place, and how much of it was unconscious? How much corruption occurred among government clerks? Where did they draw the line, and why did they draw it there? Who paid eager journalists to write lies, and who paid them to write the truth? How much awe did the rubber tappers in the *kampongs* and plantations of Kelantan and Java in fact feel toward the *tuans* they bowed to every morning? How many local customs no longer visible, or proscribed outright, were in fact thriving? How much hoodwinking of officialdom was resorted to, connived at, or promoted by the local religious leaders? What was the true reputation of the native teacher in the Christian mission school, not among the missionaries but among the children and their parents? How many young converts—like Hastings Banda of Nyasaland, later an elder of the Church of Scotland—also subjected themselves to the initiation ceremonies of their tribe? And when revolt broke out, as it did in Natal in 1906 and in Nyasaland under John Chilembwe in 1915, what were its real causes?

These questions were all as unanswerable, and in one sense as simpleminded, as the one that might serve to cover them all: what went on after dark?

From the Atlantic "middle passage" of slave-trading days, between two continents, there had been no escape by sea. From the twentieth century's middle passage between two worlds there was no escape at all. There was no way home to a home that was gone, or going. Tradition meant little in a context that allowed aliens to create "traditional" authorities, chiefs on salary; or where a black man like Felix Eboué from French Guiana could appear in the Congo or the Sudan as a French colonial official, "as convinced of his superiority as if he were a dolichocephalic blond."[34] The *évolué* was looked on as a man who had stopped moving: he was not an *évoluant*. But this was to his advantage when the society in which he had involved himself had itself stopped evolving in a way desirable to anyone. Eboué behaved as he expected others to behave—in other words, well at all times, especially in those of crisis. As a natural result, when he was governor-general of French West Africa in 1941 he declared against the Germans' satellite government of France at Vichy and so gave to "Free France" its first solid base of operations. "A great Frenchman," said General de Gaulle, Eboué died a Companion of the Liberation and is buried in the Panthéon, himself a keeper of the flame.

To people of his color, the wisdom of the way Eboué took is still a matter for debate; but his instinctive support for the "civilization" that the French had always proclaimed as their own but that many of them had failed to defend made Senegal's Léopold Senghor (who met Eboué's sons in a German prison camp at Poitiers and later married his daughter) hail him in a poem as "the lion who stands and says no!" A socialist Catholic, Senghor always advised *les noirs* to assimilate but not to be assimilated. In roots lay spiritual strength —although he confessed he was unable to write poems about Africa while actually living there, so different was the reality around him from his ideal. His continuing aim he summed up in 1961, when he was president of the Republic of Senegal:

Our ultimate task is to bring about a symbiosis of our African-Negro, or more precisely, Negro-Berber values, and European values—European values because Europe contributes the principal technical means of the emerging civilization. Indeed, all the values from either side cannot be retained.[35]

But Senghor's ideas, like Eboué's, were those of an exceptional man and offended other literate promoters of *négritude* (blackness) who were still trying to find out what people wanted in order to give this desire a voice.

Blacks changed as rapidly as did the western world they gravitated toward. In their birthplaces the western world altered the context they had known and changed both itself and the context at a pace nobody could measure. In some areas the changes represented by the input of foreign habits triggered local response, in some they were not far from sacrilege. Sociologists and anthropologists "on the spot" may sometimes be able to trace change as it happens and graph it, but historians are never so lucky, finding nothing of all this in documents, which are artifacts of a particular kind, made for a specified purpose. Historians may also suspect that their colleagues are making unwarranted claims, treating everything they stumble on as "evidence" of value without knowing (and no blame to them) what it is evidence of. Delavignette made gentle fun of the "man looking for lip plugs in the Bobo country," speeding by car on metaled roads from one preserved village to another. The truth is, as he says, indigenous societies can no longer be studied apart from the territorial administration.[36] The past is simply not there for study, whatever lip plugs and other such shards survive. But of course this "truth," to those who have retained their own traditions and have "survived" as living witnesses to the fact that they indeed possess a past, is one more piece of western arrogance. They do not see themselves as so many remnants of folklore, ripe for footnoting in an anthropological textbook. Here is an area of disagreement not likely to contract. To study Indonesian nationalism primarily as a result of the implanting of western values must henceforth be dismissed as "woefully inadequate," says Harry J. Benda. But what would be joyfully adequate? The evidence remains debatable, since there is no consensus on what anything is evidence *of*. Indonesia's own *Sarekat Islam* uttered its assertive call in 1921: "Socialism, communism, incarnations of Vishnu Murti, awaken everywhere: Abolish capitalism, propped up by the imperialism that is its slave! God grant Islam the strength it may succeed!" "This Hinduized Communist Manifesto and Islamic oath," says Bernard Dahm very truly, "could certainly not have appeared in any place on earth but Java."[37]

The inquirers, as outsiders, do not get much help from the autobiographies of colonial leaders either. These leaders write with a purpose. They tell what they declare is an inevitable tale. They do not admit that there was ever, in colonies, any other point of view than their own; because if they did so, they would be casting doubt on their claim to be the true representatives of their people. They are sure that what they learned from the record of other nations is of value and ask their kin to take this sense of value on trust. At best, then, inquirers can hazard an educated guess about certain things that were widespread. They may fairly suppose that the universal imperial principle of law and order was accepted not because it was imperial but because it was useful, that the benefits it conferred were too obvious to be refused by the Syrian shopkeeper in Senegal, the East Indian retailer in Kenya, and the Chinese merchant in Singapore. They can calculate that the doctor's black bag was a passport that would be respected even in hostile hill country, and that the utility of a good road system would be approved by anyone needing to transport a cash crop to market. But this is all divination. They cannot be sure.

The fact that they cannot does, however, provide one clue to the solution of the related problem: why, if there was a train of powder to light, had nobody yet managed to find the fuse? The answer is, surely, that the controlled did not constitute anything which could properly be called a "society" at all. The structures being built, the natural products of empire everywhere, were states, not nations. Imperialists did not go nation building. Since empire was seen by its controllers as an institution, and not as a stage in a political jouney toward something entirely different, it created what it intended to create: a local polity within defended bounds, governed according to metropolitan rules, with due allowance made for prevalent conditions. "How were things done?" was therefore a more important question than "Who did them?"—but if the second question had to be asked, it was immediately clear there was only one possible answer to it. Mao Tsc-tung gave this answer, one that any imperialist would have approved, when he said that what was borrowed from the West had to be integrated with the characteristics of the nation and given a definite national form before it could be useful.[38] Exactly so: this made sense when a Chinese leader, with millennia of ascertainable history behind him, said it. But was it sensible for someone from Sierra Leone or the Chad territory or Oubanghi Shari or the Bechuanaland protectorate or Dutch New Guinea to say it? Kwame Nkrumah in the Gold Coast might be right to declare that the outcome of empire was the creation of a political kingdom, but there was no point to such a statement unless it was also obvious who was the rightful king.

When this had become obvious, when after 1957 the Gold Coast had become Ghana, Nkrumah remembered his flourish and, to the scandal of the many Bible readers in his parish, had it carved on the plinth of the statue he set up to himself outside the Law Courts in Accra: "Seek ye first the kingdom of politics and all else shall be added unto you!" There was exhilaration and drama in this; its effects were not cancelled by the fact that Nkrumah was ousted from power by a coup on February 24, 1966. They underline the common sense of the view held by the Nigerian scholar Peter P. Ekeh that the "fight" for independence in African colonies was a struggle for power between two bourgeois classes, the alien administrators and the local elites they had created in their own image: "In the long run, however, it is the African *bourgeois* class which had the advantage in the struggle by persuading the lay African that it had finally acquired the charismatic qualities with which Western education endowed its recipients."[39]

Meanwhile, much the same struggle was being carried on in Asia, where "kingdoms of politics" had also to be created before the claims of the new kings could be recognized. In Burma and in Java, nationalism was indeed seen as the ideology asserting "that the state is the political expression of the destiny of an undivided body of cultural and linguistic kinsmen."[40] As Harry J. Benda noted, the intelligentsia in both countries, who had been condemned to the oppositionist fringe of colonial life and were aloof from modern economic life, were able to envisage independence only in terms of eliminating the alien overlordship and the aliens' capitalist economy: "Sociologically and ideologically *étatisme* if not socialism provided the *intelligentsias* with a logical, perhaps the only logical, prescription for national salvation: and, though inspired by conscious visions of modernity, such 'national socialism' could in fact be nourished by long, often hidden, traditional roots."[41]

In colonies the getting of office, or of a post in an office, was commonly seen by the aspirant less as a job to do than as a role to play and a status to enjoy. An expectant elite might claim, but it could not prove, that it held a moral position of authority in an emergent nation. Everything lacked sharp outlines: the expectancy itself, the claim, the morality, the position, the authority, and the nation. Educated men found themselves not so much at the head of their communities as beside them: indeed not so isolated from the people as the alien controllers, but separated from them nevertheless because the educated occupied a different position within a fabricated caste. They objected to the social futility of their own role but could not yet appeal to the communal sense that alone would have given both edge and drive to their complaint.

The strength of the imperialists lay in their awareness that they had such a sense. They were a cohesive group with a distinctive purpose, and they knew it. They knew, too, that formless and rootless opposition was really no opposition at all. Vigilance was certainly necessary but not a nervous fussiness. So counting "subversive elements" was a useful exercise, never an imperial policy. It was clear to all the imperial authorities, indeed to every governmental authority after the days of October 1917, that "the Reds" might be behind whatever trouble broke out anywhere, since fomenting trouble was their declared business. It would always be necessary to root out conspiracies and crush them. Conspirators, however, must not be dignified with the name of rebels. Rebellion itself could never be recognized as such but must go under labels like unrest, disturbance, and agitation. Imperialists knew, better than many, that ideas were contagious. They were particularly so at a time when the world's communications were improving, a fact that enabled the intelligentsia bred everywhere under colonial conditions to get to know one another, usually in Paris or London, where they could study one another's pamphlets before issuing more of their own. Tactics could be borrowed from anyone and anywhere. In the 1890s Tilak had borrowed his "no rent" campaign from the files of the Irish Land League. In the 1920s the Indian Congress adapted the Irish invention of the political boycott, and Ireland's Eamon de Valera was able to count on the cordial support of the New York branch of the Universal Negro Improvement Association. But such contagion would become dangerous, it was believed, only if authority weakened its precautions and failed to follow through on its principles and practices. This must not happen. And why should it?

Anyone who brings oneself to frame such a question knows its unspoken companion: why shouldn't it? People do not usually examine or even talk about principle until others have raised the subject. They then have to define it to satisfy themselves as well as their critics, and if they have long entrenched themselves in routine they may find this difficult to do. (Every religion has warned its communicants about the vital immediacy of this problem). In a time full of question, much of it was inevitably self-questioning. The power structure that had fashioned the nineteenth century had managed, although battered, to survive the world war that in the second decade of the twentieth century it had generated within Europe. The assumptions that had supported it, particularly the claim that progress was one of the natural laws, indeed one of the inalienable rights of man, had been badly shaken. How badly, nobody could tell. This uncertainty made caution the watchword and fashioned policies that edged away from political and social experiment. It was clear that an explosion was very easily triggered. If this happened, it would bring everything down. It would mean "the end of civilization." Not the enemies outside, but those within, were the people to be feared most; for if these were to succeed, everyone who had ever nursed a grievance would certainly rush in to present it. It was not so much the colonies' "unquenchable hearth" that troubled conservative governments but the fear that someone would find a pile of combustible materials next door, or in the basement of one's own house, and so bring about "the fire next time." Timidity about the future was commonly expressed in condemnation of the past and detestation of the present: thus it was hard to find, among those who thought at all, an unthinking assurance about anything at all.

Not only the mental and physical exhaustion caused by a four-year war of attrition had produced this result but also the realization that the efficiency hitherto assumed to be both the justification and the natural accompaniment of all western action had turned out to be illusory. For who could honestly say, on the most practical level of strategy and tactics, that the war had been ably fought by anyone save the unfortunate soldiers of all countries who were dragooned into it? What had victory achieved for common people who had long been taught and had come to believe that their governments knew what they were doing? A maimed man in a mean street was not likely to conjure up images of the wasteland or Castle Despair, but these images multiplied among the literary, deepening in color every year, and all of them set within a context of apology and self-recrimination. The war was everyone's fault, the peace was everyone's fault, society was at fault. Against this emotional background the Bolsheviks staged their emotional challenge in the guise of rationality, and the colonized came forward to publicize their emotional complaints.

What they wanted, now and for the immediate future, was recognition. They needed to be caught sight of. They needed to stay visible. They intended to become part of the world's conscience, as once Mordecai the Jew staying at the king's gate had stayed in the king's mind. They needed, above all, to be assured that they themselves at least, their presence if not their dreams, existed as a reality beyond the area of their own fervency. Power they did not strive for: it was something so far off that it could hardly be identified even in dreams. In the summer of 1917 Mao Tse-tung placed a "small ad" in a Changsha newspaper, saying he would like to meet "young persons who are interested in patriotic activities and prepared to work and make sacrifices for our country."[42] Getting attention and spreading the word—these, at least, were things that could be done, and done now.

They got attention. They did these things. Thus for good reasons did the party of independence in Egypt always keep its name Wafd, a delegation: the delegation that planned to lay the Egyptian "case" against Britain before the Powers assembled at the Versailles peace conference in 1919, Powers whose representatives had been heard to declare their total belief in President Woodrow Wilson's doctrine of self-determination. The result was foreseeable by everyone, including the leaders of the delegation. Its chief, Saad Zaghlul, was deported to Malta in March 1919, and a British foreign office official, filing the matter, minuted that "the extremist leaders ought never to have been received by Sir Reginald Wingate [British high commissioner in Cairo] except for the purpose of being told not to make fools of themselves."[43] The imperial displeasure was meted out impartially. Wingate was not deported, but he was offered a type of exile in the government of the Straits Settlements in Malaya. This demotion, as expected, he refused; and, although he lived until 1953, he was never officially employed again.

But the rejection of the delegation, the refusal of its right to exist at all, made the Egyptian case a cause. As Zaghlul put it, anyone afterward who said that the Wafd was a party demanding national independence was a criminal, for such a statement implied that there were other parties in Egypt that did not want independence.[44] This newly discovered visibility of men who were ready to make a career as international nuisances added to the embarrassments of the imperial master, whose position was already compromised because, in public if not in private, he was compelled to mime the gestures of the professional self-determinants. To give approval to the sudden apparition on the map of Europe of ethnic regions like Albania and Latvia, while continuing to deny any juridical reality to the ancient peoples of Egypt, Ireland, and India, was not really a tenable position. Was it possible that the surface of the world within the imperial framework, the 84 percent of global ground, was in truth a surface only—something lacking depth of soil, which one hour of storm might blow away?

This question, like others then being raised, was rhetorical. No storm came. Imperialism seemed secure, a solid piece of the apparatus essential to the management of the business of the century. Its manipulators agreed that this management must be done according to principle and must not ignore appeals made to their better nature: Gandhi told Romain Rolland in December 1931 that he wanted to develop world opinion so that England would be "ashamed to do the wrong thing."[45] (The right thing, clearly, was to speed India on its road to independence.) The political nonconformists in colonies could not cohere because they were too few in number, and too scattered in geography, to do so. The tactic that served them best was the one they had already adopted: to go on airing their sense of personal frustration, with the hope of eventually converting it into a general accusation of social injustice. They could not match the confidence that, at least on the surface, their imperialist adversaries still showed. The strategic and the economic power, both the guns and the butter, were still on the same side. It seemed that Cecil Rhodes has been right after all, right to say that empire was basically a bread-and-butter question. From whatever angle it was looked at, this was true. Empire was the public expression of the way things were, the way its rulers agreed they should be.

The western working classes whose interests Rhodes had had in mind profited from empire. Asian and African peasants to whom bread and butter were things unknown (and whose interests Rhodes had not been thinking about at all) could not be said to have profited from it, but they certainly survived under it in greater numbers than ever before. So what was to be gained by smashing the imperial structure? Nothing of value would be found in its rubble. Empire provided some sort of home, if only an orphanage, for progress. It was the only shelter from which people might look and say they saw, however dimly over however far a horizon, a time when, and a place where, famine and ignorance and poverty and disease would not be forever accepted as the inevitable facts of universal life. The colonial elites saw the future as obscurely as everyone else did; but they saw it more consistently, they looked toward it all the time. Better bred, better fed, better schooled than their compatriots, they believed what they had been taught, that there was such a thing as progress, which brought benefit to all mankind. They believed that progress was effected by change. Change by definition was something good, for if it did nothing else it would break into, and with luck break up, the conditions of stagnancy and fatalism that lay around them.

But they did not believe in changing things beyond recognition. (Very few people do.) But because they did not, they fell under the lash of M. N. Roy, who had no time for the bourgeois cant of progress, no belief that any change short of demolition was worth consideration. His raking criticisms are worth examining both for their own sake—no other Communist wrote so incisively in a language not his own and kept so clear of jargon—and for the light they throw on the problems that faced the "bourgeois nationalists" in India who were never sure where or when they would ever find a following. They would have been far more disturbed by what Roy said had they not seen that his dilemma was much like their own. He too was sending messages into a void.

Roy looked on Hinduism—the bedrock of both Tilak the terrorist and Gandhi the pacifist—as an ideology of social slavery. What India needed was not the ministrations of moderates but the surgery of someone like Turkey's Kemal. The violence that Gandhi always deplored was not a western innovation: the East would have to renounce most of its gods and goddesses before it could think of denouncing violence per se. What good could India's Congress ever do—burdened as it had been since 1908 with a constitution, foisted on it by the same moderates, which declared that its objectives were "to be achieved by constitutional means, by bringing about a steady reform of the existing system of administration, and by promoting national unity, fostering public spirit, and developing and organizing the intellectual, moral, economic and industrial resources

of the country"? Roy accordingly bombarded Congress with mani-
festos and denounced it through editorials in his newspaper, *The
Vanguard of Indian Independence*, founded on May 15, 1922, with
a £200-per-month subsidy from the Comintern. He told Congress
that ignorant workers and peasants did not understand political
theories any more than they cared for spiritual abstractions. Better,
then, to hoist the banner of *Swaraj* (self-government) and rally the
people under it with the slogan "Living Wages to the Worker and
Land to the Toiler!" The native army, which maintained British
dominion in India, was recruited from among the poor peasantry.
A program of agrarian revolution would therefore win the troops
to the cause of national freedom. Who could not see the common
sense of this? Many, unfortunately, as Roy was ready to admit. There
were men who called themselves nonviolent revolutionaries. One
might just as well speak of a vegetarian tiger.

Congress was looking about for other examples to follow, but
even when it found them it did not understand them; or pretended
not to. American independence, Roy reminded its members, had
been conquered not in Philadelphia but at Bunker Hill, not by the
vote of the people's representatives assembled in Congress but by
the soldiers in the field. Austrian troops had quit Italy not because
the followers of Cavour had cast their votes against them, but because the troops of Garibaldi had made it too hot for them to stay.
Cromwell had not sent ballot boxes all over England before he dissolved parliament and killed the king. Not the moderate Girondins
but the rabid and unconstitutional Jacobins had carried through the
French Revolution. And, to come up-to-date, British troops had been
forced to evacuate Ireland not because the Sinn Fein independents
had refused to take their seats at Westminster but because of the
stubborn resistance of the republican fighters. But clearly, middle-
class elites had no desire to arm the masses — and, indeed, they
would have been fools to do so. Nehru said in April 1923 that Congress needed a more revolutionary program. Roy wholly agreed: but,
what was it to be? Surely, Nehru and his kind would never find one.
"Let us remember that most people like to talk of revolution and
direct action, but have no desire to participate in it."

Roy was ready to allow that Lenin, wrong perhaps in some things,
had been right in most things. He had known, for example, that

the English workers perceived themselves to be at the center of an empire, prosperous because of the existence and exploitation of colonies. They were therefore too well-off to be revolutionary material. They were always ready to bargain with capitalism, always willing to stay in its orbit. When capitalist employers frightened themselves with specters of the growing power of trade unionism, they misunderstood what they saw. They were not looking at specters at all; they were looking at projections of their own image. Workers would have formed no unions had they not been so determined to become part of the terms of trade. Marx's call for the workers of the world to unite in order to lose their chains had been answered by a majority of workers in the industrial world who insisted on having new chains to wear. This was as true in a backward colony as in a back street. Colonial subjects, like the industrial proletariat, were part of a system they thought it was in their own interests to maintain. But if England was deprived of its colonies, its industrial condition would be no better than that of the countries on the European mainland. Its rates of exchange would fall as catastrophically as theirs had done and were still doing. There would be no terms of trade worth speaking of. People would be forced to think again, since only necessity brings most people to think at all. England could be made as ripe for Communism as France and Italy were. Now was the time, Roy urged Congress. Its members were trapped in a state of political bankruptcy because they were unable to make the needs of the common people their own. Congress was unable to recognize what these indeed were: which was not to say that it did not know what these were. It pretended instead that all its high-sounding demands for administrative and fiscal reform reflected the interest of common people. Its leaders had used politics as a ladder for reaching an agreeable social position, but there was never much room on a ladder, and they did not really suppose that others could keep on climbing to the plateau they had managed to colonize so comfortably. Perhaps some of the "grand old men" of the moderate party really did think that intellect and learning were their inviolable mandates for leading the people. But to Roy, this was nonsense, largely political pedantry which could produce only petty reformism at best. Several thousand "noisy, irresponsible students" and a number of middle-class intellectuals, followed by an ignorant mob momentarily incited by fanaticism, could never become the social basis for the political organization of a nation.

If the mob was ignorant, this was not solely the responsibility of the foreign ruler. India's own religious and social institutions had long contributed to ignorance and might be said to have formed it. No wonder then that the main aim of the peasantry was to achieve two meals a day, something that 90 percent of them did not manage to enjoy. Congress was merely, as Roy insisted, the political apparatus of the propertied class, and the exploitation of the disinherited by the propertied was the only agency of Hindu-Muslim unity. The possible end of foreign domination, therefore, was not by itself a sufficient inducement for the people at large. Congress's call for the boycott of foreign cloth was a futile gesture, for the poor would buy foreign cloth rather than go naked. Gandhi's thesis of simplicity was the romanticism of a highly educated man, with no appeal to anyone with sense. "The *charka* [spinning wheel] has been relegated to its well-deserved place in the museum"—at least in the minds of all those who were closer to reality than Gandhi. City life had opened new visions to the workers hitherto resigned to their miserable lot as ordained by Providence, and they were the least likely to confuse Gandhi's pastoral Arcadia with Utopia. Nor were they ready to follow his call for noncooperation with the *raj*. How could they, when government clerks would starve without their salaries, miserable though these were, and would never stoop to manual work?

Roy summed all this up in a hortatory lecture to the Glasgow socialists who read the *Glasgow Socialist*. The call for India's self-determination, which British socialists supported, merely encouraged the idea of bourgeois nationalism. British workers would do better to denounce the masked imperialists who by supporting this call disgraced their name. Workers must cease to be duped by the imperialist cry that the masses of the East were backward races that must go through the hellfires of capitalist exploitation—the same fires from which the British worker, too, was struggling to escape. But this was typical of imperialist conduct the world over. Successful hoodwinking was one of its most profitable businesses. Meanwhile, the so-called leaders and self-styled representatives of these Indian workers were rushing off in every direction but the right one, which of course they would never take since it led to their own de-

struction. Their cry for "self-government within the empire" was
as hollow as their other pretensions. One day they would be allowed
to have precisely this, since whatever arrangements were made about
it might be relied on not to interfere with the final authority of
British imperialism in India. An editor himself, Roy knew whose
decision was always final.

So all the argument and aspiration then current about the blessings of "dominion status" were so much camouflage. For Indians,
the status of equal partnership within a British Commonwealth of
Nations was a myth, one made to beguile the western-oriented,
Whitehall-influenced upper classes. The partnership in view, if any,
was a junior partnership. The business it joined—the exploitation
of the country—would stay the same.[46] England now wanted from
India what it had always wanted from India. Surely, no one needed
to point out, even to the self-deceiving moderates, that "England
did not conquer India in order to 'civilize' her." Above all, talking
about all this ad nauseam was a cheapening exercise, and Roy felt he
had to applaud Gandhi himself when the latter declared in 1927 that
Congress had sunk to the level of a schoolboys' debating society.[47]

But the approval was momentary only. Roy could never stomach
the advice Lenin had given him, to think more about how to carry
forward the Indian masses under Gandhian leadership than about
errors in Gandhi's social philosophy. It is not surprising that modern
Indian socialists, who revere Gandhi, do not want to conjure with
the name of Roy—who tended, says one of them, "to generalize
from his limited experience as a hunted Bengali terrorist."[48]

Yet that his generalizations had a great deal of truth to them is no
doubt why they can still put the Indian intelligentsia on the defensive. Roy accurately described the assumptions and the predicament
of the colonial elites, both in India and elsewhere. They hoped to
effect a change in management eventually. The British had at least
made India a state, even if they had not made it, since they had
never wanted to do so, a nation. All other European colonies had
been given the same kind of framework, the same steel support. A
native bureaucracy therefore had to be ready to take over—or more
accurately, to accept when it was handed over—the bureaucracy
created by the alien controller. Then the elite among the controlled
would desert the office stool for the Cabinet desk. In Roy's sour

view they would do this less for genuinely "national" reasons than for reasons of their own. They would replace the corporal's stripes with the general's stars, and they would most certainly not disband the army. To these ends they sought to redirect toward themselves their people's habit of conformity and, like white liberals in a similar situation, never stopped to consider whether the changes they were promoting might not also work upon this habit. They wanted to bring their compatriots to a point where they were ready to reject the dominance of the alien whites, but they had no intention of altering what the whites had been doing for so long and so successfully. Success was the most splendid weapon in the imperial armory—and it must therefore be included in the legacy, when this came to be enjoyed.

It might make pragmatic sense to look on "the end of empire" as part of a sleight of hand policy, indeed a piece of "office politics" on a tremendous scale. But this made no emotional sense, had no appeal at all. That a state, and the machinery of a state, was not the same thing as a nation; that it was an artificial organization, geared to achieve specific purposes and these alone, was something well known to those in a native elite whose training in nationalist agitation had been obtained in the interstices of an alien administration. Their principal ambition had been, on grounds of ability as much as on those of "natural right," to make their way into its various chambers. They had dealt for so long with adminstrators, aliens though these were, that they had come to see through their eyes and therefore to look on India as mainly an administrative problem than as a political or national issue. The members of this elite knew they could bring no true bill against the imperial controller if they could not prove they spoke for the millions, for a corporate society, one with an identity as strong and self-righteous as the alien's. (As many found out after World War II, one alternative route to success in this lay through trade unionism, which was accustomed to the practice of having a few delegates in a trade union congress cast their votes confidently for, say, a million electrical workers.)

So although imperialists might find politics rough, very often their opponents who claimed, as they had to, that they were nationalists speaking for a nation, found it much rougher, the more so because they could not afford to lose face by publicly recognizing that their chief business was less to confront the imperialists than to convince their own people. Moreover, nationalist politics threatened to displace many "nationals" who were quite content (or at any rate not prepared to appear overtly discontented) with their local position of importance. Several of these belonged to the conformist constituency that saw assertion not only as a luxury but also as a danger. Later, Frantz Fanon would call this entire tribe, a worldwide fraternity to be found in every empire, "men in masquerade"—but this again is a literate, literary view of a predicament, from one who had fought (although he never came to believe he had won) his personal battle. The men themselves did not think they were masquerading. "Collaboration"—a word that before World War II had not achieved its ill fame—was not thought of as a form of betrayal by those who practiced it: for what was there to betray?

Because so many thought this, Gandhi, whose personal history in South Africa had not included any collaboration with a governmental machine, constantly upbraided his compatriots for what he called their "awful habit of simulation."[49] This habit had increased both the confidence and the ignorance of India's rulers, he was sure. (Yet the more perceptive among them had sized up the habit well enough. Tell them what they want to be told, give them an answer that will please them, and then perhaps they will go away and leave us alone—all the imperial memorialists illustrate this custom of the people they had in their charge.)

The political nonconformists, by contrast, were always trying first to break out of the masquerade and then to break it up. They looked for a role without a mask. They wanted to find for themselves a place in the morning, beyond what Algeria's Ferhat Abbas poignantly called *la nuit coloniale*. On this, the colonial memorialists provide a wealth of testimony. To be treated as negligible—which is what imperialism does, without thinking, to its subordinates—is truly a shocking experience. But only the educated, those who understood what things might be, because they had seen how things were beyond the village, knew this shock. The villagers did not share the experience. Since they hardly ever met white people, they did not know what whites thought and cared less for what they expected. Such heedlessness and ignorance among their kin the educated saw as an enemy greater, because longer lived, than any imperial ruler.

They also took the view from above. They knew that the ruler would never have been able to come among them, never have existed at all, if this heedlessness had not been there below them. Only education could bring awareness, self-respect, and all the possibilities of life. Without it nothing worth doing would ever be done. For long the whites had owned both awareness and self-respect—and see, see what they had done with them!

This was why Marcus Garvey so constantly and so fervently insisted that "on the day when the black man by his own initiative had lifted himself from his low state to the highest human standard, he would be in a position to stop begging and praying, and demand a place that no individual, race, or nation will be able to deny him."[50] (*Ceteris paribus*, this was the call of Theodor Herzl, the herald of Zionism; and of Saad Zaghlul, crying from Egypt.) And where was this position, to which nothing would be denied? Why, in a nation of his own, within which his own race could work out its destiny and measure itself, from an equal status, against all others. The "highest human standards" must find a public context before anyone would recognize them. This context was the nation, in the era when the League of Nations commanded great prestige at Geneva. The nation had become the accepted symbol throughout the world of the fact that a people had arrived, that they were there, and must henceforth be taken into everyone's account. It was a true diagnosis of the future: for blacks, among them those in the Ras Tafari movement in Jamaica, would hold tenaciously to the memory of Ethiopia's Emperor Haile Selassie, wearing his dignity as an imperial robe and in the presence of the League's Assembly defending his country against imperial aggression.

Dignity: it was a unifying theme. In empires it was monopolized by the controllers. The English when speaking Hindi or Urdu used the imperative tense. The colonial French addressed the natives in the second person singular. The Dutch resented it when the Indonesian spoke Dutch to them. Pidgin English and a bastard Portuguese served as a form of communication in eastern latitudes, but how much respect could someone who obeyed the call to come *chop-chop* expect to receive? When an old man, Jomo Kenyatta was to recall how in 1921 his countrymen the Kikuyu in Kenya would gather round a reader of Garvey's newspaper, *Negro World*—which, although banned in the British colonies in the West Indies and in Africa, circulated widely there under cover.[51] Here was a message that came, literally, from another world. A symbol of the future of this other world was the paper's refusal, unique among black newspapers of the time, to carry advertisements for hair straighteners and bleaching creams.

Dignity: it was the theme of the 1920s, and it was a theme that, once stated, could not be recalled. It found its way into odd corners, lodged itself in unexpected places, and sometimes expressed itself in strange circumstances. Abd-el-Krim, the Rif leader who between 1921 and 1924 challenged the imperial forces of Spain and France, claimed it for his own. He recognized that the French had given Morocco order, security, and economic prosperity—"but I shall bring the same benefits, with the further advantage that I am a Muslim; and so it will be from a leader of their own faith and not from an infidel that the Moroccans shall receive these blessings."[52] No one questioned that they were blessings. Dignity was also the theme of four Pan-African Congresses, as well as of the 1927 Congress against Imperialism. People, as Georges Hardy remarked, were declaring their wish to be admitted into the human family without reserve or compromise, without outbursts of indignation or smiles of derision.[53]

Another and a better name for dignity, in Frantz Fanon's opinion, is authenticity. No masquerader, by definition, could attain this. Fanon accordingly calls in question Dominique Mannoni's celebrated *Prospero and Caliban* (1947), which took a psychiatrist's view of the condition of the Malagasy of Madagascar: the patient on Mannoni's couch was someone else, since the true Malagasy had died long ago when descended upon by General Galliéni and his French army.[54] An outsider, however intelligent, would never diagnose successfully. Stupidity could do no worse: indeed it might do better, by unwittingly exposing the truth. Certainly, army habits did not change much over the next century. In September 1945 a British general arriving hastily to occupy Saigon in the place of the Japanese was confronted with something he had never heard of called the Vietminh. He did not want to hear of it now. "They came to me and said welcome and all that sort of thing," he recalled six years later. "It was an unpleasant situation, and I kicked them out."[55] This soldierly appreciation of an awkward political situation well reflects the attitude that those whom one does not know are not, in any real sense, people at all. Lay figures are not supposed to come to life. Any evidence indicating they have done so will not be accepted. There is no trafficking with the impossible.

Because they knew that the foremost of the rights of man was the right to be recognized as such, the colonial leaders continued to insist on their own distinctiveness, to follow Gandhi's regular advice and say no. Only by doing this could they convince the controllers that the controlled existed as human beings, could they prove that they were not just an unpleasantness that could be "kicked out." Appeal could be made to a famous precedent. People in a colonial situation had said no before. What was looked for now had once been demanded, by whites, from whites. Decolonization was a process dating back to 1776. It had been obtained by violence, and the victory then won had not confined itself to the field of action alone. The tale of the defeat of imperial dominance, English and Spanish, had become part of the national essence in both American continents. It had also become part of the "organized memory of mankind" elsewhere. Western Europeans were brought up to believe that, in particular, the revolution in North America against the British Imperial Power had set up a landmark for the human spirit. It was a happening that in its time looked forward and upward. It had cleansed the present and had improved the prospect for people everywhere. It was a genuine revolution, with a true ideological content. Its leaders turned their backs on restoration and reconstruction and went out on a new track. They set out to build in America a better society, organized according to truer principles. The new republic of the United States was designed to embody moral idealism and purpose of a kind that, in the opinion of its citizens, the subjects of the European dynasties would never understand. The republic's founding fathers stepped out of the context of the old world and its ways. They distrusted power itself, since history was nothing but a record of its abuse. They also distrusted history, because it had been handed down by the self-serving and their admirers. It was George Washington's hope to raise in America a standard to which the wise and honest might repair. It was Thomas Jefferson's faith that happiness was obtainable and could be pursued only in a free society that was an independent state. These ideals are hard to find among the twists of political fortune in the twentieth century: but there they were on the record, and it was a record anyone could cite.

What was not on the record was as significant as what was. The philosophical pioneers of colonial rebellion had not appealed to any right of "emancipation." In turn, their British opponents never thought of claiming that they had emancipated anyone. Emancipation, like development, is something that happens to someone at somebody else's behest. In emancipation somebody is striking the fetters from someone. Twenty years after the "Americans" had successfully fought for their liberty—in the process applying this new name to themselves, which both laid claim to a continent and buried their status as British subjects—the freemen who were building a society in Australia's New South Wales were still calling convicts who had worked out their "time" and were now at large among them, "emancipists." This drew attention to their original state of bondage and sought to remind them that, even in a free society, they did not have the right to think of themselves as equals of those who had never been behind bars. Throughout the nineteenth century, emancipation was to remain an initiative in the hands of authority. It was an act of grace and favor, in the old monarchical tradition; for even as it conferred a benefit, it attested to a virtue. Magnanimity might in the long run prove to have a price excessively high for others to pay, as it did when in 1909 the British "emancipated" the defeated Boers from colonial status and at the same time consigned to their nonmagnanimous care the destinies of the Bantu majority in South Africa: but in the short run it looked good, felt good, and proved that at least some of the lessons of the American and French revolutions had been adapted with success.

With the great precepts of "the Revolution" on his banners, Napoleon's wars set out to "liberate" peoples by enclosing them within a French Empire that took upon itself to decree, because it alone understood, the shape that the future should assume. When Napoleon was defeated, these humanitarian and nationalist colors were caught up by other hands, not all of them on the Left. The cry that people had rights which should be expressed and preserved in the constitutions of the states they lived in, once heard, could not go unheeded by any authority wanting to keep control of events, security of tenure, or serenity of mind. The rescue of the unfortunate from the circumstances to which their own weakness bound them became a respectable aim among the fortunate, and paternalism came into vogue. On two notable occasions, in 1833 and in 1861, it reached the statute books. Imperial acts interfered draconically with the rights of property in the name of the rights of man when the British government emancipated all slaves within the empire and when Tsar Alexander II liberated the serfs in all the Russias. Imperial authority had the keys at its belt, and enjoyed the privilege of choosing which one to turn at any time in a particular lock. Illiberal jailers elsewhere, like the Austrians, were to be forced to conform to this modern conduct: and Italian nationalism, making its presence felt and its victory assured under French and English patronage, stated a principle that others, in time, would call upon.

Animating this liberal power of emancipation was the doctine of improvement. Education and progress, civilization and civility, belonged to it. These became entrenched in the philosophy of the privileged. They decorated all the imperialists' prospectuses, even though they did not always inform their practices or appear on their daily agenda. When in 1858 India passed from the control of a commercial company to that of the British Crown, the royal proclamation announcing this assured all the new Indian subjects that color and creed would be no bar to their advancement. This was not true: but again the principle, once stated, could not be recalled. The idea that people trained within an imperial system might one day be fit to take up positions of consequence was not thought inconceivable. Indeed, was thought unlikely, and nobody bothered to appoint any particular day for this event to happen. This was not, or not always, hypocrisy: for a belief in progress is usually accompanied by an attachment to progression, to a due order of cause and event. Things take time.

By the middle of the nineteenth century liberalism had become both a symbol and a trophy of success. Not only was it right, it also paid off: great dividends, both moral and commercial, accrued from it. And, as good liberals, they could deny neither the duty to propagate their faith nor the likelihood that it would be enthusiastically received. Although Sir Henry Maine had his doubts that much good would come of this kind of proselytization, he was certain it was necessary to proselytize. Of India he said in 1868, "If British rule is doing nothing else, it is steadily communicating to the native the consciousness of positive rights, not dependent on opinion or image, but capable of being actively enforced."[56] By the middle of the twentieth century it seemed to the natives' posterity, who had become fully conscious of these positive rights, that the hour to enforce them had arrived. But who could enforce them? In what way? What context would best preserve them?

This, at least, was no longer a mysterious philosophical exercise. The question had already been answered, in very concrete terms. Physical rebellion by the subjects of King George III in one case, and of King Louis XVI in another, had hoisted the banner of freedom long since, and the doctrine that people had positive rights had marched beneath it to famous victories. A state of independence was the prerequisite for liberty: the nation-state would embody and enliven all the rights in liberty's gift. Even happiness might prove to be one of them—at any rate, Thomas Jefferson had thought it capable of pursuit. Thus all "right-thinking" people could appeal to celebrated precedents. Surely, then, these needed only to be appealed to again, this time by people who were not white. Independence, sometimes going under its new name of self-determination (that presupposed that the self would want to be independent) was more widely publicized after 1919 than ever before, so much so that it appeared to be one of the most fundamental rights of man—if a man was to call himself such at all. Imperialists had always taken their own rights not only to be self-evident but to be self-evidently just, and their history of achievement was closely studied. In their different times and places Mao and Castro, Nasser and Sukarno, Nkrumah and Weizmann, Nehru and Bourguiba read up on imperial history and edited its text according to the lessons they wanted to teach from it. The European and American national struggles, the Irish, Polish, Egyptian, and Slav "questions" all provided much to draw upon. The *Philosophy of the Revolution*—the title of Nasser's autobiography (1955)—was a philosophy that belonged to everybody, a doctrine all could grasp.

The Russian Revolution of 1917 made it even more exciting. After all, it was the propertied and the bourgeois who had benefited from freedom, who had inherited what had been won in 1776 and 1789.

But "the days of October" brought the dispossessed into view and promised everything to those who owned nothing beyond their own ambitions. But the communist dogmas that accompanied their arrival proved less essential than doctrinaires thought, for it had long been a custom in the world beyond Europe for European notions to undergo a change, to be transmuted by those who transmitted them into a form and style of messianic populism whose themes centered on the tenets, which must ever be vague, of "social justice." The spokesman for these ideas aimed not to take a particular "party line" to its logical conclusion but to uncover, identify, and foster a communal sense of oppression and wrong. They set out to canalize the emotions of the crowd. They intended to make people realize what it meant to be the prisoners of, the prisoners in, a colonial situation. They wanted to fire them with a resolve to be free of it. A doctrine understood or a doctrine misunderstood, a type of socialism whose parentage would not have been recognized by the orthodox European socialist, were all pressed into this cause.

The American and the French revolutions had been the landmarks of the eighteenth century. The triumph of Italian nationalism, *Risorgimento*, was the landmark of its successor. The Russian Revolution seemed to point toward yet another kind of triumph in the twentieth century, that of nonwhite colonial assertion, which would make a landmark of its own. To do this it needed to say nothing new or revolutionary. It had only to promote the ideas already at large, to call on ideals already expressed in a whole library of western political literature. It had no need to fashion some new ideology. The justice of its cause was—surely?—plain to all. Those in the colonial situation had only to repeat the declarations of 1776 and 1789, to underline the heady universalist creed of 1917, and to insist simply that their imperial controllers, who preached they wanted only to promote the common good, practice their own doctrine and let their peoples go.

These things were said to willing ears. Other also thought that what was said should relate, and be seen to relate, to what was done. The British knew it was because they had so openly proclaimed that their domestic liberalism applied to colonial policy as well, that the politics of complaint had spread so far within their empire. They agreed with Edward Wood, who returned from an official inspection of the West Indies in 1922, advising that it was bad policy "to withhold a concession ultimately inevitable until it has been robbed by delay of most of its usefulness and all of its grace."[57] *Bis dat qui cito dat*: he gives twice who gives quickly. The colonial complaint was more about pace than about sincerity, but too slow a pace made the sincerity suspect, and gradualism as a theory of movement struck the impatient as another name for stagnation. British colonies inevitably and invariably produced programs for their salvation that had a British ring to them. The Trinidad labor leader A. A. Cipriani, who retained the rank of captain from his war service in the British West Indian Regiment, was from 1925 advocating an eight-hour day, old-age pension, a minimum wage, compulsory education, heavier taxes on the oil industry, and the abolition of racial discrimination. That these were all rejected by the newly formed local legislature was to be expected: that they would all remain entrenched on the agenda of complaint was also to be expected.

Similarly, the Nigerian National Democratic party led by Herbert Macaulay from June 1923 carried a banner proclaiming "Right, Truth, Liberty, and Justice." It was able to do this in the certainty that it would never find itself confronted with the opposing colors of "Wrong, Lies, Slavery, and Tyranny." Nigeria had developed fast. Its northern and southern protectorates had been amalgamated as recently as 1914 and since then had lived two very different lives. In the north the British exercised their rule through the Muslim chiefs, who naturally wanted to perpetuate the beliefs, customs, and institutions under which they had always lived. This system of governance was practiced, to a point of veneration, under the name of "indirect rule." It had been invented, and continued to be blessed, by the long-lived Lord Lugard, and as a result, as one maverick official pointed out, "no more damning remark could be made in the annual secret report on an officer than that he was 'direct,' or not sufficiently imbued with the spirit of Indirect Rule."[58] In this paternalistic enclave, progress was not expected to occur nor the politics of complaint to find either form or forum. And this expectation was met.

In Lagos and the south it was another matter. The educated Africans there were the type whom Edgar Wallace's *Sanders of the River* (in fiction) and Lugard (in life) chiefly distrusted. Wallace's creation

(1908), like all stereotypes, was to enjoy a long career: in an Alexander Korda film epic of his story, made in 1934, the American black singer Paul Robeson played the loyal native and the Kikuyu Jomo Kenyatta earned a pound a day as an "extra," as an unreconstructed tribesman thumping a shield and beating a drum, in a cast of hundreds rounded up from all quarters of London including the West African Students' Union (WASU).[59] Sanders's opinions are worth repeating since they make it obvious why they were so complained of:

> By Sanders' code you trusted all natives up to the same point, as you trust children, with a few notable exceptions. The Zulu were men, the Basuto were men, yet childlike in their grave faith. The black men who wore the fez were subtle, but trustworthy; but the browny men of the Gold Coast, who talked English, wore European clothing, and called one another Mister, were Sanders' pet abomination.

Educated Africans never changed their opinion that the "northern" system of indirect rule was just a device employed by the colonial administration to keep Africans in their place, a place which would forever be at the far end of Sanders's telescope. They asked for participation in the business of government. Through resolutions passed by the British West African Congress held at Accra in 1920, they insisted that a legislative congress be established in each West African colonial territory. They pressed for a university, for an elective franchise, and for an end to racial discrimination in the Civil Service.

To the governor, Sir Hugh Clifford, all this was so much "loose and gaseous talk," the sort of thing to be expected from people who were bemused by "political theories evolved by Europeans to suit a wholly different set of circumstances arising out of a wholly different environment." Two years later, although the environment could hardly be said to have changed, he was compelled by the Colonial Office to change his stance, if not his views. He established a legislative council for Lagos and the southern protectorate, remarking as he did so that this would provide "the politically-minded sections of the public with a legitimate outlet for their energies and aspirations."[60]

Thus the outlet was recognized, with whatever misgivings, as being legitimate. The complaint was recognized as valid, the assertion as reasonable. Participation in government was allowed to be a proper ambition. The language of Marcus Garvey was let pass without comment when it echoed in the declaration of WASU itself, founded in 1926, that among its aims was the assertion of Africa as a whole. Africa, it stated, should step "into her rightful place as a unit in the powerful army of the human family." Similarly, when the Nigerian Youth Movement was revivified in 1926 by Nnamdi Azikiwe (who had met and admired Garvey in the United States) and by H. O. Davies (who had met and admired Harold Laski at the London School of Economics), the aims of its charter were two: to obtain local autonomy for Nigeria within the British Empire and to enjoy equal status with the other (white) members of the British Commonwealth. By this time these aims surprised nobody. They were indeed seen as inevitable. This was clearly the route that nationalism was destined to take. It would be a long road. Nobody should rush along it, since it had so many pitfalls. But there it was.

Where was it exactly? Maps had not been issued. Estimated times of arrival, at defined positions, had not been set. Imperialists could certainly point to a number of official documents stating that eventual self-government was the policy being followed and that the interests of "the natives" were paramount; accordingly, they were often inclined to think that no further comment from any quarter was needed. The passage of time would by itself prove their sincerity. Not unexpectedly, there were those who did not see time as an impartial oracle; they saw it as something the privileged were able to manipulate to suit themselves. "Loose and gaseous talk" was not necessarily the monopoly of one side to this dispute. Much time had passed, but still the same things were happening.

The connection between England and India, according to Gandhi on February 14, 1916, was clearly based upon an error: "But she [England] does not remain in India in error. It is her declared policy that India is to be held in trust for her people. If this be true, Lancashire must stand aside." Only when Lancashire's grip had been pried loose would the distortion in the Indian textile economy cease—for as Nehru noted, until 1926 there was "the unique spectacle of the Government of India taxing goods manufactured in India itself."[61] It was no answer to say that the British government in Britain could not control the production and marketing of cotton, could not tell Lancashire magnates what to do, and when to do it, in the private sector of industry. Indians suffered publicly from the privacy of these men. If something was wrong, a government could, indeed should, put a stop to it: the matter was no sooner stated than solved. India had endured this process of "Drain" too long. It was a much-used metaphor, and it implied that if better judges of what should be done with the available resources were put in charge of the system, the flushing out of it of so much that was valuable would be prevented. What did "Drain" consist of, in the imperial structure? The taxation of the local population; the customs receipts obtained from trading with a third country; the maintenance, in part from local sources, of the imperial government, with its administration, its army, and its foreign personnel; the pensions payable to this personnel; the bill for imperial wars; requisitions, forceful expropriations, and forced labor. Funds raised under all these headings left the country. This action was part of the "tragic memories of past history."[62] But in the right hands, might it not also be made the firm basis of a true, a national government?

Colonial leaders wanted to have more to distribute for their peoples—but more of the same, more of what was now going on, more of what was around, since there was nothing else available and no technique accessible to make anything else available. To make this distribution possible, they had to get control of the machine that ran the system. Garvey's litany said it all for them: "Now come the Irish, the Jew, the Egyptian, the Hindu, and, last but not least, the Negro, clamouring for their share as well as their right to be free."[63] Shares, like rights, were more easily claimed than defined. Not asked was the question "Who would decide when to start dispensing what proportion of the goods that were wanted?" But the program made it clear that a bill was being presented, in the expectation that it would be paid.

Moreover, the victorious Great Powers were constantly claiming that World War I had been an entirely necessary and salutary conflict, since its aim and achievement alike had been to crush German domination. But, if German domination was so wicked and wrong, were not all other kinds of domination equally so? If it had been right and proper for China to abrogate in wartime the extraterritorial rights there of Germany and Austria, why would it not be so for it to abrogate everybody else's in peacetime? Why should African territories be passed around like parcels, merely because one set of white men had defeated another set of white men? Why should Africans not be allowed to manage their own affairs, and why should the question of allowance exist at all? The American-Negro spokesman W. E. B. du Bois had in May 1915 made his own assessment of the war. He saw it as the result of jealousies engendered by the recent rise of armed national associations of labor and capital, whose aim was to exploit the wealth of the world, wealth obtainable mainly outside the European circle of nations. The forcible removal of Germany from this circle would change nothing for the better, for Germany's "share," like Turkey's, would be used to aggrandize the possessions of its conquerors. Such language was repeated in one of the resolutions passed at a Pan-African Congress which du Bois managed to organize in Paris for two days in February 1919. This stated that "the natives of Africa must have the right to participate in the government as fast as their development permitted, in conformity with the principle that government exists for the natives, not the natives for the government."[64]

Nobody, then, began with a right to dominate anybody, to exclude anyone, or to form circles around anything. The Germans complained that they had done what they had done because they had been driven to it by their enemies' policy of encirclement—but was not this encirclement, a ring around the world, the very policy that from the outset had been used to corral all the colonial peoples? In Garvey's view these peoples now had merely to fall into line and state their imperatives. All this was wrong, all of it must stop. The Negroes (Garvey's word) must have a country and a nation of their own, and the only country they could have was Africa. What were the Negroes, he asked, in the eyes of the world that encircled them? Another distortion only. They were people of dark complexion, "who [have] not accomplished anything, and to whom others are not obligated for any useful service." This very lack of self-help and self-reliance had created the prejudice against them. There was no white supremacy beyond the power and strength of the whites to hold themselves against the others. Indeed, there was nothing innate, no particular virtue in anybody. No black was good enough to govern the white. No white was good enough to rule the black. This was true of all races and peoples. But there was no force like success:

The Negro will have to build his own government, industry, art, science, literature and culture before the world will stop to consider him. Until then, we are but wards of a superior race and civilization, and the outcasts of a standard social system.

Until when? Garvey wrote on March 22, 1923, that the next world war would give Africa the opportunity for which the Negroes—could they only be free of these conformists, "our modern Uncle Toms" —were preparing.[65]

Just then (1923) René Maran's *Batouala*, a tale by a black man telling how it was for another black man in Oubanghi Shari, excited *tout Paris* and collected the prestigious *prix Goncourt*. Attention was being paid—or, at least, heads were turning. They did not turn far enough for the novel's most recent editor, who remarks reprovingly that a modern reader will be disappointed that it does not contain more protest and that "a more vivid description of the horrors of French colonial rule," with "a more sympathetic portrayal of traditional African society," is not given.[66] But in 1923 French officialdom was horrified enough to ensure that *Batouala* was banned throughout their African empire. But the style of criticism that had been found remained *à la mode*. André Gide and André Malraux were among the potentates who joined the process of *exposé*: Malraux wrote in 1933 that, having lived in Indochina, he personally could not conceive that a courageous Annamese could be anything but a revolutionary.[67] The language of Voltaire continued to lend itself to the puncturing of pretension, and in the 1930s Paris's Latin Quarter became the headquarters for issuing theories of *négritude* and of a genuine universalism, which, if they seldom got south of Marseilles at the time, served to incubate African political theories for the time that was coming. But it was still true, as Senghor's biographer points out, that Frenchmen's criticism of French society never failed to surprise these young men from French Africa and the French Caribbean, who had come from a world where all such criticism was, literally, unheard-of.[68]

Every intellectual finds something to say about the general human condition. The particular colonial condition attracts even more voluble anathema. While French *assimilés* were making their analyses and Garvey was prophesying increasingly in the style of the Baptist church he had long ago quit, Ho Chi Minh's tone remained what it had always been, one of simple denunciation. In him clarity of mind did not mute the force of indignation. The eight-point program he presented in 1919 to the victor Powers at Versailles included equality between rulers and ruled, and basic civil rights. Colonization was, obviously, an act of violence committed by the stronger against the weaker. It was time for all such distinctions, and therefore all such violence, to disappear. The Imperial Powers spoke constantly of their duty, but what did this mean? It was plain enough: it meant markets, competition, interests, and privileges. "Trade and finance are things which express your 'humanity.' Taxes, forced labor, excessive exploitation, that is the summing-up of your civilization." Behind the mask of democracy, as he said in 1924, French imperialism had transplanted to Annam the whole cursed medieval regime, including the salt tax — surely a curious proof of any claim to modernization. The image of dedicated patricians putting things right according to higher principles was equally bogus. The French exported their proletarians to conquer the proletarians of the colonies. On the Senegalese, other dupes of French pretension, had been pinned the sad distinction of having helped French militarism massacre their brothers of the Congo, the Sudan, Dahomey, and Madagascar. Algerians had fought in Cochin China, Annamese were garrisoned in Africa. In the world war itself more than a million colonial peasants, the majority of them black men but close to a hundred thousand Annamese, had been dispatched to Europe to shoot white peasants and workers. What sense, never mind what justice, could be found in all this? What morality, when the French promoted the demoralization of their colonies, and therefore their continuing weakness, by promoting the sale of alcohol and opium? What higher creed, when the Catholic mission alone occupied one-quarter of the area under cultivation in Cochin China? Where the profits went was plain to see: those of the Bank of Indochina, which had amounted to 126,000 francs in 1876, had reached 22¾ million francs by 1923. What was said at home, who said it, and what political colors were flown made no difference to policy abroad. This was equally true, Ho noted, of the English: Ramsay MacDonald at the head of Britain's first socialist government in 1924 was no less active than Tories like Baldwin and Austen Chamberlain in suppressing the peoples of India and the Sudan.

None of this had a reason or right to exist, and it would never find any. Ho summed up thirty years of diagnosis when he issued on September 2, 1945, the Declaration of Independence of the Democratic Republic of Vietnam, which freely quoted the American declaration on inalienable rights, on life, liberty, and the pursuit of happiness. These were principles as valid now as they had been on the day they had been written. What did they mean? Simply that "all the peoples on the earth are equal from birth, all the peoples have a right to live, to be happy and free."[69]

Statements of this kind served effective notice on the western Powers that it was their own ideals which their imperialisms were charged with betraying, their own hopes which their crimes had brought low. As Bertrand de Jouvenel commented, Ho Chi Minh was merely playing a role against France that was taken from a French script.[70] The script had long been in the public domain, its English translation and its American version equally available. Aguinaldo in the Philippines had read it and had tried to get the play produced, or at least to drive his people out of the audience onto the stage. So had Jamal-ad-Din "al-Afghani," the Muslim reformer, who in the 1880s had watched the English at work in Egypt, a work they should not have been there to do, among people who should not have allowed them to do it. Al-Afghani had pinpointed the reasons for English success in the world: they were "steadfast, ambitious, stubborn, persevering, and proud."[71] So must Muslims become. So must Negroes become. So must Chinese become. So must everyone become.

Victorian English schoolmasters would have been delighted to know how far their creed had spread, the creed that saw the world as one great school for building character, whose prizes went not to the swift but to the dedicated and the disciplined. The central point of the assertion now being made was that people should not allow themselves to be used and that if they were in a position where they could be used, they must get out of it. People should look others in the eye. This assertion was most fiercely and consistently made in an area that was never officially "colonial" at all, one not enclosed by the imperial framework. In the voices that came from China these assertions were joined with another assertion centuries old, one declaring that the Chinese were superior to all peoples, and that if they had fallen on evil days, this was their own fault. Yet there was no error so grievous that it could not be corrected by persons of pure and uplifted mind, who had only to discover the true path to travel it once more. For China, "the Revolution" had not the overtones it had in Europe. Its revolution was intended to reverse the course of recent history, which had permitted foreign war vessels to ride in its harbors and range its rivers, which had allowed foreign devils to control its customs and regulate its trade while spreading an alien creed. China's revolution was devoted to expelling these foreigners. The Chinese, under whoever's leadership in the first fifty years of the century, were not revolting against conditions of misery and poverty. Not despair but hope urged them on. They were determined never to lose control of the future, for to lose this was to lose also any identification with the past, and with that, all sense of themselves.

To gain the future they first had to reorganize the present. There was only one way of doing this. They had to follow western techniques, not because these were intrinsically or spiritually "better" but because they worked. These techniques had built the framework of western power and still sustained it. The Big Hairy Ones had condemned themselves to a life of airs without graces, of enterprise without serenity, of courage without fortitude—but their major advantage was a grasp of the practicable, whose essence others too could distill once they had learned how to set up a modern laboratory. If the despised Japanese could go to western school and come out of it with their spirits and their selves intact, it went without saying—surely?—that the Chinese could do this also.

In grappling with this, the Chinese were trying to find their own answer to the question that everywhere confronted "backward" peoples judged by the powerful as irrelevant. Since their leaders genuinely believed that it was time for a change, the Chinese did not see change as their enemy; they thought time was their ally and that the changes, when they came, would not shatter their society as they had shattered others. Westerners continued to hold power in China; but they had not the assurance to walk at will through the land doing as they pleased, and they never thought they had, or even that they had any right to have, any such thing. They still used the Chinese; they still set up and profited from facilities in China; but they could not safely ignore the fact of Chinese assertion—and they did not suppose they could. The Chinese Empire, to the surprise of itself and everybody else, had survived the nineteenth century despite all the imperialist harpoons wedged in its flanks: the Chinese Republic, launched in 1911, was for the next four decades to thrash about and lose much more blood. But the West was never able to wound it mortally.

For since China, unlike India, had never been colonized, it retained its international position. Every Power trafficking with China, and in China, had been careful to issue assurances—less indeed to placate the Chinese than to blandish one another—that the integrity and independence of China was of primary importance. That almost all the European treaties mentioned this, no matter what concessions they wrested, proved that every European Power doubted its reality: but every Power wanted this reality to be true. Chinese "integrity" was to be preserved so that it could be effectively exploited. Were China to be officially partitioned as Africa had been, it would spoil every prospect for profit. Business could never be conducted where the balance of power had been broken, in conditions similar to the English Wars of the Roses or the German Thirty Years War. "Big stick" policies plainly would get nobody anywhere worth reaching. So, Chinese Empire or Chinese Republic, the westerners stayed faithful to their roles, making deals among themselves about China but determined to keep China in existence as a place about which deals might be made.

In 1901 the scholar Liang Ch'i-chao wrote an article "On the Development of Imperialism and the Future of the World in the Twentieth Century."[72] The prospect as he saw it was plain but uninviting. It therefore had to be looked at from a new angle. If in the new century China was, as the metaphor went, "awakening," it would not do so in a bed provided in a house owned by aliens. If democracy would help it clear the house, democracy it would try. If socialism supplied a key, or communism revealed unexpected backstairs, these it would use also. In July 1921 the founding fathers of the Chinese Communist party met in the French concession in Shanghai: but it was customary, as an Old China Hand remarks, "to repair to the relative security of an imperialist enclave in order to plot against one's fellow-countrymen in power or one's imperialist hosts."[73] Sun Yat-sen, China's pioneer revolutionary, was prepared to try any remedy for China's ills, first Ford and then Marx: when no American Lafayette appeared, but only American gunboats on the Yangtze and at Canton in 1923, he was ready to see "our faces turned towards Russia." But this was in keeping with the general acceptance in China of the new doctrines of pragmatism, which their popularizer, John Dewey, was present to expound to Chinese youth in 1920. Sun was prepared to see Chinese faces turning toward Russia, but not Chinese minds. In this he was no distance from Mao Tse-tung himself, who told Edgar Snow in 1936 that the Communists were certainly not fighting for an emancipated China in order to turn the country over to Moscow. That this attitude became well known in Moscow explains Stalin's comment in 1944 that the party Mao led was composed only of "margerine Communists."[74]

Americans were false friends. Russians were unpredictable and, what was much worse, inefficient. The Japanese were predators, but this was no surprise. In Chinese eyes the chief foreign encumbrance was still the presence of Great Britain, its first invader. It was Great Britain, reported the British vice-consul in Canton, "with her subject peoples and her history of conquest in India and Egypt, who is constantly denounced in the press and by the student-body as an 'arch-imperialist' and the oppressor of China."[75] Britain's role as the imperialist ringmaster, however deprecated by a new generation of diplomats, did not seem, in China's opinion, to have changed much. Joseph Chamberlain had declared in 1898 that any port in China occupied by a foreign nation was to be, ipso facto, a treaty port open to all on precisely similar conditions; and since then England's unique position as moneylender and exporter to the world had allowed it to profit more by the application of this free trade principle than by any system of preferential tariffs and trade wars.[76] Free trade had always been an imperial policy, beloved by merchants who detested the thought of expenditure on naval bases. It was also an option open only to the Power that could afford to take it. As the manifesto of the First Congress of the Kuomintang (National People's party) expressed it in January 1924, "After the country was thrown open to international commerce, foreign imperialism came in like an angry tide. Armed plundering and economic pressure reduced the country to a semi-colonial status and caused her to lose her independence."[77] The Americans had been very ready to copy the British practices. They were not then as rich as the British but were equally ambitious, and the thought of the treasure that could be obtained from the China market was enough to give a consistency to American policy thereafter that it would otherwise have lacked. The United States, like England, insisted that whatever China granted to others be granted also to itself—for example, foreign control over the China tariff, consular jurisdiction, and the dispatch of naval patrols. Secretary John Hay's "Open Door" notes of 1899 and 1900 were therefore not addressed to China at all but to the other Powers, who did not suppose that the United States proposed to do anything new to preserve the integrity of China other than join the ring of those who were already guarding it. They were right.

When in 1915 Japan served its Twenty-One Demands on China, Secretary Lansing minuted that it would be "quixotic in the extreme to allow the question of China's territorial integrity to entangle the United States in international difficulties." Quixotry was henceforth kept at bay in the State Department. When visited by Baron Ishii on November 2, 1917—the same day Arthur Balfour issued his declaration on Zionism, as quixotic an act as can be found on the imperial books—Lansing affirmed the Open Door policy but agreed that Japan had "special interests in China, particularly in the part to which her possessions are contiguous."[78] Whatever this last sentence meant, the Japanese construed it to mean that their own "China policy"—which did not include a genuine cameraderie with European Powers, because these would doubtless agree to give Japan only the smallest share of whatever was being distributed—could be pursued without causing any international complication. As the Powers met at Versailles in 1919 to solve all the questions of the day, China found itself cast, as usual, as a "question," with Japan in a high place among those ready to give it an answer. China had already submitted its own "Questions for Readjustment" to the Peace Conference, thus serving notice on the Imperial Powers that if justice and adjustment were their aims, there was ample scope for both of them in China. There was, for example, the question of dispossessing the Japanese from Shantung, a province they had wrested from the Germans which was certainly not German but the "cradle of China," the birthplace of Confucius and Mencius. Yet although Woodrow Wilson allowed that there was "a lot of combustible material" in

China and that Hay's policy of the Open Door had proved to be "not the Open Door to the rights of China but the Open Door to the goods of America," the Supreme Council at Versailles decided that it could not enter into a discussion of "issues of a broader character." Indeed, they would have found this hard to do in the Shantung business, since the Japanese had taken care to publicize that Britain, France, and Italy had in February 1917 signed secret treaties that promised to support the claims of Japan "in regard to the disposal of Germany's rights in Shantung."[79]

As a direct result of the rebuff at Versailles the May Fourth Movement ignited at least some of these combustible materials. Here was a true nationalist movement, and although the fire it ignited did not cause an explosion, it never entirely sputtered out. The Powers' writing off of Shantung brought out the students in Peking on May 4, 1919, and thereafter local agitation spread to become a movement indeed, one that shifted and surged in a kaleidoscope of conflicting ideas of western science and democracy, communism and agrarian reform, student power and labor participation, the reorganization and strengthening of the political parties, and an antiwarlord movement. The whole was set within the context of anti-imperialism, for imperialism was the one thing all Chinese leaders, whatever their other hostilities, agreed lay at the root of every problem in China. No longer was it a time to appreciate the ironic implication of Ch'ên Tu-hsiu's remark, made in June 1919: "What is politics, after all? Everybody must eat—that is important."[80] The Chinese had always thought it was important to eat, although time and chance had often prevented this. It was still important, but so, now, was "politics," since only politics could bring about what was needed, a restructuring of the entire life of the country. The Powers could still form their rings, of which the Nine-Power Treaty made in 1922 was the latest in the tradition of attending to China without listening to what it said. Yet they were showing some signs of unease, some faint awareness that at the far side of all their "China policies" was bankruptcy, if nothing worse. Significantly, the government of Great Britain embarrassed its *confrères*, particularly the United States, when on Christmas Day, 1926, it issued a curiously breast-beating statement:

The Powers should yet recognize . . . the essential justice of the Chinese claim for treaty revision. . . . H. M. Government attach the greatest importance to the sanctity of treaties, but they believe that this principle may best be maintained by a sympathetic adjustment of treaty rights to the equitable claims of the Chinese.[81]

But this recognition that the claims were equitable still did nothing to alter the treaties, nothing to prevent the Japanese from putting their own imperialist "China policy" into full military motion in Manchuria from 1931, and nothing to ameliorate the turmoils into which China fell during the next two decades.

But China's "nationalism" remained something actual. This name, so loosely thrown about, so often laid claim to elsewhere, in its case described a living condition. China's course in these years was not enviable, but its attitude was something others could learn from. It was not an actor's attitudinizing: it expressed something real. China was both a nation and a civilization. The events of the century had proved that it was not a state, with an effective government: this lack had brought on all the troubles that still plagued it. India, by contrast, was a state, whose condition of statehood had been imposed and supervised by the British. Two centuries of direct alien rule had given India the supportive "steel frame" that China now so badly needed. India was governed by a system of bureaucratic administration that the British had not invented, since they had adapted it in the 1860s from China's model, a civil service recruited by examination. They had worked on it, making it ultimately the most effective government in Asia. So the question facing India's elite — "Was India a nation?" — was one unknown to the Chinese. But in what way was India a nation? How could it be made into a nation? How could the diverse peoples of India, the majority of them illiterate, learn to read the script de Jouvenel spoke of, when they knew nothing of western aspirations? Their principal characteristic was patient acceptance: they had never shown desire for change. How were such people to be worked upon?

India's intelligentsia believed, while they pondered these questions, that if they were to rely on nationalism, it would be as much an artifact as the machinery of the *raj* itself. What was instinctive in China would have to be implanted. They had to construct a community and then breathe life into it, force it to "awaken," make it indeed a "movement" whose course would command attention and respect. Here Chinese tactics could serve them — and so indeed could

those of the Irish and the Egyptians. To go looking for positive elements like nationhood and nationalism was plainly to enter a maze,
for it was clear to all competent observers, whether Hindu, Muslim,
or British, that there was no general agreement concerning either
the reality or the utility of these abstractions. The negative approach
was more promising. To call for independence, to stress the anomaly
of the foreign presence, to draw attention to the aliens' shortcom-
ings, to capitalize on their faults — all these things could be done, and
doing them would summon up an audience that at the least was
interested and at best might be converted to activity within the area
of these politics of complaint. But in fact the audience for which
these activities were staged was the *raj* itself, whose "better nature"
Gandhi wanted to win over to his side. Thus making telling points,
organizing strikes and hunger marches and spectacular crowd scenes
became the regular employment of the sophisticates who, genuinely
convinced that the aliens were an excrescence and a stumbling block
to Indian progress, delighted in contriving situations that would
show them in their worst light — one that showed them standing
still, not knowing what to do next.

   This was certainly the tactic of Jawaharlal Nehru — and of his
Tunisian friend Habib Bourguiba, who found that the French were
even more susceptible to ridicule as a style of opposition than the
pragmatic English. Although both men knew what the world looked
like from the inside of a jail — where "we read books for which we
had no time outside," said Nehru — they asserted that the view from
beyond the walls, in the open air, was worse. There they were still
prisoners of circumstances, locked within the same ineffectiveness
that the aliens had imposed upon the scene. Here was the true white
man's burden: the deadweight of inertia. Aliens continued to deny
the right of self-assertion to those who did not have the power to
make it good, but they had not noticed (apparently) that they had
lost their own self-assertiveness and were no longer doing anyone
any good. The acceptance on which they had for so long depended
was now being withdrawn. The potential for action, if not yet passed
into the hands of the controlled, had at least entered their consciousness. The controllers could hardly win a war for the minds of people
so long as they denied that a battle was being waged.

   "Even the terrors and misery of the battlefield," said Nehru with some exaggeration, since he had not experienced either, "are better than the peace of the graveyard." Inertia had brought the imperialists to a standstill, irresolute in a developing, changing situation that, above all others, demanded from them the free play of acumen and imagination, qualities they had always boasted they possessed. What was the use of living in a western imperial context that promised nothing save the eternal perpetuation of the status quo? The alien rulers would neither look for opportunity nor grant it to others. Amid their self-imposed routines of administration, they took life at a gentle pace, "bridging the mental as well as the physical world between breakfast and a large curry lunch."[82] Ho Chi Minh habitually listed the bad practices of French imperialists in order to denounce them, but he saw these as evidence at least of activity. The most unscrupulous Frenchman overseas never doubted his right to be where he was. But what could be said of this infuriating nullity, kept alive by aliens who, devotees of sound governance, had stopped thinking constructively about the future and who compounded this sin of omission by protesting that all would be well if only a handful of agitators would stop agitating?

Where irony ended, indignation took over. The western-educated expected more of government than it could ever provide, either in India or anywhere else: but they had of course been taught even more positively than the English in England that a constitutional government responsible to the people, supported by an able and incorruptible civil service, was one of the foremost products of the human mind—applicable everywhere. They did not claim equality of knowledge in these matters; they claimed the right to get the experience to get this knowledge. What justice was there, or even common sense, in a situation that denied them participation in the administration of their own country?

In putting the question they were only following one of Lord Curzon's many exhortations to improvement. "If there was one subject," he had pronounced,

which an Indian boy should be encouraged and even compelled to learn, it appears to me to be history. Deductive logic will never enable him to draw *correct* deductions as to British rule in India. History will, or at least may.[83]

History now had: and those who had learned from it did not lack deductive logic either.

They also knew how to assess the change that had come over the imperial attitude itself. They read the literature of disillusion that emanated from the West. They read the condemnations of imperialism made by the imperialists' kin. They read the writers who everywhere saw dust and ashes littering a wasteland, for whom twilight was the best illumination to be hoped for, and this not fervently. Everything said had a faintly apologetic ring to it. As an unusual Palestine policeman remarked in 1938: "Should those who control the forces of order take to thinking, even a little, that rebellion is justified, the control is liable to puzzle those who are controlled."[84] The controllers of the forces of order were not thinking this a little, they were thinking it a lot. In their turn, the controlled were not so much puzzled about the way things were going as delighted about the speed with which they were doing so. They had always been certain that their main enemy was not this policy or that statesman but the imperial assurance, the whole firmament of imperial assumption, itself. If time was eroding this, then all they had to do was stand and wait and keep saying no as Gandhi advised.

Gandhi increasingly saw his role as that of the watcher on the threshold and to the annoyance of congressmen often deprecated political action lest it disturb the course of what time had already decreed. Attending a Round Table Conference at London in 1931, he deployed metaphor with ominous effect. Here they all were, English, Hindus, and Muslims, able to sit around a table to parley and negotiate about the future of India "while there was still a little sand in the glass."[85] Indeed this was an age where metaphor abounded. Nobody wanted to give things their right names, as these were usually harsh and often frightening. So it was a time of appeasement, of eleventh hours followed by darkness at noon, of quiet on the western front, and the construction of other mental Maginot lines of varying degrees of thickness. Seen of course in the distance by the farsighted were clouds no bigger than a man's hand, which were soon to be racked and riven by winds of change, which would gather themselves into the gale of the world. Words, like everything else, wore a mask. Was it possible that behind the mask of imperialism was nothing at all? The Irish and Egyptians were saying so, Chinese still caught up in the battle against it were sure it was true. In Palestine imperial indecisiveness made itself most manifest, for there, opposed to two implacable purposes, what could imperialism do, save preach its antediluvian doctrines of law and order, to which nobody would agree to subscribe? From a British officer in Palestine came a reading of the runes that everybody could agree with, on whatever side of the imperial wall they found themselves: "If we behave as we did in Palestine, and sink to ruminating about our purpose in an armchair, instead of taking it with us up the hill against the wind, it will soon receive no more respect than the hobby of an old man, who cannot stop talking about it."[86]

To a critical eye the British Empire particularly was in no shape to go uphill against the wind. It had now taken to itself a new and noncommittal name, one popularized by its white colonials to compensate some feelings of inferiority carried over from robuster days. But what, in other eyes, did the British Commonwealth stand for? Nehru diagnosed its purposes at Lucknow in August 1928. It stood for one part of the world dominating and exploiting the other—dominating India, Malaya, and much of Africa. One knew well who shared the wealth in common. Should India assist England and its English dominions, autonomous states all, in this career of exploitation? Clearly not. At the time there was much talk about dominion status for India, but it was just talk. Since India was not an English dominion, any status allocated to it would not be English either. This was not surprising, for if a genuine autonomous status was ever granted to India, it would necessarily entail the breakup of the British Empire as it then stood:

You will get Dominion Status the moment you make it clear to the British people that unless it is granted, they will stand to lose much more. You will get it when they feel it will be hell for them in India unless they agree to it. You will not get it by logic or fine phrases.

Nehru repeated the theme at Lahore the following year. The British Empire could not be a true commonwealth so long as imperialism was its basis and the exploitation of other races its chief means of sustenance. The empire was in fact undergoing a process of dissolution. In the days of Clive and the East India Company, the English had come to India on the crest of a wave of new impulse in the world—but where was the wave, where was the impulse now? Because they were now incapable of doing anything else, they were indeed still doing what they had always done—trying to make their moral standards correspond with their material interests. But the process was now obvious to everyone. Empire had now become old-fashioned, an irrelevance in the world. What could it do? What problems could it solve? In India it did nothing, and its greatest success was to make nothing happen. This kind of conduct did not solve problems; it merely promoted more of them. Stale platitudes kept proper company with antique attitudes. There were tremendous national and cultural differences between the different countries of Asia as well as of Europe—"but there was no such thing as East and West except in the minds of those who wish to make this an excuse for imperialist domination, or those who have inherited such myths and fictions from a confused metaphysical past."[87]

In such a way was the Emperor declared, by the best-educated and most perceptive of his subjects, to have no clothes at all.

The next task, therefore, that faced the leaders of colonial dissidence was to make a national cause. The question now had been asked far and wide—"Who are these people and why are they in charge of us?" The problem now was one not of definition but of technique. A collection of individual rancors and frustrations did not make a cause. But clearly, a national rancor, a communal frustration, did. The matter must be taken to the marketplace. To be effective politics must be brought to the people: the people must be politicized. Everything must be politicized. Grievances must be inflated and published at large to become all-embracing. Everyone must be assembled in a common purpose. The dilemma of the elites had not lessened, for they were still, like their masters, compelled to travel areas of darkness, avoiding the comprehension gaps.

To politicize the people was one more task that must be done facing uphill and against the wind. W. E. B. du Bois's experience was typical. When organizing his Pan-African Congress at Paris in 1919, he had trouble even renting accommodations. He had had "to corner black soldiers on leave, black students from Africa and the United States, and black functionaries in the French colonial system."[88] By these means he managed to collect a total of fifty-seven "delegates," who at once busied themselves proposing amendments to the Covenant of the League of Nations. But it was still all hole-and-corner, everything done in back rooms whose rental was overdue, without enough paper clips and with dust on the files. Other African congresses were convened in 1921, 1922, and 1929, but there were never more than a hundred people present until the fifth conference was held at Manchester, in 1945.

At the eastern end of this spectrum Sukarno in the Dutch Indies had learned that there was no magic wand. He had only a handful of supporters to count on, and if his audience sometimes swelled it could as easily vanish. Unlike the British and the French, whose troubles in foreign policy in this era steadily worsened, the Dutch believed that they had no European defense problem to cope with, then or in the future, and so they thought they could afford to give their undivided attention to their empire and its profits. They had in their opinion erased a criticized past by instituting a new "Ethical Policy" in 1901, "ethical" being an adjective of particular interest, since it made clear that even the most pragmatic and unwatched empires knew in what style imperial governance had now to appear. The welfare of the natives was currently at the head of the agenda, but it was still an imperial agenda. *Sarekat Islam*, originally a movement intended to safeguard the interests of Javanese merchants, had become a program for the purification of religion. But it found out that such purification was not easily achieved in a society that religion did not control and whose officers and police were mainly Eurasians who regarded Islam as the underdog's creed. So the movement issued its first call for independence in 1917 and by 1919 could count, even if it had not the means to summon or to muster, 2.5 million members. On May 23, 1920, the Communist party of the Indies (P.K.I.), which by definition could not admit that any religious route to success existed, was founded and thereafter kept up a career of quarrel with *Sarekat Islam*: Trotsky's views were never welcome in the Indies—"the putrescent tissues of Islam, which will vanish at the first puff, fail even to realise the importance of the Eastern woman, who is to be the great centre of future revolution."[89] P.K.I.'s call was for justice. It spoke to this theme, in the name of "Indonesia" and in the voice of the veteran Marxist Hendrik Sneevleit, at the Second Congress of the Comintern in 1920. It thereafter took the vanguard in the policy of independence.[90]

Justice was, however, one of the abstractions that kept inescapably bourgeois connections. It was natural that a nationalist party, conscious every day of the week of the injustice of its own subordinate position, should raise it, but it was equally natural that it had no appeal in Moscow. P.K.I. got no help there. Stalin himself, in a speech delivered at the University of the Peoples of the East in May 1925, criticized its leaders as being overeducated sectarians who were out of touch with the real forces that animated the people. Experience had shown, the Comintern told the P.K.I.'s delegates, that in not a single country of the world could the proletariat count on success without obtaining the active support of the majority of the peasantry.[91] In the Indies the majority of the peasantry stayed mute. It may have been true that adhering to Islam at the grass-roots level made the acceptance of colonial rule as a legitimate and lasting form of government impossible "in the mind of even the least sophisticated villager,"[92] but no means was found of successfully impressing this sentiment on the Dutch, and no machinery devised could break through the blank and contemptuous response to agitation that the Dutch, proud of their imperial machine, everywhere displayed. Educated Indonesian dissidents who had never expected anything from Moscow gathered in another group, the Indonesian National party (P.N.I.), founded on June 4, 1927, by Hatta with Sukarno as its chairman. But they could make no headway either. The Dutch, ruling 18 million people, of whom 95 percent were illerate, held that Sukarno and his kind constituted just another small and unimportant set of agitators, confused in their thinking and absurd in their claims. They dealt with them accordingly, without being troubled by (perhaps never even finding out about) English styles of unease or French doubts about the future. They were never to change their minds, never to think themselves wrong. In 1947-48, when the Indies crumbled around them, they were to remain convinced that they had been pressured out of their legitimate property by a combination of rhetoric and double-dealing, preached and practiced at their expense by the Americans and the British.

So in the interwar era, when Gandhi and Nehru were successfully drawing to themselves the world's attention, the spotlight played only fitfully on Sukarno. He was therefore right to remark in 1927 that it was useless "to wait for help from an airplane from Moscow or a caliph from Istanbul." He spoke in the aftermath of a Communist rebellion in Sumatra and Java, which the Dutch had promptly suppressed. The P.K.I. was outlawed, and thirteen thousand people were arrested—but this had less politicized the people than convinced them that the imperial authority had powers of reprisal it was very ready to invoke and that to give it no further reason to invoke them thus made sense. The Dutch then proceeded equably to outlaw the P.N.I., jailing its leaders and in 1936 rejecting even a mild request from moderates that a conference be convened to discuss plans for the "evolutionary development of Indonesia over a 10-year period towards self-government within the limits of the existing Dutch constitution."[93] Sukarno, Hatta, and Sjahrir stayed in jail until 1942. When help finally came, it was not through any upsurge from an indignant populace. A magic wand was waved after all—not in Moscow or in Istanbul but in Tokyo, on whose imperial decree these became the first "prison graduates" to take over a national leadership.

But the fact that the major Imperial Powers throughout the 1930s were preoccupied with their international position, and were trying to cope with the rise of what was obviously another and more unpleasant edition of imperial Germany, was of great use to the cause of colonial assertion. Even if it could not be said that the "movements" were moving far, it became clear to the elites that they were at least on their way. Since home governments did not want to spend their valuable and overcrowded time on the affairs of colonies, something of a pattern emerged and established itself. Trouble in colonies, if sufficiently publicized, would be followed by some kind of appeasement from the metropolis. When an accumulation of social and economic grievances erupted in riot and arson in the British West Indian sugar plantations and when the continuing Arab-Jewish quarrel in Palestine steadily worsened, ameliorating Royal Commissions were quickly appointed and sent out to deal with both. This naturally encouraged the conviction among dissenters that their dissent would find attention and that increasingly it was entrenching itself on the agenda of politics.

Thus the interwar era ended with the realization among both controllers and controlled that "colonial policy" had become something to be worked out. It was no longer something that a colonial Power could assume it had, without stopping to think about what exactly it was. Old-style imperialist assumptions were gone. There was now a "colonial question," which entailed more than the occasional handling of some specific problem in one particular territory. Genuine, committed imperialists were no longer to be found. Curzon had protested in 1922, while watching his colleagues paring down expenses and cutting imperial ties all over the world, that their actions would ruin the future. He complained to a like-minded ambassador, Sir Percy Loraine in Tehran, that he had warned the Cabinet a score of times. " 'You are destroying the work of a century.' But the answer was, 'the House of Commons won't have it,' while the C.I.G.S. [Chief of the Imperial General Staff] chimed in with, 'the sooner you are out of those places the better.' " Another official, Sir Eyre Crowe, told Loraine that Great Britain was a state disarmed, with a public opinion opposed to all employment of force whatever — equally for a right, as for a wrong, cause.[94] Yet even then the soldiers and the politicians were seeing the future more clearly than Curzon, Crowe, and Loraine, whose diagnoses were accurate enough as far as they went. Of course, the very fact that those in charge could discern the shape of things to come made these things come in this shape that much nearer and that much sooner. As professionals, the soldiers were ready, if never eager, to carry out whatever strategy was devised for them by the politicians; but since throughout the 1920s and 1930s peace-committed politicians handled the whole matter of strategy very gingerly indeed, nobody assumed that any plan for the future was likely to come to fruition. No longer was the future seen as a colonial territory. Rather was it envisaged as a morass that sensible people would do well to keep clear of. Since common sense insisted that this was not a practicable policy, expedients and appeasements were promoted to the top of the agenda. The politicians were right to believe that the democracy they represented was not interested in maintaining at a very high price large portions of the world's surface as a private preserve. Costs were therefore kept down, and the work of imperial maintenance was made as invisible as possible. Since any sudden uproar would reveal what was afoot, uproar was to be avoided. If it could not be avoided, its causes must be at once investigated, hastily and with an expression of apology.

The resolve to do as little as could be contrived was accompanied by the inclination to tolerate others — even others who were obviously set on bringing about a state of affairs in which much would have to be done. "After all, why not?" was the question that flourished in this context. Why not give Ireland, or at any rate most of it, to the Irish, who would grind their axes forever if they were not appeased? Gladstone's opinion had been that the story of Anglo-Irish relations contained "an old and inveterate dishonour":[95] why not accept this verdict and arrange matters so that England would have as few relations with Ireland as possible? Why not give Egypt a monarchy that was not independent but might in quiet times be made to seem so, and why not try to make quiet times the rule, not the exception? Was it not racism to deny to Japan the empire in China it seemed to want—or, according to Japan's argument, to need? The opinions of Premier Hughes of Australia were reckoned as too intolerant to be considered at all. He had written to Balfour on September 11, 1918, that the Japanese were "everywhere, and working assiduously. We too must work in like fashion or retire like my [Welsh] ancestors from the fat plains to the lean and rugged hills."[96] He said much the same in public. But—working assiduously at what, exactly? And, anyway, who could stop the Japanese? Best to bury these matters amid the memoranda of diplomacy. British governments at least did not have to cope with the social and political intensities of the French, whose Communist deputies in Paris telegraphed on September 10, 1924, their congratulations to Abd-el-Krim "on the brilliant victory of the Moroccan people over the Spanish imperialists," adding their hope that the Moroccans would continue, in company with the French and European proletariat, the struggle against all imperialisms including the French, until Moroccan soil was completely free.[97]

Encouragement of the forces of disorder was usually not so blatant. It had become a commonplace that the imperial positions were more vulnerable to sapping from within than to siege from without. Looking over the ruins of his official residence and his burned library in 1931, the governor of Cyprus, Sir Ronald Storrs, saw this as one more end product of a system that had launched "fresh generations of youth sedulously indoctrinated with disloyalty"[98] from the secondary schools into the professions. He was right, and the remark could have been made at any time during the past thirty years. Cyprus's legislative council was shut down, but no government had any means of dispersing the ideas that had promoted the riot in the first place. The ideas were, however, still contained, and they would have remained containable had the framework itself held firm. But it did not. A siege from without was now to be mounted, and while this was being dealt with nobody had time to handle the sapping from within. Even in 1942, when Congress served notice on the *raj* to "quit India," it still had no power to enforce this. But the war that engrossed the Imperial Powers between 1939 and 1945 had a cumulative effect. It was fought all over the world, and every colonial territory felt its impact. At the end of World War I the center of gravity in public affairs had remained in Europe, and as a direct consequence the European Powers had not only kept, but had also added to, their empires. At the end of World War II the center of gravity shifted. The satellite colonies of Europe did not inherit Europe's power: but they found out, finally, that since it would be neither confidently nor consistently used against them, they could make their own assumptions about their future without fearing a successful contradiction. The point of all their assertion could now be driven home.

But even while they were doing this, imperialism was finding itself a new base, in a new framework of affairs.

THE NEW CONTROLLERS

The effect of World War II on the international state
system. The new "Great Powers" and their views.
The American imperialism of idealism and the impact that it made. The world perceived as caught
between forces of good and evil. The making of a
new framework.

5

THE NEW CONTROLLERS

A war fought for gain is described as aggressive, or unjust, by those whose assets are its intended prize. A war fought to keep what its instigators won long ago is described, usually by themselves, as defensive, or just.

At the end of World War 1, two allies who had waged it with different ends in view looked on victory and the prospect it presented from expectedly different standpoints. Curzon at the British Foreign Office told the Japanese ambassador on July 18, 1919, that any policy of "seeking a preferential position was out of harmony with the spirit of the times."[1] The war, he cautioned his caller, had changed things. Ah so: the Japanese view, though unexpressed at the time by Baron Chinda, was that the war had indeed changed things but not nearly enough. It had not changed, for instance, England's preferential position. Nobody heard Curzon or his colleagues offering to relinquish this merely because it jarred with the spirit of the times. The empire of Japan, which had recently arrived at world status and was determined to exploit it, neither needed nor wanted governess-like advice that was very clearly designed to keep yellow people in what the white people of British and other empires thought was their place. For the one empire, victory was a terminus. For the other, it was a stage on a journey.

In war all contestants proclaim victory as their principal aim, whether they want to win a trophy or to keep one. They do not confess their other ideas. Whatever hopes and discontents have been turning over in the minds of their citizens who are doing the actual fighting, national governments do not usually announce their firm resolve to attain, once victory has righteously blessed their arms, a world transformed out of all recognition. Governments see victory as the stage they must reach in order to regain and enjoy the past, a past that it is now much more possible to enjoy because the trouble-maker whose presence and politics made the actual past so tense a time has been disposed of. The true business of the future is to improve upon the past—not to launch its inheritors into uncharted seas but to set them sailing in familiar waters, this time assisted by far more accurate charts. Paradise regained is an old and potent enchantment. That no country in the twentieth century was ever able to return to what its leaders rosily called "pre-war conditions" or "normalcy," either after 1919 or after 1945, did not make the hope that it might yet manage to do so any less attractive to those for whom the past had been a time of privilege, and who feared that the future might hold for them nothing but a state of reduction and loss. They knew well enough that the people who were forever proclaiming the need to invest in change were the same people who had never invested in anything whatever, people for whom the old days had never been good.

The matters that had been on the political agenda during and after World War I, and had never been dealt with to anyone's satisfaction, were still on the agenda a generation later. To have and have not was still the issue. Curzon was no longer there to invoke the spirit of the times, but plenty of his successors were very ready to do so, particularly the controllers of his British Empire, who were as determined as he had been to maintain it. The organization of Western Europe, Ernest Bevin told the House of Commons in 1948, needed to be economically supported. The framework had to be reinforced. This policy involved England's closest possible collaboration with the Commonwealth and British "overseas territories" (the Labour party's preferred name for the colonies), and with the colonies of the French, the Dutch, the Belgians, and the Portuguese. No conflict existed between the socioeconomic development of these territories to the advantage of their peoples, and the development of the territories as a source of supply for Western Europe. In fact, their continuing contribution was essential if the balance-of-payments problem was to be coped with in any reasonable manner.[2] Here clear notice was served that not only the British Empire but all the European empires had to stay in existence, had indeed to strengthen themselves in whatever ways were available to them. Sukarno's statement, made in 1926, was still true: "no one simply hands over his rice-basket, if that means his undoing."[3] The days after World War II were the days of rice-basket politics. The problem of how to fill the basket and keep it filled was the first priority in the collective imperial mind.

To so advantageous a task the Great Powers brought their best efforts. They refurbished imperial assumptions that might be old but were still seductive. Robert Delavignette, director-general of ENFOM (*l'Ecole nationale de la France d'outre-mer*) took a ranging paternalist view that proved how deeply *le Lugardisme* had managed to penetrate French official thinking. In December 1949 he noted how Great Britain was envisaging the formation in Africa of vast black dominions, which would one day, probably later rather than sooner but certainly, become members of a reorganized and expanded Commonwealth. France of course would remain faithful to its long tradition, continuing to regard its overseas territories as an integral part of the national community. But these were merely two different approaches to an identical goal. The goal was no less than "the administration of the future, the administration which will bring together humanism and authority." More splendid even than in the past, therefore, was the career that lay before the dedicated colonial administrator. He was "the unknown electrician in the power-house of a new order of life," a new order as much for Africa as for either France or Britain.[4]

Thus far had come the idea of the Coprosperity Sphere, exported from its original habitat of Japan. In Europe the Japanese were thought of as the wrong people to have conceived it. Their attempts to carry it out had justly come to grief, but their hardheaded practicality appealed as strongly as ever to others who had to reckon that economic woes lay in wait for them around every political corner. Empire had long been accustomed to disguising its true *raison d'être* beneath trappings of another type; but in these new, harsh, and lean days why should this pretense be kept up? Japan's attitude, which had caused Curzon to purse his lips in 1919, was in the 1940s what it had always been: to get on, to get ahead, to get rid of competitors, to put the world within a framework of the old kind but under new imperial supervision—its own. Field Marshal Tojo set it all out with precision in 1941. The world, he ordered, "is to be divided into the great East Asian zone, the European zone (including Africa), the American zone, and the Soviet zone (including India and Iran), though Australia and New Zealand may be left to England—to be treated in a similar manner as Holland."[5] Those opposed to this grand design, one Napoleon himself might have thought ambitious, had to summon all their forces to break it.

Yet thirty years after the Japanese had been defeated, the problem of challenge they had set had not been resolved. How, exactly, were rival Powers to coexist in the world, without their rivalries wrecking the framework that contained them all? By the 1970s the United States had apparently reached the position of a satisfied nation, wishing to retain its power without having overtly to exert it, since it had become clear that any exercise of power, done for whatever motive, created enemies. The People's Republic of China had inherited Japan's original role as an aspirant steadily gaining self-confidence, but China was still [1975] controlled by old men who remembered the "Long March" that had brought the country to its present place of authority and respect; what China would do with this place no one knew. Japan seemed content to play its part, and with great success, in the western framework of economic co-prosperity. The plans of the Soviet Union, true to Russian tradition, were clear to nobody beyond its borders and possibly not even to the Politburo in the Kremlin. But it was judged to be in keeping with whatever spirit governed these latter times for the leaders of the nations to meet regularly at "summits," less to accomplish anything specific than to reassure themselves that nothing new, and by definition dangerous, either had been done or was being scheduled for the future. On February 27, 1972, the American president Richard Nixon and China's foreign minister Chou En-lai issued a joint communiqué which announced that it would not be in the interests of the peoples of the world for any major country to collude [*sic*] with another major country against other countries or for major countries to divide the world into spheres of interest.[6] If this was whistling in the dark, at least there was some harmony to it. The reference to the popular interest was a recognition that power had more assessors than ever before and that it had to ally itself, or be seen as trying to ally itself, with the long-known but still amorphous concept of the general will.

By the 1970s Japan was (so it seemed) securely under American influence, but it was by Japan's own doing that the theater of imperial operations in the "Far East" had become so greatly extended and now included so populous an audience, all ready to cheer the actions of nationalism. This had certainly not been its original intention, as Tojo's map of the future made plain. He was an alumnus of the old school, the school founded and staffed by those who dealt in zones and spheres long before they thought of people. But Japan turned out to be the last of the blessed, the last inheritor of all the imperialist assumptions. Empire as the world had known it went with it down to defeat.

No omen had warned of this. In March 1942, after the British had surrendered Singapore and some 92 thousand British, Indian, and Australian troops, every Japanese child was given a box of caramels, cakes, and sweets by a rejoicing government. The box was small, but the symbol was great: it represented the glorious prizes that the imperial forces of Japan were then seeking and winning. They marched into the European empires in the East to make them spoils of war. The children enjoying the caramels would presently grow up to enjoy the mastery of eastern Asia. In the meantime, their paternalist parents would purify and reanimate the taken territories according to the proper principles, which Japan alone owned. "Asia for the Asians," a slogan invented by China's Sun Yat-sen, had been appropriated by the Japanese and proclaimed on the banners of their army as it entered Burma, there to commandeer the rice crop. The preposition used—"for," not "by"—accurately defined the prospect before everyone. Asians would need leadership before "Asia" could ever be said to belong to them in any serious and spiritual sense, before Asia could indeed be said to exist at all. Only Japan could supply this leadership. Men like Tojo, graduates from his school, would long be needed, to make Asia's future safe.

"To the victor, the spoils!" is an age-long gleam in an age-old eye.

No glint of ideology is to be found in it, or the sparkle of anything fit to be described as revolutionary. It is only a flashier reflection from the comfortable doctrine that has governed the politics of Australia in this century, the principle of "me too"—throw those rascals out and we'll do it better, but what we do will be the same sort of thing. Imperialists, committed to the grand manner and the noble cause, naturally avoided such homespun language, but they owned no more intricate philosophy. The eastern world that the western Powers in their insolence had made over to suit their particular commercial conveniences was now, under Japanese direction, ejecting the westerners. But there would be no change in this world's role of satellite. Western technology, on whose utility Japan itself had thrived for eighty years, was now proved to be indeed a jinn who would serve any master who put his hand to the levers of the machine. As part of the great Coprosperity Sphere these lands would become even more of a going concern than the Big Hairy Ones had managed to make them. But management was still the essential thing. The framework imperialism had built was therefore not to be wantonly thrown out with the imperialists who had built it.

Power in the hands of Japan would, accordingly, establish a true system of authority amid the ruins of the system that had always been false. The foundations of that system were still serviceable. Of this process and attitude the city of Singapore was a fitting symbol. When it changed hands, it became Shonan: but it was not destroyed or even seriously interfered with. Chinese and Malays and Hindus continued to do there what they had always done but under the eye of a different policeman. Singapore was not dealt with as Baghdad had once (1258) been dealt with by Hulagu the Tartar. Hulagu's hordes had sacked the city, slain its inhabitants, and razed its buildings before riding back into their own world, back into their own context. In the fifth decade of the twentieth century there was no other world to return to. No escape route led out of the world the West had made. And had such a route existed, the Japanese, intent above all else on inheriting the success that the mandate of heaven in its mysterious wisdom had heretofore seen fit to bestow upon the aliens, would not have taken it.

For the races subject to the West, or, like Japan itself, satellite in its orbit, had lived too long in these fixed positions to be capable of envisaging some other way of living, within some other system. Japan in 1941 did what Italy had done thirty years previously. Italy had gone to Libya "for the national conservation of an immense surplus of population and to cease playing the role of Cinderella assigned to her by other people."[7] Italy's actions in the second decade of the century had accurately registered the strength and the appeal of European imperialism: Japan's actions in the fifth decade registered its weakness. But the appeal was still the same. One may legitimately wonder how much Japanese attitudes would have altered, once they had established themselves among the peoples they planned to include within their Coprosperity Sphere. Japan's original declaration, that steps would be taken to abolish the influence of all European, American, and Communist ideas, called down a plague on every contemporary imperial house. But since Japan was so much more "Asian" in outlook than were the Asiatics among whom it descended, had the "proper and suitable frame of government" it intended to impose actually been constructed, historians might well have found themselves recording what they cannot in fact record, a genuine colonial revolution.

From the outset the Japanese were determined not to create an intellectual proletariat. They planned to limit the number of college graduates, the unemployables who, as other imperial experience proved, found the time and the inclination to devise embarrassment for government in the name of liberalism or nationalism or humanity or whatever. That they thought this proved how carefully they had watched what had happened in the western empires. But what had surprised western imperial governors lay in wait for them also. Legitimacy, like every other abstraction, depends on the point of view. The Japanese had not sufficiently understood the degree of disrepute under which colonial status everywhere now labored. They found that the "true fatherly attitude" of which Tojo spoke—and which, he assured Burma's Ba Maw at Singapore in 1943, would henceforth govern all Japanese conduct—would never win any new adherents. Listened to was the song, not the singer. Burmese in particular dismayed the Japanese by taking a regrettably "British" view of independence. They seemed to suppose they had a right to administer their own affairs—and to have a free press besides! To this strange assertion the Japanese bleakly retorted that "natives will have to reconcile themselves to such pressure as is unavoidably involved for them in our acquisition of resources." Famous gardeners, they knew that gardens were not created by allowing weeds to proliferate at will. They brought with them no admiration for Asian races as such, peoples with roots indeed but who had not grown, peoples on whom the sun had not shone, peoples from whom the mandate of heaven had very obviously been withheld, and for very good reason. The level of the Annamese, to take one example, was low as a race. Their political capacities were weak: this must be so, since very recent history had proved that the capacities of their French masters were feeble indeed. The same held true for the Indonesians and for others who had been for too long contaminated with the vices of the conquered. Plainly, all of them would need Japanese protection, guidance, and example for years to come.[8]

Japan's actions made it clear that, although it had picked up all the useful twentieth-century gadgetry, it had retained the assumptions of its nineteenth-century mentors. When its soldiers pushed into the European eastern empires, it had every intention of matching theory with practice. The soldiers' brutality, as they set about ordering things as they were ordered to do, illustrated the depth of what the Japanese high command knew as "sincerity." People who rejected an obvious superiority were obviously inferior people. They had no right to complain about what was decreed by their betters as best for them. They had no right to insult Japanese conceptions of chivalry and honor by showing resistance and making objections, however feeble. Because they had no dignity, they had no essence. They deserved nothing better than, literally, to be pushed around. Prisoners of war, in particular, were so much cattle, since their sense of honor should not have allowed them to become prisoners in the first place.

The Coprosperity Sphere, under its originators, was not equipped with the acoustics necessary to hear any politics of complaint.

One man bred to the anti-imperialist tradition, and long unhampered in its exercise, found this out when he transferred his activities from the British to the Japanese imperial sphere. Subhas Chandra Bose, intent on making use of any enemy to the *raj*, eventually was himself used by the enemy. In May 1939 he had resigned his position as president of the Indian National Congress in order to form a

"Forward Bloc." He had tired of what he called Congress's milk-and-water opposition to the *raj* and of Gandhi's increasing woolliness of mind.

Compare, he urged his readers, the inspiring articles written by Gandhi in *Young India* in 1921 with the stuff now being turned out weekly by his *Harijan*. Bose reckoned he knew better than anyone how to act in what Nehru, that other timeserver, had once called "a dissolving period of history." Dissolution was a process that could be actively assisted. The better to assist it Bose quit India before Congress had geared itself to pass its own "Quit India" resolution in August 1942. From March of that year he took to the Berlin radio, no longer rehearsing the politics of complaint but proclaiming the recipe for revolution. All Indians who worked to strengthen British hands in wartime were betraying the cause of their motherland. If by doing so they hoped to get some kind of reward, they would be disappointed, for the British were steadily losing not only their power of reward but their power to do anything at all. Bose declared that Britain and its empire were fast becoming, as the war went on, a colony of Franklin Roosevelt's American empire. He broadcast with cheerful malice a matter on which English newspapers had not chosen to comment. An old imperial privilege, extraterritorial rights, had resuscitated itself—and had done so in the home of its founder. The American government had successfully insisted that its forces based in the British Isles be given these rights, which kept its nationals beyond the jurisdiction of British courts. Egyptians and Chinese might take note.

While in Berlin, Bose arranged a celebration of India's Independence Day—a fiction invented by Nehru in 1930—on January 26, 1943. Germany's foreign minister Ribbentrop was affably present: Rashid Ali of Iraq and the mufti of Jerusalem were in hopeful attendance. Bose dismissed the accusation that he was supping with the devil. If so, he was in good company—for what was Winston Churchill, long the archenemy of Indian aspirations and of Bolshevism alike, doing in a Russian alliance? In times of dissolution and destruction the devil was certainly abroad, but one might as well make use of his presence. Bose told his listeners he had very carefully studied the struggle for liberty that the world had experienced during the last two centuries: "but I have not as yet discovered one single instance when freedom was won without outside help of some sort."[9] The devil's help would suffice, if none better could be found. The Japanese doubtless had their own plans, but so did Bose. Traveling first to Tokyo and then to Shonan (Singapore), he became president of the Indian Independence League and next formed an "Indian National Army," some 20,000 soldiers drawn mainly from the 45,000 Indian troops of the British Malayan Command that had surrendered in February 1942. Tojo gave Bose a nucleus for an empire of his own when in November 1943 he granted him the use of the Andaman and Nicobar islands in the Indian Ocean. But thereafter the tide turned against the Japanese: Bose lost what control he had had of events, and his life in 1945.

But that he had made his point is evident from a memorandum sent by the commander in chief of the forces in India, General Auchinleck, in February 1946. This was addressed to all senior British officers and marked "strictly personal and secret, not to be passed through any office." "It was no use," Auchinleck warned,

shutting one's eyes to the fact that any Indian officer worth his salt is a nationalist, though this does not mean . . . that he is necessarily anti-British. If he *is* anti-British this is as often as not due to his faulty handling and treatment by his British officer comrades.[10]

Thus clearly had a British officer, bred in all the conventional places amid all the conventional attitudes, come to accept the facts of a new situation and to be very cautious how he framed his assumptions for the future. That the imperial framework was not going to survive the second world war as it had the first was plain to the soldiers involved in it, always the most practical of empire's servants. It was not nearly so plain to empire's civilian controllers, the politicians, although the same kind of evidence had been steadily accumulating in areas wider and more complex than any soldier, however hard pressed, could know.

In August 1941 the third article of a joint statement that became known (first of all in American editorials) as the "Atlantic Charter" stated that the president of the United States and the prime minister of the United Kingdom respected "the right of all peoples to choose the form of government under which they live: and they wish to see sovereign rights and self-government restored to those who have been forcibly deprived of them." This rhetoric resounded in the ears of other peoples than those under German domination in the "enslaved Europe" on which Churchill's mind and energies were fixed, for the roll of those in the extra-European world who had at one time or another been "forcibly deprived" of control over their own societies was long indeed. Afghans could look across India to Siamese in self-congratulation, but who else was left?

If such were in reality the rights of men that the Great Powers now said they believed in and would promote, it was to be expected that they would be called upon to act according to their profession of them far more rapidly and completely than had their political predecessors during the 1920s and 1930s. The Covenant of the League of Nations was also, certainly, a high-sounding piece of idealism, but its articles had been inserted into the Treaty of Versailles, a document whose reputation for idealism never stood high even among those who wrote its terms and imposed them on the vanquished. The Wilsonian principle of self-determination had been let loose into a world whose Powers did not respect it, and the men at Geneva who made it their cause were not those to whom the responsibility for national government was ever entrusted. The imperial Powers had remained in charge of the global system of communications and thus in control of the kind of messages that had passed through it from one place to another. By 1945 their privileges had been buried under an accumulation of events which no one, privileged or other, had had time to evaluate. Although hostilities were over, incendiary bombs still seemed to be blazing in scattered outlying districts, and the call for fire brigades was already louder and more constant than the authorities, who had not yet had time to inventory their surviving equipment, wanted to hear or felt they could cope with.

Those who had "won the war," or had at any rate managed not to lose it, retained the old and ingrained assumption that victory would return to them their full rights in their imperial properties. But the people who lived within these properties had used their accustomed position of bystander to good effect while the war waged around them and among them, saying not a word about its method, direction, or result. They were now ready to heed the words their elites had long been speaking to them, ready to make leaders of men who had never been sure where they could find a following.

Taking inventory was not exhilarating. Immediately after the cease-fire in both Europe and Asia (VE Day, May 8, 1945; VJ Day, August 12), plain facts could not be ignored. In eastern Asia particularly, the Great Powers had clearly lost their claims to greatness, their pretensions to the lordship of humankind. They had been trounced and evicted by the Japanese. That the latter had finally been defeated made no difference, for they had not been forced to quit by any exercise of their enemies' conventional warrior virtues. No bayonet charge littered them lifeless on the battlefield. They vanished one morning, but still in good military order, as a result of some magic explosion that had occurred in two cities few outside Japan had heard of. White men returning to properties they had been thrown out of in humiliating circumstances could not regain the context of prestige to which they had been accustomed. The concept of prestige had in part been based on personal conduct, in part on the knowledge among the majority that somewhere behind the *tuan* was an armory filled with powerful weapons, which he could deploy where he chose. This now seemed a mirror image from another age. The image itself could not be restored. Whites were, they had proved, exactly like other people — they made mistakes, they behaved badly, they pretended things were other than they were. It was therefore implausible, to say the least, for the Powers which had for so long held the East in fee to set out to collect the fee all over again, to argue that this particular part of the world was unable to face the future, or life itself, without their tutelage — since it had managed to survive the immediate past in better shape than had Europe itself.

Implausible or not, the case was argued. Behind the image of "Free France" throughout the war had lain the assumption that a freed France would be a France arrayed in its old imperial splendor *outre-mer*. De Gaulle had declared on December 8, 1943, that when victory was attained France intended to carry out, of course in free and close association with the peoples of Indochina, "the mission with which she is charged in the Pacific."[11] For thirty years Ho Chi Minh and others had been asking what mission, and who had charged her with it? Answers now had to be given.

Rhetoric had in fact passed from the stock-in-trade of the controlled to that of the controllers. Churchill had grumbled privately when the Atlantic Charter was issued, how states that owned no overseas colonies or possessions were capable of rising to "moods of great elevation and detachment" about the affairs of states that had. But, himself an ironist, he knew that irony was no weapon against the anticolonial fervors the American government and press were then propagating, and it was with these firmly in mind that he rose in London's Guildhall in November 1942 to make his celebrated declaration that he had not become the king's first minister in order to preside over the liquidation of the British Empire. He knew too that he was surrounded by those who were not troubled—or were at least saying at the time that they were not troubled—by such a prospect. He had only to look around his own Cabinet room or along his own front bench, where sat the leaders of the Labour party, now in national coalition.

Labour had been in full cry after the enemy imperialism for a long time. *Labour and the New Social Order*, a pamphlet of 1918, had approved the continuing existence of the British Empire so long as there was within it a progressive development of "Home Rule all round." *Labour and the Nation*, issued in 1928, had highlighted the necessity for paternalist care of the native races' welfare. In *Labour's Peace Aims*, written by Labour's leader Clement Attlee at the outbreak of the war in 1939, the clear message was that Labour repudiated imperialism. But Attlee did not think that the British Commonwealth was imperialistic. He told the West African Students' Union on August 16, 1941, that indeed yes, the Atlantic Charter applied to Africa; and that "we in the Labour party have always been conscious of the wrongs done by the white races to the races with darker skins." But he agreed that the accepted colonial policy, however mysterious it might seem to others and however much it might irritate the audience that faced him (the angriest in London), was precisely what Churchill had said it was: a progress toward self-government and independence within the Commonwealth.

The British Labour party was therefore glad to hail the prospect of a future of continuing paternalism. It would have been false to its past had this not been so—since clearly the welfare of the people, whether they lived in the homeland or in distant properties belonging to it, could be neither ensured nor insured unless common-sensible and farsighted men were present to make and underwrite all the necessary arrangements. But outsiders had heard all this said before, and too often. It was now much later than these old-style paternalists thought. The world they had known was vanishing fast. What would take its place nobody could tell, but that it would need more effective guidance was plain. The time of the outsiders was arriving, a time when they would fix a new frame for the new events which would certainly pass by the old controllers into an area beyond their understanding.

Greatest and most confident of the outsiders was the United States of America. (Soviet Communism was also formidable, but confidence had never been one of its foremost attributes). The Americans' view of empire was an essential component of their own view of themselves, since their country would never have come into existence at all had empire been something to cherish and admire. Americans had never cared to understand the modern distinction that official Englishmen insisted on between empire and Commonwealth. Americans doubted the existence of any such distinction. Words were only words: all over the world the British imperial properties and institutions still stood, and in them all the old kinds of imperial business went on. That the British Right agreed with the British Left on the need to maintain this state of affairs and on the tactics necessary to do it was no surprise: it proved only that the British international posture did not now depend, had never depended, and would never depend upon the political complexion of a British government. In Washington detailed knowledge of the agglomeration of countries that now called itself the Commonwealth, but which even its member nations were chary of describing as an institution (a fact which was suspicious in itself), was confined to particular desks within the State Department, usually manned by minor officials or by those on their way to higher things.

Moreover, even if the Commonwealth was taken at the valuation of its own effusive publicists, as a place where equals associated in autonomous harmony, the place they met in was still a white man's club. On the veranda of this club—the institution notorious everywhere as the most exclusive of all the white man's contrivances—the controllers of half the world sat at their ease. Fanning themselves with their liberal principles, they looked out upon an estate tilled by innumerable native subjects, whose lives they would continue to control for the greater glory of the gross national product of the metropolis.

This straight outlook troubled one young emissary from the State Department, John Paton Davies. Writing from India in 1943, he warned that any American commitment to restore Britain as a first-class Power after the war would only lay the groundwork for a future war between revolution and counterrevolution:

Britain can be a first-class Power only as it has the Empire to exploit. Imperial rule and interests mean association with other peoples on a basis of subjugation, exploitation, privilege and force. It means a constant struggle between the urge to revolt and the compulsion to suppress.

This opinion was reinforced by what he saw in Tehran when the Allied leaders conferred there in November—December of that year. Roosevelt, Stalin, and Chiang agreed that Indochina should not be returned to the French—"but Churchill was determined that the French and the Dutch should get back their colonies."[12]

This was true. Churchill, although accustomed to complication and inured more to failure than to success during a long political life, knew that although determination had its limits, a display of it could often convince the hesitant and the less committed that only one course was available. He did not divorce strategy from politics, or the present from the future, any more than did the Soviet leaders or Chiang and his warlords. To him the fact of European empire signified order and stability in the world: indeed, it was because men had gone out from Europe to build empires that order and stability had become widespread and were now assumed, even by the most insistent nationalist, to be necessary to the conduct of affairs. To keep what had been won, to hold fast to a position of power, had been his and his country's dominant and instinctive reason for going to war, however reluctantly, against the Germans in 1939, the Italians in 1940, and the Japanese in 1941. As he was to write to Anthony Eden on December 31, 1944, "'Hands off the British Empire!' is our motto, and it must not be weakened or smirched to please sob-stuff merchants at home or foreigners of any hue."[13] It would therefore be the duty of the victorious, if they were going to enjoy something more than an armistice, to restore the old imperial order. The future must assume the shape of the past, for only by so doing could it take care of the past and preserve its heritage. The agenda would be complex, the amount of work needed to carry it out prodigious. But when victory was gained, the last thing sensible people needed to have set before them at a peace conference was a clean sheet. For this was an idealistic image, to the point of foolishness. Any kind of modish notion (like a corollary to Woodrow Wilson's theory of self-determination, or some global extension of Franklin Roosevelt's domestic panaceas of a New Deal or a Works Program Administration) might be dictated by enthusiasts who had long been incubating their contrasting plans for utopia—sketching these out, perhaps, in a café in Paris in the 1930s, behind the bars of a Senegal jail, or at the counters of a Dutch bank in Indonesia.

This was certainly the Eurocentric view, the view from the old world. It had also become an old-time view. That the world, the time, and the view were all changing, an old inhabitant like Churchill knew well enough. He coped with the present—and splendidly so—a time of crisis. He had no great interest in the future, which he did not expect to enjoy. Even at the height of his power and fame he knew that courage, like other gifts, might be overtaken. In 1950 he set down, in the third volume of his highly subjective *History of the Second World War*, the relief he felt on December 7, 1941, when he heard that the United States of America had, at gunpoint, entered the war: "So we had won after all!"

Relief, a transient emotion, is usually succeeded by feelings more complex. It was so here. The exercise of European power, the accustomed practices of European imperialism, the belief in a natural Eurocentricity to international affairs, now had to live at risk from a take-over by the republic in the West. By November 1943 the American domination of what both partners termed the Anglo-American partnership had become definite, and the success of the working wartime alliance depended on the fact that the British government *"had* to agree with the Americans, and, realizing their position, yielded gracefully." This was not publicized outside government circles; but Churchill, as William H. McNeill has pointed out,

recognized that if he insisted upon a course of action distasteful to the United States' government, the Americans could always afford, however reluctantly, to quarrel openly with him, and then bring economic pressure to bear against him which no British government could stand. Britain could afford no such luxury, and had always therefore to stop short of any action that promised to alienate American sympathy and support.[14]

If these were indeed the facts of life, Americans saw little risk in their perpetuation. There was nothing for anyone to fear in a future that Americans would be on hand to direct. They now understood that their absence from the European scene in the interwar years had proved ultimately dangerous both to the world at large and to their own national security. They would not run that risk again. From Europe and the larger world that was, at least for the moment, Europe's patrimony, they would no longer be absent. Since their very presence would be a reassurance, they, as liberators, expected to be welcomed. They saw nothing of imperialism in this, only an assertion of common sense. They knew imperialism for what it was: an open conspiracy among the powerful to deprive people the world over of their inalienable right to be free. Everyone could now see what havoc this conspiracy had deservedly wrought, what disasters it had predictably led to. Of course a better route existed, toward a better destiny. But this was not a new route—Americans had already traveled it. They had only to encourage others down the same road.

These assumptions were the natural product of American history. Americans had been preserved, as Dean Acheson later expressed it, in "a cocoon of history."[15] They had grown up within a unique context of order and stability, neither of which had been dependent on direct control by a powerful central government. They had made their own remarkable progress at their own speed. The expansion of the United States from sea to shining sea had in fact been protected more by the blessing of geography than by the spell of the Monroe Doctrine (to which, for example, Napoleon III in Mexico had paid no attention whatever) and more by the preponderance of the British Navy in international waters than by either. The success of this expansion had been welcomed by everyone because it formed yet one more element within the framework of the world order that had been established in the nineteenth century. The contrast with Latin America had only to be drawn to make this point even sharper. Latin Americans appeared to have preserved themselves by accident. Their history had wrapped them in no cocoon. Instead, it had taken the form of a melodrama, punctuated by a series of financial collapses and constitutional and social upheavals which nobody in Europe's officialdom had ever bothered to count.

As a result an entire hemisphere had remained outside the context of world order and world consciousness, living a life nobody knew about. The Great Powers did what they wanted to do without bothering what the best minds in Rio or Lima or Buenos Aires thought about it.

But the northern republic was reckoned to have earned its passage and gained its place among the just — among the industrious, the civilized, and the commercially sound. And, of course, the uncolored.

The citizens of the republic were well aware of the condescension with which Europeans looked upon them and were happy to condescend toward Europe in their turn. Americans, feeling free in both senses of the word — free from outside interference and free to build their society as they wanted it — expressed their sense of superiority by having as little as possible to do with the politics of Europe, and they did not object when European diplomats rated a posting at Washington as much on a par with one to Brussels or Madrid. A staple of American editorials was delivering homilies to erring foreign governments, homilies which none but American citizens, and perhaps not too many of them, read. President Theodore Roosevelt developed some wistful ideas that the United States, or more accurately himself, should play a larger part on the world stage, but Americans of his time were in no mood to indulge him. In 1917-18 the American government became the associate, but not the formal ally, of those fighting against the Kaiser's Germany. The experience did not change the mood, as Woodrow Wilson found out when Americans refused to rise to the spectacular opportunity he gave them in 1919 and 1920 to bring their weight to bear upon the European center of events.

But an equally spectacular opportunity, given them by the Japanese one Sunday morning, Pacific time, in the fifth decade of the century, could not be refused. Americans were brought into Europe's antifascist struggle, to their own enormous surprise — a fact Europeans would be slow to forget, since in their own opinion it made the attitudes struck on America's moral platform (to which their attention was later so often directed) something less than true and the platform itself less than firm. Churchill, although somewhat bemused by Roosevelt, assessed Americans in general as spectators who contrived not only to avoid seeing most of the game but also to misunderstand the part of it they did see. He could not, for instance, ever find either sense in or point to the official American attitude toward Chiang Kai-shek, because this attitude presupposed three things that were simply not true: that Chiang was a statesman, that China was a Great Power, and that the view from Chungking was as important in the present and as significant for the future as that from Washington, London, or Moscow.

But this was yet another case in which Churchill could only record his view and see it shelved by his confident allies.

American politicians naturally objected to such conservative wrongheadedness in someone whom otherwise they were very ready to admire. They allowed that Churchill was, perhaps, entitled to his eccentricities, since he was so obviously not a common man. But what was not common should not be any longer valid. China held the place it did in American thinking because it was marked as a favored base from which the desired future should begin. It was the place where a Chinese democracy, guided by Americans, would bring to Asia, the continent so long held as a fief by predatory imperialists, every possibility of progress and happiness for six hundred million people. It was more symbol than place. The incoming dynasty, the one that would govern the future, would be formed by common people everywhere. Imperialists like Churchill (if indeed there were any such left) would find themselves stragglers, without a base of operations or even a place to stand. Common men, in whom true wisdom reposed, had a natural distrust of power. They would never look on its politics as a great game and would never stoop to play it. The twentieth century, even after five decades, had not yet properly begun: but when it did begin, in the opinion of Roosevelt's vice-president Henry A. Wallace,

No nation would have a God-given right to exploit other nations. Older nations will have the privilege to help younger nations to get started on the path to industrialization, but there must be neither military nor economic imperialism. The methods of the nineteenth century will not work in the people's century which is now about to begin. . . . There can be no privileged people.[16]

How such a condition of affairs could come to pass without the industrial elders paternalizing in the old style over their agrarian juniors, and how long Powers so privileged would be able to continue exercising their privileges without arousing all the old-style

objections to them among the unprivileged, Wallace did not state—
probably because he did not know, never having had to think the
matter through.

In wartime public men habitually see the future *couleur de rose*
in order to elevate the public morale. Political rhetoric expands its
own empire, whose most exotic colonies have always lain in tropics
where the hot airs blow. Tomorrow is not just another day, it belongs to another era. Nobody either has time to think anything
through or wants to do so, since the fate of everything, today as
well as tomorrow, is in the hands of military men whose success is
going to depend on their capacity to exploit the mistakes made by
their professional colleagues "on the other side of the hill" and on
the chance (a fair one) that the latter will make more mistakes than
themselves. Neutral civilians free to traverse both sides of the hill
are likely to find what they went to look for on either slope. In 1940
the Republicans' presidential candidate, Wendell Willkie, on his return from a very rapid world tour reported to American audiences
that he had found the "dread of imperialism" everywhere. He defined freedom as "the orderly but scheduled abolition of the colonial
system."[17] He spoke for the accepted American view of any system
but its own: for even an orderly abolition presupposes the presence
of someone who has both the freedom and the authority to organize
its schedule. President Franklin D. Roosevelt himself, professional
friend of freedom, had long-standing anticolonial views. He had declared in 1928 that "there never has been, there isn't now, and there
never will be, any race of people fit to serve as masters of their fellow men."[18] As masters, no: but perhaps there was still a place for
marshals and sheriffs. Some men might have to be put on duty to
look after their fellows. Although he had earlier—during a negotiation with Britain for U.S. facilities at Caribbean bases in return for
overage destroyers—refused to consider taking on any American
responsibility for the "three million headaches" that inhabited the
British Caribbean islands, Roosevelt allowed in 1941 that there were
"many minor children among the peoples of the world who need
trustees in their relations with other nations and peoples."[19]

Neither of these free-floating thoughts had ever been unknown
in London and Paris.

Roosevelt's picture of the future was airy to a degree, but it was not wrought from heedlessness or lack of principle. Roosevelt disliked his own present. He had done much to alter its conditions in his present-day America: now, caught up in a power struggle not of American devising, he saw a chance to preside over new ways for the world in a time beyond. Sincerely believing in both the sense and the morality of Wilson's doctrine of self-determination, he saw no point in making plans for the continuance of a world governed through the interlocking diplomacies of the Great Powers. Such a world would go on behaving as it had always behaved, which was badly. It would lurch into conflict again one day, since all it knew was self-interest. Some nervous hand would always find some convenient trigger on some inconvenient frontier. Such a world had to go. The virtue of this present war was that it gave people of goodwill the opportunity to clean all of this world up in order to throw most of it out. Self-determination must therefore wait until the war was over. And *then* would be the time to bring out the plans; for not only Nazi Germany and imperial Japan, but also the context of rivalry and ambition that had produced both, would have unconditionally surrendered.

In thinking along these lines Roosevelt, far abler and much more knowledgeable about the actual habits of the world the United States lived in than his predecessor Wilson, his adjutant Wallace, or his opponent Willkie, fairly represented a national American judgment, even though he realized better than most how difficult it would be to translate such ideas into terms other peoples would understand. The American confidence that the four freedoms listed in the Atlantic Charter might be applied to all humanity could not cross the Atlantic without running a blockade. One of humanity's homes was in the Soviet Union. But the Russian people had not been heard from in centuries. Moscow dealt as little in idealism as St. Petersburg had done, and accordingly its official judgment on the implications of the charter was taken on the same pragmatic level as Churchill's, as one of its pronouncements shows: "Practical application of these principles will necessarily adapt itself to the circumstances, needs, and historic peculiarities of particular countries."[20] It would indeed. From such a level anyone seeking to view tomorrow's sunlight playing upon broad uplands was bound to be disappointed. But disappointment had no part in the American forecast:

disappointment and cynicism were two sides of the same coin, and it was not a coin in American currency. Americans saw themselves as fighting to put right a world that others had set wrong, even if a great many who were drafted resented having to spend "the best years of our lives" doing it. They thought of their comrades-in-arms, when they thought of them at all, as foreigners who had not had the luck (or the sense) to be born and brought up in the free air of the western hemisphere—as misguided in the present and incompetent to deal with the future since their judgment was inevitably blighted by the errors of their past. Of course such people thought freedom divisible and liberation ominous. But the truth was, obviously, that the imperial power which the Atlantic Charter pilloried was as much an enemy as the past itself. Indeed, it was the same enemy. Territorial empires were the products and the symbols of so many delusions of grandeur. Because they were built on the proscription of freedom as a principle, they must themselves be proscribed.

That there were other kinds of empire available to the powerful was a fact that lay concealed, at least from those determined not to look for it.

No hypocrisy imposed itself on the American thinking on these themes. Regarding the United States's interests in Latin America and China, no one in government or in missionary circles had ever believed that American influence, when put to work, had done anything but make life better for its recipients. That a majority of British, French, and Dutch officials had thought exactly the same thing, also without hypocrisy, about what they did in their own empires was beside the point to critics who began from their own special point—there was no way power could be used beneficently by the self-interested, and if undeniable benefits did result, these were accidental by-products of a system otherwise designed.

True, the doings of the United States in Latin America had posed a dilemma of definition for Washington. The first four decades of the century had seen an "almost constant battle over the terms on which inter-American relations were to be conducted," as David Green remarked in his evocatively titled work, *The Containment of Latin America* (1971).[21] This battle had been waged internally in U.S. government circles, not bilaterally with Latin American governments. There had never been any dilemma of purpose. It was right (who could deny it?) to open doors and let in light. Since the turn of the century, the entire doctrine of the Open Door had centered on the principle that commercial competition was normal and healthy, something in the clear interests of Americans and Peruvian *peons* and Chinese peasants alike. In the presence of this competition, stimulated by its impulses, deprived people would come to live and learn to love ordered and happy lives; in the process they would become the kind of neighbors and customers that sensible people — that is to say, democratic westerners — would want to have.

This set of assumptions, long treasured by Americans as self-evidently just and as part of their heritage but never closely analyzed by them and never clearly brought to international attention, was in the era following the second world war to be imposed upon events and in time would build a new framework around them.

The destiny that is manifest to many is never obvious to all. Americans were to discover in their turn what the nationals of other Great Powers, happy also in the possession of unquestionable assumptions, had found out before them: that everything could be questioned in societies where the dissident were not confined in labor camps and that there were others who did not think as they did and saw no reason to do so. European governments had lived too long in an imperial context not to know imperial power when they saw it. Whether it had a hard center to it in the Soviet style or a soft center to it in the American style was beside the point. The physical powers of persuasion available to both sides in the age of atomic power were recognized as more or less equal. Of course it would matter very much to the two protagonists, if they became antagonists, who owned the more and who the less; but it would be only an academic question to those who got in the way of any resolution to this problem. At the far side of this kind of persuasion lay destruction. All of the European countries found themselves in this predicament after 1947, because they were beleaguered in no-man's-land between the front lines of a "Cold War" between the United States and the Soviet Union, a war about whose strategy and outcome they would have little to say — assuming they would survive in sufficient numbers to say it.

It was this general, disseminated sense of grievance that underlay the anti-Americanism which accompanied the growing obtrusiveness of American power, growing to the point where it became a fact of everyone's life. One element in the grievance was a recognition that Europe now seemed to have become relegated to a colonial future —a recognition so bitter for France's General de Gaulle that he determined on principle that France should take a political line athwart that of the United States whenever it was practicable to do so. European imperialists had long known that it was a sense of powerlessness which animated and accounted for all the twentieth-century upheavals in their satellite territories. That the European states, reckoning themselves the peer group of the United States and the superiors of the Soviet Union, should now experience the same impotence was an irony only the entirely detached could appreciate —and perhaps only the Irish and the Swiss, whose security had always been other people's responsibility, could bring themselves to so rarefied a point of detachment (not that they tried). The Powers of Europe did not want to lose control of their future to the greatest of innocents abroad, to an imperialist state which did not even know it was one, which had no sense of history and no other experience of the world to draw upon, and which seemed to think that when every troublesome issue had been put in the form of a "question," the answer to that question would present itself.

They did not want these things—but, as their own colonial subjects had done, they learned to live with them. For the majority of European peoples the alternative leadership of the Soviet Union was not an alternative anyone would want. For this reason anti-Americanism in the third quarter of the century never became a solid political movement in Europe. Nonetheless, a pervasive attitude developed which prevented many American plans from working out and sometimes caused them to die on an agenda: President Lyndon Johnson's complaint to Prime Minister Harold Wilson in 1968, that all he wanted from the British in Vietnam was a battalion of the Black Watch, expressed a long-standing exasperation in Washington that America's so-called friends were not really friendly to America's hopes or ready—as they preferred to put it—to pull America's chestnuts out of what they thought an American fire.

The attitude was based on the judgment, sometimes reached with prejudice but sometimes well considered, that these powerful strangers, bounding onto the international stage and protesting their goodwill—a claim which was, save in the sourest of ideological circles, generally accepted—were incapable of taking the next but essential step of thinking through the consequences of their innocence. To suspect Russia, under whatever type of tyrannous government, of imperialist plans that were simultaneously sinister and clumsy was no new exercise for Europeans: it was on the Americans, with whom there was little European tradition of active diplomacy, that suspicion centered. The fear that the Americans, confronting enemies —first the Russians, then the Chinese, perhaps on a dark day both— whom they did not really understand and who in turn were equally bewildered by them, would do the wrong thing for what they judged to be the right reasons was very real in the chancelleries of postwar Europe. Men in these corridors had long since worked out a variety of ways to deal with duplicity: they had no sure equipment with which to cope with ignorance. They found out that Americans learned the rules of the imperial game very fast—yet, while they were learning they still had the time to correct all mistakes except the cataclysmal. This was a crucial point. The United States could afford to write off to experience what European governments dared not experience. The latter had no "risk capital" to invest and no time to play with.

This European distrust had its own history, as do all such assumptions. Europeans' ignorance of American ideas and methods was extensive. They knew something about the American sense of mission but not much about what missionaries so indoctrinated might want to do. They had not been taught that optimism was a natural right, and they neither understood nor welcomed the American faith that any future worth having should follow, for everyone's sake, an American example. The American attributes they knew best were those that had for so long and so unflatteringly been portrayed in Hollywood movies—few of which had ever spent time or footage on anything other than romance or violence or mixtures of both. As a result, the foreign image of American action was formed of peculiar materials, including the fear that the instinctive attitudes of the late Theodore Roosevelt or of the live Douglas MacArthur would be briskly processed into policy, and that gung-ho marines with command-decision powers would decide the immediate course of events—and, by this decision, the fate of mankind itself. A fatal button would be pressed because at the time it seemed to some manly mind the manliest thing to do. (The movie *Dr. Strangelove* [1964], describing such events, was an enormous success in Europe.) This nightmare alternated with one deriving from the other camp, in which the sound of Russian tanks, starting up by the Oder before a march to the Bay of Biscay, came clanking into everyone's dreams.

These were the pessimisms to which Western Europe had to accustom itself, from the time of the inauguration of the North Atlantic Treaty Organization in 1949 until the Soviet-American confrontation in the Cuban missile crisis of October 1962. Trip-wire politics made everyone nervous. Europeans realized that the context of their security depended on someone else's steadiness of nerve. But nobody knew how steady were Washington's nerves on a given weekend; and when a doubt existed on so great a scale, nobody wanted to give anyone else the benefit of it. The remark of an apocryphal Pole, that the fate of Europe now lay in the hands of the cowboy and the *moujik*, was passed around in the 1950s not only at café tables and cocktail parties but down chancellery corridors as well.

Successive American administrations passed from surprise to annoyance at this reaction to their benevolent intentions. The trip wires held: Berlin stayed a crisis point but one that never came to climax. Sensible men continued to outnumber fools, and the resolute the nervous. Americans therefore came to believe that jealousy of their superior technological skills lay at the root of the hostility —a jealousy which was meanly but effectively summarized in the jibes current for years about "coca-colonization" and whatever other habits the youth of Europe had picked up which their parents could attribute to foreign influences. Americans did not think anyone had earned the right to this degree of petty malice. The most recent history of the Europeans proved that for all their boasted insight into the essence of everything, they had not been able to prevent much of their vaunted civilization from collapsing in ruins around them. Their present position, their physical and economic security, depended almost entirely on American money and American troops. Although nobody much liked this situation, it had to be endured, for Europe needed the United States and the United States needed Europe. Since this was the reality, why quarrel about it?

The common sense of this indeed appealed to the majority (but never, ever, to the minority) of those involved. Moreover, since American politicians had never expected their European counterparts to understand accurately what they did, they were prepared, if not pleased, to tolerate misrepresentation. One price to be paid for "liberating" Europeans, for watching them "recover," was to have to hear their nonsense. They were free to take up their untenable positions, since these, too, would be protected by American troops.

But such positions were not intended to be so readily available, with the same impunity, to American citizens.

Imperialism had always had its enemies and on the whole had known how to cope with them. A Great Power that denies any capacity for or intention of imperializing, being itself an anomaly, must find its policies in a condition of confusion, and opponents to them hard to classify, since even treason cannot be defined until everyone is clear what exactly is being betrayed. After the late 1940s Americans were in fact doing precisely what Europeans supposed them to be doing: entering a new world and establishing their presence there. Amid its complexities American statesmen, all men of goodwill, found their feet—but they were also politicians who on their home ground had to conjure up simple explanations in order to convince a majority of their party supporters that they were putting their feet in the right places, and that in the process they had not been contaminated. In a new country the sensible pioneer is one who reckons on the appearance at any time, in any guise, of a possible enemy. The American view of Communism as a worldwide conspiracy encouraged the belief that some of its conspirators might well have infiltrated the United States and that the American way of life in all its decencies was threatened far less by foreign soldiers on a distant front than by subversive ideas within its frontiers, ideas which might burrow their way into American society along its lines of least resistance. Not all of these could be discovered even by the most vigilant. But these vigilant were quick to guess who was most likely to keep a map of them. Who but the unorthodox of all sorts and persuasions? These were people more likely indeed to be found outside the ranks of the American Communist party than within them, since identifiable Communists lost most of their menace simply by being identifiable and therefore orthodox enough in their own way.

When in Moscow during 1942, Roosevelt's traveling confidant Harry Hopkins had told Molotov, perhaps with some malice aforethought, that the Communist party in the United States was made up of "disgruntled, frustrated, ineffectual, and vociferous people — including a comparatively high proportion of distinctly unsympathetic Jews."[22] It was a categorization with a future. Ten years later, when the Soviet Union had deserted the wartime causes of the United Nations and had revealed itself in what were now seen to be its true colors, a large body of public opinion in the United States was eager to believe that there were still many such people around, as unsympathetic as ever but of course no longer nameable as Jews, since anti-Semitism had become taboo; and that if these were not actual card-carrying members of the Communist party, they were at least Commies and pinkos, "soft on Communism" because of a lack of both character and common sense if for no more sinister reason, and fellow-traveling with the party along a line laid down in Moscow, a line that ran directly athwart the interests of the United States.

Opinions hardened, sometimes to the point of petrifaction, on both sides of this line, as the Cold War and its camps were established. The diplomacy of this war and the politics of its establishments relate to the theme of this book only insofar as they helped create a context in which the extant, formalized, territorial styles of imperialism dissolved and new styles took over. That the war should have developed a conspiratorial context of its own on the side — including questions like "Who was supposed to have duped whom?" "Who lost China to the Communists in 1949?" "Who chose Korea in 1950 as the first battleground for a trial at arms?" and "How many names were in fact on Senator Joseph McCarthy's notorious 'list' of Communists in Washington's high places?" — was an explicable outcome of a kind of situation in which people start up suddenly to look for their enemies in the darkness, only to fall over many things, including their own feet, in the process. The record of these collisions belongs to the domestic history of the United States in the 1950s. The most significant thing about them is that although they complicated this history, they did not unbalance it. A decade after "McCarthyism" had been discredited — a process which was not, however, accompanied by a general absolution of everyone it had slandered—"middle" Americans who wanted to believe that the president of the United States, any president of the United States, knew what was likely to happen in world affairs since he had so much more information about them than they had were beginning to allow that a "Left" not in the pay of the Kremlin might exist after all. But no sooner had at least some of the middle classes done so than they were assailed by the flanking attacks of a "New Left" which was neither the product of mild disagreement nor the importation of sinister foreign notions but anti-American of its own accord, calling down anathema not only on American foreign policy but on the capitalist establishment of which this policy was a part, on the American way of life itself.

The members of this group—which could not develop any close-knit organization—were mostly patriots. They were not, however, patriots of the present-day United States, whose draft cards they burned and whose police they called pigs. They "belonged" in spirit to a United States that would exist if the wrongheads and exploiters on the far side of thirty ever allowed it to come into being. This would be a "greener" and certainly a cleaner America, with all its pollutions gone forever. It would be an America true to its idealist principle, pried at last from the grip of parents who were impossible to live with, since they believed in the necessity of bankers, the Central Intelligence Agency, political parties, and all such self-serving, timeserving institutions. It would be an America in which people "did their own thing" in fraternities, whose heroes ranged from Trotsky to Che Guevara, from Herbert Marcuse to Buddha, Krishna, and Stokely Carmichael. That would be an America in which civil rights were not embalmed in documents displayed in the glass cases of imposing Washington temples honoring the past, but were alive and well and available from day to day to all the citizens of the republic, wherever bred, of whatever color. From this republic to an eager world beyond, waiting for such a doctrine, would be a natural step. There was nothing intrinsically wrong in the idea of a manifest destiny; but it must be ensured that America head toward a destiny far other than that which its out-of-date, money-motivated imperialism had wrought for it and which in time would bring it to grief, as other powerful and heedless empires had, deservedly, come to grief.

Accordingly, in the late 1960s, as American colleges doubled their enrollment with young men who preferred not to be drafted into the armed forces, a quarrel developed in American society unlike any that had ever resulted from similar situations in Europe. Dissidence had an international record. Every European government could refer to a long history of political dissension: the police files had always been filled. In every generation some people had made it their business, and sometimes their career, to inveigh against crime in high places, to expose villainy among the powerful. But even as these radicals made such charges, they could not claim they had been betrayed—since to be betrayed is first to have given one's trust. Far from doing this, they had readily assumed that men in power would forever be up to such mischief. That was what power did to men, that was what they wanted power *for*. That all power tended to corrupt became the liberal maxim of an entire era. The other part of the maxim, that absolute power corrupted absolutely, radicals were ready to accept, without once imagining it could ever apply to them. Their general reaction to power as they saw it, always from below, was that the authorities of the day had outguessed and outgunned them. Their consequent resolve was to do some better guessing and get some better guns.

In America radical critics mounted a different kind of attack, starting from different premises. Their position was that no discovery of villainy ought to be possible, because in the American system no villainy ought to exist. But since wrongdoing was unthinkable, what was to be thought when it was found out? Not simply, as a European might have supposed, that bad or foolish men had been exposed in the midst of their nefarious folly—but that something had gone wrong with the American system itself. This thought was so startling and shocking that by the late 1960s every confrontation had taken the form of a tableau in which the just faced the unjust, who in turn exposed the injustice they saw on the other side—and, as patriot railed at patriot and the young at the old (those age thirty and over), nobody amid the uproar heard anyone else say anything of value.

The charges thrown about thus became equally stereotyped, whether they concerned duplicity in foreign policy or innocence in foreign policy, the playing of power games or incompetence in the playing of them, or governmental support (or lack of it) for the fascist regimes of unknowable countries in the name of democracy or of the Free World or of national security or of a combination of all these. Such actions could be defined, every one of them, as un-American activities, from which no one could come out with clean hands. America's domestic politics had long known and respected a tradition of exposé, sometimes called muckraking. There had been many occasions when eager reformers had in everybody's best interests unmasked and confronted crooks and thrusters in public life in order to pillory them as enemies of society, betrayers of all that was best in the American way. But to be forced to indict America's international stance as an extension of the same type of aberrant conduct dismayed and embittered those who felt this compulsion as severely as it did those who indignantly denied that any such culpability existed. George Washington's warning against foreign entanglements, one which had never been forgotten, was once more reissued, with the emphasis placed not on the inconveniences or the dangers they entailed but on the immorality they conferred. One answer made to this particular charge—that it might be both possible and right to export to the outside world Washington's personal ideal of a standard to which the wise and honest might repair—did not deflect it.

Thus American power in the postwar world was asserted to a growing accompaniment of discordant chorus. To take one example: in 1969 the American student editors of Fidel Castro's speeches were able to remark without fear of contradiction from their (possibly not many) readers that the role of such noted liberals as John F. Kennedy, Adlai Stevenson, and Arthur Schlesinger, Jr. in the United States's attempt to crush the Cuban Revolution at the Bay of Pigs in April 1961 had pushed more and more students out of the liberal wing of democratic politics into protest politics "and finally to the point where they saw the American government as the principal enemy of the majority of the people in the world"—this, in an introductory essay which concluded with the rusty invocation "Power to the People!"[23] Such a paean of dispraise, if it was heard at all, must have served only to confirm the opinion in Kansas City, or wherever else middle America amid all its silences was presumed to live, that no "real" Americans would spend their time poring over the speeches of a declared enemy of the United States in the first place and that nothing good could come of traducing the flag and mocking the ideals of the American republic.

Less noisy but more effective were the charges brought by the academics and publicists who, having grown up during the earlier stages of the Cold War, stopped in their bivouacs to make new assessments of it.

These all invoked the name of empire and discovered the practices of imperialism.

In the bibliography to his book *The Cold War in Asia* (1974), the Japanese-American scholar Akira Iriye remarked that United States's expansionism, imperialism, and colonialism had become subject to searching scrutiny.[24] Few would have thought these topics could be scrutinized, since they had not been supposed to exist, only a dozen years previously. Another detached outsider, an Iranian, decided that this exercise was now possible because in the major cities of the capitalist nations a revolutionary avant-garde was using the leisure made available to it by the welfare state to study its environment: namely, the capitalist consumer society.[25] The very detachment of these sharp diagnoses effectively underlined both the emotional commitment and the intellectual energy of the historians of their own times who began to produce their revisionist views of the context that had bred them. They elected different villains to star in the same piece, but they agreed that the "real" conflict, the one being waged behind the ideological facades of freedom versus tyranny, sprang from the expansionist requirements of American capitalism. They brushed aside the consensus view, popular since 1945, that the United States had been reluctantly driven by the pressure of outside events to assume a position of world power. (Imperialism might be shy and retiring, but it was never reluctant.) Historians followed the lead of Professor William Appleman Williams, who followed the race that had been run back to a particular starting pistol, the one whose loud report J. A. Hobson had been there to hear and record—to the "Open Door" Notes on China issued by Secretary Hay in 1899 and 1900. The policy governing these, when combined with the ideology of an industrial manifest destiny, had become the history of American foreign relations thereafter.[26]

This thesis was regularly to be drawn upon by those who saw

American foreign policy as perpetually, because inevitably, money motivated, intent on fashioning a framework for self-interested action. This framework would forever include American colonialism —a term used to describe the system that promoted monopolistically regulated trade and investment at higher rates of profit than those obtaining in the home economy. Foreign sponsors for this view were easily found. Fidel Castro was certainly one. Competition, he observed, was the name given to the fight among producers of the same product for a limited market. The fight did not aim to feed the needy, but to feed those who were able to buy, and no aid was given to anyone who did not so qualify. It was no wonder, then, that the promoters of such policies, "with their sleepless merchants' and usurers' minds, naturally believed that revolutions could be bought, sold, rented, loaned, exported and imported like some piece of merchandise." Castro, bred an academic, produced this and other diagnoses in tones of reason, as one who spoke a truth self-evident, when he addressed the United Nations's General Assembly in New York on September 26, 1966. If a being from another planet arrived there, he told it, a being who had read neither Karl Marx's Communist Manifesto nor the cables of the United Press, the Associated Press, nor any other monopolistic publications; and if he were to ask how the world had been divided, and saw on a map that the wealth of the world was shared among the monopolies of four or five countries, he would assuredly say without further consideration that the wealth of the world had been badly distributed, that the world was being exploited.[27] Here once more was the colonial assertion, the accusation of robbery, the voice from below, this time raised in a forum founded on the premise that all the nations should have an equal say in ordering their own and the world's affairs.

It was, however, a forum which had had ample time since its foundation in 1945 to discover that things on paper had not much to do with things in practice. Many hearing Castro agreed with him that "stabilization" was a technical term meaning American control, and that the entire doctrine of the containment of Communism was still, and would remain, an imperialist doctrine.

And certainly one of its most easily recognizable features, in the eyes of the same critics foreign and domestic, was the presence of the long-publicized and long-sought-for Open Door.

American hopes for the universal benefit to be found beyond this portal had indeed been consistent since the turn of the century. But a policy that other Powers had been ready to accept as serviceable in the special circumstances of China was not one they reckoned necessary in areas closer to home, traditionally in their orbit, areas where an extant pattern of control could be easily extended. The American dismay expressed when the British and the French signed their joint Iraqi oil deal at San Remo in 1920 has already been noted. What the United States wanted, and in fact supposed it deserved, (as a new associate to the victorious Allied cause), was to be made welcome in places of commercial privilege that the imperialist enterprise of others had already exploited. It was asking too much—and it was refused, more or less politely but certainly firmly. "In practice," according to a recent (1975) official study of this phase of America's oil policies, "the Open Door policy was merely a convenient label for a policy which was essentially aimed at expanding American interests abroad."[28] But pragmatism of this order was a late growth: such crisp candor, a product of greater experience in a school of harder knocks, would have shocked opinion in the 1920s, however willingly oilmen everywhere would have privately agreed with its common sense.

In the meantime, Americans continued to find their enterprise confronted with closed doors. The rebuff in the Middle East was repeated in Indonesia, also in 1920, when the Anglo-Dutch petroleum consortium Royal Dutch Shell granted itself the monopoly of whatever the Jambi field in Sumatra would produce. This was, as another, less pragmatically inclined historian of America's international oil epic observed, "a clear violation of the Open Door"[29] —a judgment which would have surprised nobody at the time. But Americans never lacked money, perseverance, and practicality; and their pattern of preference was also set in 1920, when the United States government broke off diplomatic relations with President Obregon's regime in Mexico until he agreed to give pledges of security for foreign investments. By 1928 American companies had gained a footing in both Iraq—by the Red Line Agreement, on a 23.75 percent basis—and Indonesia; by 1934 they had also imposed themselves on Kuwait in the Persian Gulf and had begun the Aramco operation in Saudi Arabia. Nevertheless, by 1943, 81 percent of

Middle East oil was still controlled by British companies, only 14 percent by American.

During World War II, however, began the "imperial presidency" which later critics were to bemoan, possibly without counting all the benefits it brought. Also in 1943, on February 18, Roosevelt declared that the defense of Saudi Arabia was vital to that of the United States and thereafter channeled Lend-Lease funds directly to this country and its king, bypassing the existing British pipeline for these funds and at the same time opening up to Aramco and other American enterprises the door that they wanted. Harold Ickes, Roosevelt's secretary of the Interior, did not fear the name imperialism: he urged the President that here was a matter for government, not for private enterprise alone. "Any realistic appraisal of the problem of acquiring foreign petroleum reserves for the benefit of the United States compels the conclusion that American participation must be of a sovereign character compatible with the strength of the competitive forces encountered in any such undertaking."[30] But in this opinion he was ahead of his time: neither American oil companies nor the United States Congress wanted to see or were willing to approve the entry of the United States government into the field of big business on its own account, swamping all competition and carrying away the system of free enterprise as it did so. There were some doors, those to boardrooms, which the men behind them fervently wished to keep forever shut.

But the Saudi Arabian door opened onto vistas other than those that led to oil fields. After the war, American confidence in the strength of American capitalism grew strong enough to encourage it to dispense with its previously protected trading and investment areas. It was therefore able to impose an Open Door policy on others, by breaking into the areas wherein these others had established their own forms of imperial protection: Britain, for example, was in no position to resist American economic pressure of any kind, as the abolition of the Red Line Agreement in November 1948 forcibly illustrated. The General Agreement on Tariffs and Trade (G.A.T.T.), signed in 1946, was accordingly the first postwar milestone on what was to be a long road, since it ensured that there would be no increase in tariff discrimination. It was a policy later heavily underlined in the European Recovery Program (Marshall Aid), which required as a condition of aid the "liberalization" of restrictions on dollar imports. American participation had indeed obtained the "sovereign character" Ickes had desired for it. By 1960 manufacturing output in the capitalist world would rise to nearly three times its prewar level.[31]

That the United States, leader of the Free World, was obtaining a handsome dividend from the part of the world it was determined to aid and protect became a major theme in the works of the American Left, and some of their ideas if not all of their venom had worked their way into the minds of many. Theodore White noted sadly in his *The Making of the President, 1968* how the view of America held by the bright young men and women who came out that year for Eugene McCarthy in New Hampshire and Wisconsin "was warped by a new mythology. They distrusted America, saw only its evil."[32] On the Left many of the charges centered on America's new imperial role: one of its members exclaimed that the imperialism let loose in the past by the British and the French, "for all its barbarous atrocities," had at least been compelled to preserve the peoples it sought to exploit. Even when it could no longer maintain its domination through military means, it had found ways of accommodating itself to the changing situation. But "American imperialism, insofar as it derives from the implacable need to justify its own myths, can make no such accommodation."[33] In America, always a myth-ridden country, people would never learn better ways while they continued to follow charismatic leaders, mythmakers who were convinced of their own rectitude: it was imperialism's particular sheep's clothing, under which it went about its usual wolfish business. Sometimes, however, according to these critics, the wolf peered out — as when in December 1962 President Kennedy told the Economic Club in New York that foreign aid was a method by which the United States maintained a position of influence and control around the world, thus sustaining a great many countries that "would otherwise definitely collapse, or pass into the Communist bloc." But what seemed clear to all in 1962 had blurred considerably by 1972. This image of the good man bearing a bag of gold was reduced in stature, and his purposes were closely scanned. Aid policies, said the author of a book whose title *From Aid to Recolonization* made his particular purposes plain, had gradually revealed themselves "as the most valuable innovation in the great contemporary mutation from costly colonial presence to more profitable indirect control."[34] The multinational corporation was one channel for this innovation, an enemy the more sinister because the macroscopic webs it spun could so often be found only with microscopes.

Thus the argument swung back and forth, while tempers kept time with its pendulum. One man's implacable needs, another man's contemporary mutations, were still another man's gibberish, and were likely to remain so as long as power was there to be analyzed by those who enjoyed the freedom to analyze it. Actually, in all these processes of revision, in all these combative theses, one kind of parochialism was being confronted with another. Those who thought the American government right to do what it did and those who thought it wrong were sharing an identical assumption—that it still had the options at its disposal, that it still enjoyed freedom to do whatever it chose to do. This assumed too much. The real point of George Washington's warning was not that foreign entanglement might bring ill or good to the republic: it was that it entangled. This was driven bitterly home when between 1965 and 1973 the greatest military Power in the world found itself unable to achieve its objective in and unable honorably to extricate itself from a country in Southeast Asia which not one in ten thousand Americans of Franklin Roosevelt's day could have found on a map. The affairs of the world still had to be weighed and balanced in a net of interlocking diplomacy: this had not disappeared with the disappearance of the power of the European states that had woven the network. No Great Power, however imperially inclined, had ever been free, unless it was on a collision course, to do exactly as it pleased to get exactly what it wanted. That the United States was more powerful than any Great Power had ever been made no difference. To think that it did, as the quarreling American schools of thought seemed to believe, was to live under an "illusion of omnipotence," to which Denis Brogan drew America's attention at the height of the Cold War.[35]

The two versions of this war that became current made separate sense. Neither ever made total sense. It was because the version of the 1950s had managed to avoid analysis, because its propagandists had labeled it un-American to analyze at all, to doubt that there were dragons in every field and Reds under all the beds, that it later came under such keen scrutiny. But it was never a matter of rational calculation alone: the stakes were too high to let nothing but reason animate the argument. What went on in the area once known to experts only as "international relations" now affected all citizens, making their daily lives dangerous and their futures problematic. About the resolution of problems of this order and relations of this kind, no one was inhuman enough to remain entirely calm. So the old armories were opened and the old weapons taken out of them. The charge of imperialism was made once again; once again, also, the old rebuttal to it was reemployed — that imperialism was just a hostile tag attached to what good and responsible people called morality and responsibility. The idea that there might be an American empire, ever expanding for everybody's expanding good, easily converted into the notion that there should be an American empire, something attractive, something necessary, as other empires in their time had been perceived by their nationals. Even the war in Vietnam could be fitted into such a context: indeed, its opponents accused that if it did not fit in this manner, it made no sense at all. The war there, wrote one enthusiast in a book frankly entitled *Imperial America* (1967), as well as the "partly derivative" developments in Burma, Indonesia, and Thailand "has raised the issue of who has the primary responsibility in South-East Asia: the United States, or Communist China."[36]

When the issue was put this way, a patriot could respond with only one answer, although the diplomat George Kennan, writing *The Realities of American Foreign Policy* in 1954, urged his readers to recognize that even benevolence, when addressed to a foreign people, represented "a form of intervention into their internal affairs, and always receives, at best, a divided reception."[37] But there is a time for academic analysis, and 1954 was not it. What was being analyzed had not yet cooled down.

Here another reminder from Carl Becker is relevant: that facts are not objective realities but mental images which, if useful and necessary to a given generation, should be accepted by it as true.[38] The discovery that there was a Cold War being waged was not invented by a generation of American hysterics, incapable of reading correctly the signs of the times. The origins of this war were rooted in what intelligent people very reluctantly assessed as the realities of their time. They accordingly saw these realities as "true," and suited their actions to them.

One of the first influential statements that defined these realities had been made by Kennan, in a memorandum originally addressed to the secretary of defense and later published in the February 1947 issue of the periodical *Foreign Affairs* under the signature X. How best to confront Communism? By containing it. Containment of Communism implied coexistence with it, but on one's own terms. The essential point was to prevent "other peoples from committing the naive and fateful folly of permitting the reins of government to be seized within their respective countries by elements that accepted the disciplined authority of Moscow." Kennan did not change his mind about the reality of "that complete sweep of dominant Soviet influence over Europe and Asia which was Stalin's initial post-war hope." It had been thwarted only by the fashioning of this containment policy. When Britain decided it could not afford to supply Greece and Turkey with a total sum of $250 million, the American Congress was asked, on March 12, 1947, to increase it to $400 million. Truman's secretary of state George Marshall admitted that this British inability to meet an imperial obligation in the Middle East was tantamount to a British abdication from the affairs of this area in the future. (This was one reality that certainly escaped the notice of the British and would continue to do so for another decade and more.) Marshall asserted that, consequently, it must henceforth be United States policy "to support free peoples who are resisting attempted subjugation or outside pressures."[39]

This was the Truman Doctrine. It generated three months later the European Recovery Program or Marshall Plan and was rounded off on January 20, 1949, by the "Point Four" program, described by Truman as a major course of action:

a bold new program for making the benefits of our scientific advances and industrial progress available for the improvement and growth of underdeveloped areas. . . . Democracy alone can supply the vitalizing force to stir the peoples of the world into triumphant action, not only against their human oppressors, but also against their ancient enemies—hunger, misery, and despair.

To clear the way toward these ends the American program of foreign aid had by 1966 reached totals of $47 billion for Europe, $27.6

billion for East Asia, $25.4 billion for the Middle East and Southeast Asia, $11 billion for Latin America, and $3.6 billion for Africa.[40]

This was a vast framework indeed, enclosing a scene full of assumptions and their consequences. As early as 1947 Dean Acheson, Truman's undersecretary (and later secretary) of state, formulated the "domino theory" which Truman's successor, Eisenhower, later made famous and handed down as wisdom to his successors. Acheson spoke of a possible future disposition of the world's surface in terms that might have impressed Tojo himself. If Communism spread, Acheson argued, the corruption of Greece would infect Iran and everything to the east. "It would also carry infection to Africa through Asia Minor and Egypt, and to Europe through Italy and France, already threatened by the strongest Communist parties in Europe." Under such an assumption was thereafter imposed the American *cordon sanitaire* made up of diverse but always serviceable materials, whether of barbed wire or of grain shipments. Among them were the rearming of West Germany, the issue of the Colombo Plan, the making of peace with Japan, the entry into a war against Communism in the Korean peninsula under United Nations's auspices, the building of "alphabet alliances" around the world, as well as direct military intervention in Guatemala and Lebanon (1958), in Cuba (1961), and in the Dominican Republic (1965) and Vietnam (1965-1973). The great globe itself, it seemed to leaders like Lyndon Johnson, was something that could be twirled at any time by an American finger—and when everyone had come to notice this, or been made to notice it by interested parties, the Cold War between the democratic West and world Communism did indeed come to take on, in the minds of those who waged it with a will and those who criticized its tactics and its purposes, the aspect of a power contest between two rival empires, of a type long familiar, whose ground plans could be studied in every anti-imperialist history the century had produced.[41] Or in every imperialist history, for that matter. The propping up of the older empires, "decaying" or not, did for a time become part of the United States's overall strategy as leader of the West; so by the time Truman's administration left office (January 1953)—which was only seven years after the supposed dawn of the century of the common man—the American government was paying nearly half of France's military bill in an

Indochina which, whatever else its inhabitants wanted, did not want the French—as a young John F. Kennedy once pointed out to an infuriated General de Lattre de Tassigny.[42]

For the policy of containing the revolutionary doctrines and practices of Communism, if it was to make sense, had to involve the defense of the status quo. This clearly had its imperfections: empire with all its apparatus was one of them. Now the dilemma that John Paton Davies and others had seen beyond the immediate horizon of World War II was staring the leaders of the Free World in the face, seriously discomfiting them. In the eyes of Americans, the original colonial nationalists, the modern expressions of colonial nationalism had always been admirable in theory—but in practice the theory lost its charm when this nationalism, seeking recognition, found avuncular friends in Moscow ready to give it and was commandeered into the cause of world revolution as a result—or, even worse, chose to join these ranks of the subversive of its own free will. This happened in the colony of British Guiana, where in 1953 the Marxist Cheddi Jagan's followers *voted* him into power, and the British government, for once as alarmed as Washington at a Communist specter in the western hemisphere, aborted the democratic constitution and outlawed his party. In such a case imperialism acted according to its natural instincts.

Americans still perceived the British, French, and other European empires that had survived the war as so many anachronisms, but the most vehement anti-imperialists in Washington or Kansas City could not and did not argue that the metropolitan leaders of these imperial systems were potential enemies of the United States, were men who had laid plans or were about to rush to put into effect the plans that others had made to dynamite the foundations of the capitalist world. Whatever else they might be, these imperialist controllers were mainly competent guardians. They could be trusted to remain so. In a world become dangerous they were certainly far more reliable than all the unknowns who lived in the other parts of the forest.

Even in the known parts of the forest the self-appointed rangers could never be totally sure everything was in order. One of these areas of doubt was, as it had always been, in the southern hemisphere, whose unknowns were not present but might be assumed to be listening somewhere when President Eisenhower's secretary of state, John Foster Dulles, presented the motion at Caracas in 1954, during the tenth meeting of the Organization of American States (O.A.S.), that the control of the political institutions of any American state by the international Communist movement would constitute a threat to the sovereignty and political independence of all the American states. The motion was passed, predictably—because it had long been accepted that Latin America made an excellent laboratory for testing elements of United States's foreign policy which, in the name of development, could be applied elsewhere in the world.[43] Since the beginning of the century a succession of American governments had treated Latin America as their particular parish, formulating and imposing policy there without referring to Latin American responses. Outside the Caribbean area there had been no taint of direct territorial imperialism, and this was the point now fastened on. There had been none because there had been no need for it. The United States got all that was wanted without it. These were assuredly, said its critics, the habits of monopoly capitalism: in Latin America it was clear to one such critic that the United States had pioneered

the forms of rule and exploitation which it is customary nowadays [1975] to call neo-colonialism. This long experience has greatly facilitated the process of turning ex-colonies of Britain and the other older imperial powers into neo-colonies of the United States.[44]

The United States still, in the 1960s, extracted, marketed, financed, or otherwise profited from copper in Chile, Peru, and Mexico; from oil in Venezuela; from public utilities in Argentina, Brazil, Chile, Peru, Ecuador, and Colombia; from all telephonic communications in Chile, Brazil, Peru, Ecuador, and Colombia; from coffee in Brazil, Colombia, El Salvador, Costa Rica, and Guatemala; from the bananas of the Central American republics; and from the cotton of Mexico and Brazil.

Americans did this and intended to go on doing it. They would not be deterred by plaints like the following from a Guatemalan—"It takes one cable from Washington—and there we are, drinking our coffee and eating our bananas!"[45] —or by Castro's perpetual commentaries from the sidelines to the effect that the O.A.S. with its "housebroken majority," or Kennedy's Alliance for Progress, were agreements between the shark and the sardine, or between one millionaire and twenty beggars—agreements which, by ensuring that no real change would ever be made, locked up the future in an imperialist vault. No wonder, then, it would be "woe to those countries, the day they try to make an agrarian reform!"[46]

It all depended, once more, on the point of view. If change was woe, it could not be progress. Change might mean Communism. It might indeed mean anything. Change itself had somehow to be contained. But what was its best container? Nobody knew; and Americans would have been glad to believe that the future could be stored in some vault or capsule of which they alone would keep the combination. (That change was not some solid substance but came with the wind and might go with it too, and thus was something nobody could summon, seize, store, or stop, was an English notion, ruefully displayed before a surprised assembly of white South Africans by Britian's Prime Minister Harold Macmillan only after the British Empire had been for the most part dismantled.) But a containment policy had to be made concrete, it had to be seen to be believed. It needed credibility, and its best evidence of this was the backing of soldiers on the ground. Therefore, as 1967 ended, the United States had seven hundred thousand men stationed in thirty countries, was a member of four regional defense alliances and an active participant in a fifth, had mutual defensive treaties with forty-two nations, was a member of fifty-three international organizations, and was giving military or economic aid to nearly a hundred nations across the globe.[47] As far as this presence could be made unobtrusive, it was done; but the elephant, as they say in Bangkok, does not easily conceal itself behind a flower. Particularly in Southeast Asia the American presence in action became painfully visible every evening on the television sets in Kansas City, once the United States had taken over, in what had been French Indochina and was now Vietnam, a shooting role in a war not cold at all. This degree of involvement, and the contortions of policy devised to explain it, brought into the open questions about the nature and purpose of America's role in the world that for two decades had been implicit. Since no explanation could satisfy everyone, President Lyndon Johnson's administration (1964-68) found itself defending a "credibility gap" it was never able to bridge.

George Ball, for example, who was then under-secretary of state, ultimately emerged from this administration's internecine quarrels over Vietnam with the reputation of a "dove." But the imperialist aviaries had always been able to find room for this sort of dove. In 1967 he argued that the United States needed to keep 100 thousand men in Southeast Asia for ten to twenty years. This did not arise "from any desire on our part to play an imperial role . . . but when the United States undertakes to help build up a nation and to provide the political assistance and security to maintain that nation against what is almost certain to be a constant effort of subversion, we have signed up for the duration."[48] European imperialists who in their time had had to present similar prophecies to the inspection of a parliamentary democracy could have told him that the first thing people want to know about a duration is how long it will last and the second thing they are sure to say about it is that the estimate given is far too long. The thought that the war in Vietnam "might well have to be repeated in comparable situations"[49] was enough to drive the majority of Americans to look for some position from which no view of any such comparable situations could ever be seen. Even John F. Kennedy, devoted Cold Warrior though he was, had allowed in November 1961 that there could not be an American solution to every world problem:[50] had he lived another decade, he would have found a host of Americans ready to agree with him as they had never done before.

Kennedy's comment perhaps betrayed the wish that things were not so, that there was indeed a solution to everything if enough time and care and thought were applied, and that on some "new frontier" a chance to apply all these would be found. It was an image to move the American heart—as French explorers' hearts had been moved that bright day a century ago on the borders of Yunnan. Americans thought themselves, in 1975 as in 1945, the best explorers for the future. What other candidates for the role were there, who were not mired in dogma and lost in tyranny?

Accordingly, for more than a generation after the end of World War II, this imperialism of idealism which had originally been constructed by Woodrow Wilson was taken as far as it could go, which was often farther than many wanted to see it come. It found itself in nominal charge of, yet only spasmodically in control of, large areas of the world which owed it only as much daily allegiance as the political traffic would bear. For the "nonimperial guardian"[51] of other peoples' independence against Communism was often confronted not only with the intricacies of an ideology but also with the contrarieties of human nature, of the kind that Wilson had never managed to take accurately into account. He had once said he wanted to compel the Latin Americans to elect good men. His successors wanted to do precisely this, all over the world. But they often found the thing impossible to arrange without at the same time arranging, and thus subverting (as in Korea and South Vietnam), the electoral process itself. They were therefore accused of having made the smoke-filled room, where power barons made their deals, one of America's principal imperial exports. But their chief trouble was Wilson's own: good men were hard to find.

Wilson's other ideas still lived. He had seen it as part of America's historic mission to bring Europe into a peaceful international order based on world law. Since the best stimulus to peace was commerce, enlarging America's foreign trade was carrying out a plain duty to humanity. When in London in 1917, his envoy Edward House had corresponded with him about the likeliest shape of this future. If the European Powers came to an understanding concerning investments by their citizens in undeveloped countries, a great deal of good and profit would accrue to these citizens as well as to the countries that needed the development. Stability would be established, investments secured, and low rates of interest guaranteed.[52] From such notions the idea of a League of Nations was no distance. Through Open Doors, using open diplomacy, this benevolent business consortium would take itself, picking up mandates for the backward everywhere. Some of Wilson's ideas were novel, but none of them were radical. He certainly thought that "the West" should remain in control of the world in the future. And why not? Westerners knew better how to do things and, more important, continued to have the will to do things—a will that was lacking everywhere else the westerner looked, as the backward condition of everywhere else proved.

Human natures not bred in the West proved contrary about this too. Here once more, from across the Atlantic, was an embodiment of the fundamentally racist assumption of imperialism, the one that

Europe had so long dealt in: the presupposition that competition of merit and a generous rivalry of liberty could bring nothing but good, a presupposition positing a basic equality of knowledge and opportunity among the competitors which did not exist. The metaphorical models, popular in economists' circles, that there are starting points and take-off points, assume the existence of an actual vehicle capable of becoming airborne, at however distant a time and a place.

American statesmen, although working within a context of international action changed out of all recognition, still used these Wilsonian concepts fifty years after his death. So too did the section of the American public that paid any attention to these matters. But none of them ever thought of doing so in the name of imperialism. They did not take to themselves in pride the name imperialist, as citizens of England and France had once done. The notion that imperialism could sensibly be said to exist in the absence of an empire did not come either fast or firmly to Americans who thought it their duty to display their principles to the world—a duty made very much clearer by the presence of an enemy whose declared aim was now what it always had been, the downfall of the free-enterprise economy on which from the outset the republic had staked its future. That the Soviet Union should have such an aim had by the mid-1950s become an axiom: indeed, it would have seemed strangely disturbing had it not, since Communist guile borne by doves of peace would have been feared more than the consequences of Khruschev's banging his shoe on a desk at the U.N. or his vow that "we will bury you."

The Russians continued to look through the telescope of their suspicions. They were certain that the stakes of the free-enterprise economy would multiply on the ground, ground not the property of the United States, as the American capitalists found themselves presented with more opportunities for their exploitation than ever before. "The real objective of the advanced industrial countries in advocating free trade was to hold the markets for manufactured goods in less developed countries and to check their industrialization." For American politicians to wave the Red Flag in their citizens' faces as a warning in order to obtain electoral support for policies that would assist capitalism in carrying out this broad aim was, again, to be expected.[53]

The Soviet Union had reason to take some comfort from this deduction concerning the mysterious habits of the American political system. Their system also moved in darkness, one which was not dispelled but increased when official Soviet circles issued statements that everything was in fact as plain as day to those who were not determined to mislead themselves by misreading Soviet intentions. Non-Russian historians of the twentieth century, whatever they make of these intentions, must if they are honest declare that they are dealing only in conjecture. Bourgeois conjecture differs from Marxist conjecture in kind but not in result. There has to date been no agreement even about what is being discussed. (Castro probably knows what Khruschev hoped to accomplish by placing Soviet missiles in Cuba during October 1962, but he has not said.)

In a recent issue of the journal *Social Sciences*, an issue specially prepared for the Fourteenth International Congress of Historical Sciences (held at San Francisco in August 1975), various Russian academic authorities reveal their view of both their own and the western world. Soviet historians quietly bury an entire history of that same Comintern which gave the authorities in all western states so much trouble in the 1920s. They remark, as if in surprise, how many of the bourgeois writers of the period, and on that period, had managed to distort even Lenin's foreign policy between 1917 and 1924, in an effort to prove that the U.S.S.R. was seeking "to export revolution." Indeed, these writers had asserted that there was no question of any Soviet policy of peaceful coexistence at the time. Of course, "these views fall very short of the truth." Truth was equally absent from western interpretations that dealt with more recent events. America's world policy was plain enough: it intended to promote the existence of imperialist blocs, among them the North Atlantic Treaty Organization (1949). This institution was designed to serve the purposes of a "Cold War," which "was being carried on by the imperialist circles against the Soviet Union and other socialist countries, and against the revolutionary and democratic movements." The journal goes on to point out the class essence of American foreign policy, a policy of expansionism defended by philosophical, sociological, and economic arguments. Even western historians, it adds, had become aware of this, but they could say little of value about the situation since their basic intellectual premise, a bourgeois idealism, was so clearly useless for any objective analysis. They could not see, what was so clear to Soviet scholars, that what needed study and explanation were the modern imperialist processes of capitalist integration like the European Common Market, processes that illustrated two tendencies in the development of imperialism: "On the one hand, an urge to deepen the integration of [these] processes and to back up economic associations with political and military alliances; and on the other, an intensification and aggravation of inter-imperialist contradictions." Whatever this might mean, or these contradictions might be, this latter-day Soviet view does not encompass the notion that there exists a rivalry in the modern world between American and Russian *power*, since imperialism is and must always remain, by definition, unknown to Soviet policy. It therefore follows that, between 1945 and 1970, the role of the U.S.S.R. in the postwar peace settlement was "to consolidate peace and international co-operation, to prevent another war, and to foil the aggressive policy of imperialism."[54]

The fact that war did not break out during these years leads to one conjecture at least—that the Soviet Union did not want one, although, because of its rooted suspicion of western intentions, it could never distinguish between behavior that would be construed as provocation and behavior that would be accepted as a normal power play according to the rules of the international game. What drove Soviet statesmen was not some grand, imperialist, ideological plan to export Communism but a resolve to guard the homeland of Communism against further damage from outside. Their country being more exhausted and injured by their "Great National War" against the Germans than anyone was then allowed to know, the Soviet government pursued its own particular policy of containment of Communism. It would contain and conserve it in order to make it safe. These activities were not called by this name or indeed by any name: it was left for Kremlin watchers to describe as policy what the Kremlin did. The Politburo extended the power of the Red Army and its political commissars into the Baltic states and into those of Eastern Europe, states which were symbolic of all the self-determinations of 1919 and 1920. They made these their patrimony, a defensive cordon for themselves, so much stockade country—a country of home farms and industrial branch plants whose produce was shipped to one destination only. These actions illustrated the Russian determination to complete a policy that the tsars had also preached and indeed had sometimes carried out, a policy to keep Holy Russia and its newest dogmas free from the contamination they would inevitably find beyond the stockade.

Soviet leaders therefore did not spend time blandishing the controllers of their satellite territories. They gave them orders and removed or drastically purged the local administrations if these orders were not satisfactorily carried out. They were quick to exploit the divisions of opinion that developed among western leaders and never admitted that similar divisions existed, or could under Marxist-Leninism ever exist, within the Soviet structure. Their structure was also an empire, although no Russian had been allowed to call it this after the days of October 1917. No one was given a view from below. No colonial assertion had been heard of since Bolshevism's earliest days, not from Soviet Asia or from Soviet Europe. As party chairman Kalinin had expressed it on October 6, 1942, so it remained thereafter—"The Caucasians have now become a social people who see in the collective system their bulwark, the foundation of material prosperity and a higher intellectual life." Perhaps the faster to introduce the peoples of the Caucasus to such advantages, American "Lend-Lease" Studebaker trucks were used to deport the Chechens and the Ingushi to Kazakhstan and Kirghizstan in February 1944. The great Shamil, hero of the Caucasian races who had held out against tsars Nicholas I and Alexander II, was after 1950, for the first time in Soviet propaganda, represented as a pure reactionary and an agent of foreign imperialism.[55]

In the West the existence of this empire under Soviet authority was not much discussed because there was plainly nothing any outsider could do about it: when an angry French or British delegate tried to return the Soviet gibes against imperialism on the Soviet delegates who had made them in the United Nations' General Assembly, the latter did not even trouble to argue the point, since there existed no such Soviet empire against which accusations could reasonably be made. While the Cold War continued, no memorialist came out of Russia to throw light on anything Russia had done. No critics initiated a debate or called down anathema on the actions of their government—or, if they did, no hint of their fate was given until Solzhenitsyn's novels began to circulate in Europe during the 1970s. The leaders of the Soviet Union had long since locked themselves away from the conception of give-and-take in anything. Their only method of accepting compromise (which they constantly did accept, over Berlin and other problems, for they did not want war) was by refusing to admit that compromise had been reached at all. What had been reached was of course the position at which they had been determined to arrive from the outset. They did not believe in bourgeois notions of progress, the programs designed to dupe and exploit whoever came to believe in them. True progress was decreed by history, and of these decrees Marxist-Leninism was the sole authorized interpreter.

For twenty-five years no one found a door to open in this wall of mutual suspicion. Dean Acheson, who was "present at the creation" of the Cold War reiterated in October 1953, when he had become a private citizen, that the purpose of American foreign policy was to maintain and foster an environment in which "our national life and individual freedom could survive and prosper." This statement, if the point about individual freedom was omitted, could have been made by any member of the Soviet Union's Politburo. But of course the point was so important that it could not be omitted. Acheson drove it home:

The tradition of 1776 is still the most powerful and attracting force in the world to-day [1953]: it is this that draws to our leadership people all over the world. Without this idea, we are to them just another powerful nation, bent upon interests which are not theirs.[56]

Accordingly, even though all the rhetoric that spoke of the duties of the watchmen on the walls of the Free World, and of the need to carry any burdens anywhere at any time, might and did become cloying, it never parted company with reality as Americans, and the "First World" of Western Europe, continued to see it.

Reality, like everything else, takes on another aspect when seen from below.

The realities of the Great Powers had never been those of the small powers or of the countries that had no power at all. When the latter looked at the world as it was at the end of yet another enormous civil war among the privileged, the ubiquitous and traditional "They" were still in charge of everything, able to dictate to their consciences whatever they chose without fear of interference from those whose existence might, or might not, be troubling these consciences. The new victors on the scene, the Americans and the Russians, were entities unknown to the subject peoples of the European empires, and on the whole they were to remain so. Certainly the powerless never threw themselves into the exercise of parsing and analyzing the policies of Washington and Moscow with anything like the zeal given this in the capitals of the West. Kremlinology, Mao watching, and pro- or anti-Americanism remained habits of the privileged. Their very existence within this circle confirmed Asian and African politicians' knowledge that white people were still pursuing their even older habit of deciding the fates of colored people. Indeed, whites were quick to assign them a new place to live, which they called the Third World: but what went on in it had a familiar aspect. Power was in the process of changing hands, but the people who were doing the confronting, the containing, the coexisting, and the talking were the same kind of people, or at any rate first cousins to the same kind of people, who had always decided what to do, when to do it, and with whom.

So although it might have been clear to India's Nehru, and perhaps to his audience of liberals at Columbia University on October 17, 1949, when he said that all the vestiges of imperialism and colonialism would have to disappear,[57] it was not at all clear at the time to great numbers of powerful people and of those who had no power whatever. Things did not disappear in this world by magic, certainly not potent things like imperialism and colonialism, which had been around as long as anyone could remember. Somebody had to abolish them: and abolition of anything depended on both a positive act of will and the strength to see it succeed. Nehru had made a nationalist assertion. But had this assertion now crossed its last barrier and become one of the assumptions of those who controlled the future? And what were these assumptions, anyway? Was it not time to examine them closely, particularly the one that assumed that the future was a slab of territory available for somebody to control? Was it true that the "immobility" of Asian and African societies, on which and amid which European imperialists had long traded, was no longer a fact of life? Would innovation in these areas now drive out the traditions that had prevented it from making any wide appeal?

Were the peoples who had been ignored because they were assumed to be powerless, or had been classified under other collective headings like "labor," now truly going to become, in Nehru's words, "the principals of history"?

And, if all this was so, had imperialism indeed reached its last stage, and was empire, its most famous visible symbol, now due to be thrown into what the Communists liked to call the dustbin of history?

THE PROSPECT AS BEFORE

Decolonization; and the shifting of power within the imperial framework.

6

THE PROSPECT AS BEFORE

After 1945 nobody had to make a point of promoting the virtues of national self-determination. The promotion had been done, the point had been taken, and it needed no lobbyists at the U.N. General Assembly—such as had crowded the corridors of Versailles at the end of World War I. (This did not, however, prevent their being there.)

Propaganda in asserting these virtues had reached enormous proportions during World War II. Every "free radio" station, every underground and resistance movement, had taken up and played national, ethnic, and even Communist arias on the theme of freedom; so that in time hope of victory and love of liberation had become synonymous terms. When Europe was "liberated" from one of its two major tyrannies, Asian and African politicians heard faintly down the wind the bells of victory tolling for them too. Freedom's famous banner, "torn, but flying," now flew above its own empire of rhetoric. What freedom signified all people thought they could tell or at least realized they should know. So even as peace amid all its rancors was breaking out, Lord Wavell's viceroyalty in India was preparing the way for a devolution of political control in the subcontinent to the leaders of what the newly elected British Labour government (July 1945) still hoped would take the form of a "Union of India," despite the burst of self-confidence that the outlawing of

273

the Congress party by the *raj* between 1942 and 1945 had given to the Muslims' project to put together a state, to become an independent republic and, they hoped, a nation, out of their several sections of British and princely India. If elsewhere there remained any colonial subjects who had somehow managed to sleep through the clamor of the second civil war waged by their controllers in half a century, any who had not "awakened" to the call of their brethren who were already up and about, active and committed, explaining and exposing, these people were now to be forcibly aroused.

This was not done only by their own kind. British and French overlords—but not the Dutch and the Portuguese, who had a natural noncombatants' desire to restore their injured status without trafficking in reconstruction designed for anyone else's benefit—were urging their subjects to face in new directions and to do unaccustomed things. The Malays, for example, were shaken into a self-conscious posture of "nationalism" by their returning British rulers, who were resolved to make them "fit" to assume responsibility for governing the Malay peninsula as an integral part of the British Commonwealth of Nations. (Since the area was inhabited by more Chinese and Hindus than Malays, this policy was to be dogged by ten years of military and political upheaval before the Chinese Communist guerrilla leadership was eliminated from the jungle and a government emerged to which power could be handed over without fear that British investments would be expropriated.)

These ideas of union—and, later, of federation, as in Central Africa (1953) and in the West Indies (1958)—were not a British monopoly. The imperialist hope was now to extend the imperial framework, to welcome within it persons and purposes hitherto excluded—but certainly to retain it. Empire would remain a going concern, if all its inhabitants got together in a spirit of companionable partnership. The French took up these ideas, announcing that universalism had never been alien to the essence of *la France d'outre-mer*. War had battered Britain, but it had split metropolitan France and had effectively taken away France's control of its properties. In the postwar era the French position was accordingly much more precarious. The British, once they had hastily surveyed their empire, refurbished their published colonial policy by putting a higher gloss on the liberalism that even its critics allowed it to contain. They were right to think they still had some options, some room to maneuver. If the French thought the same, they were wrong. Syria and Lebanon had claimed their independence in 1941; and the French—galled the worse because they had never lost their suspicions, incubated in the nineteenth century, that the crafty British, given half a chance, would somehow steal a Levantine march on them—had to stand by and watch the area become a British military theater of operations. They were never able to reoccupy it. The same thing happened in French North Africa, where the Anglo-American command was indifferent to the machinations of the nationalist groups, provided they did not interfere with the command's strategic dispositions.

This was the immediate and unpleasant history with which the Fourth French Republic had to cope in 1945. It created the French Union, combining the *Départements d'Outre Mer*, which included the Antilles and Algeria, with the *Territoires d'Outre-Mer*, which consisted of West and Equatorial Africa, Madagascar, and the Pacific islands. This single entity constituted the republic; and all its residents were citizens. The union also included the "associated States," the protectorates of Tunisia and the Union of Indochina. Here was followed the model of the British dominions before 1919: the states had full autonomy, save in foreign policy. But the world of 1945 did not resemble the world of 1919, and these new and nice French distinctions seemed, in the opinion of many new citizens, to smack of an *ancien régime*, which would ultimately reveal its true intentions. The French Union became a French Community when in 1958 the Fifth Republic was born, but this framework was still, as will be seen, too narrow to enclose the realities of the day. It was a day that did not accommodate principles of community, come somewhat too late.

For colonial assertion, confident it had the world's attention, was now self-assured enough to make its case. Colonial leaders knew that the imperial framework had been weakened to the point of collapse. This had not been true in 1919. Then the victors had intended to reestablish what they could of the pre-1914 condition of authority and the convention of its acceptance. They had not heeded the colonial complaint that the condition was not what it might have been nor the convention what it should have been. In 1945 the victors realized that their victory, its results uncertain in

Europe, was still flimsier beyond Europe's bounds. They knew that the assertions coming from all quarters, serving notice that things must now be managed differently and have another outcome, needed to be carefully assessed if any fruits of the victory were to be maintained. The colonial question was now high on the political agenda of the metropolis, as it had never been before.

Many things the privileged had been accustomed to had been either lost or stolen: they would never be sure which. Of course, they would not be compensated for their loss. The only certainty was that things were not now, nor would they be, what they had been. Reconstruction, not mere restoration, was the task. Such a task needed what it had always needed—knowledge, will, room, time, and money: and these it did not have and would not find.

The reputation of empire, its presence both on the map and in the mind of man, had always given to its controllers places from which to look toward the horizon. From their new position in the world this could no longer be seen. Imperialists were mainly conservatives, thinking of their empires as a matter more of sentiment than of policy. Having to deal with empire as a political problem, and with colonial nationalism as an integral part of the problem, was something new. Having to find justification continually for what they had long done instinctively was something disturbing. Colonial nationalism had been recognized hitherto as a minor or counterpoint theme in the imperial symphony: to see it transposing itself, to hear it becoming a major statement, caused consternation. The British, for example, were dismayed when told that their actual domination of Africa was on a par with Hitler's projected domination of Europe. They were shocked to hear Hastings Banda, who returned to his homeland of Nyasaland in 1958 after a thirty-year, self-imposed exile, declare at mass meetings that he was like Moses come home to his people—and to watch him six months later leading them in open revolt. Imperialist philosophy, such as it was, had usually been ready to evolve in response to a changing world situation, but not at the speed that was now forced upon it by all the nationalist agitations that took hold of the "combustible materials" the Comintern had identified twenty years earlier. Sentiment and gradualism were two more, and not the least significant, casualties of World War II.

So was the habit of authority. Only the Americans, not burdened by concepts of empire or by a guilty memory of imperialism, could afford to produce a series of confident plans for the future. They did not greatly care if some plans contradicted others, since they were sure even the future would work in their favor and sort out these contradictions. To them, therefore, was left the dreaming of all the agreeable dreams: a century for the common people to enjoy, new frontiers for them to reach, great societies for them to build while they waged war on poverty. European governments, by contrast, did not publicize either their dreams or their plans, because they did not seriously believe that anything much could come of them. With no clear prospects, they thought it pointless to issue a prospectus that might prove fraudulent. So their politicians claimed statesmanship only by announcing a policy of caution. They had all been proved wrong in the past, and they knew that everyone knew this. When foresight can be dismissed as guesswork, it is better to stay clear of it. In the European countries' present condition—impoverished and needing simple necessities, like imports for which they could not pay—nothing much seemed possible save survival, and how to achieve even this with any degree of comfort was not at all obvious. Europe had once again, and quite possibly once too often, dissipated its wealth (not merely its money) "in smoke and explosions."[1] It was time to calculate the extent of the mess and then do whatever possible to mop it up.

Accordingly, anyone who claimed to know the shape and style of the future was listened to, although less often with respect for what he was saying than from a sense of futility and lack of self-esteem. As had happened often enough in empire's history, men who were sure they were right did not find it hard to win a following from other men who were confident of nothing. In these conditions, the voice that sounded the most assured carried the farthest distance and could bill what it said as wisdom. Privilege therefore now had to justify itself, and appeasement was back in style. Nehru's grave reminders to the West of both its sins and its promises of reparation rang in many ears as the clear intimations of reason and duty. The nature of the war had made many people wonder whether progress meant anything, had any reality. The reputation of civilization itself—the famous crock of gold that was of course the prize to be found at the end of every imperial rainbow—did not stand high among the civilized who had somehow managed to survive the "gale of the world" without discovering from what quarter it had come. A generation unable to think well of itself did not think much, or expect much, of the future. People began to think that one set of ideas about the future was as good as—i.e., no better than—another. Perhaps, then, it was time for adjusting to ideas which, since they had never been tested, could not be said to have failed.

In this atmosphere, the colonial leaders who had long publicized their politics of complaint were ready to be appeased and to take over a stage whose present occupants were supposed to be equally ready to quit. But, as in any theater, a transformation scene so complex needs skillful direction, otherwise every movement leads to impact and all communication becomes tumult. This direction was lacking and would not be found: a strategy of take-over was never to be accepted and adopted through the colonial world. Noise and collision were always at anyone's call. Yet certain tactical patterns of confrontation were to repeat themselves.

One pattern proved both useful and attractive: cries from the territory for *uhuru* or *merdeka* (freedom); boycott, strike, and riot; arresting and jailing "the ringleaders responsible," with suspension of habeas corpus; indignant questioning of all this in the metropolis; appointing an official commission of inquiry; its report on "the disturbances," with recommendations of a liberal kind; implementing these recommendations; granting amnesty for those in jail; their emergence shoulder-high and their metamorphosis into national heroes; dispatching juristic experts to the territory to draw up a new, representative, Westminster-model constitution; elections; and the triumphal victory and appearance on the front bench of the national heroes. This precise pattern was followed in the Gold Coast. Kwame Nkrumah, jailed for taking "positive action" in 1949, was appointed "leader of government business" by the British governor-general in February 1951 and six years later, dispensing with the governor-general, appointed himself *Osagyefo*, or leader of the people. Upbraided for his Gold Coast policy by Kenyan settlers when he visited them in 1950, Labour's colonial secretary, James Griffiths, made his position on all this perfectly clear: "And what was the alternative, man? Bloody revolution, that's what it was!"[2]

The British set this style in decolonization because it was inevitable they would, once they had decided to leave and to partition the Indian subcontinent, as well as to invite the resultant states, both of which were clearly headed toward republicanism, to remain within the Commonwealth. Why this decision was made is clear if we imagine a history of events that might have accompanied any other decision. Britain could not have "held down" India by military means, for had this attempt been made, as Auchinleck and all senior officers knew, the army would have either shredded away or turned its guns on its alien commanders. The loss of the Indian army made everything east of Suez a power vacuum, and all the soldiers' attempts to find alternative bases in the Mediterranean, in the Middle East, and in the Red Sea and Indian Ocean soon came to nothing. Exhausted and insolvent as a result of the war, Britain had not the means to marshal and maintain flying squadrons of military police and firemen, ready and willing to "keep the peace" in restive colonies everywhere and confined to bases in inevitably hostile territory. To attempt any such policy would certainly have brought down on Britain's head prolonged uproar at the United Nations (a situation with which, perhaps, it would have coped) and, more important, the United States's liberal wrath, with which it could not have coped at all. Absence of troops, money, and friends had never been a basis for launching a successful foreign policy and it was not so now. European nations unable to balance power on their continent, caught as it was in conditions of Cold War between the two extra-European super Powers, could not hope to balance it in the world at large. The last effort at this exercise was the intervention by Britain and France in the Israeli-Egyptian quarrel of October-November 1956, when these two European governments, still thinking imperially, dispatched parachutists to "hold" the Suez Canal. The immediate uproar, which came from India and Canada as well as from the United States, ensured that the troops were back at their bases before a fortnight had passed. That this liberal embarrassment was something peculiarly western was underlined by the actions of the Soviet Union, then busy invading Hungary to get rid of a Communist government there which showed signs of nationalist assertion. A similar uproar greeted this adventure, but the Soviet Union paid it no heed whatever.

The dismantling of empire and the abdication from imperial power took the name decolonization, but this name carried more positive overtones than it had a right to. It was less a policy than a reaction to events that could no longer be brought under control. It was at best a process, during which positions were reached with the knowledge, concealed as long as possible from everyone concerned, that they would be given up under pressure. Calling this a policy is as euphemistic as calling rebellion unrest. Empire had always had a recognizable role to play on the world's stage: decolonization's was to exit from it. In Britain's case it could, however, be made to appear, and it certainly was, that Britain was heading merely toward a companionable greenroom, called the Commonwealth. It could be made to appear that this had always been its intention. It could be made to appear that another imperial script which had long been in the public domain was being followed. The empire's white colonies that had become dominions had done so without upsetting anyone's *amour-propre*. It could therefore be made to appear, and again it certainly was, that at the end of the road leading from the empire stood another institution, liberal and therefore multiracial, in which all the graduates from the old imperial structure would be glad to reside and make their presence felt. The central purpose of British colonial policy, as stated in a white paper on *The Colonial Empire, 1947-48* drafted by Labour's first colonial secretary, Arthur Creech-Jones, was simple: "It is to guide the colonial territories to responsible self-government within the Commonwealth, in conditions that ensure to the people concerned both a fair standard of living and freedom from oppression from any quarter."[3] But this policy of guidance was not going to have enough time to ensure any such things. What had been assertion had become confrontation, and all acts of confrontation set off a chain reaction which did not wait for years to pass to have its effect.

When this colonial policy statement was made the British still thought they lived within the imperial context and owned the imperial privileges of room and time. They saw no need to justify the course they were following, since surely everyone could see it was fair. They were convinced that the program of colonial development, practiced in the open and organized to promote everybody's welfare, both economic and political, would attract and occupy further generations of the controllers and the controlled. The immediate scene was one of action, even of bustle. Empire had perhaps, according to a famous joke, been founded in a fit of absence of mind, but its future now clearly demanded presence of mind, in the best minds it could get. The staff of England's Colonial Office therefore expanded greatly while the colonies were becoming daily news in ways never before known. Getting rid of the empire, remarks one observer, with due reference to one of Professor Parkinson's laws, seemed to need "far more administrative effort and a far greater bureaucratic establishment than was required for gaining or keeping it."[4] This was not surprising. Every issue that arose in a colonial territory now presented a social as well as a political aspect. The natural response of an educated bureaucracy was to increase the number of "experts" on call, to "deal with" both the issue and the aspects. Sociology provided the framework for an ongoing exercise, perpetually producing problems and challenging intelligent men of goodwill, whose parish would never diminish.

Accordingly, between the late 1940s and the late 1950s there were "something like twenty [colonial] constitutions being revised, and we have had to create a queue for the assistance of the legal adviser."[5] To queue at all is to believe in order and trust in time. How much time was available was the debatable point, one argued much more sharply by "men on the spot" than by metropolitan officials, to whom the intricate, self-generating problems of a particular colonial territory often had all the fascination of an acrostic. Kenya's settler spokesman Michael Blundell noted of a colonial conference to which he was summoned in January 1959 at Chequers, the British prime minister's country retreat, that the officialdom he met with there apparently still thought time was something elastic and that this elastic belonged exclusively to officials. According to the tentative timetable they discussed in his presence, it was possible, but not necessarily inevitable, that Tanganyika would achieve its independence by 1970, Uganda "shortly thereafter," and Kenya "much later, probably after 1975."[6] It all depended on which official one talked to and what bent his mind had taken. Five years before, an internal Colonial Office report had already accepted as fact that "the last European settler could not be far behind the last European civil servant."[7] Or perhaps it depended on another fact, that one man's instinct is another's last gasp: as Lord Melbourne, Queen Victoria's girlhood mentor, had once remarked of the outcome of the Catholic Emancipation question, "all the damned fools in England predicted one set of things, and all the sensible men in England another set, and all the damned fools proved perfectly right, and the sensible men perfectly wrong."[8] On the colonial emancipation question, who made sense and who did not was to remain a matter for debate.

Interoffice memoranda do not often talk the language of public speakers and statements. After World War II, as after World War I, the British government devised a scheme, designed to run for forty-four years, for ex-soldiers to settle in Kenya. On November 1, 1954, Kenya's governor Sir Evelyn Baring, who presumably had not read the Colonial Office's internal reports, soothed anxious settlers there by reminding them of one recent public statement, made by the colonial secretary, Oliver Lyttelton:

H.M. Government are not likely to lend themselves to encouraging people to come if they intend to betray them. They [the settlers] will be entitled to feel confidence in the possession of the homes they have built for themselves and for their children.[9]

Four years later his successor, Alan Lennox-Boyd, said the same thing to soothe Conservatives arriving for their annual party conference at Blackpool. These men may have meant what they said, but they did not control the clock. The "timetable" tactics used in India — the Attlee government had announced in February 1947 that the *raj* would quit by June 1948, thus galvanizing Nehru (for India) and Jinnah (for Pakistan) into constructive action — were too attractive not to be seized by colonial leaders everywhere, who wanted the credit of achieving national independence for themselves, not for their undeserving posterity. Lyttelton assured himself and his parliamentary critics who were busily assailing his scheme to build a Central African Federation in 1953 that the first duty of a government, of any government, was to deliver peace and order; but his successors found that they had to settle for their own peace and quiet. By the time Malaya and Ghana (the Gold Coast) had achieved national independence in 1957, "all that mattered was that an indigenous political élite, with some degree of local support, should exist and be willing to take over."[10] After the general election of

October 1959, Harold Macmillan's government was resolved to get out of Africa on the best terms possible, and his famous "wind of change" speech delivered in South Africa in February 1960 signified this to the world at large.

How able was the indigenous political elite, and how much support could it command, were not matters investigated with any thoroughness. When the whole process was nearly completed, Iain Macleod, the last Conservative colonial secretary to square to its problems, asked the question and promptly answered it in an article he wrote for *The Spectator* on January 31, 1964: "Were the [colonial] countries fully ready for independence? Of course not." Pragmatism had thus won one of its more dubious days, under Conservative rule, in diverse places like the Sudan in 1952, Egypt in 1954, Nigeria in 1960, Cyprus in 1961, Sierra Leone in 1962, and Kenya in 1963. The Central African Federation endured for a decade, and then in 1963 split into its components: Malawi (Nyasaland), Zambia (Northern Rhodesia), and Rhodesia (Southern Rhodesia). In the last named country the settlers speedily underlined the truth of one of Michael Blundell's comments about his compatriots in Kenya—"It is interesting to note that when the settlers of Kenya were about to indulge in some desperate action to demonstrate their contempt for Colonial Office rule, they invariably prefaced it by singing God Save the Queen in order at the same time to show their loyalty"[11]—for by 1965 Rhodesia's white men had issued their Unilateral Declaration of Independence and set out to confront a future in which apparently there would be no clocks. By that year the Colonial Office had disappeared into the Commonwealth Relations Office, which had been absorbed back into the Foreign Office by 1970.

In the midst of the incomprehensible, as Joseph Conrad points out in *Youth* (1902), anything can occur. During these years the incomprehensible was expanding its empire, whose bounds were never determined, whose news came from no headquarters, whose internal development no one could keep track of, since no one was responsible for any of its affairs. France and the Netherlands and Belgium, who had no "Dominion status" to confer that anyone in their empires wanted, did not follow the British pattern, but they were to reach, or be forcibly brought to, the same conclusion.

For the "orgy of nationalism," which Northern Rhodesia's Roy

Welensky in 1957 saw occurring within the British Empire in Africa, could not help but affect others there who had been bred up within imperial frontiers.[12] In Welensky's white man's country, loyalties were given not to the events of the 1950s and 1960s but to those of the 1890s, the world of Cecil Rhodes and Joseph Chamberlain. Elsewhere lived other emigrants from a modern world whose governors certainly did not believe, although they might often find it politic to declare, that Jack was indeed as good as his master. The Belgian Congo remained an empire unobserved: it had made no headlines since 1908. It was still a place of paternalism, ruled by a trinity of guardians: the State, the Church, and the rubber and mining companies. No assertion had ever been heard from the Congo, since no elite had ever been trained there; and politics had been kept so far at bay that even the Europeans in the territory had no political rights. But during World War II the capital of Léopoldville had grown from 40 thousand to 100 thousand, and after the war *évolués* were being heard from, asking at first for simple things, like equal pay for equal work. In Europe the Belgian government was necessarily aware of the international temperature in colonial affairs, and in 1955 a liberal Belgian, A. J. van Bilsen, produced a thirty-year plan for further education in and political development of the Congo. This was greeted with general incredulity: but its production certainly guided thinking in quarters which nobody could clearly identify yet, and did it fast: for, "whereas in 1956 the *évolués* were asking for planned emancipation by gradual stages, in 1959 they were demanding independence for 1961."[13]

But this still seemed like so much jungle drumming to many — certainly to the director of the tourist bureau for the Belgian Congo and Ruanda-Urundi, who in 1958 at Brussels issued a booklet which spoke in a language Leopold II might have used. In its preface the honorary vice-governor-general of the Congo regretted that the ignorance of his fellow countrymen, to say nothing of foreigners, in matters concerning the Congo was so very evident. He therefore wanted to commend the booklet particularly to the attention of Belgian young people, since the Congo offered "infinite scope to their imagination and to their endeavour." The scope was in fact finite, despite the proofs he gave of all Belgium had done to promote the principles of what the French-speaking world was finally prepared to honor as *le Lugardisme*. Belgium had developed "this virgin territory for the benefit not of the metropolis alone but of mankind as a whole and, more especially, the peoples whose guardianship was entrusted to her."[14]

What peoples, exactly? They had always had names but they had never had faces; whatever thoughts they had, few whites had ever bothered to discover. Since no native elite had been created among the Congolese to guide the reception of European ideas, emotions simmered below in peoples who had never learned how to express themselves in terms others could grasp, peoples who found no public outlet for the conflicting feelings that the experience of imperialism brought as a matter of course. In the Congo the "revolution of rising expectations" was a matter of first principles, and these principles were not political. They centered on a desire for the good things in life, all of which were owned by the white men—post and place and privilege, mansions and women and cars. This revolution had fermented unseen. It did not surface in complaint, and when the lid finally blew off showed itself to be a compound of rage and hatred which swamped and boiled over everything the imperial structure depended upon: paternalism, Europeans, common sense, civility, polity, and every other doctrine western civilization had ever propounded. Fittingly, a post-office clerk, Patrice Lumumba —who had indeed been in jail, but for peculating the petty cash, not for "positive action" in the style of Nehru and Nkrumah—ignited the series of events in 1959 which by 1961 had loosed an unpaid and envious native *Force Publique* and by this token created a new state on the ruins of one of imperialism's largest monuments.

That so great a disaster could overtake an empire, anyone's empire, and anything done by empire, was thought impossible by all the imperial controllers when they set out to appease the present and, by so doing, to keep at least some lien upon the future. Looking around their new world, the Imperial Powers had admitted they had difficulties, but they had not yet thought of themselves as beleaguered. Their pessimism was never deep enough to make them believe that rationalism itself was one of the imperialist privileges, that common sense was an exception to the general rule, or that within a modern political structure, so carefully tended, all hell could break loose. They had long spoken about "civilization" more than they had thought about it, but they had never supposed the whole notion was false. They did not much like the world they found themselves in, but they could not believe that it was inhabited by total strangers, who had learned nothing after a tutelage of over eighty years. They did not want it proved to them that racism had been at work and in the end would produce nothing more than another version of itself. So they had started out to deal with the known and the familiar, to put back in order the machinery they had invented. But they knew, too, that machines would not run by themselves, that mechanics as well as managers were needed to look after them, and that both would have to learn to work in a different climate. And what lubricant could be relied on, now that the clerks, the soldiers, and the policemen were listening to the voices that told them it was not only right but possible to withdraw their services?

Here were more questions than answers, and more common than either were metaphors—a form of speech which always thrives in times of uncertainty, in times when hard facts are indeed as abundant as usual but no interpretation of them is commonly accepted. Here was "a change in the wind." (The other metaphor, "the wind of change," was the term that politicians took up and popularized because, although nobody knew what it meant, it seemed to hold a promise and a hope. It apparently was coined as early as 1948 by the English novelist Elspeth Huxley, writing of West Africa in *The Walled City*.) The change had been observed during the war even by those who were least willing to alter their course because of it. On May 6, 1944, Lord Halifax, at the time British ambassador in Washington, had thought it right to remind a skeptical U.S. audience that "simple self-determination would not work in the case of Palestine and India because of the existence there of religious and racial problems."[15] Since then these problems had not diminished, and neither had the skepticism: for the skeptics continued to think that if the problems were ever to be solved, it would not be by an alien arbiter, who could have no genuine interest in their solution, having no genuine interest in those who propounded it. A month after he spoke, Halifax wrote home to Leopold Amery, secretary of state for India, sadly describing "the well-intentioned but ignorant drift of thought in [American] intellectual circles."[16] Some drifts of thought might be ignorant, but others were directed by a human agency that knew exactly what it was about. The fact of war, like the prospect of being hanged within the fortnight, concentrates the mind and stimulates the imagination. As at no other time, it allows the young men who have been dismissed as idealists and the older men who have not been recognized as serious to propagate their views as orthodoxy, no more than straight common sense. Radicals come up "from below" and assert themselves against the tenets of the status quo in much the same style and for much the same reasons as do the colonial elites. That this practice was dangerous a conservative like Amery well knew; for even as he received Halifax's complaint, he was minuting crossly how the overseas services of the British Broadcasting Corporation, an institution originally designed (1923) as a pillar of every establishment extant, were creating the worldwide impression that Nehru, Gandhi, and Congress were *entitled* to speak for all India—"it was bad enough to have to contend with the misrepresentation of American correspondents!"[17]

But this impression deepened, to the point where it became an entrenched assumption. The times favored this as never before, as one contrast with the previous postwar period shows. On December 17, 1918, some sixty sergeants of the British West Indian Regiment had founded, while in Italy, a "Caribbean League," one of whose aims had been the "right of the black man to govern himself in the Caribbean": simultaneously, another West Indian group in London had formed a "Society of Peoples of African Origin," with a journal called *The African Telegraph*. The sergeants had been jailed, the league proscribed, the society abandoned, the *Telegraph* cut. Such peremptory treatment was not possible now. Although an empire's controllers could and did continue to argue that such kinds of assertive behavior were unearned claims to privilege, the simple proscription of this behavior was no longer feasible. They made a better case when they insisted in the face of such behavior that empire could still do much for its subjects, since empire remained the place of power, the home of enterprise, and the center of wealth. The term "viability" began to be heard at large. The question was asked: "Is colonial nationalism, of the type being publicized on all sides, viable?" On what economic foundation could it rely if it was determined to pursue to the bitter end its political quarrels with the "colonial situation"—which was, after all, the situation that had bred whatever prosperity the colony could boast? And this argument the colonial elites could not easily dismiss. Not all their members were so charmed with the idea of independence that they wished to cut every connection, commercial and other, that pumped into their countries what vitality they had.

Behind both the argument and its acceptance lay an old assumption indeed, one which had also long commanded consent—that possession was nine points of the law.

The lawgivers in the postwar world sat on a familiar bench. It seemed that if they drew themselves together and kept up appearances, they might yet find their way. But law, power, and weakness were not the terms in which their sense of reality now expressed itself. These terms had never been popular. The audience to which every public document was now addressed was known to be permantly encamped on the side of liberty and justice—although encamped on mysterious sites no explorer had ever mapped, since in each generation different names had been given to the definitions of both. But it was possible and sensible to assert the facts of life, though these had to be read between lines rather than on them. The Charter of the United Nations Organization was one such document, signed at San Francisco on June 26, 1945. Its second article asserted the right of a nation to be the sole judge and regulator of its internal affairs. This surprised nobody, since if the clause had not been there no nation would ever have agreed to sign the Charter. Among these internal affairs the Imperial Powers naturally included the business conducted within their overseas properties. They had always reckoned such business a domestic matter—no outsider had ever been summoned to arbitrate the Irish question, for example— and they saw no reason to change their minds after fighting a war one of the chief aims of which was to retain what they had. Trespassers must still be prosecuted—and if liberal and humanitarian ideas were among these trespassers, and were now preparing to penetrate every ground they claimed to be within the patrimony of public conscience, the Imperial Powers thought it better that those who had experience handling this conscience, as they had of handling everything else, should stay in charge of the tactics by which these ideas were deployed.

Accordingly, Article 73 was also in the Charter to remind everyone that idealism had not been forgotten by those best qualified to
guard it. It declared that the signatories to the Charter, including
of course the Imperial Powers, regarded it as "their sacred mission
. . . to grant the political aspirations of native peoples, and to aid
them in the gradual development of their free political institutions."
How seriously this pledge was taken the memorialists of the day
do not tell, but the use of the word "sacred" is suspicious and even
then probably did more harm than good. Certainly a mission, a right
to grant (or not grant), and policies of gradualism, aid, and development, were all well-thumbed terms taken from the political diction-
aries of the 1920s. Those who listened to their cataloging now were
much the same people who had listened to their cataloging then,
with much the same expression on their faces.

Leadership was therefore still a western monopoly; only westerners were equipped to understand and implement it. Since there
had been no change of mind, there was no change of habit. Things
had once more to be put in their proper places. People, too. Consequently, it was not surprising that the year 1945-46 was known in
Asia as the reoccupation. (Only the Filipinos, who had been com-
batants in and not spectators of the war, called it the liberation.)[18]
Yet the self-appointed leaders knew they could not afford to lose
face by turning their heads too often to see if anyone was following
them. Victory always walks cautiously, picking its way among the
rubble. Europe itself was littered with it. The empires owned by
Europe were less materially damaged, but they had been left in a
physical and a psychological vacuum. Nothing could be more dangerous, since people easily accustom themselves to an absence of
instruction. The vacuum must be filled: the customary agents were
ready to fill it. No doubt the future would present its problems, but
these would not be made simpler by indecisiveness in the present,
a time, as always, to be seized and used. In 1919 some of the Imperial
Powers had had to decide quickly what to do with the African and
Asian properties belonging to another Imperial Power, properties
which had been left derelict as a result of the world war. In 1945
the Powers had to take care of their own properties. So the conference of the Soviet, American, and British leaders that convened at

Potsdam on July 23, 1945, decided that these three Powers had rights of general disposal and that French Indochina south of the sixteenth parallel should be put under British command.

Ho Chi Minh's Vietminh, which had been established in 1941 to rid the country of "French and Japanese fascists" and which was then in power at Hanoi and Saigon (a condition not to be repeated until thirty years had passed), was recognized by nobody except perhaps by the Office of Strategic Services of the U.S. army, which that summer was still parachuting instructors into the peninsula to train Ho's soldiers. Possibly Ho was confused by this state of affairs, and accordingly, when issuing his Declaration of Independence of the Democratic Republic of Vietnam on September 2, 1945, he took care to remind the world that "we are convinced that the Allied nations, which at Tehran and San Francisco have acknowledged the principles of self-determination and equality of nations, will not refuse to acknowledge the independence of Vietnam." The French in Indochina would understand (or so he assured them in October) to what extent the existence and imposition of colonialism had misused the reputation of France, by bringing on the Annamese "disastrous calamities—forced labor, *corvées*, salt tax, compulsory consumption of opium and alcohol, heavy taxes, complete absence of freedom, incessant terrorism, moral and material sufferings, and ruthless exploitation."[19] Ho had said these things before—indeed they were all lifted from speeches and articles that had doubtless been yellowing in his drawer for years. But it was a new experience for colonial Frenchmen to have these things said to their faces, on what they still thought of as their patrimony, by someone they had always regarded as a rebel, in circumstances they assessed as ridiculous.

The experience would, however, become familiar, if never welcome. "Do not keep the air of the conqueror," General LeClerc was told when he took over the command in Indochina on January 28, 1946, from the British forces that had been keeping the French place warm: "You have lost all the battles."[20] From the colonial standpoint the lost battles were far more significant than the won war. Victors might choose to remember only what Churchill had called the "turning of the tide," but observers of the victory remembered also the day the tide had gone out—and, aware of the natural habits of a tide, were willing to wait, in the certainty it would happen again. The Great Powers had all lost their greatness at each other's hands: France, Britain, and the Netherlands had been defeated in 1940, the United States in 1941 and 1942, the Soviet Union between 1941 and 1943, Italy in 1943, and Germany and Japan in 1945. Prestige, like heaven's mandate, could belong only to those to whom defeat was unknown. No pretensions could take its place. But that such a direct and wounding comment could be made about the past—the past, imperialism's core country, the heart of its power! —and to the French in particular, a people whom the misfortunes of war had relegated to the sidelines and who consequently were more determined than anyone to restore things and to ignore all the clamor about new ideas, winds of change, and trends of the times— was clear evidence that the colonial assertion of the 1920s and 1930s had developed a truculence which, if left uncontradicted, would carry everything before it.

What could contradict it?

A generation of the French army, from 1945 to 1961, certainly thought it had both the right and the ability to do this. Not only was this army anxious to take up once more the burden of empire, but it was also determined to purge the past of all stains on its honor, and no amount of rhetoric from Annamese or from left wingers at home and abroad—none of which was new—would make it swerve from either task. France *outre-mer* had managed to stand for a French presence in the world when France's presence in Europe had been submerged: in May and June 1940 all the Third Republic's colonial commanders in chief had continued to resist, but after the capitulation of June 17 the army had, true to another of its traditions, closed its ranks in support of the state and taken its orders from the Vichy government and from Marshal Pétain so long as both had some semblance of authority. When the war was over, the army had become an amalgamation of de Gaulle's Free French forces and of the regular African army, and this contingent was "to pass on *in toto* to the post-war Army the reactionary ideology adopted by the Vichy regime."[21] Its officers cordially welcomed the coming of the Cold War, which drew the lines of ideological battle, and which officially stamped all subversion as originating in Moscow.

They had long believed this, and they saw no reason not to be delighted with a condition of international affairs that raised the amount of military credits available for operations to reestablish French rule in Indochina from 3.2 billion francs in 1945 to 308 billion francs in 1951. In their view Ho Chi Minh, since he had been recognized by Peking and Moscow in January 1950, was not the authentic representative of the Vietnamese people. But Emperor Bao Dai, as President Truman agreed, was. Military defeat at Dien Bien Phu in 1954 did not alter many minds in an army that could count 92 thousand killed in a worthy cause. The Indochina experience, brought to a halt by the Powers at Geneva that year, was reckoned the only true French passport to bring to the task of returning Algeria to its French senses. The case was even stronger there, since Algeria was part of France itself. Algerian nationalism thus constituted one more advance guard of the Communist conspiracy, and it was pointless to compromise with such. See what had happened when civilian Frenchmen, who were apparently capable of believing any nonsense, had thrown away all French advantages in Morocco and Tunisia in the same abominable year, 1954. No matter what paper safeguards for French interests Pierre Mendès-France had obtained there, the French found themselves confined to an anteroom and before another year had passed saw the door even to this shut on them — and they were out, gone. Of course, in reality the Muslim population of the Maghrib was warmly attached to France, whatever campaign of fear the Front du Libération Nationale (F.L.N.), or whatever it chose to call itself, might choose to mount.

This bitter quarrel between the military and the civilians about the nature and duties of the present, so vividly illustrated in French imperial affairs, was only one aspect of the larger contradictions that harried those who were then in charge of an empire, a state, or an army. Ideology, with all its rigidities and ground rules, had always known the world was hostile. It expected to have its nonconverts, and because it was this honest in its outlook, ideologists thought it vastly easier to cope with determined enemies than with the unclarity of purpose of those who held no convictions whatever. French soldiers who believed in "pacification" for the honor of France and the good of mankind even as they went to work in the torture rooms of Constantine could never believe in the integrity of anyone else. Reality was what one mind saw as obvious, and if trend meant anything, it could mean only that those who said they were following it had no minds of their own to begin with. This argument was of course rejected outright by all those who saw military men less as guardians than as warders, and'in a Europe that had recently seen militarism carried to its absolute extremes, these people were in the majority. Reappraisal and reassessment, the rejection of dogma and of the kind of men who were happiest when they did not have to think at all, had become habitual in government and educated circles even before any colonial issue had elevated itself from the agenda to the headlines.

The first forum of debate on the matter was an open one indeed, given worldwide publicity. The trial at Nuremburg of German war criminals, a trial instituted and conducted by the victor Powers, was based on the premise, one that had never before been a support for the apparatus of jurisprudence, that it was not acceptable for men to give or to take orders conflicting with the principles of decency, morality, and humanity. That if this premise had been consistently applied in history no nation could ever have mustered either a government or an army did not trouble this generation, which let lawyers puzzle out its implications. The important point was to redefine decency, morality, and humanity: and to broadcast their elements afresh. The conscience of intelligent people everywhere was still sore. Their feelings could be moved more readily than their reason. For over a century an upright, homebred intelligentsia had thought of imperial power as a questionable factor in maintaining a civilized world order. Now they were ready to answer their question and to diagnose this power as a type of poison.

The findings of those who looked through this microscope were much the same everywhere, whatever the time of the day or the place of the laboratory. Cambridge University's Eric Walker had written in *Colonies* in 1944 that "countless decent folk who know little or nothing of the history of colonial Empires have come to believe that it is an offence against the public and private morals to attempt to govern a colonial Empire at all."[22] If empires were bad, imperialism were worse. Elie Kedourie in 1970 confirmed Walker's view, although he found fewer decent folk to tally. In the years since the war he had seen the development of a fashionable western sentimentality, that Great Powers were intrinsically nasty and small powers inevitably virtuous. In particular, he identified influential orientalists and commentators on Middle Eastern affairs among those who, from their base at the Royal Institute of International Affairs at Chatham House, had been most successful in spreading a deep sense of guilt among the English intellectual and political establishment, finally making it incapable of taking any decisive, or even necessary, action.[23] George Kirk, one orientalist who felt free from such guilt, had already acidly pointed out the natural result of its influence. Errors made were those of omission, not commission. During the decade 1945-55 in the Middle East—in Egypt, Palestine, Persia, and Iraq—Britain had elected to bring down the curtain on dramas it had written and produced: no wonder, then, that it had had to leave these various theaters with a red face, with offensive cries from Nasser, Ben-Gurion, Mossadegh, and Kassem hurtling after it.

Kirk quoted the diatribe issued in Egypt by Musa Alami, whom he reckoned an Arab "moderate." After the British, tiring of the perpetual Palestine harassment, had in February 1947 handed over the whole "question" to the United Nations, thus precipitating both the partitioning of the country and the first of what was to become a series of Arab-Israeli wars, Musa in October 1949 wrote down what he saw as "the lesson of Palestine." This lesson was plain:

The prime causers of the disaster were the British. It was they who gave the Jews the Balfour Declaration in 1917 with its "national home," and then opened the doors to them. British protection and patronage enabled the Jews to make Palestine their home, and to multiply. Under the protection of British arms Jewish colonies were founded and extended, and Jewish immigration flourished. Under the wings of the British Mandate Jewish terrorism hatched and grew, and was trained by British hands until it became an organized military force. During all this the British prevented us [Arabs] from arming, and shut our eyes to the arming of the Jews, until the time came when they were strong enough to stand on their own feet. Then the British withdrew and announced their neutrality. Thus the British were the prime causers of the disaster, and on them lies the responsibility.[24]

This particular "moderate" indictment was wrong on some counts and failed to include others that would have strengthened its case: but the point was not what it said but that it was said at all, that it was delivered as a judgment against an Imperial Power that had always acted as sole judge of its conduct and had never admitted another competent court of investigation could exist. Non-Europeans who had never found room or time to indulge in either sentimentality or fashion (the natural privileges of the comfortable), were quick to drive home the advantage presented them by the guilt feelings of their masters. Men off-balance morally were more easily unseated politically.

That World War II had been an imperialist war launched by the European Imperial Powers for their own distinctively European and imperial ends was something not disputed among those who lived in many of the areas where much of it had been fought. These areas were colonial, all of them: French and Italian North Africa, British and Italian East Africa, British-controlled Egypt and Iraq, the American Philippines, everybody's Melanesia and Micronesia, and the Dutch East Indies. "The same old game . . . the actors are the same, and the results must be the same," wrote Nehru to Gandhi on February 4, 1940.[25] The "great game" which had been invented by the Victorians for their advantage and pleasure was still being played by the same players for the same reasons. When peace came, as it would when they had reached a state of exhaustion after a stiffer contest than usual, there apparently was no reason why, after a suitably restorative interval, the game should not resume.

Or was there a reason? Nehru had made his comment during the period of "phony war," before any of the contestants had got to grips. Six months later everything looked different and would stay that way. What happened thereafter in India could be used as a textbook for the tactics of assertion. A planned program of civil disobedience had been begun there by the Congress on October 17, 1940. Nehru had been arrested by the *raj* on October 31 and had been given a four-year prison sentence: but he had been released on December 4, 1941, three days before the Americans entered the war. By February 1942, while the eastern empires were indeed tumbling like dominoes before the Japanese onslaught, he was describing the Allied cause in general and the British war effort in particular as "an arrogant imperialism which is indistinguishable from fascist authoritarianism." To him the Atlantic Charter was a pious and nebulous expression of hope, stimulating nobody, since in fact and

in intent it was not addressed to anybody. The people who controlled India from Whitehall and from Delhi were incapable of understanding what was happening, much less of dealing with it. A true
war strategy would require the sacrifices not only of the lives of
brave men but also of racial prejudices, of inherited conceptions of
political or economic domination and the exploitation of others, of
the vested interests of small groups that hindered the growth and
development of others. Where now, he demanded, were the vested
interests of Hong Kong and Singapore? The "Quit India" resolution
passed by Congress on August 7, 1942, he described as "the voice
of the entire oppressed humanity of the world."[26] The *raj* then
locked him up, from August 9, 1942, to June 15, 1945, and outlawed the Congress party itself. But the questions the *raj* had refused
to answer in war now returned in peace in full volume and from all
quarters. How long could the rest of oppressed humanity be penned
in jails by imperial jailers? And in what jail, or in what Sherwood
Forest, could they be confined and named outlaw? These were the
problems facing the controllers in the future. For the controlled, in
their own view the oppressed, what counted was the present, whose
difficulties were the most obvious. To them, oppression, not appeasement, seemed to be back in style.

Many of empire's first agents in Asia had been soldiers; so were
many of its last. The early pioneers had usually had enough common
sense to realize that, if they were to survive and prosper as a handful among the many, they must regulate their conduct to suit the
events of the day and to bend with a wind when it blew. For the
last arrivals this was still serviceable behavior: pragmatism does not
alter from one era to another. Returning soldiers, now dispatched
from Europe to reoccupy the imperial forts, were not abreast of the
literature on nationalism or in the habit of reading the weightier
editorials. Their knowledge of the politics of complaint was sketchy,
and they could not contribute much to the debate then current
about alienation and a world gone awry. But they knew what policemen always know—that complaint takes noisy forms, all of which
are contrary to the preservation of good order and military discipline. If a street became so crowded with agitators that the law abid-
ing could not pass, the soldiers' business was to clear it: and to do
so they would use whatever means were at hand.

The Dutch East Indies was the first disputed property to which they came. On August 17, 1945, two days after the general Japanese surrender, Sukarno proclaimed the independence of Indonesia. On September 29, British troops landed at the capital Jakarta, which they continued to call Batavia; and, as they did simultaneously at Saigon in Indochina, they employed both Indian and Japanese troops to help them maintain the necessary law and order. They did not choose to involve themselves in what they regarded as "local politics," and their very disinterest did Indonesian nationalism a particular service: for by recognizing Sukarno's regime as the de facto government in the islands, the British commander in chief created a situation which compelled the Dutch and the Indonesians to negotiate with one another, however bitterly, while the British were in the chair. The troops did not leave until November 30, 1946, and by then the Indonesian nationalist cause had gained unprecedented worldwide attention.

Yet these military expeditions and dispositions, these arrangements of local deals, which attracted little public attention in Britain, also made it clear to the world's observers that the basic imperial attitudes had not changed. Paternalism was still the mode. It was present even in those who criticized its current activities, for it can certainly be distilled from General Douglas MacArthur's announcement that his blood boiled when he saw "America's allies deploying Japanese troops to reconquer the little peoples [*sic*] we promised to liberate. It is the most ignoble kind of betrayal." Predictably, Nehru told *The New York Times* that he thought the same.[27] The charge puzzled the British, who indeed had no imperial plans of their own in Indochina and Indonesia. But to the critical eye this made the business so much worse, that the British should consider it a natural and fraternal task to occupy territory in the East until the Dutch and the French had managed to organize enough shipping and soldiery in Europe to take over what they thought of as their customary places of power in their own empires.

The Dutch, once arrived, were not involved in a brisk police action but were plunged into a colonial war and were unable to establish any firm footing until a military truce had been arranged on January 17, 1948. In the meantime, developments in the Cold War had done them a favor, for they were encouraged by the terms of the Marshall

Plan issued in the summer of 1947—the plan which, as it is seen in hindsight by all who liken the Cold War to a duck decoy, was "the major thrust to preserve the capitalist system in a post-war crisis-ridden world."[28] Capital certainly was given to the Dutch. The plan allocated $506 million to growth in the Netherlands and allowed that $84 million of this amount might be used by the Dutch government "for the development of" Indonesia. But both the favor and the truce turned out to be temporary: the latter broke in December 1948, and, as a British observer noted, "by a strange irony January 1, 1949, the day on which it had been agreed that all Indonesia should be fully self-governing, saw the erection of a wire cage on Manubing Hill on the island of Banka—the total area in which the Prime Minister [Hatta] and his cabinet were allowed to take their exercise."[29]

The Dutch, with 140 thousand troops in the islands, resumed the battle until they were compelled to admit defeat in the spring of 1949. The compulsion was less military than moral and political. Their dilemma at the United Nations was acute, and their position in the State Department even worse, because Acheson warned Foreign Minister Stikker that unless the Netherlands accepted the position the Indonesians desired them to take, Marshall Aid might well be withdrawn.[30] For the respect spectators accord to a knockdown, "clean" fight is not granted to a war of attrition and increasing atrocity, as the Dutch were the first, but by no means the last, in this era to find out. The sense of public outrage began to stir and the alarm to sound in a western world then eager to take up the colors of all free peoples who were not Communists. Since Sukarno in Indonesia had all his life been fighting a running battle with the Communists, and had recently quelled a P.K.I. rebellion, Washington did not think it politic to see him and his cause cut down. Nor was it.

Thus the Dutch discovered that the cold shoulder could be turned even on a Cold War colleague. Colonialism could be publicly disavowed when it menaced only a particular colonialist government and not the opinions or the security of the democratic West as a whole. With such a situation in mind, Walter Lippmann publicly repeated, on January 10, 1949, the arguments about India that John Paton Davies and others had earlier used in private correspondence. America's friends in Western Europe, Lippmann urged, must try to understand why we cannot and must not be maneuvered, why we dare not drift, into general opposition to the independence movements in Asia. . . . They should try to realize how disastrous it would be to them, and to the cause of western civilization, if ever it could be said that the western union for the defense of freedom in Europe was, in Asia, a syndicate for the preservation of decadent Empires.[31]

Could such a thing be said? Indeed it could, and increasingly it was. Lippmann's use of the term "syndicate" struck a sinister note, since it evoked the image of organized crime. Were imperialists, then, nothing but a lot of *mafiosi*, their boasted paternalism merely the self-serving of so many dons and godfathers?

Empire had been designed as a system of world order; as a consequence of their pride in this, imperialists had claimed that they were fulfilling the necessary role of guardian, carrying out a mandate which only the powerful could honor. But now empire's reputation was gone, and the occupation for the imperialist fast diminishing, because empire had clearly failed in its primary task. It had not maintained order. Its law was not respected. It had not expanded the horizon for its subjects. It had not even been able to command their adherence, let alone their loyalty. Chinese in Malaya, Chinese in Hong Kong, Malays in Malaya, Burmese in Burma had not risen as one man to support their imperial protectors when the latter were attacked and displaced by an alien enemy. In the imperial milieu, as seen from below, one foreigner was much the same as another, equally self-centered. Foreigners were met, as they had always been, by an equal egocentricity from those over whom they set themselves. Indonesians could not be supposed to have developed much love for the Japanese between 1942 and 1945: but when they took over and maintained the governmental substructure in their own islands, they at once furthered their own aims, effectively supported the Japanese, and certainly proved that they had no love whatever for the Dutch and that they had not hidden away for the duration of the occupation loyalties which would now be brought out afresh in good condition. These facts were too obvious to be ignored by European critics who were sometimes quicker than their imperial subjects to conclude that the imperial system needed not so much reappraisal as demolition. Criticisms easily dismissed previously as mere impertinence were now sifted and weighed for the truths they contained, in however granulated and minuscule a form. Even the supporters of empire knew that if it did not somehow find a better system of "public relations," if it could not justify its presence in the world as the world had now become, it would certainly be forced out of existence by a combination of its guilt and the predilections of its powerful friends.

But no adequate way of presenting an imperial case occurred to imperialists, as they watched their numbers dwindle. One chief result of the loss of power was the decline of imagination. Indeed, there had never been much of this evident in the heyday of empire, though imperialism as a creed had insisted on its dogged attachment to concepts like trusteeship and development. These had lived—and, as it now turned out, were to die—in a customary condition of comfortable vagueness. Hubert Deschamps was referring in particular to colonial administration during the interwar years of the century when he described the typical situation as one of *plénitude territoriale et incertitude doctrinale*, in a period when nobody had made plans (as opposed to daydreams) *à longue portée*:[32] but this was true of the entire European imperial experience, whose administrators were always more interested in peace and quiet, balancing books, and transporting goods to the world's market than in the political education of those they lived with. Policy, as has been noted, was always "in short supply"; and here the end of empire had some affinity with its beginnings. People will make arrangements for a birth. They will for a funeral. It is what happens in between that is left to chance. The record of empire underlines this. As Robert Heussler pointed out,

At the start of each colony's association with England, policy was important, for there had to be a reason to move forward. At the end of the colonial time, similarly, there was a rationale of going away. In between, the landscape was dominated by a system, not a policy.[33]

This system, one of *immobilisme*, was now under indictment.

As a result, affairs that had the merit of moving were granted more attention than they sometimes strictly deserved. In the late 1950s people in the Western world continued to listen closely to those outside who had a great deal to say about the future. In 1955 an Afro-Asian conference, the first of its kind, gathered at Bandung in Indonesia. Three-hour harangues were commonplace there. Nothing new was said and nothing was arranged that was afterward carried out. In 1956 a congress of black writers and artists assembled at Paris, only a stone's throw from the cafés where many of them had in the 1930s issued their accounts of *négritude* and the human condition. In 1959 Moscow followed the trend by setting up an "Africa Institute," whose curriculum was often to startle blacks who had learned their Marxism in European and colonial universities and were therefore accustomed to a free exchange of ideas. Every such gathering perceived itself as part of a "Movement," and it continued to be a movement more away from something than toward something, as was inevitable at the time. What faced its members, it was said on one of these occasions, was "the massive task of reshaping the past in order to forge the future."[34] As Walter Bagehot once said of Oxford University, this meant well but not much. Certainly, nobody had to provide explanations; and the fact that such unfounded assertions could be made was less important than the fact that the longtime assertions were now also recognized as unfounded.

Territorial imperialism, which had never had any real ideological content beyond the national self-interest of the particular Imperial Power, had no friends in public places. High places had always got this message quickly; as early as January 1921, the "Indian," soon to be "African," expert Lord Hailey had remarked that "in an eastern country success in administration depends quite as much on the maintenance of a general atmosphere of obedience to authority and acceptation [*sic*] of the existing order of society as it does on the definite enforcement of statute law or the working of the administrative machinery."[35] From the existing order of society, this general atmosphere now evaporated, and the acceptance was withdrawn.

The ability to cut losses with grace depends on the amount of the loss and the degree of the shock. A shock can be cushioned only if cushions are available. The bureaucracies of large states could absorb many of the redundant imperial officials, and so could remoter colonies not yet awakened by all this uproar, colonies like Fiji and the Maldive Islands. Or generous pensions, "golden bowlers," could be found for those not thought career-worthy. In Asia, therefore, the alien official could afford to spend a few years "working himself out of a job," and take reasonable pride in the skill and amiability with which he did so. When he left, he did not leave his kin behind. In a continent of millions, there had never been implanted sizable segments of Europe, "settler colonies" to which the end of imperial control would signify not a self-congratulatory lesson in liberal political science but the death of the settlers' hopes and, possibly, of themselves. In Africa, other peoples' losses were to be cut, for in the north, the east, and the center of this continent such colonies existed.

In 1954, the year that the French quit Indochina, there were 850,000 settlers—*colons* if one was French, *pieds noirs* if one was not—living among the 9 million Muslim inhabitants of French Algeria. (This fact also presented particular facets to those who looked at it: to the *colon* Algeria was not *outre-mer* at all but an extension of metropolitan France across a Mediterranean river.) By the law of September 20, 1947, Algeria was ruled by a governor-general responsible to the minister of the interior. Ninety percent of the country's industrial and commercial enterprises were in *colon* hands. In such a situation, even statistics assumed an emotional color and could be read as telling the oppressor's tale: "the *colon* agrarian area was equipped with 19,509 tractors, the Muslim sector with 418"; and, as late as 1956, of 864 high administrative posts only 8 were held by Muslims.[36] On February 10, 1943, while the French, Americans, and British were all coursing the country on their military business, Ferhat Abbas produced a manifesto on behalf of his Union Populaire Algérienne. This manifesto advocated a policy of *rattachement* rather than of *assimilation* and called for an autonomous Algerian republic federated to a renovated French Republic. De Gaulle, as the leader of "Free France," strove for the second goal but not for the first. Accordingly, the ordinance he issued on March 7, 1944, which revived the spirit of the Popular Front's lost Blum-Violette legislation of 1936 by envisaging the grant of full citizenship to 60 thousand Muslims, was dismissed by Abbas and his *Amis du Manifeste* as "out-dated." Thereafter, dates signified different things to different people; and VE-day in Europe (May 8, 1945) was marked in Algeria not by glad rejoicings but by a furious battle at Sétif between *colons* and Muslims which officially claimed the lives of a hundred Europeans and over a thousand (unofficially, over 8 thousand) Muslims.

This set the pace for a series of events directed by the French in Algeria, who from 1947 to 1958 gave orders to Paris. It ensured, too, that all the "new wave" of Algerians prominent in the Front du Libération Nationale at the time of its final triumph in 1961 — including Ahmed ben Bella, who was twenty-six years old in 1945 — traced their revolutionary determination back to that day in May.[37]

It has been claimed that, until 1956, the only point on which virtually all of France concurred was that Algerian independence was unthinkable and unmentionable — a claim which proves its own uncertainty, since logically who can utter a thought that does not exist?[38] Once the Fourth Republic had made everyone in the overseas territories a citizen, even French liberals like Mendès-France could not think of Algeria as anything but "irrevocably French." In Algeria sedition was found more easily than nationalism, for no Muslim movement there had ever spoken with the authority of Néo-Destour in Tunisia or of the Istiqlal in Morocco. Ferhat Abbas himself had in 1934 declared that he could not find an Algerian fatherland. But he now had his nationalism forced upon him, and so did others, for *colon* behavior, a composite of fear and rage, was of a kind that welded even the most disparate groups of those wanting to make themselves heard. Younger men combined within the interstices of the older groupings, and whenever some of the leaders were arrested in the towns, others appointed themselves in the hills. A general revolt, fomented by a Comité Révolutionnaire pour l'Unité et l'Action, broke out on November 1, 1954. "At one o'clock this morning," Cairo Radio reported excitedly, "Algeria began to live a worthy and honorable life."

Jacques Soustelle, who became governor-general on January 26, 1955, believed that worth and honor belonged only where they had always belonged, in French hands, and opened his term of office with the announcement that, whatever happened, the destiny of Algeria was French. But the destiny of Algeria was no more French than that of Indochina. Soustelle read the future better when he declared in 1957 that it seemed, alas, "as if there are some who would like to replace what they call French colonialism — a colonialism that has built roads, bridges, and harbors in Algeria as well as schools, hospitals, and dispensaries — by a kind of neo-colonialism, though it does not call itself that, which appears to be exclusively concerned with profits, oil, and dollars."[39] An Algeria given over to bomb outrages was relinquished to the excesses of General Massu and his paratroops on January 7, 1957, and from that point became inextricably entangled with the political confusions and the military misconceptions that strangled the Fourth and released the Fifth French Republic, finally allowing de Gaulle to make his assertions the politics of the day and to impose his solution on the affairs of not only *Algérie française* but the French Empire as a whole. A realist in his romantic way, he was ready to accept the argument that *Le Monde* of Paris, not his favorite journal, had been putting forward for a long time. Réné Service had written, soon after the Algerian revolt broke out, that the truth of the matter was that metropolitan France was incapable of assimilating the 40 million people who belonged to countries that were and would remain economically retarded. To believe otherwise was mere sentimentality. It was time to discard mental lumber of this kind. It was time for thought. It was certainly time to scrap once and for all the idea of a civilizing mission, for "this most generous of myths has been destroyed by the facts of the twentieth century."[40]

What was this myth? And what were these facts?

Cynical journalists do not run states, and what was sentimentality to the columnists of *Le Monde* was in other quarters a defeat of the spirit. One of its recent examiners says that myth in the French context should not be interpreted "as imputing a false or irrational character to the ideas in question"[41] —but to make this point is to allow that many such interpreters have always been about. Myth and common sense have never kept company. The myth was embodied in the vision, one held by virtually the entire French elite, that an indissoluble link existed between the metropolis and its colonies. The link was indissoluble because it was not concrete but, supposedly, spiritual. The vision spanned a wider horizon than any that would ever be seen from actual territory, for its boundaries were the "common universe of discourse" that was the patrimony of people of goodwill. Where such people had been bred and educated did not matter. No one need list the benefits that resulted for all concerned, since these spoke for themselves in the French language, the language that was the heritage of every native of this universe. The development, *la mise en valeur* of France and its colonies, would make good the extension of the great movement that was Europe's pride, the Enlightenment itself — for Europe would remain, to men like Albert Sarraut, "the illustrious cradle of everything that was quality." Lyautey, another son of France, had preached and practiced all his life that only a *classe dirigeante* could recognize this quality and could know best how to reveal its essence and its texture. It was de Gaulle's own theme, the one that guided his life and permeates his memoirs: "To me, France cannot be France without grandeur." And this grandeur had nothing to do with counting hectares of ground across the map of the earth. On this as on other themes, the last words said were echoes of the first.

In 1874 the most influential of France's imperialist seers of the nineteenth century, Paul Leroy-Beaulieu, had written in his *De la colonization chez les peuples modernes* (a book which became a political bible and was in its fifth edition by 1908) that for France colonization was "a matter of life and death. Either France will become a great African Power, or in a century or two she will be a secondary Power in Europe, she will count in the world for little more than Greece or Roumania counts in Europe." Ten years later Jules Ferry was translating this into political terms, hammering it home, trying to make it a commonplace "Nations, in our time, are great only according to the activity they develop."[12] And in Ferry's time it did indeed become a commonplace and has remained one throughout our own. His English contemporaries Curzon and Chamberlain and Milner put the same argument to the anti-imperialists around them, men whom they saw as eccentrics, purblind men who were potential inhabitants of a "Little England" which, with no role to play, would be confined to the narrowest of corners, doing the least of things. For what message could *un peuple casanier*, a homebound people, ever deliver that anyone would hear? What life could they live that anyone would ever take for an example? What pride could they find that would carry them safely though the emergencies lying in wait to test every generation?

To "count" in the world. This had always been empire's principal reason for existing. Empire had made it a principle of life, had made it the justification for everything done by imperialism. This was a nation's passport to right of entry and right of passage, right to rule and right to pride. Only such a passport could transport time travelers safely into the future, a future wherein they would never be lost.

These assumptions, their rhetoric only slightly changed by the passage of seventy years, underlay the Fourth Republic's construction in 1946 of a French Union and received their first shock when Syria and Lebanon denounced the mandate under which they had existed, but not lived, for a generation. The shock waves radiated undergound thereafter, but never far under it, for this action proved to be a prologue to another twenty years of colonial assertion. Here was yet another case where a national destiny could not be made manifest to those who had conceived their destiny in other terms. "If only," Habib Bourguiba wrote from Tunis on June 29, 1946, to Ferhat Abbas, then exiled in Cairo, "If only France made an effort to understand us!"[43] Both these men genuinely admired the French world, but they perceived themselves as already freemen of it. They wanted to be truly thought of as such: France should recognize the value of what men like themselves brought to the French world. But this was asking too much. The French never realized the amount of understanding expected of them. Why, anyway, should they have to make any such effort? Their view was that effort was the business and the duty of those they had enlightened, so that they might keep their place in the light.

Enlightenment also takes its place among the myths born in Europe and displays the same characteristics. Myths are particular and peculiar artifacts: that is to say, they are peculiar to particular people. In the political world they are inevitably nationalist, part of an exclusive territorial equipment. They have significance only for those who have invented them and who therefore know how to use them. What they signify and symbolize will not translate into terms that anyone else will understand. So the French prophets who assumed that they spoke for the people of a universal country found out—late in the evening but still much earlier than Leroy-Beaulieu and his disciples had reckoned—that the people would not honor them because the people did not recognize this country as their own. They had their own traditions and symbols, which they had preserved the more resolutely because nobody else, certainly not the alien prophets, would admit that such traditions and symbols existed. Since the universalist myth had not been created by those it was designed to benefit, it seemed to these people only a cloud of fiction, thrown up by the self-serving to cover realities that dared

not disclose either their true names or their real purpose. From beyond the bounds of the French Republic, of the French Empire, of
the French Union, and of the French universe—indeed from the
other mysterious universe, once epitomized as "darkest Africa"—
came a genuinely universal comment, one that spoke for the truth
of a situation recognized throughout the colonial world. Joseph
Kasavubu's Alliance des Bakongo (Akabo) on August 24, 1956,
made its position, and this situation, plain: "Only one claim justifies
colonization, and that is consent."[44]

Privilege is fact, not fiction. It is not confounded by myth, since
nothing about it is the least bit romantic. Consent is never volun-
tarily given it, since every doctrine based on rights denies its right
to exist. On all imperial proving grounds the assumptions of the
European *classes dirigeantes*, assumptions so often masked at home
by subtle social arrangements which avoided definition wherever
they could, had always been apparent. The people who spoke of
quality could never assume that it was other than rare or that anyone except themselves would ever recognize it. Their program of
"law and order" had ensured the peace of their group by maintaining the subservience of all others. Empire presupposed that a society
existed and that its ordered and orderly elements would not change
—or should not, if the ruling classes stayed true to their principles
of rule. It imposed such a society where it went: and it wanted to
think no more about this.

While Leroy-Beaulieu was analyzing the nature of colonization,
Fitzjames Stephen in England was parsing the principles of *Liberty,
Equality, Fraternity* (1874). He found them all philosophically un-
sound and called them all practically dangerous. They had hard and
knifelike edges, which old societies could pare or cover up. But in
new societies, working under imposed rules, they were constantly
exposed. He noted that the law in England had been accepted for
centuries, and because this was so "the lions under the throne" need
never roar. But in places where nothing could be taken for granted,
roaring was essential and had to be done on a regular basis. No room
for compromise existed, since compromise was, in the upshot, com-
promising to those who held power. Stephen knew the Indian scene
firsthand. There the English had never been proselytizers. But they
had found, as everyone who has to deal with legislation must find,

that laws have to be based on principles and that it is impossible to lay down any principles of legislation "unless you are prepared to say, I am right, and you are wrong, and your view shall give way to mine, quietly, gradually, and peaceably; but one of us two must rule and the other must obey—and I mean to rule."[45]

This was the true imperial style. When so displayed, the entire principle of "law and order" clearly belonged, as did Mercator's projection, to a distinctive kind of mental geography and to a particular world view—a view that was to be seen only from the windows of the privileged.

Certainties of this sort no longer existed by the middle of the twentieth century. The windows of the privileged were starred and shattered by all the uproar that had broken out beyond them. It was the day of democracy, and since its dawn imperial power and all the other appurtenances of privilege had lived at risk. That this would come about had been forecast by every nineteenth-century commentator of any standing. What a thinking oligarchy had stored, an unthinking democracy would scatter. Tocqueville had remarked that he was not more disposed to fall beneath the yoke because it was held out to him by the arms of a million men. Sir Henry Maine had insisted that the doctrine of natural rights was only the divine right of kings in a new dress and that the opened way to democracy might be only a way "into a receptacle of loose earth and sand." Even then, Power had been questioned: the fact that one political business of the day had been known as "the Irish question" proved it, for this matter had been concerned less with the destinies of the Irish people than with the assumptions of their English masters. "Say where the line should be drawn," Daniel O'Connell had cried, "which determines that servitude should end, and liberty commence!" If there has been only one definition of servitude, there have always been as many definitions of liberty as there have been democrats.

Karl Marx had warned that theory becomes a practical force when it is absorbed by the masses. One need not refer to Russian history alone to prove him right. But no one at any given time can accurately chart the rate of this absorption. No one can tell when the man whom Lord Acton once called the "international extraterritorial universal Whig" is about to carry all before him—or even when he did. Yet clearly the rise of European empire, its place in the world and its reputation in the history books, was the product of homebred assumptions about authority, assumptions which one generation of rulers dearly wanted to pass on intact to a posterity of its own kind. The disappearance of this empire resulted from the counterattack motivated by yet another assumption about authority: the one first set out two hundred years ago by British subjects in America who questioned their status. This assumption stated that true sovereignty, and therefore all privilege, properly belonged in the hands of the people. Although this entire question—"which people, who among them, how many of these?"—may never be resolved, the casualties to the status quo that this clash of assumption brought about are very remarkable and have forced themselves on everyone's attention in the thirty years that have passed since the end of the second world war.

For in these years the masses on which Karl Marx had spent his thought did indeed begin to "absorb." The assertions of the spirited and the ambitions of the nonconformists transferred themselves as practical possibilities into the awareness of at least some of the conformists—who switched their normal heedless obedience from one set of controllers to another, in the hope rather than the trust that these new leaders knew what they were about. As they did this, and were seen to do this, privilege became uneasy and began to blandish. Assertion, once so risky, became a commonplace and took a more truculent tone, since it expected to be appeased.

A direct chain of causation can therefore be traced that links phenomena (some of them fleeting) of these times like: the civil rights movement in the United States; the rise of a separatist nationalism in Scotland, Wales, and Quebec; the presence of over 141 nations, each with its labeled desk and team of delegates, at the U.N. General Assembly; the diminution of the influence of the churches; the emergence of a teen-age culture and of the industries that feed it; the student power movement; the black power movement; and, possibly the most telling of all and with the longest future, the women's liberation movement, since it seeks to emancipate one half of the human race from the colonial rule of the other half. The siege trains of these movements were laid against not only the walls of all the empires but the parks and pales of privilege everywhere. It is a continuing campaign, and its tactics are predictable, for its strategy was

laid down in a script written by John Wesley and George Whitefield
—those "Jack Cades in cassocks." To read what they said is to understand why the ruling class of their day could not accommodate
within the clerical or any other establishment either them or the
Methodist movement they led (although indeed it tried). "If the
one is rich and the other poor, does not justice stand afar off? . . .
Perhaps the hazard is greater among us, than either among Jews,
Turks, or heathens." Perhaps it was, and is, indeed.

Fifty years ago Arnold Toynbee wrote that the founding of the
Turkish Republic was a monument to the ascendancy that the
modern civilization of the West had established in the contemporary
world.[46] This thought might also cover these other republics that
now make up the tally at the U.N. Yet if the image of a monument
now seems fanciful, and westerners on the whole avoid making large
claims for the degree of their civilization, Toynbee's reference to
modernity still needs to be thought through. To be modern, as David
Apter observes in his *The Politics of Modernization* (1961), means
to see life as alternatives, preferences, and choices.[47] But of course
those able to see life in such a way are living proof that their position is privileged. Their next obvious step is to try out the alternative,
realize the preference, and clinch the choice. The step may be obvious; but for the majority in a world populated more by the hungry
than by the fed it remains formidably difficult.

Difficult—but perhaps not impossible. The habits of imperialism in this century have so long been under the closest scrutiny
that they hold little mystery. The mystique that the white race
was a superior one, and therefore naturally entitled to its superior
position, has been exposed as another imperialist myth. No longer
respected by nonwhites, it can no longer be capitalized upon by
the whites. The latter have accordingly withdrawn to firmer stances,
to reliance on more tangible kinds of capital. But wealth need not
recognize a color line either. In 1959-60 the turnover of the Uni-
lever Corporation was £1,800 million—almost twice the combined
national incomes of Ghana and Nigeria at the time—but the capital
employed by the corporation's main African subsidiary, the United
Africa Company, was £125 million. This was a sum equal to the
total gross fixed capital investment of the same two countries in
any year.[48]

Of course, this was then the customary state of affairs — resented by most, profiting some, surprising none. But at the same time, in May 1960, the Arab League first proposed that Arab governments with oil in their lands should agree on a plan for jointly regulating supplies and prices.[49] Yet, because the Arab League since its birth in 1944 had been a league in name only, it took another thirteen years before the fact of a state of Israel, established in an area of the Middle East reckoned by the Arabs as their own, brought the Arabs to forget their differences and weld their purposes. The Arab-Israeli "October war" of 1973 was likely to remain a landmark even in a century not short on landmarks; as a direct result of the Egyptian defeat, the Arab oil producers announced they would cut their crude production by 5 percent each month and place an embargo on oil shipments to the United States and the Netherlands. It was not a final action: but the fact that it was taken at all served sharp notice of change and gave to the Organization of Petroleum Exporting Countries (O.P.E.C.) — formed at Baghdad in August 1960 by Saudi Arabia, Kuwait, Iraq, Iran, and Venezuela, and growing in number since — a position of status and respect in the eyes of the members of the industrial world who had fashioned its frame and had thought there could be no other keeper of it.

Prophetically, William d'Arcy's original concession from the shah of Persia, dated May 21, 1901, had spoken of sixty years as a time to reckon with — "a special and exclusive privilege to search for, obtain, exploit, render suitable for trade, carry away and sell natural gas, petroleum, asphalt and ozevite throughout the whole extent of the Persian Empire for a term of sixty years." And, sixty years later almost to the month, O.P.E.C. was able to take as high a tone. The first resolution it passed stated that its "members can no longer remain indifferent to the attitude heretofore adopted by the oil companies in effecting price modifications." They agreed on this, as J. E. Hartshorn points out, because they believed that since the institution of the fifty-fifty profit-sharing system in Saudi Arabia in 1950, the eight major companies that controlled oil operations had, "in continuing bad faith, posted" lower prices for Middle East crude than they were in practice able to realize; so that the half-share in profits on these posted prices accruing to the host governments in the Middle East had been artificially depressed over a period of years.[50]

Protest of this kind had been made before but in a wrong climate for its success. D'Arcy's concession had indeed been unilaterally annulled in 1932, but at the end of a year of negotiation between the shah and the Anglo-Persian Oil Company it was extended for yet another sixty years, to 1993. More serious trouble had hit the company in 1951, when Premier Razmara, taking a stand against nationalization, was assassinated and succeeded on May 1 by the nationalist Muhhamad Mossadegh. Mossadegh nationalized the company, but he found the combined pressures of the international oil interest too much for him and saw Iran's oil production fall from 32 million tons in 1950 to 1 million in 1952. By 1954 a consortium, which left the Anglo-Persian Oil Company, now the British Petroleum Company, with a 40 percent interest, had been arranged: moreover, as the official U.S. account already quoted puts it ingenuously, "with the assistance of the U.S. Central Intelligence Agency, the Shah had by this time [August 13, 1953] deposed the radical Mossadegh."[51] By 1967 the British government was still holding 51 percent of the equity in British Petroleum: to most Persians, says an admiring biographer of the corporation, "perhaps to ninety-nine per cent of those who ever meet a European, the British people are British Petroleum."[52]

No wonder, then, that the radical cry in the Middle East was "legislate, not negotiate"[53] — a program carried out in Libya, which struck oil in the 1950s but avoided the big companies, these notorious agents of foreign imperialism, by giving to seventeen different "independents" the use of eighty-four concession areas: carried out also by Iraq's Colonel Kassem in 1961, who followed the Mossadegh line; by Libya's Colonel Qaddafi in 1969; and repeated, and due to be repeated, elsewhere.

In the modern industrial world which is imperialism's legacy, oil is as much a symbol as a substance. It is a barometer that tells the western weather, and it is one all people watch, wherever under the sun they stand. It is commonly agreed that war had long ago proved to be too serious a matter for soldiers. There is no such agreement about the business of oil and oilmen, but much the same notion that occurred to Harold Ickes thirty years ago is feeling its way toward acceptance and may yet become assumption. One may be sure that more than statistics, prices, and barrels were in the mind of

Shaikh Abdullah Tariki of Saudi Arabia when he made a point that imperialists as well as anti-imperialists will need to consider more than ever as this century runs out its time:

We are the sons of the Indians who sold Manhattan Island. We want to change the deal.[54]

The game, however, would remain the same.

NOTES

NOTES

Foreword

1. Jacques Berque, *French North Africa*, p. 19.
2. Carl Becker, *Everyman His Own Historian*, p. 250.

Chapter 1

1. Alfred Milner, *England in Egypt*, p. 379; Theodore Roosevelt, *The Winning of the West*, II, 56.
2. J. A. Hobson, *Imperialism*, ed. Philip Siegelman, p. xvi.
3. Bahman Nirumand, *Iran*, p. 7.
4. Speech in Havana, February 4, 1962, in M. Kenner and J Petras, eds., *Fidel Castro Speaks:* p. 115.
5. Hobson, *Imperialism*, pp. xvii-xviii.
6. Quoted in Eric Ashby, *Universities*, p. 241.
7. *With Prejudice* is the title of the autobiography of Marshal of the Royal Air Force Lord Tedder (London: Cassell, 1966).
8. Sir Charles Johnston [ex-governor of Aden], *The View from Steamer Point*, p. 13, writing of Robert Heussler, *Yesterday's Rulers*; Sir Roy Harrod, *Topical Comment*; pp. 3-4; Ross Terrill, *R. H. Tawney and His Times*, pp. 232-33; Sir Cecil Kaye, *Communism in India*, ed. Subodh Roy, p. 1; Frances Fitzgerald, *Fire in the Lake*, p. 6.
9. Selwyn Ryan, *Race and Nationalism in Trinidad and Tobago*, p. 493.
10. *Ibid.*, pp. 497-98.
11. Alan Scham, *Lyautey in Morocco*, p. 2.
12. V. G. Kiernan, *The Lords of Human Kind*, p. 35.
13. *Ibid.*, pp. 9, 50.
14. W. R. Crocker, *Nigeria*, p. 20.
15. John Masters, *Bugles and a Tiger*, p. 134.
16. Kiernan, *Lords*, p. 253.
17. Walter Laqueur, *A History of Zionism*, p. xvi.

317

18. Joseph Schumpeter, *Imperialism*, ed., Bert Hoselitz, p. 105.

19. L. H. Gann and Peter Duignan, *Burden of Empire*, p. 45.

20. *Ibid.*, p. 127.

21. L. H. Gann and Peter Duignan, *Colonialism in Africa, 1870-1960*, II, *The History and Politics of Colonialism, 1914-60*, p. 27.

22. Godfrey Uzoigwe, "Pre-colonial Markets in Bunyoro-Kitara," *Comparative Studies in Society and History*, 14, no. 4 (September 1972), pp. 422-426.

23. Quoted in Geoffrey Barraclough, *An Introduction to Contemporary History*, p. 235.

24. Judith M. Brown, *Gandhi's Rise to Power*, p. 19.

25. John S. Bastin and Harry J. Benda, *A History of Modern South-East Asia*, p. 14.

26. T. S. Eliot, *Notes towards a Definition of Culture*, p. 41.

27. Louis de Carné, *Voyage en Indo-Chine* (Paris, 1872), quoted in Virginia Thompson, *French Indo-China*, p. 266.

28. C. Wright Mills, *The Sociological Imagination*, p. 161.

Chapter 2

1. H. G. Wells, *The War that Will End War*, quoted in W. Warren Wagar, ed., *H. G. Wells*, p. 60.

2. Keith Thomas, "History and Anthropology," *Past and Present*, no. 24 (April 1963), p. 7.

3. Sir James Fitzjames Stephen, *Horae Sabbaticae*, II, 119.

4. Arnold J. Toynbee and Kenneth P. Kirkwood, *Turkey*, pp. 5, 75.

5. Giovanni Giolitti, *Memoirs of My Life*, pp. 349-350.

6. *Ibid.*, pp. 123, 250, 263, 276.

7. M. M. H. Macartney and Paul Cremona, *Italy's Foreign and Colonial Policy, 1914-37*, pp. 301, 319-20.

8. Michael Grant, *The World of Rome*, p. 41.

9. *Hansard's Parliamentary Debates, Fifth Series* [hereafter 5 *Hansard*], August 16, 1909, col. 1003.

10. Quoted in Homer A. Jack, ed., *The Gandhi Reader*, p. 135.

11. Foreword by Cecil Hourani to Jean Duvignaud, *Change at Shebika*, p. xiv.

12. J. L. Garvin, *The Life of Joseph Chamberlain*, II, 579.

13. *Selected Speeches and Statements of the Quaid-i-Azam Mohammed Ali Jinnah*, ed., M. R. Afzal, pp. 49-50.

14. John Paton Davies, Jr., *Dragon by the Tail*, p. 264.

15. David C. Gordon, *The Passing of French Algeria*, pp. 36, 39.

16. Jean Suret-Canale, *French Colonialism in Tropical Africa, 1900-45*, p. 83.

17. Winston S. Churchill, *Great Contemporaries*, p. 314.

18. Arnold J. Toynbee, *Survey of International Affairs, 1925*, pp. 99-100.

19. W. H. Elsbree, *Japan's Role in Southeast Asian Nationalist Movements, 1900-45*, p. 7.

20. Bertrand Russell, *The Problem of China*, p. 82.

21. Sir Meyrick Hewlett, *Forty Years in China, 1898-1938*, pp. 1-2.

22. Sir Reginald Craddock, *The Dilemma in India*, p. x.

23. P. M. de La Gorce, *The French Army*, p. 458.

24. J. S. Ambler, *The French Army in Politics, 1945-1962*, p. 290.

25. Toynbee, *Survey, 1925*, p. 151.

26. Peter Calvert, *The Mexican Revolution,* pp. 34 35.

27. Ian H. Nish, *Alliance in Decline,* p. 7; Russell H. Fifield, *Woodrow Wilson and the Far East,* p. 61.

28. Harry N. Howard, *The King-Crane Commission,* pp. 87-89.

29. Elspeth Huxley, *White Man's Country,* 2nd ed., II, 84; H. S. Morris, *The Indians in Uganda,* pp. 178-179.

30. Macartney and Cremona, *Italy's Policy,* p. 282.

31. *The Killearn Diaries, 1934-46,* ed. Trefor E. Evans, pp. 71, 131.

32. Lord Winster, 5 *Hansard* (House of Lords) 161, April 13, 1949, col. 1224.

33. L. S. Amery to Lord Linlithgow, June 17, 1942; Nicholas Mansergh and E. W. Lumby, eds., *Constitutional Relations between Britain and India,* II, *The Transfer of Power in India,* p. 225.

34. Quoted in Geoffrey Barraclough, *An Introduction to Contemporary History,* p. 77n.

35. 5 *Hansard* 437, May 16, 1947, col. 1965.

36. David Halberstam, *The Best and the Brightest,* p. 225.

37. Bernard B. Fall, *The Two Vietnams,* 2nd revised ed., p. 225.

38. Adolf A. Berle, Jr., *Latin America,* pp. 1, 23.

39. Tamas Szentes, *The Political Economy of Underdevelopment,* p. 199.

40. John K. Fairbank, in his introduction to Akira Iriye, *Across the Pacific,* p. xii.

41. William R. Roff, *The Origins of Malay Nationalism,* p. 12.

42. David Lowenthal, *West Indian Societies,* p. 201.

43. N. S. Carey Jones, *The Anatomy of Uhuru,* p. 82.

44. Valentine Chirol, *India,* pp. 83-84, 190.

45. *The Selected Works of Mahatma Gandhi,* ed. Shiraman Narayan, XLVIII, 227-29.

46. Guy de Lusignan, *French-speaking Africa since Independence,* p. 11.

47. Jawaharlal Nehru, *An Autobiography,* p. 420.

48. Paul Eltzbacher, *Anarchism,* pp. 13-14.

49. Sir Michael E. Grant Duff, *A Memoir of Sir Henry Maine,* pp. 233, 252.

50. R. J. Hammond, *Portugal and Africa, 1815-1910,* pp. x, 335.

51. *Report of the Royal Commission on Palestine, Cmd.* 5479 (London: H.M. Stationery Office, 1937), p. 147.

52. Robert Nisbet, *Social Change and History,* pp. 191-93.

53. Harry Magdoff, *The Age of Imperialism,* p. 59.

54. Romesh C. Dutt, *The Economic History of India in the Victorian Age,* 2nd ed., pp. 603-4, 613.

55. Albert Sarraut, *Grandeur et servitude coloniales,* p. 21.

56. Gunnar Myrdal, "The 'Soft State' in Underdeveloped Countries," *Unfashionable Economics,* ed. P. Streeten, p. 230; John White, "Observing Development," *South Asian Review,* 6, no. 1 (October 1972), p. 49.

57. Robert Nisbet, *The Sociology of Emile Durkheim,* p. 18; Emile Durkheim, *The Rules of Sociology and Method,* ed. G. E. G. Catlin, 8th ed., pp. 19-21, 31.

58. Quoted in John Gross, *The Rise and Fall of the Man of Letters,* p. 286.

59. Eric Ashby, *Universities,* p. 52.

60. *Ibid.,* pp. ix, 225.

61. *Report of the Royal Commission on Higher Education in the Colonies,* Cmd. 6647 (London: H.M. Stationery Office, 1945), p. 93.

62. Ashby, *Universities,* pp. 154, 203, 426n.5; Chirol, *India,* p. 202.

63. Dorothy Norman, ed., *Nehru,* I, 220; Krishna Kripalani, *Rabindranath Tagore,* p. 203.

64. Norman, *Nehru*, I, 346.

65. Toynbee, *Survey, 1925*, p. 176.

66. Richard Symonds, *The British and their Successors*, pp. 63-64; Norman, *Nehru*, I, 235; Fall, *Two Vietnams*, p. 39.

67. W. R. Crocker, *Nigeria*, pp. 151-152.

68. Judith M. Brown, *Gandhi's Rise*, p. 357.

69. Gilberto Freyre, *The Portuguese and the Tropics*, p. 51.

70. Norman, *Nehru*, I, 20.

Chapter 3

1. *The Killearn Diaries, 1936-46*, ed. Trefor E. Evans, p. 207.

2. *Ibid.*, p. 215.

3. Robert Engler, *The Politics of Oil*, p. 1; Dean C. Tipps, "Modern Theory and the Comparative Study of Societies: a Critical Perspective," *Comparative Studies in Society and History*, 15, no. 2 (March 1973), pp. 199-203.

4. Hollis Lynch, *Edward Wilmot Blyden*, pp. 150-51; K. K. Ghosh, *The Indian National Army*, p. viii; H. D. Perraton, "British Attitudes towards East and West Africa, 1880-1914," *Race*, 8, no. 3 (1967), p. 226.

5. Sir Charles Lucas, ed., *Lord Durham's Report on the Affairs of British North America*, II, 38.

6. Sir Francis Tuker, *Gorkha*, p. 102.

7. Pierre Guillen, *The Entente 1904 as a Colonial Settlement*, pp. 23, 38.

8. George Orwell, *Collected Essays, Journalism, and Letters*, eds., Sonia Orwell and Ian Angus, II, 113.

9. H. W. Nevinson, *A Modern Slavery*, reprinted in D. F. Joyce, ed., *Slavery in Portuguese Africa*, pp. 10-11.

10. E. M. Winslow, *The Pattern of Imperialism*, pp. 92-93.

11. D. K. Fieldhouse, *Economics and Empire, 1830-1914*, pp. 5, 84, 380-81, 476.

12. H. N. Brailsford, *The War of Steel and Gold*, p. 164; V. G. Kiernan, *Marxism and Imperialism*, p. 18.

13. Kiernan, *Marxism and Imperialism*, p. 67; review of Fieldhouse, *Economics and Empire*, by Richard Wolff, *American Historical Review*, 80, no. 4 (October 1975), p. 941.

14. D. C. M. Platt, *Finance, Trade, and Politics in British Foreign Policy, 1815-1914*, pp. xiii, 76, 154-55, 178, 180.

15. John Strachey, *The End of Empire*, pp. 122-23.

16. Platt, *Finance*, p. 3.

17. George Woodcock, *The British in the Far East*, pp. 25, 31.

18. *Ibid.*, p. 129.

19. *Ibid.*, p. 99.

20. L. H. Gann and Peter Duignan, *Colonialism in Africa, 1870-1960*, II, *The History and Politics of Colonialism, 1914-60*, p. 349.

21. H. G. Wells, *Works*, IV, *Anticipations and Other Papers*, Chap. 4.

22. Jawaharlal Nehru, *An Autobiography*, p. 21.

23. J. de V. Allen, "The Malayan Civil Service, 1874-1941," *Comparative Studies in Society and History*, 12 (1970), pp. 161-163.

24. *Hansard's Parliamentary Debates, Fifth Series* [hereafter 5 *Hansard*], 41, July 25, 1912, col. 1402.

25. Sir T. Raleigh, ed., *Lord Curzon in India, 1898-1905*, II, 332; Lynch, *Blyden*, p. 243; Sir Alexander Carr-Saunders, *New Universities Overseas*, p. 19.

26. Suret-Canale, *French Colonialism in Tropical Africa, 1900-45*, pp. 97-98, 100-7, 307-9; A. S. Kanya-Forstner, *The Conquest of the Western Sudan*, p. 171.

27. Elie Kedourie, *The Chatham House Version, and other Middle Eastern Studies*, p. 99.

28. Kanya-Forstner, *Western Sudan*, p. 264.

29. Flora Shaw (Lady Lugard), *A Tropical Dependency*, p. 1.

30. Ronald Hyam, *Elgin and Churchill at the Colonial Office, 1905-08*, pp. 406, 418; Robert C. Gregory, *India and East Africa, 1850-1939*, p. 111

31. Ronald S. Cunsolo, "Libya, Italian Nationalism, and the Revolt against Giolitti, *Journal of Modern History*, 37, no. 2 (June 1965), p. 203.

32. James Duffy, *Portugal in Africa*, p. 132; William Cadbury and Joseph Burtt, *Labour in Portuguese West Africa*, p. 24.

33. Eric A. Williams, *Inward Hunger*, p. 16.

34. Arnold J. Toynbee, *Survey of International Affairs, 1925*, pp. 99-100.

35. Fritz Fischer, *Germany's Aims in the First World War*, p. 9.

36. For these and other views, cf. David H. Burton, *Theodore Roosevelt*, pp. 68-70, 115, 180.

37. Stephen Koss, *John Morley at the India Office*, p. 102.

38. C. J. Lowe and M. L. Dockrill, eds., *The Mirage of Power*, III, 593-95.

39. Kedourie, *Chatham House Version*, p. 17.

40. November 18, 1890; India Office archives, London, MS. European Papers, Section D, folios 558/3. I owe this and two other references from these archives to Dr. Murray Hogben.

41. David G. Gordon, *The Passing of French Algeria*, p. 18.

42. Eric Ashby, *Universities*, pp. 71-72.

43. Dorothy Norman, ed., *Nehru*, I, 277-78.

44. James Dodds, *Records of the Scottish Settlers in the River Plate, and their Children*, p. 125.

45. Quoted in W. H. Auden, ed., *G. K. Chesterton*, p. 125.

46. W. H. Russell, *My Diary in India in the Year 1858-9*, I, 180.

47. C. S. Goldman, ed., *The Empire and the Century*, pp. 160-61.

48. John Buchan, *ibid.*, p. 39.

49. 3 *Hansard* 190, November 26, 1867, cols. 211, 214.

50. J. A. Hobson, *Imperialism*, ed. Philip Siegelman, p. 229.

51. *Ibid.*, pp. 37-39, 74, 77-78, 117, 312.

52. E. Berkeley Tompkins, *Anti-Imperialism in the United States*, p. 223.

53. Hobson, *Imperialism*, pp. 85, 89, 98, 225.

54. Earl of Cromer, *Modern Egypt*, II, 54.

55. Theodor Herzl, *Diaries*, ed. M. Lowenthal, p. 382.

56. Wilfrid Scawen Blunt, *My Diaries*, II, 98.

57. Fieldhouse, *Economics and Empire*, p. 461.

58. *Ibid.*, p. 467.

59. Henri Brunschwig, *French Colonialism*, pp. 31-32.

60. Theobald von Bethmann-Hollweg, *Reflections on the World War*, p. 167; A. P. Thornton, *Doctrines of Imperialism*, pp. 77-78.

61. J. Chesneaux, "Stages in the Development of the Vietnam Nationalist Movement, 1862-1940," *Past and Present*, no. 7 (April 1955), p. 103.

62. Carr-Saunders, *New Universities Overseas*, p. 31.

63. *Report of the Special Mission to Egypt*, Cmd. 1131 (London: H.M. Stationery Office, 1921), pp. 6, 8, 16.

64. H. J. Simson, *British Rule, and Rebellion*, p. 31.

65. Sir Walter Lawrence, *The India We Served*, pp. 37-38.

66. Bertrand Russell, *Problem of China*, p. 180.

67. Dwight D. Eisenhower, *Crusade in Europe*, p. 457.

68. Harry Magdoff, *The Age of Imperialism*, p. 14.

69. Conor Cruise O'Brien and W. D. Vaneck, eds., *Power and Consciousness* (London: University of London Press, 1969), p. 20.

70. John Gerassi, *The Great Fear in Latin America*, new revised ed., p. 43.

71. Quoted in Edwin Lieuwen, *United States Policy in Latin America*, p. 42.

72. Graham H. Stuart, *Latin America and the United States*, 5th ed., pp. 50, 152.

73. Lloyd C. Gardner, *Economic Aspects of New Deal Diplomacy*, p. 41.

74. Quoted in Edwin Lieuwen, *Arms and Politics in Latin America*, p. 10.

75. David Green, *The Containment of Latin America*, p. 140.

76. Henry N. Howard, *The King-Crane Commission*, pp. 32-33, 37, 99.

77. Isaiah Friedman, *The Question of Palestine, 1914-18*, pp. 279-80.

78. Lowe and Dockrill, *The Mirage of Power*, III, 548.

79. Doreen Ingrams, ed., *Palestine Papers, 1917-22*, pp. 77, 98.

80. Quoted in Christopher Sykes, *Cross-Roads to Israel*, pp. 68, 95.

81. Ingrams, *Palestine Papers*, p. 61.

82. *Ibid.*, p. 27.

83. *Ibid.*, pp. 22, 27, 43, 61.

84. Quoted in Walter Laqueur, ed., *The Israel-Arab Reader*, p. 262.

85. *Peel Report*, Cmd. 5479 (London: H.M. Stationery Office, 1937), p. 119.

86. Ben Halpern, *The Idea of the Jewish State*, pp. 325-26.

87. Ingrams, *Palestine Papers*, p. 45.

88. Simson, *Rule, and Rebellion*, p. 310.

89. Halpern, *Jewish State*, p. 358.

90. Herzl, *Diaries*, pp. 278, 290.

91. Ingrams, *Palestine Papers*, p. 19; Halpern, *Jewish State*, pp. 272-73.

92. 5 *Hansard* 341, November 24, 1938, col. 1987-92; 5 *Hansard* 433, February 25, 1947, col. 1906.

93. Ian H. Nish, *Alliance in Decline*, p. 145.

94. Chow Tse-tsung, *The May Fourth Movement*, p. 20.

95. R. Craig Brown and Ramsay Cook, *Canada, 1896-1921*, pp. 289-90.

96. Stephen W. Roskill, *Hankey*, II, 28-29.

97. Aaron S. Klieman, *Foundations of British Policy in the Arab World*, p. 28.

98. *Ibid.*, p. 51.

99. William B. Cohen, "The Colonial Policy of the Popular Front," *French Historical Studies*, 7, no. 3 (spring 1972), pp. 372, 376.

100. Walter G. Langlois, *André Malraux*, p. 112.

101. Virginia Thompson, *French Indo-China*, p. 438.

102. Cohen, "Popular Front," p. 377.

103. H. G. Wells, *Experiment in Autobiography*, II, 669.

104. Cohen, "Popular Front," p. 385.

105. Lowe and Dockrill, *Mirage of Power*, III, 536-41.

106. Krishna Kripalani, *Rabindranath Tagore*, p. 266.

107. Ho Chi Minh, *Ho Chi Minh on Revolution*, ed., Bernard B. Fall, p. 10.
108. Kenneth Robinson, *The Dilemmas of Trusteeship*, p. 7.
109. Josiah Wedgwood, 5 *Hansard* 341, March 21, 1938, col. 2049.
110. 5 *Hansard* (House of Lords) 41, col. 155; Cmd. 1922 (1923), p. 36.
111. Cmd. 1131, pp. 19-20.
112. Klieman, *Foundations of British Policy*, pp. 126, 134-35.
113. Judith M. Brown, *Gandhi's Rise to Power*, p. 231.
114. Toynbee, *Survey, 1925*, pp. 216-17, 249, 252.
115. Cheddi Jagan, *The West on Trial*, p. 170.
116. Orwell, *Collected Essays*, II, 217-218.
117. Jagan, *West on Trial*, pp. 173-75.

Chapter 4

1. A. W. Singham, *The Hero and the Crowd in a Colonial Polity*, pp. 193, 307.
2. Cf. A. P. Thornton, "Small-Island Men," *International Journal*, 6, no. 3 (1969), pp. 590-600.
3. Quoted in Louis L. Snyder, *The Dynamics of Nationalism*, p. 336.
4. Quoted in K. K. Aziz, *The Making of Pakistan*, pp. 105-6; Aziz Ahmad, *Islamic Modernism in India and Pakistan, 1857-1964*, p. 167.
5. J. N. Wolfe, ed., *Government and Nationalism in Scotland*, p. 189.
6. Valentine Chirol, *Indian Unrest*, p. xiii.
7. A. W. Griswold, *The Far Eastern Policy of the United States*, p. 59.
8. Charles A. Beard, *The Idea of National Interest*, p. 255.
9. W. H. Elsbree, *Japan's Role in Southeast Asian Nationalist Movements, 1900-45*, p. 6; Russell H. Fifield, *Americans in South-East Asia*, p. 3.
10. Theodore Friend, *Between Two Empires*, pp. 9, 39, 206.
11. Brian Weinstein, *Eboué*, p. 8.
12. H. M. Stationery Office, London, Cmd. 8655-7 (1897), p. 10.
13. Robert Delavignette, *Freedom and Authority in French West Africa*, p. 13.
14. Quoted in Paul Eltzbacher, *Anarchism*, p. 10.
15. November 15, 1910; India Office Archives, MS. European Papers, folios 116/67, p. 6.
16. Symonds, *British and their Successors*, p. 74.
17. Homer A. Jack, ed., *Gandhi Reader*, pp. 117-20.
18. J. P. Haithcox, *Communism and Nationalism in India*, p. 23.
19. Ho Chi Minh, *Ho Chi Minh on Revolution*, ed., Bernard B. Fall, p. 6.
20. Eltzbacher, *Anarchism*, p. 89.
21. Robert Conquest, *The Soviet Deportation of Nationalities*, pp. 19-20.
22. Sir Cecil Kaye, *Communism in India*, ed., Subodh Roy, p. 125; Conquest, *Soviet Deportation*, p. 25.
23. Haithcox, *Communism and Nationalism*, p. 43.
24. Sankar Ghose, *Socialism and Communism in India*, p. 124.
25. B. R. Nanda, ed., *Socialism in India*, p. 18.
26. Branko Lazitch and Milorad M. Drachkovitch, *Lenin and the Comintern*, I, 384-87.
27. Xenia J. Eudin and R. C. North, *Soviet Russia and the East, 1920-27*, p. 196.
28. J. E. Casely Hayford, *West African Leadership*, ed., Magnus J. Sampson, p. 15.
29. Aaron S. Klieman, *Foundations of British Policy in the Arab World*, p. 81.
30. Jawaharlal Nehru, *Selected Works of Jawaharlal Nehru*, ed., S. Gopal, II, 251, 281.

31. Walter Laqueur, *The Soviet Union and the Middle East*, p. 76; Ho Chi Minh, *Ho on Revolution* , p. 127.

32. Quoted in C. Grove Haines, ed., *The Threat of Soviet Imperialism*, p. 11.

33. Kaye, *Communism in India*, p. 276.

34. Delavignette, *Freedom and Authority*, p. 26.

35. J. L. Hymans, *Léopold Sédar Senghor*, pp. 57, 88.

36. Delavignette, *Freedom and Authority*, pp. 12-13.

37. Harry J. Benda, preface to Bernard Dahm, *Sukarno and the Struggle for Indonesian Independence*, p. vii; Dahm, *Sukarno*, p. 39.

38. Jerome Ch'en, *Mao and the Chinese Revolution*, p. 9.

39. Peter P. Ekeh, "Colonialism and the Two Publics in Africa: a Theoretical Statement," *Comparative Studies in Society and History*, 17, no. 1 (1975), p. 102.

40. Lloyd A. Fallers, "Populism and Nationalism: a Comment on D. A. Low's 'The Advent of Populism in Buganda,' " *Comparative Studies in Society and History*, 6 (1973), p. 447.

41. Harry J. Benda, "Political Elites in Colonial South-East Asia: an Historical Analysis," *Comparative Studies in Society and History*, 19 (1973), p. 245.

42. Ch'en, *Mao*, p. 49.

43. Elie Kedourie, *Chatham House Version and other Middle Eastern Studies*, p. 109.

44. Albert Hourani, *Arabic Thought in the Liberal Age, 1798-1939*, p. 221.

45. Mohandas K. Gandhi, *The Selected Works of Mahatma Gandhi*, ed., Shiraman Narayan, XLVIII, 397.

46. Kaye, *Communism in India*, pp. 14, 29, 73, 75, 130, 149, 188, 192.

47. Haithcox, *Communism and Nationalism*, pp. 21, 91.

48. Nanda, *Socialism in India*, p. 4.

49. Jack, *Gandhi Reader*, pp. 204-5.

50. Howard Brotz, ed., *Negro Social and Political Thought, 1850-1920*, p. 210.

51. Theodore G. Vincent, *Black Power and the Garvey Movement*, p. 133.

52. David S. Woolman, *Rebels in the Rif*, p. 170.

53. L. H. Gann and Peter Duignan, *Colonialism in Africa, 1870-1960*, II, *The History and Politics of Colonialism, 1914-60*, p. 425.

54. Frantz Fanon, *Black Skin, White Masters*, p. 94.

55. Bernard B. Fall, *The Two Vietnams*, pp. 64-65; George Rosie, *The British in Vietnam*, p. 135.

56. Sir Michael E. Grant Duff, *A Memoir of Sir Henry Maine*, p. 244.

57. E. F. L. Wood, *Report on Visit to the West Indies and British Guiana*, Cmd. 1679, p. x.

58. W. R. Crocker, *Nigeria*, p. 217.

59. Jeremy Murray-Brown, *Kenyatta*, p. 187.

60. Gabriel O. Olusanya, *The Second World War and Politics in Nigeria, 1939-1953*, pp. 16-17.

61. Gandhi, *Works*, XIII, 222; Nehru, *Works*, II, 251.

62. Quoted in Tamas Szentes, *The Political Economy of Underdevelopment*, p. 189n.28.

63. Marcus Garvey, *Philosophy and Opinions of Marcus Garvey*, ed., Amy Jacques Garvey, Part 2, p. 118.

64. W. E. B. du Bois, *W. E. B. du Bois Speaks*, ed., Philip S. Foner, pp. 251-52.

65. Garvey, *Opinions of Garvey*, Part 2, pp. 25, 36.

66. Réné Maran, *Batouala*, trans. Barbara Beck and Alexandre Mboukou, pp. 2-3.

67. Walter G. Langlois, *André Malraux*, p. 200.

68. Hymans, *Senghor*, pp. 85, 97-99.

69. Ho Chi Minh, *Ho on Revolution*, pp. 55, 70, 143.

70. Rupert Emerson, *From Empire to Nation*, p. 19.

71. J. M. Ahmed, *Intellectual Origins of Egyptian Nationalism*, p. 16.

72. Akira Iriye, *Across the Pacific*, p. 84.

73. John Paton Davies, Jr., *Dragon by the Tail*, p. 108.

74. Foster Rhea Dulles, *American Policy towards Communist China, 1949-1969*, p. 17; Davies, *Dragon by the Tail*, p. 306.

75. W. Roger Louis, *British Strategy in the Far East, 1919-39*, p. 115.

76. Griswold, *Far Eastern Policy of the U.S.*, p. 45.

77. Dorothy Borg, *American Policy and the Chinese Revolution, 1925-38*, p. 17.

78. Dulles, *Policy towards China*, p. 17; James B. Crowley, *Japan's Quest for Autonomy*, p. 22.

79. Borg, *Policy and Chinese Revolution*, p. 7; Chow Tse-tung, *The May Fourth Movement*, pp. 86-87.

80. Chow, *May Fourth*, p. 232.

81. Borg, *Policy and Chinese Revolution*, p. 231.

82. Dorothy Norman, ed., *Nehru*, I, 79; Nehru, *Works*, II, 260-61.

83. Eric Ashby, *Universities*, p. 82.

84. J. Simson, *British Rule, and Rebellion*, p. 222.

85. Nicholas Mansergh, ed., *Documents and Speeches on British Commonwealth Affairs, 1931-52*, p. 227.

86. Simson, *Rule, and Rebellion*, p. 327.

87. Norman, *Nehru*, I, 172, 309.

88. Vincent, *Black Power*, p. 56.

89. Kaye, *Communism in India*, p. 272.

90. G. M. Kahin, *Nationalism and Revolution in Indonesia*, p. 51.

91. Harry J. Benda, *Community and Change in South-East Asia*, p. 26.

92. Harry J. Benda, *The Crescent and the Rising Sun*, p. 13.

93. Kahin, *Nationalism in Indonesia*, pp. 91, 95.

94. Gordon Waterfield, *Professional Diplomat*, pp. 62, 77.

95. *Hansard's Parliamentary Debates, Fourth Series*, 8, February 13, 1873, col. 1273.

96. Ian H. Nish, *Alliance in Decline*, pp. 258-59.

97. P. M. de La Gorce, *The French Army*, p. 213.

98. Arnold J. Toynbee, *Survey of International Affairs, 1931*, p. 363.

Chapter 5

1. Chow Tse-tung, *The May Fourth Movement*, p. 29.

2. *Hansard's Parliamentary Debates, Fifth Series*, 446, January 22, 1946, cols. 398-99.

3. Bernard Dahm, *Sukarno and the Struggle for Indonesian Independence*, p. 63.

4. Robert Delavignette, *Freedom and Authority in French West Africa*, p. 8.

5. Akira Iriye, *Across the Pacific*, p. 209.

6. Akira Iriye, *The Cold War in Asia*, p. 1.

7. Quoted in Ronald S. Cunsolo, "Libya, Italian Nationalism, and the Revolt against Giolitti," *Journal of Modern History*, 37, no. 2 (June 1965), p. 200.

8. W. H. Elsbree, *Japan's Role in Southeast Asian Nationalist Movements, 1900-45*, pp. 6, 19, 24, 39, 60.

9. Subhas Chandra Bose, *The Testament of Subhas Chandra Bose, Being a Complete and Authentic Record of Netaji's Broadcast Speeches, Press Statements, etc., 1942-45*, ed., "Arun," pp. 22-23, 29, 49.

10. Sankar Ghose, *The Indian National Army*, pp. 309-11, 314.

11. F. C. Jones, Hugh Borton, and B. R. Pearn, *Survey of International Affairs, 1939-46*, p. 264.

12. John Paton Davies, Jr., *Dragon by the Tail*, pp. 276, 284.

13. Iriye, *Cold War in Asia*, p. 87.

14. William H. McNeill, *Survey of International Affairs, 1939-46*, p. 756.

15. Dean Acheson, *This Vast External Realm*, p. 10.

16. Quoted in *The Times*, London, May 23, 1942.

17. Quoted in *The New York Times*, October 27, 1942.

18. Foster Rhea Dulles and G. E. Ridinger, "The Anti-Colonial Policies of F. D. Roosevelt," *Political Science Quarterly*, 70 (March 1955), p. 4.

19. John Lewis Gaddis, *The United States and the Origins of the Cold War, 1941-47*, p. 24.

20. *Ibid.*, p. 3.

21. David Green, *The Containment of Latin America*, p. 17.

22. Gaddis, *Origins of the Cold War*, p. 56.

23. M. Kenner and J. Petras, eds., *Castro Speaks!* p. ix.

24. Iriye, *Cold War in Asia*, p. 194.

25. Nirumand, *Iran*, p. 7.

26. William Appleman Williams, *The Tragedy of American Diplomacy*, pp. 145, 148; K. T. Fann and D. C. Hodges, eds., *Readings in United States' Imperialism*, p. 10.

27. Kenner and Petras, *Castro Speaks!* pp. 36, 99.

28. Robert B. Krueger, *The United States and International Oil*, p. 40.

29. Gerald D. Nash, *United States' Oil Policy, 1890-1964*, p. 63.

30. Krueger, *U.S. and International Oil*, p. 50.

31. Michael Barratt Brown, *After Imperialism*, p. 292.

32. Theodore H. White, *The Making of the President 1968*, p. 87.

33. Fann and Hodges, *Readings in Imperialism*, p. 321.

34. Tibor Mende, *From Aid to Recolonization*, p. 71.

35. Denis W. Brogan, "The Illusion of Omnipotence," *Harper's Magazine*, 205 (December 1952), pp. 21-28.

36. George Liska, *Imperial America*, p. 41.

37. George Kennan, *Realities of American Foreign Policy*, p. 57.

38. Carl Becker, *Everyman His Own Historian*, p. 245.

39. Walter LeFeber, *America, Russia, and the Cold War, 1945-71*, p. 43.

40. Daniel Boorstin, *The Americans*, p. 579.

41. Ronald Steel, *Imperialists and Other Heroes*, pp. 7, 22.

42. G. M. Kahin and J. W. Lewis, *The United States in Vietnam*, p. 33.

43. Williams, *Tragedy of American Diplomacy*, p. 148.

44. Paul A. Baran and Paul M. Sweezy, *Monopoly Capital*, p. 183n.5.

45. I heard a Latin American delegate (Guatemala) say this at a conference on Caribbean affairs in Jamaica, January 1970.

46. Kenner and Petras, *Castro Speaks!* p. 35.

47. Ronald Steel, *Pax Americana*, p. 10.

48. Quoted in Steel, *Imperialists*, p. 71.

49. Liska, *Imperial America*, preface.

50. Williams, *Tragedy of American Diplomacy*, p. 7.

51. E. Friedman and Mark Selden, *America's Asia*, p. 50.

52. N. Gordon Levin, *Woodrow Wilson and World Politics*, pp. 4, 28.

53. Richard Freeland, *The Truman Doctrine and the Origins of McCarthyism*, p. 31.

54. *Social Sciences*, 6, no. 2 (20) (Moscow: U.S.S.R. Academy of Sciences, 1975), pp. 84, 86, 89, 93, 162.

55. Robert Conquest, *The Soviet Deportation of Nationalities*, pp. 19-20, 33-34.

56. Acheson, *Realm*, p. 27.

57. Dorothy Norman, ed., *Nehru*, II, 494.

Chapter 6

1. Stephen W. Roskill, *Hankey*, II, 544.

2. Michael Blundell, *So Rough a Wind*, p. 83.

3. *The Colonial Empire, 1947-48*, Cmd. 7433 (London: H.M. Stationery Office, 1947-8), p. 17.

4. J. M. Lee, *Colonial Development and Good Government*, p. 64.

5. D. Goldsworthy, *Colonial Issues in British Politics, 1945-61*, p. 17.

6. Blundell, *Wind*, pp. 261-262.

7. N. S. Carey Jones, *The Anatomy of Uhuru*, pp. 24, 361.

8. W. E. H. Lecky, *Democratic Government*, II, 1.

9. Blundell, *Wind*, p. 65.

10. Goldsworthy, *Colonial Issues*, pp. 24, 361.

11. Blundell, *Wind*, p. 124.

12. Colin Leys, *European Politics in Southern Rhodesia*, pp. 246, 249.

13. Ruth Slade, *The Belgian Congo*, p. 17.

14. Roger de Meyer, *Introducing the Belgian Congo and Ruanda-Urundi*, p. 9.

15. Dorothy Norman, ed., *Nehru*, II, 130.

16. June 4, 1942; Nicholas Mansergh and E. W. Lumby, eds., *Constitutional Relations Between Britain and India*, II, *The Transfer of Power in India*, pp. 177-78.

17 *Ibid.*, p. 276.

18. Theodore Friend, *Between Two Empires*, p. 241.

19. Ho Chi Minh, *Ho Chi Minh on Revolution*, ed., Bernard B. Fall, pp. 153-54.

20. W. H. Elsbree, *Japan's Role in Southeast Asian Nationalist Movements, 1900-45*, p. 101.

21. P. M. de La Gorce, *The French Army*, p. 345.

22. Eric A. Walker, *Colonies*, pp. 2-3.

23. Elie Kedourie, *The Chatham House Version, and other Middle Eastern Studies*, pp. 3, 6.

24. George Kirk, *Survey of International Affairs, 1939-46*, pp. 13-14.

25. Norman, *Nehru*, II, 7.

26. *Ibid.*, p. 75.

27. George Rosie, *The British in Vietnam*, p. 94; Norman, *Nehru*, II, 95.

28. Harry Magdoff, *The Age of Imperialism*, p. 123.

29. Woodrow Wyatt, *Southwards from China*, p. 175.

30. G. M. Kahin, *Nationalism and Revolution in Indonesia*, p. 415.

31. *Ibid.*, p. 405.

32. Hubert Deschamps, *Les méthodes et les doctrines coloniales de la France*, p. 173.

33. Robert Heussler, *Yesterday's Rulers*, p. 64.

34. L. H. Gann and Peter Duignan, *Burden of Empire*, p. 105.

35. R. Kumar, ed., *Essays in Gandhian Politics*, p. 305.

36. David C. Gordon, *The Passing of French Algeria*, p. 39.

37. Edward Behr, *The Algerian Problem*, p. 51.

38. D. Bruce Marshall, *The French Colonial Myth and Constitution-Making in the Fourth Republic*, p. 2.

39. Dorothy Pickles, *Algeria and France*, p. 10.

40. *Ibid.*, p. 53.

41. Marshall, *Colonial Myth*, p. 4.

42. Quoted in *ibid.*, pp. 33, 35.

43. *Ibid.*, p. 122.

44. Réné Lemarchand, *Political Awakening in the Belgian Congo*, p. 158.

45. Sir James Fitzjames Stephen, *Liberty, Equality, Fraternity*, ed., R. J. White, p. 90.

46. Arnold J. Toynbee and Kenneth P. Kirkwood, *Turkey*, p. 1.

47. David E. Apter, *The Politics of Modernization*, p. 10.

48. Michael Barratt Brown, *After Imperialism*, p. 235.

49. *Ibid.*, p. 245.

50. J. E. Hartshorn, *Politics and World Oil Economics*, pp. 30, 312.

51. Robert B. Krueger, *The United States and International Oil*, p. 55.

52. J. R. L. Anderson, *East of Suez*, p. 56.

53. Hartshorn, *Politics*, p. 25.

54. *Ibid.*, p. 312.

SOURCES

SOURCES

A comprehensive bibliography on imperialism, whether or not it was called "selective," would make a large book, possibly in three volumes. A bibliography on the history of the European empires might well occupy six.

I have therefore simplified a problem I had no hope of solving. In Section I, for the reader's convenience, I list *the sources that are quoted in the text and gathered in the notes*: sources which are, accordingly, "useful."

The concept of utility depends on subjective judgment. So in Section II I list *the sources referred to but not quoted* — in the sense of having considered what they say, whether or not I agree with it — *in the preparation of this book*. A reader who began at the Foreword and has reached this page will know my opinion that those who write on this subject — and not only on this subject — are, to some degree, conditioned by the time they live in, by race, nationality, class, ideology, and the personal idiosyncrasies that these attributes produce. The selection in Section II aims to underline this point.

A third section, of books that were read and considered but not used, would merely occupy space: so it does not appear here. Its absence, however, comments more severely on my judgment than on the books omitted.

I. Sources Quoted in the Text

Acheson, Dean. *This Vast External Realm*. New York: Norton, 1973.

Afzal, M. R., ed. *Selected Speeches and Statements of the Quaid-i-Azam Mohammed Ali Jinnah*. Lahore: Research Society of Pakistan, University of the Punjab, 1966.

Ahmad, Aziz. *Islamic Modernism in India and Pakistan, 1857-1964*. London: Oxford University Press, 1967.

Ahmed, J. M. *Intellectual Origins of Egyptian Nationalism*. London: Oxford University Press, 1960.

Allen, J. de V. "The Malayan Civil Service, 1874-1941," *Comparative Studies in Society and History* 12 (1970), pp. 161-69.

Ambler, J. S. *The French Army in Politics, 1945-62*. Columbus, Ohio: Ohio State University Press, 1966.

Anderson, J. R. L. *East of Suez: a Study of Britain's Greatest Trading Enterprise* [British Petroleum]. London: Hodder and Stoughton, 1969.

Apter, David E. *The Politics of Modernization*. Chicago Ill.: University of Chicago Press, 1965.

Ashby, Eric. *Universities: British, Indian, African; a Study in the Ecology of Higher Education*. London: Weidenfeld and Nicolson, 1966.

Auden, W. H., ed. *G. K. Chesterton: a Selection from His Non-Fictional Prose*. London: Faber, 1970.

Aziz, K. K. *The Making of Pakistan: a Study in Nationalism*. London: Chatto and Windus, 1967.

Baran, Paul A., and Sweezy, Paul M. *Monopoly Capital: an Essay on the American Economic and Social Order*. New York: Monthly Review Press, 1968.

Barraclough, Geoffrey. *An Introduction to Contemporary History*. London: Watts, 1964.

Barratt Brown, Michael. *After Imperialism*. London: Heinemann, 1963.

Bastin, John S., and Benda, Harry J. *A History of Modern South-East Asia: Colonialism, Nationalism, and Decolonization*. Englewood Cliffs, N.J.: Prentice-Hall, 1968.

Beard, Charles A. *The Idea of National Interest: an Analytical Study in American Foreign Policy*. New York: Macmillan, 1934.

Becker, Carl. *Everyman His Own Historian: Essays on History and Politics*. New York: F. S. Crofts, 1935.

Behr, Edward. *The Algerian Problem*. Harmondsworth: Penguin Books, 1961.

Benda, Harry J. *The Crescent and the Rising Sun: Indonesian Islam under the Japanese Occupation, 1942-45*. The Hague, W. van Hoeve, 1958.

————. *Community and Change in South-East Asia*. New Haven, Conn.: Yale University Press, 1972.

————. "Political Elites in Colonial South-East Asia: an Historical Analysis." *Comparative Studies in Society and History* 19 (1973), pp. 46-52.

Berle, Adolf A., Jr. *Latin America: Diplomacy and Reality*. New York: for the Council of Foreign Relations, Harper and Row, 1962.

Berque, Jacques. *French North Africa: The Maghrib between Two World Wars*. London: Faber, 1967.

Bethmann-Hollweg, Theobald von. *Reflections on the World War*. London: Duckworth, 1920.

Blundell, Michael. *So Rough a Wind*. London: Weidenfeld and Nicolson, 1964.

Blunt, Wilfrid Scawen. *My Diaries*. 2 vols. London: Secker, 1919.

Boorstin, Daniel. *The Americans: the Democratic Experience*. New York: Random House, 1973.

Borg, Dorothy. *American Policy and the Chinese Revolution, 1925-38*. New York: for the American Institute of Pacific Relations, Macmillan, 1947.

Bose, Subhas Chandra, ed. "Arun." *The Testament of Subhas Chandra Bose, Being a Complete and Authentic Record of Netaji's Broadcast Speeches, Press Statements, etc., 1942-45*. Delhi: Rajkamal Publications, 1946.

Brailsford, H. N. *The War of Steel and Gold*. London: G. Bell and Sons, 1914.

Brogan, Denis W. "The Illusion of Omnipotence," *Harper's Magazine* 205 (December 1952), pp. 21-28.

Brotz, Howard, ed. *Negro Social and Political Thought, 1850-1920*. New York: Basic Books, 1966.

Brown, Judith M. *Gandhi's Rise to Power: Indian Politics, 1915-22*. Cambridge: at the University Press, 1972.

Brown, R. Craig, and Cook, Ramsay. *Canada, 1896-1921: a Nation Transformed*. Toronto: McClelland and Stewart, 1974.

Brunschwig, Henri. *French Colonialism, 1871-1914: Myths and Realities*. London: Pall Mall Press, 1966.

Burton, David H. *Theodore Roosevelt: Confident Imperialist*. Philadelphia: University of Pennsylvania Press, 1968.

Cadbury, William, and Burtt, Joseph. *Labour in Portuguese West Africa*. London, 1909. Reprint. New York: Negro Universities Press, 1969.

Calvert, Peter. *The Mexican Revolution*. Cambridge: at the University Press, 1968.

Carey Jones, N. S. *The Anatomy of Uhuru: an Essay on Kenya's Independence*. Manchester: Manchester University Press, 1966.

Carr-Saunders, Sir Alexander. *New Universities Overseas*. London: Allen and Unwin, 1961.

Casely Hayford, J. E. *West African Leadership: Public Speeches Delivered by J. E. Casely Hayford*. Edited by Magnus J. Sampson. Ilfracombe: Arthur H. Stockwell, 1951.

Ch'en, Jerome. *Mao and the Chinese Revolution*. London: Oxford University Press, 1965.

Chesneaux, J. "Stages in the Development of the Vietnam Nationalist Movement, 1862-1940." *Past and Present* no. 7 (April 1955), pp. 111-15.

Chesterton, G. K. *G. K. Chesterton: a Selection from His Non-Fictional Prose*. Edited by W. H. Auden, London: Faber, 1970.

Chirol, Valentine. *Indian Unrest*. London: Macmillan, 1910.

———. *India*. London: Benn, 1926.

Chow Tse-tsung. *The May Fourth Movement: Intellectual Revolution in Modern China*. Cambridge, Mass.: Harvard University Press, 1965.

Churchill, Winston S. *Great Contemporaries*. London: Cassell, 1937.

Cohen, William B. "The Colonial Policy of the Popular Front." *French Historical Studies* 7, no. 3 (Spring 1972), pp. 370-75.

Conquest, Robert. *The Soviet Deportation of Nationalities*. London, Macmillan, 1960.

Craddock, Sir Reginald. *The Dilemma in India*. London: Constable, 1929.

Crocker, W. R. *Nigeria*. London: Allen and Unwin, 1936.

Cromer, Earl of. *Modern Egypt*. 2 vols. London: Macmillan, 1906.

Crowley, James B. *Japan's Quest for Autonomy: National Security and Foreign Policy, 1930-38*. Princeton, N.J.: Princeton University Press, 1966.

Cunsolo, Ronald S. "Libya, Italian Nationalism, and the Revolt against Giolitti," *Journal of Modern History* 37, no. 2 (June 1965), pp. 46-50.

Curzon, George Nathaniel. *Lord Curzon in India, 1898-1905: a Selection from His Speeches as Governor-General and Viceroy*. Edited by Sir Thomas Raleigh. 2 vols. London, 1906.

Dahm, Bernard. *Sukarno and the Struggle for Indonesian Independence*. Ithaca, N.Y.: Cornell University Press, 1969.

Davies, John Paton, Jr. *Dragon by the Tail: American, British, and Japanese Encounters with China and with One Another*. New York: Norton, 1972.

Delavignette, Robert. *Freedom and Authority in French West Africa*. London: Oxford University Press, 1950.

Deschamps, Hubert. *Les méthodes et les doctrines coloniales de la France*. Paris: Gallimard, 1968.

Dodds, James. *Records of the Scottish Settlers in the River Plate, and Their Children*. Buenos Aires, 1897.

du Bois, W. E. B. *W. E. B. du Bois Speaks: Speeches and Addresses*. Edited by Philip S. Foner. New York: Pathfinder Press, 1970.

Duffy, James. *Portugal in Africa*. Harmondsworth: Penguin Books, 1962.

Dulles, Foster Rhea. *American Policy towards Communist China, 1949-69*. New York, Crowell, 1972.

Dulles, Foster Rhea, and Ridinger, G. E. "The Anti-Colonial Policies of F. D. Roosevelt." *Political Science Quarterly* 70 (March 1955), pp. 1-10.

Durkheim, Emile. *The Rules of Sociology and Method*. Edited by G. E. G. Catlin, 8th ed. Chicago, Ill.: University of Chicago Press, 1938.

Dutt, Romesh C. *The Economic History of India in the Victorian Age*. 2nd ed. New York: B. Franklin, 1970.

Duvignaud, Jean. *Change at Shebika: Report from a North African Village*. New York: Bantam Books, 1970.

Eisenhower, Dwight D. *Crusade in Europe*. Garden City, N.Y.: Doubleday, 1948.

Ekeh, Peter P. "Colonialism and the Two Publics in Africa: a Theoretical Statement." *Comparative Studies in Society and History* 17, no. 1 (January 1975), pp. 100-105.

Eliot, T. S. *Notes towards a Definition of Culture*. London: Faber, 1948.

Elsbree, W. H. *Japan's Role in Southeast Asian Nationalist Movements, 1900-45*. Cambridge, Mass.: Harvard University Press, 1953.

Eltzbacher, Paul. *Anarchism: Exponents of the Anarchist Philosophy*. Berlin, 1900. Reprint. New York: Libertarian Book Club, 1960.

Emerson, Rupert. *From Empire to Nation: the Rise to Self-Assertion of Asian and African Peoples*. Cambridge, Mass.: Harvard University Press, 1962.

Engler, Robert. *The Politics of Oil: a Study of Private Power and Democratic Directions*. New York: Macmillan, 1961.

Eudin, Xenia J., and North, R. C. *Soviet Russia and the East, 1920-27: a Documentary Survey*. Stanford, Calif.: Stanford University Press, 1957.

Fall, Bernard B. *The Two Vietnams: a Political and Military Analysis*. 2nd rev. ed. New York: Praeger, 1967.

———, ed. *Ho Chi Minh on Revolution: Selected Writings, 1920-66*. New York: Praeger, 1967.

Fallers, Lloyd A. "Populism and Nationalism: a Comment on D. A. Low's 'The Advent of Populism in Buganda.'" *Comparative Studies in Society and History* 6 (1973), pp. 445-50.

Fann, K. T., and Hodges, D. C., eds. *Readings in United States' Imperialism*. Boston: P. Sargent, 1971.

Fanon, Frantz. *Black Skin, White Masters*. New York: Grove Press, 1967.

Fieldhouse, D. K. *Economics and Empire, 1830-1914*. London: Weidenfeld and Nicolson, 1973.

Fifield, Russell H. *Woodrow Wilson and the Far East: the Diplomacy of the Shantung Question*. Hamden, Conn.: Archon Books, 1965.

———. *Americans in South-East Asia: the Roots of Commitment*. New York: Crowell, 1973.

Fischer, Fritz. *Germany's Aims in the First World War*. New York: Norton, 1967.

Fitzgerald, Frances. *Fire in the Lake: the Vietnamese and the Americans in Vietnam*. Boston: Little, Brown, 1972.

Freeland, Richard. *The Truman Doctrine and the Origins of McCarthyism*. New York: Knopf, 1972.

Freyre, Gilberto. *The Portuguese and the Tropics*. Lisbon: Executive Committee for the Commemoration of the Fifth Centenary of the Death of Prince Henry the Navigator, 1961.

Friedman, E., and Selden, Mark. *America's Asia: Dissenting Essays on Asian-American Relations*. New York: Vintage Books, 1971.

Friedman, Isaiah. *The Question of Palestine, 1914-18: British-Jewish-Arab Relations*. London: Routledge and Kegan Paul, 1973.

Friend, Theodore. *Between Two Empires: the Ordeal of the Philippines, 1929-46*. New Haven, Conn.: Yale University Press, 1965.

Gaddis, John Lewis. *The United States and the Origins of the Cold War, 1941-47*. New York: Columbia University Press, 1972.

Gandhi, Mohandas K. *The Selected Works of Mahatma Gandhi*. Edited by Shiraman Narayan. Ahmedabad: Navajivan Publishing House, 1968-

Gann, L. H. and Duignan, Peter. *Burden of Empire: an Appraisal of Western Colonialism in Africa South of the Sahara*. New York: Praeger, 1967.

————. *Colonialism in Africa, 1870-1960*. Vol. 2, *The History and Politics of Colonialism, 1914-60*. Cambridge: at the University Press, 1970.

Gardner, Lloyd C. *Economic Aspects of New Deal Diplomacy*. Madison, Wis.: University of Wisconsin Press, 1964.

Garvey, Marcus. *Philosophy and Opinions of Marcus Garvey: or, Africa for the Africans*. With a new Introduction by E. U. Essien-Udom. Edited by Amy Jacques Garvey. 2nd ed. 2 vols. in 1. London: Frank Cass, 1967.

Garvin, J. L. *The Life of Joseph Chamberlain*. 3 vols. London: Macmillan, 1932.

Gerassi, John. *The Great Fear in Latin America*. New rev. ed. New York: Collier Books, 1965.

Ghose, Sankar. *Socialism and Communism in India*. Bombay: Allied Publishers, 1971.

Ghosh, K. K. *The Indian National Army: Second Front of the Indian Independence Movement*. Meerut: Meenakshi Prakashan, 1966.

Giolitti, Giovanni. *Memoirs of My Life*. London: Chapman and Dodd, 1923.

Goldman, C. S., ed. *The Empire and the Century*. London: 1906.

Goldsworthy, D. *Colonial Issues in British Politics, 1945-61*. Oxford: at the Clarendon Press, 1971.

Gopal, S., ed. *Selected Works of Jawaharlal Nehru*. New Delhi: Orient Longmans, 1972.

Gordon, David C. *The Passing of French Algeria*. London: Oxford University Press, 1966.

Grant, Michael. *The World of Rome*. London: Weidenfeld and Nicolson, 1960.

Grant Duff, Sir Michael E. *A Memoir of Sir Henry Maine*. London: 1892.

Green, David. *The Containment of Latin America: a History of the Myths and Realities of the Good Neighbor Policy*. Chicago, Ill.: Quadrangle Books, 1971.

Gregory, Robert C. *India and East Africa, 1830-1929*. Oxford: at the Clarendon Press, 1971.

Griffiths, Sir Percival J. *To Guard my People: the History of the Indian Police*. London: Benn, 1971.

Griswold, A. W. *The Far Eastern Policy of the United States*. New York: Harcourt, Brace, 1938.

Gross, John. *The Rise and Fall of the Man of Letters: Aspects of English Life since 1880*. London: Weidenfeld and Nicolson, 1969.

Haines, C. Grove, ed. *The Threat of Soviet Imperialism*. Baltimore, Md.: Johns Hopkins University Press, 1954.

Haithcox, J. P. *Communism and Nationalism in India: M. N. Roy and Comintern Policy, 1920-39*, Princeton, N. J.: Princeton University Press, 1971.

Halberstam, David. *The Best and the Brightest*. New York: Random House, 1972.

Halpern, Ben. *The Idea of the Jewish State*. Cambridge, Mass.: Harvard University Press, 1961.

Hammond, R. J. *Portugal and Africa, 1815-1910: a Study in Uneconomic Imperialism.* Stanford, Calif.: Stanford University Press, 1966.

Harrod, Sir Roy. *Topical Comment: Essays in Dynamic Economics Applied.* London: Macmillan, 1961.

Hartshorn, J. E. *Politics and World Oil Economics: an Account of the International Oil Industry in its Political Environment.* 2nd ed. New York: Praeger, 1967.

Herzl, Theodor. *Diaries.* Edited by M. Lowenthal. New York: Grosset and Dunlap, 1962.

Heussler, Robert. *Yesterday's Rulers.* Syracuse, N.Y.: Syracuse University Press, 1963.

Hewlett, Sir Meyrick. *Forty Years in China, 1898-1938.* London: Macmillan, 1943.

Ho Chi Minh. *Ho Chi Minh on Revolution: Selected Writings, 1920-66.* Edited by Bernard B. Fall. New York: Praeger, 1967.

Hobson, J. A. *Imperialism.* Edited by Philip Siegelman. Ann Arbor, Mich.: Ann Arbor Paperbacks, University of Michigan Press, 1965.

Hourani, Albert. *Arabic Thought in the Liberal Age, 1798-1939.* London: Oxford University Press, 1970.

Howard, Harry N. *The King-Crane Commission: an American Enquiry in the Middle East.* Beirut, Khayats, 1963.

Huxley, Elspeth. *White Man's Country: Lord Delamere and the Making of Kenya.* 2 vols. 2nd ed. London: Chatto and Windus, 1968.

Hyam, Ronald. *Elgin and Churchill at the Colonial Office, 1905-08: the Watershed of the Empire-Commonwealth.* London: Macmillan, 1968.

Hymans, J. L. *Léopold Sédar Senghor: an Intellectual Biography.* Edinburgh: Edinburgh University Press, 1971.

Ingrams, Doreen, ed. *Palestine Papers, 1917-22: the Seeds of Conflict.* London: Murray, 1972.

Iriye, Akira. *Across the Pacific: an Inner History of American-East Asian Relations.* New York: Harcourt, Brace, and World, 1967.

———. *The Cold War in Asia: a Historical Introduction.* Englewood Cliffs, N.J.: Prentice-Hall, 1974.

Jack, Homer A., ed. *The Gandhi Reader: a Source Book of His Life and Writings.* Bloomington, Ind.: Indiana University Press, 1956.

Jagan, Cheddi. *The West on Trial: My Fight for Guyana's Freedom.* New York: International Publishers, 1966.

Jinnah, Mohammed Ali. *Selected Speeches and Statements of the Quaid-i-Azam Mohammed Ali Jinnah.* Edited by M. R. Afzal. Lahore: Research Society of Pakistan, University of the Punjab, 1966.

Johnston, Sir Charles. *The View from Steamer Point: Three Crucial Years in South Arabia.* New York: Praeger, 1964.

Jones, F. C., Borton, Hugh, and Pearn, B. R. *Survey of International Affairs, 1939-46: the Far East, 1942-46.* London: Oxford University Press, 1955.

Kahin, G. M. *Nationalism and Revolution in Indonesia.* Ithaca, N.Y.: Cornell University Press, 1952.

Kahin, G. H., and Lewis, J. W. *The United States in Vietnam.* New York: Dial Press, 1967.

Kanya-Forstner, A. S. *The Conquest of the Western Sudan: a Study in French Military Imperialism.* Cambridge: at the University Press, 1969.

Kaye, Sir Cecil. *Communism in India, with Unpublished Documents from the National Archives of India, 1919-24.* Edited by Subodh Roy. Calcutta: Edtions Indian, 1971.

Kedourie, Elie. *The Chatham House Version, and other Middle Eastern Studies.* London: Weidenfeld and Nicolson, 1970.

Kennan, George. *Realities of American Foreign Policy*. Princeton, N.J.: Princeton University Press, 1954.

Kenner, M. and Petras, J., eds. *Fidel Castro Speaks!* New York: Grove Press, 1969.

Kiernan, V. G. *The Lords of Human Kind*. London: Weidenfield and Nicolson, 1969.

―――. *Marxism and Imperialism: Studies*. London: Arnold, 1974.

Killearn, Lord. *The Killearn Diaries, 1934-46: the Diplomatic and Personal Record of Lord Killearn (Sir Miles Lampson), High Commissioner and Ambassador, Egypt*. Edited by Trefor E. Evans. London: Sidgwick and Jackson, 1972.

Kirk, George. *Survey of International Affairs, 1939-46: the Middle East, 1945-50*. London: Oxford University Press, 1954.

Klieman, Aaron S. *Foundations of British Policy in the Arab World: the Cairo Conference of 1921*. Baltimore, Md.: Johns Hopkins University Press, 1970.

Koss, Stephen, *John Morley at the India Office*. New Haven, Conn.: Yale University Press, 1969.

Kripalani, Krishna. *Rabindranath Tagore*. London: Oxford University Press, 1962.

Krueger, Robert B. *The United States and International Oil: a Report for the Federal Energy Administration on U.S. Firms and Government Policy*. New York: Praeger, 1975.

Kumar, R., ed. *Essays in Gandhian Politics: the Rowlatt Satyagraha of 1919*. London: Oxford University Press, 1971.

LaFeber, Walter. *America, Russia, and the Cold War, 1945-71*. New York: Wiley, 1972.

La Gorce, P. M. de. *The French Army: a Military-Political History*. London: Weidenfeld and Nicolson, 1963.

Langlois, Walter G. *André Malraux: the Indo-China Adventure*. New York: Praeger, 1966.

Laqueur, Walter. *The Soviet Union and the Middle East*. New York: Praeger, 1959.

―――. *A History of Zionism*. London: Weidenfeld and Nicolson, 1972.

―――, ed. *The Israel-Arab Reader: a Documentary History of the Middle Eastern Conflict*. New York: Citadel Press, 1969.

Lawrence, Sir Walter. *The India We Served*. London: Cassell, 1928.

Lazitch, Branko, and Drachkovitch, Milorad M. *Lenin and the Comintern*. 2 vols. Stanford, Hoover Institution Press, 1972.

Lecky, W. E. H. *Democratic Government*. 2 vols. London, 1899.

Lee, J. M. *Colonial Development and Good Government: a Study of the Ideas Expressed by the British Official Classes in Planning Decolonization, 1939-64*. Oxford: at the Clarendon Press, 1967.

Lemarchand, Réné. *Political Awakening in the Belgian Congo*. Berkeley, Calif.: University of California Press, 1964.

Levin, N. Gordon. *Woodrow Wilson and World Politics: America's Response to War and Revolution*. New York: Oxford University Press, 1968.

Leys, Colin. *European Politics in Southern Rhodesia*. Oxford: at the Clarendon Press, 1960.

Lieuwen, Edwin. *Arms and Politics in Latin America*. New York: for the Council on Foreign Relations, Praeger, 1965.

―――. *United States' Policy in Latin America*. New York: Praeger, 1965.

Liska, George. *Imperial America: the International Politics of Primacy*. Baltimore, Md.: Johns Hopkins University Press, 1967.

Louis, W. Roger. *British Strategy in the Far East, 1919-1939*. Oxford: at the Clarendon Press, 1971.

Lowe, C. J., and Dockrill, M. L., eds. *The Mirage of Power*. 3 vols. London: Routledge and Kegan Paul, 1972.

Lowenthal, David. *West Indian Societies*. London: for the Institute of Race Relations, Oxford University Press, 1972.

Lucas, Sir Charles, ed. *Lord Durham's Report of the Affairs of British North America*. 3 vols. Oxford: at the Clarendon Press, 1912.

Lusignan, Guy de. *French-speaking Africa since Independence*. London: Pall Mall Press, 1969.

Lynch, Hollis, *Edward Wilmot Blyden: Pan-Negro Patriot, 1832-1912*. Oxford: at the Clarendon Press, 1967.

Macartney, M. M. H., and Cremona, Paul. *Italy's Foreign and Colonial Policy, 1914-37*. London: Oxford University Press, 1938.

Magdoff, Harry. *The Age of Imperialism: the Economics of United States' Foreign Policy*. New York: Monthly Review Press, 1969.

Mansergh, Nicholas, ed. *Documents and Speeches on British Commonwealth Affairs, 1931-1952*. London: for the Royal Institute of International Affairs, Oxford University Press, 1953.

Mansergh, Nicholas, and Lumby, E. W., eds. *Constitutional Relations between Britain and India*. Vol. 2, *The Transfer of Power in India*. London: H.M. Stationery Office, 1971.

Maran, Réné. *Batouala: a True Black Novel*. Translated by Barbara Beck and Alexandre Mboukou. Washington, D.C.: Black Orpheus Press, 1972.

Marshall, D. Bruce. *The French Colonial Myth and Constitution-Making in the Fourth Republic*. New Haven, Conn.: Yale University Press, 1972.

Masters, John. *Bugles and a Tiger: a Volume of Autobiography*. New York: Viking Press, 1956.

McNeill, William H. *Survey of International Affairs, 1939-46: America, Britain, and Russia: Their Co-operation and Conflict, 1943-46*. London: Oxford University Press, 1953.

Mende, Tibor. *From Aid to Recolonization: Lessons of a Failure*. London: Harrap, 1973.

Meyer, Roger de. *Introducing the Belgian Congo and Ruanda-Urundi*. With preface by A. Moeller de Laddersons, Honorary Vice-Governor-General of the Belgian Congo. Brussels: office de publicité, 1958.

Milner, Alfred. *England in Egypt*. London, 1893.

Morris, H. S. *The Indians in Uganda*. Oxford: at the Clarendon Press, 1968.

Murray-Brown, Jeremy. *Kenyatta*. London: Allen and Unwin, 1972.

Myrdal, Gunnar. "The 'Soft State' in Underdeveloped Countries." In *Unfashionable Economics: Essays in Honour of Lord Balogh*. Edited by P. Streeten. London: Weidenfeld and Nicolson, 1960.

Nanda, B. R., ed. *Socialism in India*. Delhi: Vikas Publications, 1972.

Nash, Gerald D. *United States Oil Policy, 1890-1964: Business and Government in Twentieth Century America*. Pittsburgh, Pa.: University of Pittsburgh, 1968.

Nehru, Jawaharlal. *An Autobiography, with Musings on Recent Events in India*. London: John Lane, 1936.

————. *Selected Works of Jawaharlal Nehru*. Edited by S. Gopal. New Delhi: Orient Longmans, 1972.

Nevinson, H. W. *A Modern Slavery*. London, 1906. Reprinted in *Slavery in Portuguese Africa*. Edited by D. F. Joyce, Northbrook, Ill.: Metro Books, 1972.

Nirumand, Bahman. *Iran: the New Imperialism in Action*. New York: Monthly Review Press, 1969.

Nisbet, Robert. *Social Change and History*. London: Oxford University Press, 1963.

————. *The Sociology of Emile Durkheim*. London: Oxford University Press, 1974.

Nish, Ian H. *Alliance in Decline: a Study in Anglo-Japanese Relations, 1908-23*. London: Athlone Press, 1972.

Norman, Dorothy, ed. *Nehru: the First Sixty years, Presenting in His Own Words the*

Development of the Political Thought of Jawaharlal Nehru and the Background against which It Evolved. 2 vols. Bombay: Asia Publishing House, 1965.

Olusanya, Gabriel O. *The Second World War and Politics in Nigeria, 1939-53.* Lagos: University of Lagos, 1973.

Orwell, George. *Collected Essays, Journalism, and Letters.* Edited by Sonia Orwell and Ian Angus. 4 vols. Harmondsworth: Penguin Books, 1970.

Perraton, H. D. "British Attitudes towards East and West Africa, 1880-1914." *Race* 8, no. 3 (1967), pp. 16-20.

Pickles, Dorothy. *Algeria and France: from Colonialism to Co-operation.* New York: Praeger, 1963.

Platt, D. C. M. *Finance, Trade, and Politics in British Foreign Policy, 1815-1914.* Oxford: at the Clarendon Press, 1969.

Raleigh, Sir Thomas, ed. *Lord Curzon in India, 1898-1905: a Selection From His Speeches as Governor-General and Viceroy.* 2 vols. London: 1906.

Robinson, Kenneth. *The Dilemmas of Trusteeship: Aspects of British Colonial Policy between the Wars.* London: Oxford University Press, 1965.

Roff, William R. *The Origins of Malay Nationalism.* New Haven, Conn.: Yale University Press, 1967.

Roosevelt, Theodore. *The Winning of the West.* New York, 1889.

Rosie, George. *The British in Vietnam: How the 25 Years' War Began.* London: Butterworth, 1970.

Roskill, Stephen W. *Hankey: Man of Secrets.* 3 vols. London: Collins, 1970-74.

Russell, Bertrand. *The Problem of China.* London: Allen and Unwin, 1922.

Russell, W. H. *My Diary in India in the Year 1858-9.* 2 vols. London, 1860.

Ryan, Selwyn. *Race and Nationalism in Trinidad and Tobago: a Study of Decolonization in a Multi-Racial Society.* Toronto: University of Toronto Press, 1972.

Sarraut, Albert. *Grandeur et servitude coloniales.* Paris: Armand Colin, 1931.

Scham, Alan. *Lyautey in Morocco: Protectorate Administration, 1912-1925.* Berkeley, Calif.: University of California Press, 1970.

Schumpeter, Joseph. *Imperialism: Social Classes.* Edited by Bert Hoselitz. Cleveland and New York: Meridian Books, 1955.

Shaw, Flora (Lady Lugard). *A Tropical Dependency.* London, 1905.

Simson, H. J. *British Rule, and Rebellion.* Edinburgh: Blackwood, 1937.

Singham, A. W. *The Hero and the Crowd in a Colonial Polity.* New Haven, Conn.: Yale University Press, 1969.

Slade, Ruth. *The Belgian Congo.* London: Oxford University Press, 1961.

Snyder, Louis L. *The Dynamics of Nationalism.* Princeton, N.J.: Van Nostrand, 1964.

Social Sciences. Vol. 6, no. 2 (20). Moscow: U.S.S.R. Academy of Sciences, 1975.

Steel, Ronald. *Pax Americana.* New York: Viking Press, 1967.

————. *Imperialists and Other Heroes: a Chronicle of the American Empire.* New York: Random House, 1971.

Stephen, Sir James Fitzjames. *Horae Sabbaticae.* 3 vols. London, 1890.

————. *Liberty, Equality, Fraternity.* Edited by R. J. White. Cambridge: at the University Press, 1967.

Strachey, John. *The End of Empire.* New York: Random House, 1960.

Stuart, Graham H. *Latin America and the United States.* 5th ed. New York: Appleton Century Crofts, 1966.

Suret-Canale, Jean. *French Colonialsim in Tropical Africa, 1900-45,* London: C. Hurst, 1971.

Sykes, Christopher. *Cross-Roads to Israel*. London: Collins, 1965.

Symonds, Richard. *The British and Their Successors*. London: Faber, 1966.

Szentes, Tamas. *The Political Economy of Underdevelopment*. Budapest: Akadémiai Kiadó, 1971.

Terrill, Ross. *R. H. Tawney and His Times*. Cambridge, Mass.: Harvard University Press, 1973.

Thomas, Keith. "History and Anthropology." *Past and Present* no. 24 (April 1963), pp. 65-71.

Thompson, Virginia. *French Indo-China*. London: Allen and Unwin, 1937.

Thornton, A. P. *Doctrines of Imperialism*. New York: Wiley, 1965.

Tipps, Dean C. "Modern Theory and the Comparative Study of Societies: a Critical Perspective." *Comparative Studies in Society and History* 15, no. 2 (March 1973), pp. 30-37.

Tompkins, E. Berkeley. *Anti-Imperialism in the United States: the Great Debate, 1890-1920*. Philadelphia: University of Pennsylvania Press, 1970.

Toynbee, Arnold J. *Survey of International Affairs, 1925: the Islamic World since the Peace Conference*. London: Oxford University Press, 1927.

————. *Survey of International Affairs, 1931*. London: Oxford University Press, 1932.

Toynbee, Arnold J., and Kirkwood, Kenneth P. *Turkey*. London: Benn, 1926.

Tuker, Sir Francis. *Gorkha: the Story of the Gurkhas of Nepal*. London: Constable, 1957.

Uziogwe, Godfrey. "Pre-colonial Markets in Bunyoro-Kitara." *Comparative Studies in Society and History* 14, no. 4 (September 1972), pp. 422-26.

Vincent, Theodore G. *Black Power and the Garvey Movement*. Berkeley, Calif.: Ramparts Press, 1971.

Wagar, W. Warren, ed. *H. G. Wells: Journalism and Prophecy, 1893-1914, an Anthology*. Boston, Mass.: Houghton Mifflin, 1964.

Walker, Eric A. *Colonies*. Cambridge: at the University Press, 1944.

Waterfield, Gordon. *Professional Diplomat: Sir Percy Loraine of Kirkharle, Bt., 1800-1961*. London: John Murray, 1973.

Weinstein, Brian. *Eboué*. New York: Oxford University Press, 1972.

Wells, H. G. *Anticipations*. London, 1901. *The War that Will End War*. London, 1904. In *Works*, Atlantic ed. London: Fisher Unwin, 1924.

————. *Experiment in Autobiography*. 2 vols. London: Gollancz, 1934.

White, John. "Observing Development." *South Asian Review* 6, no. i (October 1972), pp. 40-45.

White, Theodore H. *The Making of the President—1968*. New York: Atheneum, 1969.

Williams, Eric A. *Inward Hunger: the Education of a Prime Minister*. London: Deutsch, 1969.

Williams, W. Appleman. *The Tragedy of American Diplomacy*. New York: Dell, 1962.

Winslow, E. M. *The Pattern of Imperialism: a Study in the Theories of Power*. New York: Columbia University Press, 1948.

Wolfe, J. N., ed. *Government and Nationalism in Scotland: an Enquiry by Members of the University of Edinburgh*. Edinburgh: at the University Press,, 1969.

Wood, E. F. L. (Lord Halifax). *Report on Visit to the West Indies and British Guiana*. Cmd. 1679. London: H.M. Stationery Office, 1922.

Woodcock, George. *The British in the Far East*. London: Weidenfeld and Nicolson, 1969.

Woolman, David S. *Rebels in the Rif*. Stanford, Calif.: Stanford University Press, 1968.

Wright Mills, C. *The Sociological Imagination*. Harmondsworth: Penguin Books, 1971.

Wyatt, Woodrow. *Southwards from China: a Survey of South-East Asia since 1945*. London: Hodder and Stoughton, 1952.

II. Sources Referred to but not Quoted

Abraham, W. E. *The Mind of Africa*. Chicago, Ill.: University of Chicago Press, 1962.

Albertini, Rudolf von. *Decolonization: the Administration and the Future of the Colonies, 1919-1960*. Translated from the German by Francesca Garvie. Garden City, N.Y.: Doubleday, 1971.

Andrzejewski, Stanislav. *The African Predicament: a Study in the Pathology of Modernization*. London: Michael Joseph, 1968.

Aron, Raymond. *The Century of Total War*. Boston, Mass.: Beacon Press, 1968.

Bauer, P. T. *Dissent on Development: Studies and Debates in Development Economics*. London: Weidenfeld and Nicolson, 1971.

Bérard, Victor. *British Imperial and Commercial Supremacy*. London: Longmans, Green, 1906.

Bonn, M. J. *The Crumbling of Empire: the Disintegration of World Economy*. London: Allen and Unwin, 1968.

Brunschwig, Henri. "Colonisation—Decolonisation; essai sur le vocabulaire usuel de la politique coloniale." *Cahiers d'études africaines* 1 (1960), pp. 44-54.

Bukharin, Nikolai Ivanovich. *Imperialism and World Economy. With an Introduction by V. I. Lenin*. London: Merlin Press, 1972.

Calvocoressi, Peter. *World Politics since 1945*. London: Longmans, 1968.

Challener, R. F. *The French Theory of the Nation in Arms*. New York: Russell and Russell, 1965.

Chettur, S. J. *The Steel Frame and I: Life in the Indian Civil Service*. Bombay: Asia Publishing House, 1962.

Crocker, W. R. *Self-Government for the Colonies*. London: Allen and Unwin, 1949.

Deutsch, Karl, and Merritt, Richard. *Nationalism and National Development: an Interdisciplinary Bibliography*. Cambridge, Mass.: M.I.T. Press, 1970.

Earle, Edward Meade, ed. *Nationalism and Internationalism*. New York: Columbia University Press, 1950.

Feis, Herbert. *Europe the World's Banker*. New Haven, Conn.: Yale University Press, 1930.

Fieldhouse, D. K. "'Imperialism'; an Historical Revision." *Economic History Review* 14, no. 2 (December 1961), pp. 18-25.

————. *The Colonial Empires*. London: Weidenfeld and Nicolson, 1974.

Galbraith, John K. *American Capitalism*. London: Hamish Hamilton, 1957.

Gifford, P., and Louis, W. Roger, eds. *Britain and Germany in Africa: Imperial Rivalry and Colonial Rule*. New Haven, Conn.: Yale University Press, 1967.

Gilbert, Felix. *The End of the European Era, 1890 to the present*. New York: Norton, 1970.

Hazlewood, A. *The Economics of Underdeveloped Areas*. London: Oxford University Press, 1959.

Hobson, J. A. *Confessions of an Economic Heretic*. 3rd rev. ed. London: Allen and Unwin, 1938.

Hopkins, A. G. *An Economic History of West Africa*. London: Longmans, 1973.

Imlah, A. H. *Economic Elements in the Pax Britannica*. Cambridge, Mass.: Harvard University Press, 1958.

Iriye, Akira. *After Imperialism: the Search for a New Order in the Far East, 1921-31*. Cambridge, Mass.: Harvard University Press, 1965.

Isaacs, Harold. *Scratches on Our Minds*. New York: Day, 1958.

Johannet, Réné. *Le principe des nationalités*. New ed. Paris: Nouvelle Librairie Nationale, 1923.

Kautsky, Karl. *The Road to Power.* Translated by A. M. Simons. Chicago, Ill.: Black, 1909.
Keddie, Nikki. *An Islamic Response to Imperialism: Political and Religious Writings of Sayyed Jamal al Din "al-Afghani."* Berkeley, Calif.: University of California Press, 1968.
Kedourie, Elie, ed. *Nationalism in Asia and Africa.* New York: World Books, 1970.
Kelly, George A. *Lost Soldiers: the French Army and Empire in Crisis, 1947-62.* Cambridge, Mass.: Harvard University Press, 1965.
Knight, Melvin M. *Morocco as a French Economic Venture: a Study in Open Door Imperialism.* New York: Appleton Century, 1938.
Koebner, Richard. "The Concept of Economic Imperialism." *Economic History Review* 2 (1949), pp. 1-29.
Kohn, Hans. *The Idea of Nationalism: a Study in Its Origins and Background.* New York: Macmillan, 1944.
Kolko, Gabriel. *The Politics of War: the World and U.S. Foreign Policy, 1943-45.* New York: Random House, 1968.
Lancaster, Donald. *The Emancipation of French Indo-China.* New York: Oxford University Press, 1961.
Landes, David S. "Some Thoughts on the Nature of Economic Imperialism." *Journal of Economic History* 12 (1961), pp. 496-512.
Legge, J. D. *Sukarno.* London: Allen Lane the Penguin Press, 1972.
Lenin, V. I. *Imperialism the Highest Stage of Capitalism.* 1917. Reprint. New York: International Publishers, 1972.
Lichtheim, George. *Europe in the Twentieth Century.* New York: Praeger, 1972.
Marx, Karl, and Engels, Friedrich. *On Colonialism.* London: Lawrence and Wishart, 1960.
Mason, Philip. *Patterns of Dominance.* London: for the Institute of Race Relations, Oxford University Press, 1970.
Moon, Parker T. *Imperialism and World Politics.* New York: Macmillan, 1926.
Murray, A. Victor. *The School in the Bush.* 2nd ed. London: Longmans, 1938.
Myrdal, Gunnar. *Economic Theory and Underdeveloped Regions.* London: Duckworth, 1957.
Nelson, Joan M. *Aid, Influence, and Foreign Policy.* New York: Macmillan, 1968.
Ngo Vinh Long. *Before the Revolution: the Vietnamese Peasants under the French.* Cambridge, Mass.: M.I.T. Press, 1973.
Omari, T. P. *Kwame Nkrumah: the Anatomy of an African Dictatorship.* London: Hurst, 1970.
Paterson, Thomas G. *Soviet-American Confrontation: Postwar Reconstruction and the Origins of the Cold War.* Baltimore, Md.: Johns Hopkins University Press, 1973.
————, ed. *Containment and the Cold War. American foreign policy since 1945.* Reading, Mass.: Addison-Wesley Publishing Co., 1973.
Pavlovitch, Michel [Mikhail Lazarevich Weltmann]. *The Foundations of Imperialist Policy.* London: the Labour Publishing Co., 1922.
Scalapino, Robert. "Nationalism in Asia: Reality and Myth." *Orbis* 10 (1967), pp. 48-52.
Seillière, Ernest. *Introduction à la philosophie de l'impérialisme.* Paris: Alcan, 1911.
Semmel, Bernard. *Imperialism and Social Reform:* Cambridge, Mass.: Harvard University Press, 1960.
Shafer, Boyd C. *Faces of Nationalism: New Realities and Old Myths.* New York: Harcourt Brace Jovanovitch, 1972.
Shonfield, Andrew. *Attack on World Poverty.* London: Chatto and Windus, 1960.

Silvert, K. H. *Expectant Peoples—Nationalism and Development*. New York: Praeger, 1963.

Stahl, Kathleen M. *The Metropolitan Organization of Britain's Colonial Trade*. London: Faber, 1937.

Suret-Canale, Jean. *Afrique noire*. 2 vols. Paris: Éditions sociales, 1961.

Udom, E. Essien. *Black Nationalism: a Search for an Identity in America*. Chicago, Ill.: University of Chicago Press, 1962.

Ulam, Adam B. *Expansion and Co-existence: Soviet Foreign Policy, 1917-73*. 2nd ed. New York: Praeger, 1974.

Vigne d'Octon, Paul. *Le Pélérin du Soleil*. Paris, 1910.

Weinberg, Albert K. *Manifest Destiny: a Study of Nationalist Expansionism in American History*. Baltimore, Md.: Johns Hopkins University Press, 1935.

INDEX

INDEX

Nkrumah, Kwame, Ghanaian leader: poli-
cies of, 171-72, 189; metamorphosis
of, 278; jailed, 285
North Africa: Anglo-American strategy in,
275; mentioned, 41. *See also* Algeria;
Ethiopia; Tunisia
North Atlantic Treaty Organization
(N.A.T.O.), 244, 265
North Sea: oil in, 25, 49
Northcote, Sir Stafford, 82
Northern Ireland, 23
Northern Rhodesia, 283
Nuremberg, trial at, 293
Nyasaland: rebellion in (*1915*), 168;
Banda returns to, 276; independence
of, 283

Obregon, J., president of Mexico, 252
O'Brien, Conor Cruise, 113
O'Connell, Daniel, 308
Oder River, 244
Office of Strategic Services, U.S. (O.S.S.):
in Indochina, 290
Oil: discovery of in Persian Gulf, 49,
120, 252; d'Arcy's exploitation of in
Persia, 91, 311; exported from Trinidad,
93; nationalized in Mexico and Iraq,
120, 191; U.S. policy in Saudi Arabia,
252; British control of in Middle East,
252; "Red Line Agreement" on, 252-
53; O.P.E.C. embargo on, 311; Arab
policy toward, 311-13
"Old China Hand": attitudes of, 50, 85,
200
'Open Door" policy: in China, 45, 113,
202, 250, 253; implications of, 241,
263; and Middle East oil, 252
Opium Combine, Shanghai, 85
Organization of American States (O.A.S.),
260
Organization of Petroleum Exporting
Countries (O.P.E.C.), 311-12
Orwell, George: *1984*, 70; in Burma police,
78; on British imperialism, 78, 84, 86;
Burmese Days, 99; relations with British
Left, 140
Ottoman Empire: Europeans in, 33; as
"sick man of Europe," 45. *See also*
Turkey

Oubanghi-Shari, French Equatorial Africa,
171, 196
Oxford University: Gandhi visits, 54;
Bagehot on, 301

Painlevé, Paul, 41
Pakistan, 148, 274, 282
Palestine: U.S. commission on, 46; Royal
Commission on (*1937*), 59; British
policy in, 120-29; indecision in,
207-8; self-determination and, 286;
mentioned, 131, 137, 138, 212, 294.
See also Zionism
Pan-African Conference (*1900*), 153
Pan-African congresses, 185, 195, 209, 210
Panama, 71
Pan-American Conference, sixth and
seventh, 118
Paris, 115, 195, 196, 209, 214
Paternalism, 21, 37, 43, 59
Pathans, 33
Patriotism, 25
Pax Britannica, 109
Peace Pledge Union, British, 140
Peel Commission on Palestine (*1937*),
124, 125, 126. *See also* Palestine
Peking, 151, 203, 291
Penang, 86
Persia, 294. *See also* Iran
Persian Gulf: oil in, 49, 120, 252
Pétain, Marshal P., 291
Peter the Great, tsar of Russia, 163
Philippines: U.S. annexation of and policy
in, 94, 151-52, 197; and World War II,
295
P.K.I. (Indonesian Communist Party),
162, 210, 212, 298
Platt, D.C.M.: quoted on Egypt, 81-82
P.N.I. (Indonesian Nationalist Party), 212
"Point Four" program, U.S., 257
Politburo, U.S.S.R., 163, 222, 266, 268
Polybius, Roman historian, 8
Popular Front in France. *See Front
Populaire*
Portugal, Portuguese: coolies in Guiana,
52; empire of, 58; labor regulations of,
92-93; after World War II, 274
Potsdam, conference at (*1945*), 289-90
Preobrazhensky, F., 160